ALL-ASIA

SOUTHEAST ASIA

VOLUME II

FarEasternEconomic
REVIEW

Published by

Review Publishing Co. Ltd,
G.P.O. Box 160,
Hongkong

Distributed by

Roger Lascelles, Cartographic and Travel Publisher
47 York Road, Brentford, Middlesex TW8 0QP.   Tel: 081-847 0935

ISBN 962-7010-39-1

Printed by
DAI NIPPON PRINTING CO. (HK) LTD
Tsuen Wan Industrial Centre, 2-5/F., 220-224 Texaco Road,
Tsuen Wan, N.T., Hongkong

WRITTEN AND COMPILED BY

Janick Bhavon (*Indonesia*)

Michael Bishara (*Brunei, Hongkong, Macau*)

Nick Cumming-Bruce (*Vietnam*)

Rowan Callick (*Papua New Guinea*)

Celine Fernandez (*Malaysia*)

Veronica Garbutt (*Philippines*)

Murray Hiebert (*Cambodia, Laos*)

Neil Kelly (*Thailand*)

Mary Lee (*Singapore*)

Editor: Michael Malik

Assistant Editor: Ron Knowles

Production Editor: Paul Lee
Henry Chiu (*Deputy*)
Winnie Law (*Assistant*)

Design Consultant: John Hull

Cover Picture: Gerhard Jörén

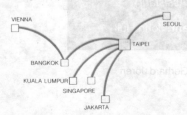

CONTENTS

Introduction ———————————————— 9

Brunei ———————————————— 15

Cambodia ———————————————— 25

Hongkong ———————————————— 35

Indonesia ———————————————— 71

Laos ———————————————— 107

Macau ———————————————— 117

Malaysia ———————————————— 131

Papua New Guinea ———————————————— 165

Philippines ———————————————— 183

Singapore ———————————————— 227

Thailand ———————————————— 255

Vietnam ———————————————— 295

SYMBOLS

Accommodation

Banks

Business hours

Climate

Currency

Customs

Dining

Dress

Entertainment

Entry

Government

Health

History

Holidays

Immigration

Language

Shopping

Sports

Tourist information

Tours

Transport

Swimming pool

Western food

Asian food

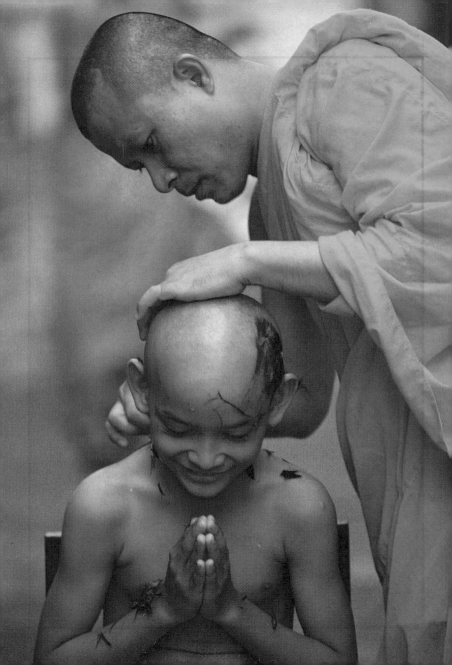

INTRODUCTION

Guide books are almost by definition out of date before they reach the reader — imagine having attempted to produce a guide to Eastern Europe or the Soviet Union in 1989. As a minor example, since the section of this book on Indonesia was printed, Jakarta telephone numbers starting with the figures 34 have all been changed to 384, while numbers which were previously started 578 now start 571 and those which used to start 5801 now start 5715. In other parts of Indonesia numbers have been completely changed, and the best advice, if looking for a hotel number, for example, is to check with the international exchange.

Prices, of course, are constantly changing and while we have endeavoured to make the prices quoted in this book as up-to-date as possible, we do not claim to be infallible. As supply and demand change constantly, some travellers might be pleasantly surprised to find there are heavy discounts available, while in other places prices may have increased. Never be afraid to ask for a discount, however, even at the most exclusive hotels. Discount fares are, of course, also available, and only those travelling on company expenses should buy an air ticket direct from an airline, since most travel agents can get you a better deal — even including their commission.

Currency rates of exchange also are unpredictable and while we quote hotel prices in US dollars, their equivalent in other currencies will change.

While we are aiming mainly at the business traveller, we have not neglected to include advice and accommodation for the budget traveller as well.

Although this is in no way a back-packer's guide, there is some advice which applies to all travellers — one of the most important is to travel light. Many travellers, even the most experienced, burden themselves with far more luggage than they really need, and there is nothing worse than having to struggle with three suitcases — even if you can find a trolley — through an airport when one would probably be quite enough if your luggage is carefully selected.

The ideal, if it can be managed, is to limit yourself to one bag which conforms to airline specifications for cabin luggage. The advantage of this is to be able to walk straight off a plane and to beat the crush at the immigration counter, while others are waiting for their luggage to arrive on the carousel.

This book will tell you the temperature range of your destination, and do not neglect to check it. If you are only visiting Southeast Asia and no other part of the continent, there is very little range of temperatures in any of the countries except in highland resorts, in Malaysia, for instance, where a light jacket or pullover is recommended for evenings. Obviously in tropical climates where temperatures can exceed 35°F (95°C), and humidity is often high, you are going to need to change your clothes possibly several times a day, so drip-dry garments — and thin cotton underwear which you can wash yourself and wear the next day — are useful to avoid not only bulk in your luggage but what can be exorbitant hotel laundry charges.

One, or even better two, changes of shoes are recommended for the tropical areas, where sudden rain can land you in ankle-deep floods even in central city areas. Always

◁ A Thai novice monk.
Photo: Ben Simmons/The Stock House

9

pack a few coat-hangers since few hotels provide enough.

Conforming to local customs is also a very important point, especially for those not familiar with Asia. Not removing your shoes on entering a mosque in Muslim countries and Buddhist or Hindu temples, for instance, is greatly insulting. It is also the custom to take your shoes off at the door when entering private houses in many parts of Asia. Just follow your host's example.

While it is quite acceptable for women to bathe or sunbathe topless in places such as Bali in Indonesia, and on private hotel beaches in many Thai resorts, it is not acceptable in most Muslim countries which include Indonesia (apart from Bali which is basically Hindu), Malaysia or Singapore. It is always a good idea to ask local advice on this.

Do not carry political literature or leaflets of any kind — Left, Right or even Centre — it is not worth the problems you may encounter.

And remember that carrying drugs, not only heroin and cocaine, but cannabis — even for your own use — can not only land you in prison, but is subject to the death penalty in Thailand, Malaysia and Singapore.

In most Asian countries it is advisable to avoid drinking water that has not come out of a sealed bottle or been boiled. If you do not drink beer or other alcohol, stick to tea.

Each chapter in this book will tell you of the minimal health certificates needed for entering a country, but you would be advised, if coming from outside Asia, to seek advice from a doctor on such requirements as anti-malaria medication — which should start before arriving in malarial regions — and other prophylactics such as any diarrhoea medicine, which can be very important for those unfamiliar with Asian food.

If travelling outside major cities, take your own soap and suntan cream. Women should carry a good supply of tampons or sanitary towels, which are often not available. Reading matter in your own language should be added to your luggage for those long flights and television-less evenings in many places.

Carry several copies of a list of dutiable goods you have with you and intend to take home, such as cameras, tape recorders or disc players, including the maker's name and any identification number — for body and lens in the case of cameras. Most countries will not require it, but those which do (such as India) can keep you for hours at the airport filling in forms. It is also always useful to have with you a supply of passport photographs of yourself for unexpected visas or passes.

Do not assume that you can take duty-free alcohol into every country just because you are a tourist. Pakistan, for instance, confiscates it on entry and though theoretically it should be returned to you on leaving the country, this is easier said than done — unless you want to spend half a day at the airport before your flight.

Finally, while several Asian countries have a deserved reputation for cheap and easily available sex, remember that AIDS is spreading fast in the region and take appropriate precautions.

This 15th edition of the All-Asia Guide comes in a new format. While there is still a complete compendium edition, it is also being printed in three sections, covering Southeast Asia, Northeast Asia and South Asia, for the convenience of those travellers only interested in one region. It is also fully colour-illustrated for the first time and the binding — a problem with some previous editions — has been improved. Another new feature is a chapter on Soviet Asia and Siberia, now becoming much more open.

The book has been re-organised so that each chapter is self-contained, including a section on local food and shopping (including precious stones) instead of one chapter on these subjects as in previous editions. The Hotel Guide also has been rearranged so that each country's hotels are listed at the end of individual chapters, instead of them all appearing at the back of the book.

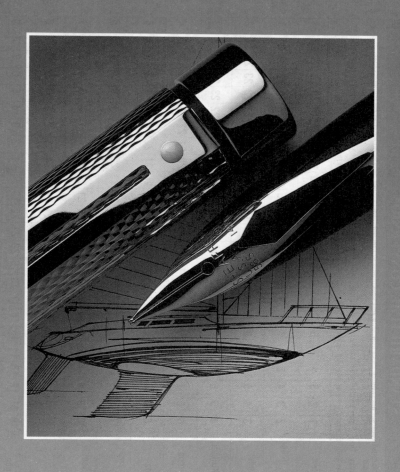

SHEAFFER.

STANDARD TIME CONVERSION

Find your location, move across columns to current hour. Move up or down the vertical column to find the time in other zones. An asterisk (*) indicates that 30 minutes must be added to the hour.

Time in blue shaded area is yesterday. Time in grey shaded area is tomorrow. (Example: when it is 10 am Tuesday in Hongkong its is 9 pm Monday in New York.)

The chart below lists Standard times only: Summer Time or Daylight Saving Time is observed in many countries, some with regional variations.

Tokyo, Fukuoka, Osaka, Seoul, Darwin*, Adelaide*	1	2	3	4	5	6	7	8	9	10	11	12	13	14	15	16	17	18	19	20	21	22	23	24
Sydney, Melbourne, Brisbane, Hobart, Port Moresby, Vladivostock	2	3	4	5	6	7	8	9	10	11	12	13	14	15	16	17	18	19	20	21	22	23	24	1
New Caledonia, Solomon Islands, New Hebrides	3	4	5	6	7	8	9	10	11	12	13	14	15	16	17	18	19	20	21	22	23	24	1	2
Auckland, Fiji, Wake Island, Kiribati	4	5	6	7	8	9	10	11	12	13	14	15	16	17	18	19	20	21	22	23	24	1	2	3
American Samoa, Western Samoa	5	6	7	8	9	10	11	12	13	14	15	16	17	18	19	20	21	22	23	24	1	2	3	4
Hawaiian Islands, Cook Islands	6	7	8	9	10	11	12	13	14	15	16	17	18	19	20	21	22	23	24	1	2	3	4	5
Anchorage, Tahiti	7	8	9	10	11	12	13	14	15	16	17	18	19	20	21	22	23	24	1	2	3	4	5	6
Los Angeles, San Francisco, Seattle, San Diego, Vancouver	8	9	10	11	12	13	14	15	16	17	18	19	20	21	22	23	24	1	2	3	4	5	6	7
Edmonton, Calgary, Denver, Salt Lake City, Albuquerque	9	10	11	12	13	14	15	16	17	18	19	20	21	22	23	24	1	2	3	4	5	6	7	8
Chicago, Detroit, Houston, Mexico City, San Jose, Managua	10	11	12	13	14	15	16	17	18	19	20	21	22	23	24	1	2	3	4	5	6	7	8	9
New York, Boston, Washington D.C...	11	12	13	14	15	16	17	18	19	20	21	22	23	24	1	2	3	4	5	6	7	8	9	10

Halifax, Bermuda, San Juan, Caracas, La Paz, Santiago	12	13	14	15	16	17	18	19	20	21	22	23	24	1	2	3	4	5	6	7	8	9	10	11
Buenos Aires, Rio de Janeiro, San Paulo, Montevideo	13	14	15	16	17	18	19	20	21	22	23	24	1	2	3	4	5	6	7	8	9	10	11	12
Part of Greenland, South Georgia	14	15	16	17	18	19	20	21	22	23	24	1	2	3	4	5	6	7	8	9	10	11	12	13
The Azores, Cape Verde	15	16	17	18	19	20	21	22	23	24	1	2	3	4	5	6	7	8	9	10	11	12	13	14
London, Dublin, Iceland, Dakar, Accra	16	17	18	19	20	21	22	23	24	1	2	3	4	5	6	7	8	9	10	11	12	13	14	15
Stockholm, Amsterdam, Paris, Rome, Frankfurt, Zurich, Lagos	17	18	19	20	21	22	23	24	1	2	3	4	5	6	7	8	9	10	11	12	13	14	15	16
Helsinki, Athens, Bucharest, Cairo, Johannesburg	18	19	20	21	22	23	24	1	2	3	4	5	6	7	8	9	10	11	12	13	14	15	16	17
Moscow, Leningrad, Bahrain, Riyadh, Nairobi, Madagascar	19	20	21	22	23	24	1	2	3	4	5	6	7	8	9	10	11	12	13	14	15	16	17	18
Gorki, Baku, Dubai, Muscat, Seychelles Islands, Mauritius	20	21	22	23	24	1	2	3	4	5	6	7	8	9	10	11	12	13	14	15	16	17	18	19
Karachi, Bombay*, Delhi*, Calcutta*, Colombo	21	22	23	24	1	2	3	4	5	6	7	8	9	10	11	12	13	14	15	16	17	18	19	20
Rangoon*, Tashkent	22	23	24	1	2	3	4	5	6	7	8	9	10	11	12	13	14	15	16	17	18	19	20	21
Bangkok, Jakarta, Hanoi, Medan	23	24	1	2	3	4	5	6	7	8	9	10	11	12	13	14	15	16	17	18	19	20	21	22
Hongkong, China, Taipei, Manila, Singapore, Brunei, Malaysia, Perth	24	1	2	3	4	5	6	7	8	9	10	11	12	13	14	15	16	17	18	19	20	21	22	23

13

BRUNEI

Islam, gas and oil dominate the tiny sultanate of Brunei, socially, physically and economically. The capital, Bandar Seri Begawan, is built round the magnificent Omar Ali Saifuddin Mosque, which overlooks Kampung Ayer, a collection of villages perched on stilts over the Brunei River.

Narrow walkways link each village and the entire network to the mainland, while fast longboats provide an efficient service for residents and visitors.

On shore, the capital is the centre of government and religion, though the economic heart of the state is 100 km away at the oil and gas fields of Seria and Kuala Belait.

Bandar Seri Begawan's magnificent parliamentary buildings and the unusual Sir Winston Churchill Museum and Aquarium stand aside in patches of greenery while nearby shophouses compete for space with office buildings, supermarkets and department stores.

The state's wealth is entirely based on oil and natural gas, giving residents one of the highest standards of living in the world with a per capita income more than 30% higher than EC residents. Moves to diversify the country's economic base are making slow progress, though almost US$4 billion was put aside for this objective in the five years to 1990. With an estimated 20-year limit on Brunei's oil reserves, these moves are likely to gather pace.

The Economic Development Board has wide-ranging powers to enter directly into joint ventures with foreign businesses. Emphasis is on the banking and financial sector and agriculture, forestry and fisheries.

The objective is to provide alternative employment opportunities as oil reserves are depleted, supplying local demand rather than building a sizeable export market. Brunei's enormous cash reserves from oil sales will be more than enough to keep the country rich for generations.

The first graduates from Brunei's new university appeared in 1989 and the student intake for 1990 was 500. The establishment of the university was part of a nation-building programme, partly intended to keep more of Brunei's educated young at home where they are needed.

Although a quiet, peaceful place, Brunei provides a few outlets for tourist and travellers prepared to exert themselves in a country not geared to the high-pressure tourism of the 1990s.

When Portugese explorer Ferdinand Magellan's ships called at Brunei on their return from the Philippines in 1521, it was the centre of a powerful empire stretching from Sarawak as far north as Manila. Finely built cannon can still be seen and sometimes bought in Brunei. They are a reminder of the sea power the sultanate once wielded over countries bordering on the southern part of the South China Sea.

Brunei's power declined, however, and during the 19th century the much-reduced territory controlled by the state was further encroached on by the White Rajahs of Sarawak and the British North Borneo Company in what is now Malaysian state of Sabah. Towards the end of the 19th century Brunei became a British protectorate and in 1906 the British Resident system was introduced. The discovery of the first Seria

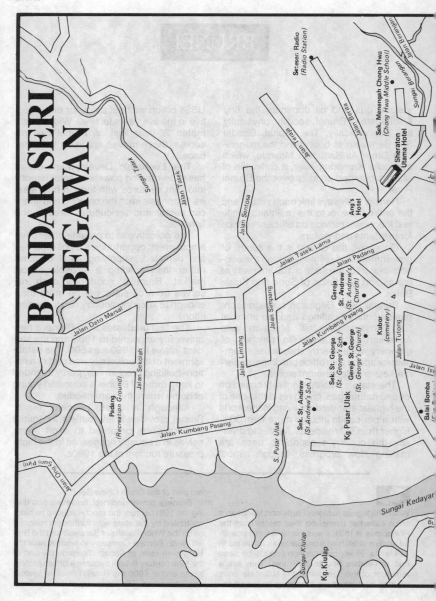

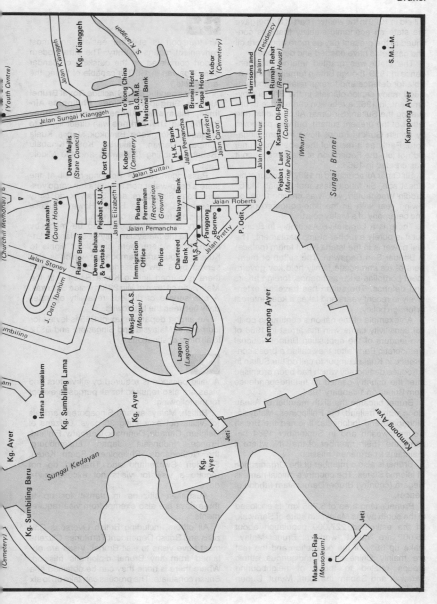

oilfield in 1929 in the western part of Brunei gave the state an economic stability that has continued to the present day as more and more oil and gas fields have opened and developed.

The state was granted internal independence in 1959, though Britain remained responsible for defence and foreign relations and provided many senior officials in the Brunei Government. In 1962 a rebellion came close to unseating the Sultan, Sir Omar Ali Saifuddin (the father of the present sultan), but was put down by British Gurkha troops flown in from Singapore. Partly as a result of the rebellion, Brunei did not join the Federation of Malaysia when it was created in 1963.

Sir Omar Ali abdicated in 1967 in favour of his eldest son, Sir Muda Hassanal Bolkiah Mu'izzaddin Waddaulah, who was crowned the following year with all the time-honoured pomp and ceremony of a Malay court.

There is a Legislative Assembly in Brunei, but it is purely a rubber-stamp parliament. The real power is in the Istana Nurul Imam (palace) in Bandar Seri Begawan. The sultan or members of his immediate family hold key government portfolios such as finance, foreign affairs and defence. The sultan has travelled extensively in recent years and takes a keen interest in foreign policy.

An example of the nation's continuing political sensitivity came with the arrest in 1988 of two leaders of the opposition Brunei National Democratic Party after they called a press conference in Kuala Lumpur to call on the Sultan to introduce democracy which had been promised after the country gained its full independence from Britain on 1 January 1984.

Brunei became the sixth member of Asean along with Thailand, the Philippines, Malaysia, Singapore and Indonesia. It joined the British Commonwealth and in September 1984 became the 159th member of the UN, where it maintains a permanent mission.

Brunei is also a member of the Organisation of Islamic States. The country's official name is Negara (country) Brunei Darussalam (abode of peace).

Brunei's land area of 5,765 km^2 is enclosed to the south by the Malaysian state of Sarawak. Of the estimated 227,000 population about 25,000 are "guest" workers. Brunei Malays make up 65% of the population and the rest are mainly Chinese and indigenous ethnic groups related to those of neighbouring Sarawak and Sabah: the Iban, Murut, Duoun and Kedayan.

Air transport is still the easiest and most convenient means of entry. The ultra-modern airport completed on the outskirts of Bandar Seri Begawan in 1973 is capable of taking the largest jets.

Airlines serving Brunei include **Royal Brunei Airlines**, **Singapore Airlines**, **Philippine Airlines**, **Malaysian Airline System**, **Cathay Pacific** and **Thai Airlines** with direct flights to Singapore, Hongkong, Bangkok, Manila, Kuala Lumpur, Darwin, Jakarta, Kota Kinabalu (Sabah), Kuching (Sarawak) and the Middle East.

Passenger vessels no longer call at the state's deep-water port at Muara but cargo vessels from Singapore and Sarawak do carry passengers to Kuala Belait. However, these vessels are few and far between.

Entry or departure can also be made by launch via the Malaysian duty-free island of Labuan, from where there are direct flights to Kuala Lumpur and Zamboanga, which is also served by a few passenger ships. Overland there is a road linking Kuala Belait with the Malaysian oil town of Miri 22 km inside Sarawak. A bus service of dubious reliability operates daily between the two towns.

An airport departure tax of B$5 is levied for journeys to Malaysia and Singapore and B$12 to all other destinations.

A valid passport is required by all visitors and visas are also required for all purposes except for the following:

British, Malaysian and Singaporean arrivals for visits not exceeding 30 days. Citizens of Belgium, Canada, Denmark, Germany, Finland, France, Indonesia, Japan, Luxembourg, the Netherlands, Philippines, South Korea, Sweden, Switzerland and Thailand do not require a visa for visits not exceeding 14 days.

Australian citizens in transit for up to three days are also exempt from visa requirements.

All others, including British Overseas Citizens and British Dependent Territories Citizens must have visas to visit Brunei. Visas are obtained from any Brunei diplomatic mission. Where there is none they can be obtained at a British consulate. The process can take up to six months.

Visitors are required to have International Vaccination Certificates. Cholera and yellow fever certificates are required for travellers over one year of age coming from infected areas.

In addition to normal personal belongings, used portable items are exempt from duty if they accompany the traveller though much is up to the discretion of individual customs officers. One quart each of wine, beer and spirits, cosmetics and half a pound of tobacco or 200 cigarettes are allowed in duty free.

Motor vehicles can be brought in from Sarawak provided the necessary exemption documents are completed and presented at the Kuala Baram customs post.

The unit of currency is the Brunei dollar (B$) which is divided into 100 cents and is on a par with the Singapore dollar. Both currencies circulate freely within the state. The Malaysian dollar is exchanged at a slightly lower rate, though some shopkeepers in Kuala Belait near the Sarawak border will accept it at almost par with the Brunei dollar. The exchange rate in 1990 stood at B$1:55 US cents. Notes in denominations of 1, 5, 10, 50, 100, 500 and 1,000 dollars and coins of 5, 10, 20 and 50 cents are in circulation. There is no restriction on the import and export of currency.

Malay is the national language, though English is widely spoken, is taught in many schools and is used in a few government communications. Several Chinese dialects are also spoken and Iban and other native languages are used in the interior.

Brunei's temperature remains fairly uniform throughout the year, ranging from 24°C (75°F) at night to 32°C (90°F) during the day. Annual rainfall is about 250 cm on the coast, rising to as much as 760 cm in the interior; the wet season is from the end of October until March, when the rain can be very heavy and sudden. Humidity is high throughout the year.

Light, easily washable clothing at all times of the year, but remember that very casual and revealing clothing can offend citizens of this Islamic state.

Forcing the pace of business negotiations is likely to backfire. Brunei deals do not progress in the manner of some Western countries and patience and courtesy will get a lot further than aggressive negotiation. This is not a one-stop, sell and sign-the-deal society.

Government and most business offices are open from 7:45 am to 4:30 pm with a break between 12:15 pm and 1:45 pm for lunch and prayers; banks open from 9 am to noon and again from 2 pm until 3 pm and on Saturdays from 9 am to 11 am. Government offices are closed on Friday and Sunday, but remain open all day Saturday.

Shops in Bandar Seri Begawan, except department stores, close on Sundays, in Seria on Mondays and in Kuala Belait on Tuesdays; shopping hours are between 7:30 am and 8 pm but vary from town to town.

BANDAR SERI BEGAWAN

TRANSPORT FROM THE AIRPORT: Buses and taxis without meters are available and bargaining the taxi price is essential; about B$15-20 is normal to the main hotels in Bandar Seri Begawan. Most hotels have courtesy bus services.

TAXIS: There are a few cabs available in the capital; none have meters and if you know where you want to go it is best to fix the fare in advance.

HIRE CARS: There is a reasonable range of services. **Avis** has offices at the airport, the Sheraton Utama Hotel, in the capital itself and in Kuala Belait. The roads between towns are good, though parking can be a problem in Bandar Seri Begawan.

BUSES: A few bus services operate to urban and rural areas and are very cheap but infrequent and not too reliable.

RIVER CRAFT: River taxis or longboats provide an efficient service to Kampung Ayer on the Brunei River and also upriver to Limbang in the neighbouring Malaysian state of Sarawak. Bargaining is in order if you hire a longboat on a private basis.

MAJOR AIRLINES
(all in Bandar Seri Begawan)

Cathay Pacific c/o Royal Brunei Airlines RBA Plaza, Jalan Sultan Bandar Seri Begawan Tel: 42222

Malaysian Airlines 144 Jalan Pemancha Bandar Seri Begawan Tel: 24141

Philippine Airlines c/o Royal Brunei Airlines RBA Plaza, Jalan Sultan Bandar Seri Begawan Tel: 22970

Royal Brunei Airlines RBA Plaza, Jalan Sultan Bandar Seri Begawan Tel: 42222, 40505

Singapore Airlines 39/40 Jalan Sultan Bandar Seri Begawan Tel: 27253

Thai Airways International 93 Jalan Demancha Bandar Seri Begawan Tel: 40500

Few organised tours are available but the state is so small and road communications are so good that it is easy to organise your own outings with a little help from a hotel receptionist. The tourist inquiry counter at the airport can provide information about what possible tour organisers are available.

The 158-room **Sheraton Utama Hotel** in Bandar Seri Begawan is the only genuine international hotel in the state and even then its service may not be as crisp as other hotels in the Sheraton group around the world. The hotel boasts a business centre offering a full range of services including advice on local business customs.

Of the other bigger hotels, **Ang's** and the **Brunei Hotel** have improved considerably, though customers should not expect the standards of service they get in other capital cities in the region. The Brunei Hotel, which was given a facelift in 1990, is pleasant and good value.

The **Hotel Capital** is also worth a try if you are looking for somewhere cheaper. It has in-house movies and a small cafeteria for house guests. A few small Chinese hotels offer cheaper service but are difficult to find without the help of a local friend or guide. In Kuala Belait the choice is pretty much limited to the **Seaview** and **Sentosa** hotels.

The number of tourist-style restaurants and bars is fairly restricted. The Sheraton's **Heritage Restaurant, Maximilian's Restaurant** at Ang's Hotel and the **Grill Room** on Jalan Sultan serve Western food. Try the Sheraton, Ang's or **Phong Mun** in the Teck Guan Plaza for Chinese food; the **Chao Phaya** in Abdul Razak Building for Thai food and the **Regent's Rang Mahel** in the Warna complex for Indian cuisine.

The Indonesian fare is quite good at the **Keri** restaurant in the Seri Complex on Jalan Tutong. Most Chinese restaurants serve alcohol; Islam restricts the serving of alcohol in the state to very few outlets and bans alcohol to all Muslims. Muslim cooking is a speciality of several of the coffee shops in the capital, with curries being especially good. At night "foodstall gardens" serve cheap, local fare.

There is little or no entertainment for tourists, other than cinemas showing mainly Chinese martial arts epics and Malay love dramas (heavily censored). The **Sheraton** occasionally hires musical groups, but there is little other live music, except at private clubs.

Brass cannon, ornamental kris (knives) and kain songket (hand-woven cloth patterned with silver or gold thread) are about the only locally produced handicrafts of interest to shoppers. A good selection and highest quality work is available at the **Arts and Handicrafts Centre** on Jalan Residency, but prices are high. The **antique store** at 48 Kampong Saba Tengah in Kampong Ayer is crammed with Chinese porcelain, Dayak carvings, brass cannons and other local treasures. It can be reached by water taxi. Locally commissioned rattan furniture is of good quality and compares favourably in price with other parts of Asia. Most consumer products are available in Brunei but other Asian countries offer wider selections at cheaper prices.

The state has some fine beaches and scuba gear can be hired in Bandar Seri Begawan and Kuala Belait. Golf, rugby and sailing are also popular and every small community has a viilage

The Omar Ali Saifuddin mosque.

Photo: Hilary Andrews

padang (square) with a football pitch.

Sports facilities for visitors can be arranged through the **Royal Brunei Yacht Club** in Bandar Seri Begawan and **Brunei Shell Petroleum** in Seria. Water sports enthusiasts should make for **Serasa Beach**.

Brunei's holidays are largely in celebration of Muslim religious events. Dates vary from one year to the next according to the moon. Other holidays, celebrating birthdays and recent political events, have fixed dates.

January 1: New Year's Day (public holiday).

Variable: Hari Raya Haji is celebrated by Muslims in commemoration of the sacrifice by the Prophet Abraham. They attend the mosque and pay visits to their friends. Those who have gone to Mecca visit the Baitullah.

January-February: Chinese New Year is celebrated by the Chinese population. People in their new clothes, visit friends and enjoy fine meals (public holiday).

Variable: The First Day of Hijrah (Muhammedan New Year).

Variable: Maulud (Tenth Day of the New Year — public holiday).

February 23: National Day.

May 31: Anniversary of the Royal Brunei Armed Forces (public holiday).

July 15: The Sultan's Birthday (public holiday).

Variable: Me'raj commemorates the ascension of the Prophet Muhammed (public holiday).

September 29: Constitution Day (public holiday).

Variable: First day of the fasting month of Ramadan (public holiday).

Variable: Anniversary of the Revelation of the Koran (public holiday).

Variable: Hari Raya Puasa marks the ending of the Ramadan Fast (public holiday, two days).

December 25-26: Christmas (public holiday, two days).

Addresses

There is no national tourist office in Brunei, but there is a visitors' information bureau at the airport. Most tourist information, however, is available at hotel reception desks.

Publications

Maps of Brunei are hard to obtain but can sometimes be bought in bookshops in the capital. The only newspaper in the state is the weekly English-language *Borneo Bulletin*. An English-language government newsletter, *Pelita Brunei*, is also available. Travel guidebooks are in short supply. The *East Asia Travel Guide* has a small but useful section on the country. *Lonely Planet's* guide book on Malaysia also includes a section on Brunei.

MAJOR BANKS
(all in Bandar Seri Begawan)

	Tel
Citibank	43983
Hongkong & Shanghai Bank	42305
Malayan Banking Bhd	42494
Overseas Union Bank	25477
Standard Chartered Bank	42386
United Malayan Banking Bhd	22516
International Bank of Brunei	21692

DISCOVERING BRUNEI

BANDAR SERI BEGAWAN

Because of its small size, the capital is an easy place to explore and with the aid of a car and a river boat you can also visit the several interesting sites just beyond the city. There is a relaxed atmosphere to the place, making it a more than pleasant interlude for the traveller who may have just come from the bustle of Bangkok or Hongkong.

The highlight of the town is the **Omar Ali Saifuddin Mosque** in the west; this is within easy walking distance from the town proper. It is partly bordered by a lagoon in which floats the **Mahaligal (Religious Stone Boat)**. That part of **Kampung Ayer** connected to the shore extends from round the lagoon into the Brunei River and visitors can venture out on to the maze of wooden footpaths.

Immediately northeast of the mosque are the **Religious Affairs Building** and the **Language and Literature Bureau Building**. Next is the **Secretariat Building** and then a little further on the **Dewan Majlis (Legislative Council Building)** and the **Lapau (State Assembly Hall)**. Some 200 yards northeast of the Lapau is the **Sir Winston Churchill Memorial Museum** a marvellous display and surely one of the strangest reminders of the days of empire to be found in the East.

Also worth a visit is the **Brunei Museum**, about 9 km from town on the Kota Batu road. It is big and air-conditioned and features — in addition to collections on natural history, traditional ways of life and Chinese ceramics — the largest oil-industry display, mounted by Shell Petroleum, anywhere in the world.

One of the most pleasant excursions available is a boat trip on the Brunei River among the stilt-houses of the various parts of Kampung Ayer. While on the water, it is worth visiting the colourful **Royal Tomb** three-quarters of a mile to the west on the north bank of the river.

Istana Nurul Iman, the lavish new palace, also lies to the west of the city. Boasting 1,788 rooms, it is larger than the Vatican and glitters on a hill overlooking the Brunei River. Marble, 22-carat gold, Philippine mahogany and the last piece of Moroccan onyx in the world have been incorporated in the ostentatious interiors. Although the palace is generally closed to the public, visitors may be able to arrange viewings through the tourism or information ministries.

UPCOUNTRY

Beyond the capital you can travel to **Seria** (100 km to the southwest along the coast) and **Kuala Belait** (another 16 km), the sites of Brunei's oil industry, where "nodding donkey" oil pumps dot the landscape.

It is also possible to go by boat and then on foot into the interior and inspect some of the few **Iban longhouses**, though such a trip is undertaken more rewardingly in neighbouring Sarawak.

The most spectacular scenery and wildlife in Brunei can be seen in **Temburong**, the easternmost district, separated from the rest of the country by Sarawak. The district capital of **Bangar** can be reached by a one-and-a-half-hour boat ride from Bandar Seri Begawan, but arrangements for visiting the interior must be made in advance.

HOTEL GUIDE

Hotel address	Phone	Fax	Telex	Cable	〜〜	🍴	🍲
A (US$100-150) **B** (US$70-100) **C** (Less than US$70)							
GAWAN							
A							
Sheraton Utama Jalan Bendahara	44272	21579	2306	SHERATON	▲	▲	▲
B							
Ang's Hotel Jalan Bendahara	23553	27302	2280	ANG	▲	▲	▲
Brunei Hotel 95 Jalan Pemancha	42372	26196	2287	BRUHOTEL		▲	▲
C							
Capitol Hotel 7 Simpang 2, Kampong Berangan	23561	28789				▲	▲
National Inn Seri Complex, Mile One Jalan Tutong	21128			NATINN		▲	▲
KULA BELIAT							
B							
Seaview Hotel Jalan Seria	32651	3301				▲	▲
Sentosa Jalan McKerron	34341						▲

CAMBODIA

Cambodia, with the architectural wonders of Angkor Wat, Bayon and other ancient temples in the country's northwest, used to be one of the most charming tourist destinations in Asia. The Cambodian people were well known for their friendliness and Phnom Penh, the capital, was an enchanting city to visit, with its elegant French-influenced atmosphere.

But in 1970, Cambodia got caught in the struggle for control of Indochina and tourism became hazardous. In 1975, the communist Khmer Rouge seized control of the country, closing it off to the outside world. During the next four years, more than a million Cambodians died — many executed but others from over work and starvation.

A Vietnamese invasion toppled the brutal regime on January 7, 1979, but continuing insecurity and difficulty in obtaining visas from the government kept Cambodia effectively off the tourist map for another decade. But beginning in 1989, Phnom Penh slowly started issuing more tourist visas.

Present-day Cambodia is only a fragment of the Angkor empire, which 800 years ago stretched into what is now Vietnam, Laos, Thailand, and the Malay Peninsula. The origins of Cambodia are believed to date back to the kingdom of Funan, a port southeast of present-day Phnom Penh which was used by traders and pilgrims travelling between China and India between the 3rd and 6th centuries. The kingdom offered tribute to China, while adopting many elements of Indian culture, including its writing system, style of dress, eating habits, and the Hindu religion.

The Cambodian monarchy is generally dated from the time when King Jayavarman II (802-850) founded his capital near Angkor and proclaimed himself "universal monarch." The Angkor empire reached its zenith during the reigns of Suryavarman II (1113-50), builder of Angkor Wat, and of King Jayavarman VII (1181-1219), a Buddhist and the builder of the Bayon temple and 100 hospitals throughout the kingdom.

Their reigns were followed by a period of gradual decline caused largely by frequent wars with the Thais, who, after defeating the Khmer, replaced Hinduism and Mahayana Buddhism with their own Theravada Buddhism. Angkor was abandoned in 1432 and the capital was moved near to what is now Phnom Penh.

Early in the 17th century, Vietnamese kings began to encroach on Cambodian territory in the Mekong River delta. The Thais advanced from the west and by the end of the 18th century had annexed much of northwestern Cambodia. The provinces of Siem Reap and Battambang were later returned, but some areas northwest of Battambang are still in Thai hands today. By the mid–19th century, Cambodia was virtually divided between Thailand and Vietnam.

Cambodia became a French protectorate in 1864, saving it from being totally swallowed up by its neighbours. The Japanese replaced the French during World War II, but in 1945, after Japan's defeat, the French returned. King Norodom Sihanouk — whom the French had installed on the Cambodian throne at the age of 19 in 1941 — and other patriots launched a campaign for independence, which was finally achieved in 1953.

In 1955, Sihanouk abdicated the throne — taking the title of prince — to enter politics and was replaced as king by his father, Norodom Suramarit. As head of state, prince Sihanouk sought to keep Cambodia neutral and from being caught in the escalating war in neighbouring Vietnam and Laos.

In March 1970, Sihanouk was ousted in a coup launched by Marshal Lon Nol, who named

◁ *Charity collectors' puppet.*
Photo: Tom Lansner

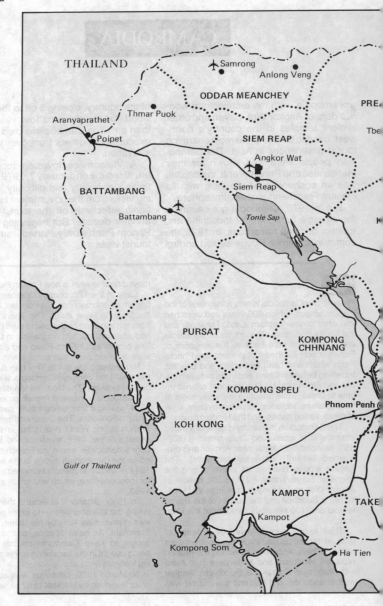

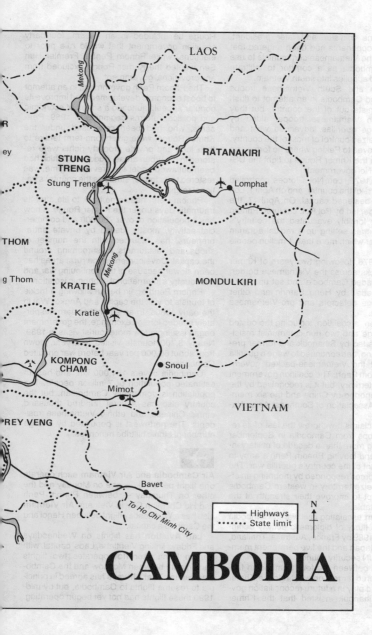

CAMBODIA

himself prime minister and later president. Sihanouk's opponents had been angered that he allowed the Vietnamese communists to use eastern Cambodia as a corridor to infiltrate guerillas and supplies into south Vietnam.

American and South Vietnamese troops soon invaded Cambodia in an attempt to flush the communists out of the country, but they failed. North Vietnamese troops, aided by Khmer Rouge guerillas, advanced west and south and seized control of most of the country. Sihanouk moved to Peking where he formed an alliance with the Khmer Rouge to fight the US-backed Lon Nol government.

By early 1975, Lon Nol's forces controlled less than 10% of the country, and on April 1, Lon Nol fled his besieged capital. On April 17, the Khmer Rouge, led by Pol Pot, captured Phnom Penh. They forcibly evacuated the country's cities and began setting up a radical agrarian society under which more than 1 million people died.

In late 1978, following two years of Khmer Rouge attacks across the Vietnamese border, Vietnam invaded Cambodia and set up a government headed by Heng Samrin and other Khmer Rouge defectors and pro-Vietnamese communists.

Since then, a coalition, including the ousted Khmer Rouge and two non-communist resistance groups led by Sihanouk and former premier Son Sann, has continued to wage a guerilla war against the Vietnamese-backed government in Phnom Penh. The coalition government controls no territory, but it is recognised by the UN and supported by China and the six members of the Association of Southeast Asian Nations.

Vietnam claims it withdrew the last of its remaining troops from Cambodia in September 1989, ending more than a decade of military involvement and leaving Phnom Penh's army to bear the brunt of the country's guerilla war. The resistance forces responded by mounting an offensive to seize territory in western Cambodia in an attempt to improve their strength at the negotiating table.

Fear of an escalating civil war in Cambodia prompted a flurry of diplomatic activity beginning in mid-1989 by France, Australia, Thailand, Indonesia, Japan and the five permanent members of the UN security council.

But talks between the four Cambodian factions foundered largely on what role the Khmer Rouge would play in a future reconciliation government. Sihanouk insisted that the Khmer Rouge be included in an interim, four-party coalition government that would rule prior to elections, while Phnom Penh's Premier Hun Sen wanted the Khmer Rouge excluded from any provisional government.

The Phnom Penh government, in an attempt to boost economic development and improve its popular appeal, launched a series of economic and political reforms beginning in 1989. Peasants, who had been collectised under the Khmer Rouge, were given long-term tenure to their land and private property rights were restored in the urban areas. Buddhism, which had been outlawed under the previous regime, was restored to its former status as the country's national religion.

Phnom Penh has come back to life after its traumatic days under the Khmer Rouge. It now has a population of over 700,000 and commercial activity, mostly fuelled by private entrepreneurs, has resumed with the number of shops and restaurants mushrooming around the capital. Development in the rural areas has been slower because of the continuing war and the country's international economic isolation.

Phnom Penh again began allowing a trickle of tourists to visit the capital and Angkor Wat in the early 1980s. In an attempt to earn desperately needed foreign exchange, the government began issuing a few more tourist visas in 1989. Nearly 3,700 tourists visited that year, down from about 60,000 per year before war engulfed Cambodia.

Cambodia covers 181,000 km^2 and has an estimated population of 7 million people. The population is dominantly Cambodian, but the country also has several hundred thousand ethnic Chinese and ethnic Vietnamese residents. The northwest is populated by a large number of ethnic hilltribe minorities.

Air Cambodia and **Air Vietnam** each operate one flight per week — one on Monday and the other on Thursday — between Phnom Penh and Ho Chi Minh City in Vietnam. **Air Vietnam** also has a Wednesday flight between Hanoi and the Cambodia capital.

Lao Aviation has flights on Wednesdays and Fridays linking Vientiane, Laos' capital, with Phnom Penh. **Aeroflot** operates two flights each month between Moscow and the Cambodian capital. **Thai Airways** has agreed in principle to resume flights to Cambodia, but by mid-1990 these flights had not yet begun operating.

Bangkok Airways and the French airline **UTA** have also been negotiating to fly to Phnom Penh from Bangkok.

Visitors can also travel from Ho Chi Minh City to Phnom Penh by road, but they need authorisation to cross the land border on both their Cambodian and Vietnamese visas. A car with a driver rented either in Ho Chi Minh City or Phnom Penh usually costs between US$200-300 in each direction. Some foreigners have been granted permission to travel on the cheap public buses between Phnom Penh and Ho Chi Minh City.

Visas are issued by the Foreign Ministry, but since there are no Cambodian embassies in non-communist countries (with the exception of India) a visitor is required to get a transit visa from Vietnam or Laos after obtaining a cable or letter from Phnom Penh authorising a Cambodian visa. The visitor can then collect a visa from the Cambodian Embassy in Hanoi or Vientiane, or from the Cambodian consulate in Ho Chi Minh City.

Visitors should specify when applying for a visa whether they plan to arrive by air or by road. At least four to six weeks are normally required to process a visa request. A visa costs about US$10.

No health certificates or vaccinations are required to visit Cambodia, but international health officials strongly advise visitors to have gamma globulin injections to protect themselves against hepatitis. Travellers are also advised to take preventative medication against malaria, particularly for trips to western Cambodia.

Avoid eating uncooked vegetables and drinking water that has not been boiled. Visitors are also encouraged to bring non-prescription medicines such as pain killers, cold cures or diarrhoea medication, because these are often difficult to obtain in Cambodia.

There are no strict regulations at present on what a traveller can bring into Cambodia. Visitors are expected to fill out a customs declaration on which they are asked to list the valuables (foreign currency, gold and jewellery, electronic equipment) they are bringing into the country. These declarations are not usually closely checked.

The official exchange rate at the State Bank, located on Achar Mean Street, was Riel 360:US$1 in mid-1990. Handicraft shops and market stalls usually pay a slightly higher black market rate.

Travellers should bring enough US dollars to pay for their expenses in Cambodia, because travellers' cheques and credit cards are not accepted.

The national language is Khmer, a non-tonal language closely related to Thai. French is in use as a second language among the educated and in most government offices. English is currently the most popular foreign language being studied.

Cambodia lies in the tropical monsoon belt and has an average rainfall of 1,560 mm, most of which falls between May and September. The remainder of the year is dry. A very hot season period immediately precedes the monsoon with temperatures rising as high as 40°C (100°F). The coolest months are November, December and January.

Light tropical clothing is best all year around, with some slightly warmer clothes for occasional cool nights in winter.

Government office hours are from 7-11:30 am and from 2:30-5:30 pm, Monday through Saturday. Meetings should be arranged early in the day, because many officials leave for other jobs later in the day. Government salaries are low, forcing most officials to have more than one job.

The State Bank is open from 7:30-10:30 am and from 2-4 pm Monday to Saturday. Markets are open from sunrise to late afternoon, while shops are open from about 7 am to 8 pm. A 9 pm curfew forces restaurants and bars to close early.

Cambodia

FROM THE AIRPORT: Most visitors to Cambodia are met on arrival by a guide and a car from the Ministry of Foreign Affairs or the Tourism Office.

CARS: Most visitors rent cars from the Ministry of Foreign Affairs or small buses from the Tourism Office to move about the capital and to travel to nearby provinces. Cars cost about US$25 per day around Phnom Penh. If a visitor travels outside the capital, he is charged about 20 US cents per kilometre or between US$150-165 per day dependent on the understanding involved. Following the economic reforms in 1989, some visitors have been allowed to hire cars (with drivers) from private owners.

TAXIS: As of mid-1990, there still were no taxis available at the airport or plying the streets looking for customers.

PUBLIC TRANSPORT: Buses charging very low fares operate over several routes on the main roads of Phnom Penh and its suburbs. Visitors should inquire at their hotel about routes.

CYCLOS: These three-wheeled pedal trishaws wait outside hotels and ply the streets of the capital looking for customers. Visitors should be sure to bargain the price of a cyclo ride in advance.

UPCOUNTRY: Foreigners travelling outside the capital need a special pass and are normally accompanied by a government guide.

Air Cambodia has regular flights to Siem Reap (near Angkor Wat) and Battambang in the northwest, Stung Treng in the north, and Kompong Som and Koh Kong in the southwest. Foreigners are expected to pay in US dollars.

Cambodian Airlines is located on Tuoth Samouth Street. This office also makes reservations and sells tickets for **Air Vietnam**, **Lao Aviation** and **Aeroflot**.

Groups should contact the General Directorate of Tourism on Achar Mean Street in Phnom Penh.

The Foreign Ministry or Tourism Office often make hotel reservations for foreigners, but more recently visitors have been allowed to look for their own accommodations.

In mid-1989, Phnom Penh had less than 400 rooms available for visitors, but this number will double when the five-star, 386-room **Cam-bodiana Hotel** is completed at the end of 1990. Construction of the hotel, plus a casino, was begun by Prince Sihanouk in the late 1960s, but work stopped when he was overthrown in 1970.

In the late 1980s, a Cambodian from Hongkong and two Singaporeans signed a joint venture with the Phnom Penh government to complete the hotel. It is located in one of the most charming spots in the city — the confluence of the Mekong, Bassac and Tonle Sap rivers. The hotel promises uninterrupted electricity and water supplies and direct-dial telephones, which are not available in city's other hotels. Rooms will cost US$75 a night.

The Cambodiana already has several nearby bungalows with three rooms each. They can be rented by visitors for US$18 per night. The disadvantage of the Cambodiana is that it is located some distance from many of the city's more popular restaurants.

About half a dozen other hotels, abandoned during the Khmer Rouge rule in the late 1970s, were refurbished earlier. The **Samaki** (formerly the **Royal**) has a swimming pool, air-conditioned rooms and private baths. Rates begin at US$16 per night for single rooms, while the bungalows behind the hotel cost US$30. The dining room serves Cambodian and French food.

At the **Monorom**, single rooms with air-conditioning and private baths cost US$16 a night. The hotel has a dining room, and there are several good, reasonably priced restaurants nearby. The **White Hotel**, a luxury apartment building during the war, offers some rooms beginning at US$17 a night.

Until recently, it has been difficult to get rooms at the **Samaki**, the **Monorom**, and the **White Hotel** because they were filled with international relief workers and Eastern European advisers. Beginning in mid-1989, many of them have been allowed to move into private villas, freeing more rooms for visitors.

In the late 1980s, several other hotels, including the **Sukhalay**, **Santipheapi**, and **Asia**, have been reopened. They offer rooms beginning at about US$16 a night. The **Sukhalay** and the **Santipheapi** also have restaurants.

The **Grand Hotel**, in Siem Reap near Angkor Wat, has also been reopened. Its rooms cost US$26.

Increasing numbers of restaurants have opened in Phnom Penh since the government introduced economic reforms allowing private

Buddha images at Bayon Temple, Siam Reap.

Photo: Tom Lansner

business in the late 1980s. Eating in Phnom Penh is far from gourmet, but the food is quite good and relatively cheap. Most of the restaurants offer simple French dishes, seafood, Chinese cuisine, and Cambodian curries and soups, which are not as hot as those in neighbouring Thailand. Imported Chinese and European beer is plentiful and cheap.

Some of the best restaurants, featuring live bands and dancing, are located on barges on the banks of the Mekong. The most well known include the **Chatamouk** and **Tonle Sap 1** and **Tonle Sap 2**.

The **Baengkak** and the **Petit Baengkak** restaurants, which are very popular with government officials, are located on the Baengkak Lake, not far from the **Samaki** Hotel. Foreigners are often overcharged at these restaurants if they do not ask for a breakdown of the charges on their bill.

In the downtown area, a visitor can eat in the **White Hotel** international restaurant, the **Seripheap**, or **Liberty**, located between the **Monorom** and **White Hotel**, the **Calamet** (or "Pepper Steak") Restaurant, situated near the **Samaki Hotel**, and the **Railway** "Restaurant."

Restaurants stop serving food around 8:30 pm, because of the 9 pm curfew. Beggars and wounded former soldiers often wait outside restaurants for alms from patrons.

A half dozen markets, selling fresh produce, cloth, antiques, and consumer goods imported from Thailand and Singapore, have reopened in Phnom Penh. The **O Rassey, Toul Thumpung** and **Central** markets are the largest and most popular with foreigners. One of the most popular souvenirs for sale in the market is the traditional silk KRAMA, or scarf. Prices in shops and markets need to be negotiated.

Shops around the downtown hotels offer traditional Cambodian crafts, such as silver boxes, silver and gold jewellery, precious stones, and baskets as well as Chinese antiques. Soapstone apsaras and heads are also for sale, but they are considered national treasures and are not often allowed out of the country.

Cambodia is famous for its deep red rubies and bright blue sapphires, many of which are mined around the western town of Pailin which was captured by the Khmer Rouge in late 1989. Formal gem mining stopped during the war in the 1970s, but individual Cambodian and Thai fortune-seekers continue to hunt for precious stones in the hills around Pailin.

Beautiful rubies and sapphires are available in shops in Phnom Penh, but shoppers are often offered authentic-looking synthetic fakes. Gem experts say that there are no simple rules for guaranteeing that a stone is authentic, unless it is examined in a laboratory. They suggest that shoppers who are afraid of being tricked should not invest large sums of money in precious stones offered in Phnom Penh.

Sporting activities in Phnom Penh are limited. Tennis is available at the **Tennis Club**, while juto, jogging, badminton and soccer are played at the **Olympic Stadium**. Visitors sometimes arrange boat trips on the Mekong or Bassac rivers.

Many Cambodian Buddhist festivals fall on different dates from one year to the next, depending on the lunar calendar.
January 1: International New Year.
January 7: National Day.
April 13-15: Cambodian New Year.
April 17: Day to commemorate the Khmer Rouge victory over the US in 1975.
May 1: Labour Day.
May 2: O Day of Remembrance for the victims of Pol Pot's brutal regime.
September or **October:** Pachom Bun. A memorial day observed by Cambodians for their departed relatives.
October: Katin, the day Buddhists offer new robes and other gifts to monks in pagodas.

CHAMBER OF COMMERCE
Cambodia does not have a Chamber of Commerce.

EMBASSIES AND CONSULATES
Only the Soviet Union, East European countries, Vietnam, Laos and India have embassies in Phnom Penh.

STOCK EXCHANGE
Phnom Penh does not have a stock exchange.

General Directorate of Tourism, Touth Samouth Street. Phnom Penh Tourism.

The National Bank is located on Achar Mean Street.

DISCOVERING CAMBODIA

PHNOM PENH
A tour of the capital should include the **Royal Palace**, which was used by Cambodia's recent kings for coronations, ceremonies and receiving state guests. The **Silver Pagoda**, on the palace grounds, is known for its silver-tile floor, a 90-kg gold Buddha, a small emerald Buddha and hundreds of religious relics.

The **National Museum**, which is being refurbished, offers an interesting exhibit of Khmer artefacts salvaged from the destruction wrought by the Khmer Rouge. **Wat Phnom**, a 200-year-old pagoda set on a hill after which the capital is named, and other recently refurbished Buddhist temples provide additional opportunities for sightseeing in Phnom Penh.

Tuol Sleng, the former Khmer Rouge torture centre where nearly 20,000 people were executed, and the "killing fields" of **Choueng Ek**, about 12 km south of Phnom Penh, introduce a visitor to the horrors of the Khmer Rouge regime.

The **Bassac Theatre** offers occasional cultural preformances, including traditional Khmer dance. By special arrangement, the School of Fine Arts will organise dance and music performances on Saturdays.

Visitors can also arrange to visit the 11th century ruins of the **Tonle Batii** 40 km south of Phnom Penh, and **Oudong**, Cambodia's 16th century capital, about 30 km northwest of the present capital.

UPCOUNTRY
Angkor Wat, the magnificent Hindu temple built by King Suryavarman II at the height of the Khmer Empire in the 12th century is again accessible to visitors, however at a price. Angkor, the world's largest temple complex, is spread over 228 km^2 and consists of sandstone temples, chapels, causeways, terraces and reservoirs. The walls of the temple are covered with thousands of carvings of battles between

The former imperial palace, Phnom Penh.

Photo: Tom Lansner

gods and demons from classical Hindu mythology, sensual dancing women called apsaras, and royal processions with kings riding elephants.

Angkor was abandoned in the 15th century as Cambodia turned to Buddhism, allowing the jungle to reclaim the temple until it was rediscovered by a French naturalist in 1861. French conservators worked to restore the temple until they were driven out by the war in the 1970s. Since then, nature has again threatened Angkor, with moss, algae and lichens disfiguring the stone, bat droppings and water seepage eroding the relief carvings and floors, and trees forcing the temple's stones to shift.

The war itself did less destruction than was often feared, though a shell damaged the West Gate, Angkor's main entrance. Only 15 of the Hindu deities in the "gallery of 100 statutes" remain. Many of the others were apparently smuggled out of the country during the chaos following the 1978 Vietmanese invasion.

Since 1986, Indian archaeologists and Cambodian workers have begun restoring the temple, scrubbing the sandstone which has been turned from a dull black almost back to its original greyish white. One of the more controversial aspects of the reconstruction involves pouring cement filler and recarving missing figures, which some archaeologists argue mars Angkor's ancient beauty. In 1989, UNESCO experts took an inventory of the temples, hoping that the UN would soon be able to help in the restoration.

Angkor remains the national symbol of Cambodia. Its picture is used on everything from money to cigarette packets, and all four Cambodian factions use it on their flags. The Khmer Rouge have three towers on their flag, which is how Angkor appears from the West Gate, while Phnom Penh's flag has five towers.

A return trip to Siem Reap, about 5 km from Angkor, costs about US$90 for foreigners travelling on a regularly scheduled flights on Wednesdays and Saturdays. Occasional charter flights organised to Siem Reap for a one-day trip can cost considerably more. Local officials charge a mandatory US$100 per person for the bus trip from the airport, a poorly-guided tour of the temple complex, and a set lunch at the **Grand Hotel**.

In recent years, visitors have often been allowed to visit nearby **Bayon** temple (Angkor Thom), with its 200 magnificent, slightly smiling stone faces. Most of the other 70 temples and monuments in the area are usually off-limits for foreigners, presumably because of security problems.

When you're flying to Hong Kong,
choose the Airline that knows it best.

Hong Kong's cosmopolitan life
style offers a dynamic blend
old and new, East and West. As doe
the Hong Kong's airline, Catha
Pacific. Combining a tradition
gracious service with more Rolls Royc
powered, wide-bodied flights to an
from our home than any other airline. T
ensure you arrive in better shape.

CATHAY PACIFIC
Arrive in better shape.

HONGKONG

This British territory on the South China coast is a unique experience. With a cosmopolitan air to rival that of New York, Hongkong is a mix of Europeans and Asians — with the Chinese vastly outnumbering their European fellow residents. The hills that split the island of Hongkong (also the name used to encompass the territory as a whole) confront their counterparts behind the Kowloon Peninsula on the mainland on one side and stand guard over the upmarket residential area of the island's "south side" on the other.

If Singapore is the ideal introductory course for visitors to Asia, Hongkong is very much the advanced and intensive programme. So much so that getting into the hustle and bustle of Hongkong too quickly can lead to an overdose of impressions, resulting in confusion and sometimes dislike.

Because of its concern with day-to-day living and a new round of fever relating to making as much money as possible before the territory reverts to Chinese control on 1 July 1997, Hongkong often fails to establish any form of rapport with visitors. Hongkong's initial impact is tremendous and, for the first-time visitor, overwhelming — shops crammed with every conceivable artifact, glitzy boutiques, superb restaurants serving some of the world's best Chinese food, a harbour crammed with ships, sampans and junks, and a feeling of tremendous dynamism and purpose.

But the territory is an area of contrasts. The Manhattan-like skyline of Hongkong Island and the frenzy of the tourist mecca in Kowloon can be left behind in a matter of minutes (traffic permitting) and a new

world is presented to the visitor. In the New Territories water buffalo-drawn ploughs can still be seen at work in the fields and peasants still use farming methods formulated by one of the world's oldest civilisations. But you may need to be fast. Such is the pace of development that anything approximating flat land is being built on.

Recreation takes second place in most Hongkong people's lives and, unfortunately, elementary courtesy and good manners generally take a back seat in the struggle to earn a living.

Despite a pre-occupation with dollars and cents, Hongkong still has very beautiful, peaceful and almost untouched places of interest. The New Territories and the many outlying islands still contain havens of tranquillity, not just for visitors but for many Hongkong people. Although they too are threatened by developers, they still provide alternatives for visitors not interested in shopping.

For the visitor just passing through there is plenty to fascinate, to bewitch and to entertain. A passing affair with Hongkong is unlikely to bring you into contact with any of its problems, except one: Hongkong is no longer cheap. The territory's commercial success has spawned an affluent middle class which demands the best in goods and services — and is prepared to pay for it. Some of Hongkong's leading retailers charge more for brandname goods than their counterparts in Paris, Rome, New York or London. In virtually all sectors, the city has become a lot more expensive than it used to be, but it does give value for money.

Hongkong has one of the highest average standards of living in Asia outside

Japan. It combines extremes of poverty and affluence, security and lawlessness, honesty and corruption, dedication and self-indulgence. It is a cocktail of human types and nationalities. For the visitor, Hongkong can perhaps offer more in a small area than anywhere else in Asia.

By the 18th century, the trading arm of Britain had reached out to touch China. Through the Portuguese settlement of Macau, the traders managed their business, going up the Pearl River to Canton for part of the year's dealings. The Chinese restricted the traders' contacts with the Middle Kingdom to trading only. They were well enough compensated for this by the silver paid for their teas and silks. But the balance of payments ran increasingly against the visitors.

Opium became the counter-measure. The drug had first been shipped into China by the Portuguese during the 17th and 18th centuries. While some found medical use, much of it was used illegally, leading the Chinese emperor to ban its sale in 1729.

The other traders moved in on Portugal, seeing in the sale of opium to China the answer to their silver drain. By 1773, with the East India Co.'s monopoly of the Bengal opium crop, the import of opium had risen to 1,000 chests a year. The import continued apace; the emperor in 1796 renewed an earlier ban, yet by 1836 more than 26,000 chests were being sold.

As the situation worsened, the Chinese demanded the cessation of the opium trade, while the British demanded recognition and the right to trade freely. It eventually led to the war after which Hongkong as a British territory was established.

Hongkong Island was ceded by the Chinese under the Nanking Treaty of 1842, confirming the occupation that had taken place during the First Opium War (1839-41). The additional 3.75 km² of Kowloon Peninsula and Stonecutters Island were ceded under the First Convention of Peking in 1860 after the Second (or Arrow) Opium War (1856-58).

Much later, in 1898, to match the territorial acquisitions of its rival trading nations on the China coast and to secure the better defence of the territory, Britain obtained the 99-year lease of the New Territories on the mainland and 235 islands — 976 km² in all.

Thus, Hongkong Island and the Kowloon Peninsula were British territory to which, in the British view, the original treaties allow China no claim. China regarded these treaties as invalid since negotiations were "unequal." But the whole of the territory is to revert to China in 1997, when the New Territories lease expires, under an agreement reached between London and Peking. This fact will dominate development over the next few years as the date draws nearer and speculation about Hongkong's future under Chinese sovereignty increases.

From the 1840s until the 1950s, apart from the Japanese occupation of 1941-45, Hongkong served as a staging post and trans-shipment centre for the trade between China and the Western world. With the Korean War and the US embargo on export of strategic goods to China, much of this trade was cut off, and Hongkong turned to manufacturing for a livelihood, also becoming a considerable financial centre, which it has remained.

By the mid-1970s, Hongkong seemed once again to have reached calm waters. Turmoil inspired by China's Cultural Revolution, which began in mid-1966, fizzled out in the second half of 1968. Hongkong returned to the more congenial task of making money, aided by a booming economy.

It was in the 1980s that Hongkong began to come of age as a sophisticated entity on the global stage. With the Chinese obsession for education, more and more families saved to send at least one of their children overseas for a Western education. As the decade wore on, the numbers of graduates flooding back to the territory with the combination of Western understanding, Chinese pragmatism and Hongkong-imbued commercial drive set the scene for making the city into one of the world's greatest commercial empires. They gave an international flavour to family wealth which had been derived almost solely from hard work in the manufacturing sector.

The picture has now changed. Although the territory has been promised a high degree of autonomy after British rule ends, the uncertainty over the future has led to a massive drain of educated Chinese to settle in the US, Canada, Australia and elsewhere, creating shortages in many professions and in middle management.

The sudden realisation of the impending change also has sparked a remarkable and uncharacteristic interest in political development

Symbols of capital: the Standard Chartered and Hongkong banks. ▷
Photo: Ashley Wright

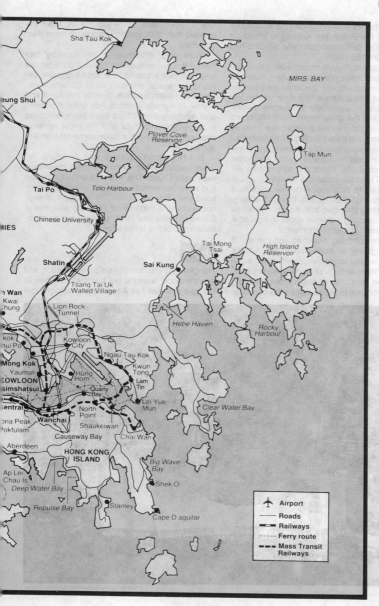

as well as money-making among the local population, and the British are rushing to introduce some form of democratic process which it had neglected for 150 years.

British colonial government was never designed to deal with a complex, modern industrial and commercial society. It was never intended to construct a socialist welfare state, and in fact many people — especially the business community — and the government itself considers that Hongkong's greatest assets have been its free economy and minimal official interference.

Taxes are exceptionally low; there are no import duties except on liquor, tobacco and some petroleum products. There are no currency restrictions. This has made the territory particularly attractive to investors and financiers as a centre for their operations and, though the commercial risk has changed little, some companies are understandably nervous about the political risk component of their investments.

Apart from clothing, watches and clocks, of which Hongkong is consistently the world's largest or second-largest exporter, other earnings come from exports of textiles, electronics, plastics and toys. Hongkong's manufacturing base is continuing to move across the border to China. The value of re-exports in 1989 exceeded that of domestic exports by more than one-third.

Increasing affluence in the territory has forced the government to plan on a bigger tax bite from indirect taxation to fund a growing demand for social services such as education, housing, health and the care of the aged and needy. Hundreds of thousands of local citizens and refugees from China have been rehoused in huge blocks of flats and the most extreme cases of misfortune can claim some aid from the authorities.

But Hongkong's history, and its future, remain bound to the whims of other countries, especially China. The whole dramatic situation has led to increased worldwide interest in Hongkong and, indeed, it could be argued that anyone wishing to experience this pragmatic mix of Sino-British culture in all its free-booting fascination had better do so soon.

Hongkong is the hub of Asia's civil aviation and sea transport network, but traffic shuts down at Hongkong's **Kai Tak** Airport from midnight to 6

The controversial Cultural Centre.

Photo: Hongkong Government Information Service

am. Entry into Kai Tak by air is an attraction in itself. Aircraft skim low over the rooftops of Kowloon and drop frighteningly on to the finger of airstrip stretching into the harbour. Aircraft coming in to land from the western end give passengers the disquieting feeling that they are about to land in the sea. Views are spectacular and it is well worth securing a window seat for the event.

An airport tax of HK$100 (HK$50 for children aged two to 11) is charged on departure from Kai Tak. There are left-luggage facilities in both the arrival and departure lounges and an unaccompanied-baggage service in the departure lounge.

A passport valid for Hongkong is required by the vast majority of people.

Holders of British passports issued in Britain do not require visas for a stay of up to six months.

Nationals of the following countries do not require visas provided their stay does not exceed three months, onward or return sea or air tickets are held (confirmed bookings not required) and they have adequate means of support while in the territory: Britain (holders of British passports issued outside Britain and nationals of depen-

dent territories), Commonwealth countries, Andorra, Belgium, Brazil, Chile, Colombia, Denmark, Ecuador, France, Irish Republic, Israel. Italy, Liechtenstein, Luxembourg, Monaco. Nauru, Netherlands, New Hebrides, Norway. Portugal, San Marino, Spain, Sweden, Switzerland, Turkey and Western Samoa.

The same regulations apply to nationals of the following countries for a stay of not more than one month: Austria, Bolivia, Costa Rica. Dominican Republic, El Salvador, Finland. Germany, Greece, Guatemala, Honduras, Iceland, Maldives, Mexico, Morocco, Nepal, Nicaragua, Pakistan, Panama, Paraguay, Peru, Tunisia, US, Uruguay and Venezuela.

Visitors in the following categories always require visas (except when in direct transit by air and when the person does not leave the airport transit area):

Nationals of Albania, Bulgaria, Cambodia, China, Cuba, Czechoslovakia, Hungary, Laos, North Korea, Mongolia, Poland, Romania, the Soviet Union and Vietnam, residents of North Korea and Iran, holders of Taiwan passports and all stateless persons.

Passengers in transit to either China or Macau enter Hongkong under such conditions as mentioned already.

Registration with the Immigration Department is required only in respect of aliens who

CONSULATES AND COMMISSIONS' TELEPHONE NUMBERS

Australia (573 1881); **Austria** (522 8086); **Bangladesh** (572 8278); **Barbados** (546 7148); **Belgium** (524 3111); **Berlize** (525 9136); **Bhutan** (369 2112); **Bolivia** (525 8446); **Brazil** (525 7002); **Burma** (891 3329); **Canada** (810 4321);**Chile** (868 1122); **Colombia** (545 8547); **Costa Rica** (566 5181); **Côte d'Ivoire** (730 7145); **Cyprus** (529 2161); **Denmark** (893 6265); **Dominican Republic** (730 3306); **Egypt** (524 4174); **El Salvador** (373 0007); **Finland** (525 5385); **France** (529 4351); **Gabon** (572 4062); **Gambia** (735 0682); **Germany** (529 8855); **Greece** (774 1682); **Guatemala** (559 0587); **Guinea** (744 5211); **Honduras** (522 6593); **Iceland** (528 3911); **India** (528 4029); **Indonesia** (890 4421); **Israel** (529 6091); **Italy** (522 0033); **Jamaica** (823 8238); **Japan** (522 1184); **Jordan** (735 6399); **South Korea** (529 4141); **Liberia** (845 4161); **Luxembourg** (823 6400); **Malaysia** (527 0921); **Malta** (739 1515); **Mauritius** (528 1546); **Mexico** (521 4365);

Monaco (893 0669); **Mozambique** (738 4400); **Nauru** (723 3525); **Netherlands** (522 5120); **New Zealand** (525 5044); **Nicaragua** (524 6819); **Nigeria** (893 9444); **Norway** (574 9253); **Pakistan** (527 4623); **Panama** (545 2166); **Paraguay** (833 6887); **Peru** (327 2311); **Philippines** (810 0183); **Portugal** (522 5488); **St Lucia** (524 5898); **Seychelles** (568 9764); **Singapore** (527 2212/4); **South Africa** (577 3279); **Spain** (525 3041); **Sri Lanka** (523 8810); **Sweden** (521 1212); **Switzerland** (522 7147); **Thailand** (521 6481); **Tonga** (522 1321); **Trinidad & Tobago** (388 1071); **Tuvalu** (522 5997); **United States of America** (523 9011); **Uruguay** (544 0066); **Venezuela** (730 8099).

For information on visa applications to the **People's Republic of China**, contact your travel agent or hotel tour desk; to **Nepal**, telephone the Royal Nepalese Liaison Office on 863 3253, to **Taiwan**, call Chung Hwa Travel on 525 8315.

have been granted resident or temporary-resident status in the colony. Those requiring visa extensions apply to the same office. The Immigration Department is on the 2nd floor of Mirror Tower, 61 Mody Road, Tsimshatsui East (Tel: 733 3111).

A valid certificate of vaccination against smallpox is not required unless you have visited a smallpox area in the preceding 14 days; likewise, no vaccination against cholera unless arriving from an infected area.

Visitors are allowed duty-free import of 200 cigarettes or 50 cigars or 250 grams of tobacco: one litre of alcoholic beverages; 60 millilitres of perfume and 250 millilitres of toilet water. Most other items are allowed duty-free entry since Hongkong is a free trading centre.

Firearms (personal property such as rifles, revolvers, etc.) must be declared and handed into custody until departure.

Motor vehicles can be imported into the colony, but for other than intending residents there is little point.

The Hongkong dollar is the legal currency with an exchange value pegged to the US dollar since 1983 at HK$7.80:US$1. There had been no change in the rate to early 1991.

Notes in denominations of HK$10, $20, $50, $100, $500 and $1,000 and coins of 10, 20 and 50 cents (bronze colour) and $1, $2 and $5 (silver colour) are in circulation.

There are no restrictions on the amount of foreign or Hongkong currency which may be imported or exported. Currency can be exchanged at banks or local money changers. There are money changers at the airport, though better exchange rates can be obtained from city exchange offices. Banks offer some of the best rates in town.

All major credit cards are accepted in Hongkong by almost every restaurant or retail establishment. In addition to normal over-the-counter services, there are a number of automated-teller installations that offer local currency against credit cards. American Express card-holders can withdraw local currency at an auto-teller machine located at New World Tower (opposite the Landmark in Queens Road, in Central). Visa card holders can get local currency at Hongkong Bank machines at the airport and eight other locations.

Contrary to many people's expectations, despite having been ruled by Britain for 150 years, few people in Hongkong speak English. Be prepared to have difficulties making oneself understood to taxi drivers and even shop assistants in many places. Some taxi drivers have a habit of not understanding any known written or spoken language when it suits them. Although English and Chinese are both official languages of Hongkong, Cantonese (a south China dialect) is the mother tongue of most of the population, and is widely used on radio, TV and in films. Mandarin and a number of other Chinese dialects are understood by a limited number of people.

Other languages are not widely understood, though most shop assistants in the tourist areas have a smattering of Japanese. Trained interpreters for almost all languages are available for hire. Hotels, business centres and the Hongkong Tourist Association can advise.

The climate is subtropical with the year more or less equally divided between a hot, humid summer and a cool — sometimes chilly but generally dry and sunny — winter. There are short autumn and spring seasons. The rain falls mainly in spring and summer; showers can be very heavy. The difference between day and night temperature is around 5.5°C on average.

From late May to mid-September, Hongkong's summer takes its toll on residents and visitors alike with temperatures up to 33°C and 90%-plus humidity. Life becomes more pleasant in late September to early December. It can get decidedly cool from mid-December to the end of February with temperatures averaging 15°C and the humidity at 75%. The temperature can, however, dip below double digits at times and visitors should include an overcoat in their luggage in winter.

Most years, typhoons affect Hongkong between May and October. But the early warning systems are most efficient. Visitors unfamiliar with the city should not stray too far from base if a typhoon signal appears imminent. Radio and television stations broadcast progress reports regularly and hotels post the signals. If you are caught out, it is possible to repair to the nearest hotel, restaurant or bar and see out the worst of the storm. The atmosphere in some bars is definitely party-like.

The greatest danger to life and limb during typhoons comes from flying debris and only fools venture out after the number eight is hoisted. Even if safely ensconced inside, common sense suggests you should stay away from windows and take reasonable precautions.

If coming solely as a visitor, in the summer men should wear light slacks and shirts; jackets are unnecessary except in the big hotels and the best restaurants in the evening. Women should wear light dresses or slacks. In winter, warmer clothing is required, especially in January and February.

Hongkong is surprisingly formal in business circles, however, and for business visitors suits for men and formal attire for women are expected.

Air-conditioning is universal in hotels and restaurants and in the better-class tourist shops. Hongkong has a justified reputation for having some of the fiercest air-conditioning in the world and it is advisable to take a jacket or wrap if going out dining.

Government offices are open from 9 am to 1 pm and 2 pm to 5 pm Monday to Friday, and on Saturday from 9 am to 1 pm. Sunday is a holiday though many shops are open. Most large commercial firms operate from 9 am to 1 pm. Some firms do not open their offices on Saturday at all. Many smaller Chinese companies operate from 10 am to 7 pm Monday to Saturday. Most banks are open to the public from 10 am to 4 pm Monday to Friday, and Saturday from 9:30 am to 12:30 pm. Some have longer hours.

The Central Post Office by the Star Ferry in Central, is open from 8 am to 6 pm Monday to Saturday. (For shopping hours, *see* **Shopping** section.)

FROM THE AIRPORT: Taxis are available (though one frequently has to wait for some time) at Kai Tak Airport. There is a fare chart indicator displayed prominently immediately outside the airport exit en route to the taxi stand. Taxis to Hongkong Island via the Cross-Harbour Tunnel charge HK$20 in addition to the fare shown on the meter (for most hotels, a total of around HK$60-70). Fares to Tsimshatsui, in Kowloon, where many tourist hotels are located, should be about HK$30. An extra HK$3 per piece of luggage may be charged if you have large suitcases.

If the taxi queue is horrendous, it may be quicker to take an air-conditioned airport bus. There are three main routes with departures every 10-20 minutes. Operating hours are from 7 am to midnight with costs ranging from HK$8-10; exact change is required. Departure is from the same area as the taxi ranks and is clearly marked. Route A1 serves about 15 hotels in the Tsimshatsui area on the Kowloon Peninsula. Route A2 heads for the Central District on Hongkong Island serving hotels from the Wanchai district through Central and ending near the **Victoria Hotel** and the Macau Ferry Terminal. Route A3 takes visitors to the Causeway Bay area, with stops outside the **Park Lane Radisson**, **Excelsior** and **Lee Gardens** hotels. There is a taped commentary on all buses alerting passengers of the destinations served from the next stop. Many stops are a short distance away from the hotels so it is not wise to use the bus system if you have mountains of luggage. Tel: 745-4466 for bus information.

Most first class hotels in Hongkong send transport to the airport for guests. On arrival, you can contact the uniformed representative of your hotel as you leave the customs area. The cost of transport to the hotel is added to your hotel bill, though some Kowloon hotels make no charge for this service.

TAXIS: Taxis are the most convenient means of transport for the visitor. In mid-1991, the flag fall on all urban (red) taxis was HK$8 for the first 2 km and 90 HK cents per 0.25 km thereafter. Waiting time was 90 cents per minute. Taxis are all metered. Make sure the meter is reset at the beginning of your journey. Drivers usually speak enough English to get you to well-known spots but if you are going out of the way, it is best to have the address written in Chinese. Taxis are scarce during peak periods, when it is raining and on horse-racing days (Wednesday and Saturday from September to May). There are an increasing number of taxi stops being introduced as main roads become more clogged. There are ranks on both sides of the harbour at the Star Ferry piers and other points. One of the surest ways to get a cab is to join the queue at

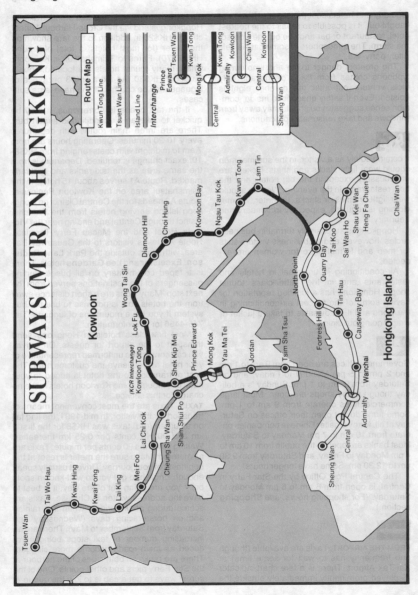

SUBWAYS (MTR) IN HONGKONG

Route Map

- Kwun Tong Line
- Tsuen Wan Line
- Island Line

Interchange

Prince Edward	Tsuen Wan / Kwun Tong
Mong Kok	
Admiralty	Kwun Tong / Kowloon
	Chai Wan / Kowloon
Central	Sheung Wan

Kowloon

- Tsuen Wan
- Tai Wo Hau
- Kwai Hing
- Kwai Fong
- Lai King
- Mei Foo
- Lai Chi Kok
- Cheung Sha Wan
- Sham Shui Po
- (KCR Interchange) Kowloon Tong
- Shek Kip Mei
- Prince Edward
- Mong Kok
- Yau Ma Tei
- Jordan
- Tsim Sha Tsui
- Lok Fu
- Wong Tai Sin
- Diamond Hill
- Choi Hung
- Kowloon Bay
- Ngau Tau Kok
- Kwun Tong
- Lam Tin

Hongkong Island

- Sheung Wan
- Central
- Admiralty
- Wanchai
- Causeway Bay
- Tin Hau
- Fortress Hill
- North Point
- Quarry Bay
- Tai Koo
- Sai Wan Ho
- Shau Kei Wan
- Heng Fa Chuen
- Chai Wan

44

the nearest hotel. Hotel guests may get priority but there is usually a doorman on duty to assist with any language problems.

Cabs may also be hailed in the street, though there are many restrictions and taxis cannot stop except at the designated areas. A yellow line drawn close to the kerb indicates no stopping at certain times of the day, usually morning and evening rush hours. A double yellow line indicates no stopping at any time.

MASS TRANSIT RAILWAY (MTR): A 38.6-km underground system which extends from Central, across the harbour to Tsuen Wan on one leg to the west. Cross the platform at one of the interchange stations along Nathan Road in Kowloon and another route sweeps around the airport and comes back across the harbour via the new Eastern harbour tunnel to join up with the Island line, which runs along the face of Hongkong Island.

Fares for the air-conditioned system range from HK$3-6. There is a bank at each station that will change notes and machines to change coins as required. The ticket issuing machine is easy to understand. Find your destination on the map on the machine. It has a price alongside the name, press the button with the corresponding value and insert coins. You receive a credit card–like ticket which is used to operate the turnstiles to get in and out of the stations. All stations have excess fare offices to make up fares if passengers have purchased a lesser value ticket than the journey demands.

Avoid rush hours — the underground is used by up to 1 million commuters each day. The system is efficient and fast. Tourists (showing your passport) can purchase a HK$20 stored-value ticket which can be used on the underground or above ground Kowloon-Canton Railway trains. The cost of the journey is deducted electronically as you leave stations (a sign flashes to indicate the value remaining).

BUSES: Double-decker serve most parts of the territory, fares ranging from a minimum of HK$1.20 for journeys in the city to a maximum of HK$4.50 (or HK$10 on race days) to the New Territories. Buses are very crowded at peak hours, but otherwise provide a reasonable means of getting about. Get a leaflet from the Hongkong Tourist Association (HKTA) for information on bus routes, stops, numbers. It is against the law for drivers to converse with passengers while the bus is in motion, though few speak English anyway.

MINI-BUSES (public light buses)**:** coloured-coded with either red or green bands, operate over many routes in the territory, providing a quick, convenient way of getting about. Fares range from HK$1 to HK$5, depending on route and time of day. Green-banded mini-buses usually have a fixed fare.

Destinations are displayed on the front, along with the price. Of special interest are those on Hongkong Island that make the run from the east end of City Hall (in the Star Ferry area) to The Peak. Turn right along the front of the Post Office as you come out of the Star Ferry and you will come to a mini-bus station on ground level, under the Exchange Square complex. Good for getting a cheap ride to Wanchai or Causeway Bay.

On the Kowloon side of the Star Ferry terminal, mini-buses run at five-minute intervals to the Tsimshatsui East shopping and hotel area.

TRAMS: On Hongkong island, quaint double-decker trams run from Kennedy Town in the west, through Central District to Causeway Bay, North Point and Shaukiwan in the east. Trams on another route head off a short way inland to Happy Valley. The standard one-way fare is HK$1.00 exact fare, pay on your way out. From the upper deck, the journey offers an excellent picture of bustling Hongkong life, and is a good place from which to photograph the city. Avoid travel at crowded peak periods. One of the best shorter journeys is to take a tram from Central to North Point (destination written on the front), a trip which ambles through Wanchai, Causeway Bay, past Victoria Park and down the backstreet market at North Point. Get off at North Point and shop or simply pay your fare and get on again for the return journey.

PEAK TRAM: The lower terminus is located on Garden Rd, a short walk up the hill from the Hilton Hotel and opposite the US consulate. A free shuttle bus service operates from the Star Ferry pier from 9 am to 7 pm daily. The journey costs HK$8 each way or HK$13 return (children under 12 pay HK$3 each way or HK$3 return). This funicular railway provides a unique view of the city — to be avoided by anyone suffering from vertigo.

TRAINS: Trains operate over two routes in Hongkong. From Kowloon (the station, Hunghom, is near the exit of the Cross-Harbour Tunnel) to the market town of Sheungshui in the New Territories, not far from the border with China. The train passes through Shatin, the Chinese University, Taipokau, Taipo and Fanling. The return first-class fare is HK$24. On Sundays, holidays and race days at Shatin, the train is unbearably crowded. Two through-train services to Canton operate daily. In addition, a Light Rapid Transit service operates from Tsuen Mun to Yuen Long in the New Territories.

FERRIES: In addition to the famous green and white Star Ferry, which crosses between Kowloon and Hongkong Island every few minutes (top deck HK$1.20, bottom deck HK$1), the

Hongkong and Yaumati ferries operate across the harbour and to outlying districts. They leave from Hongkong Island piers in Central (Star Ferry pier area or 400 m to the west of the piers), from Wanchai, North Point and Shaukiwan, and cross the harbour to points in Kowloon and the New Territories such as Yaumati, Shamshui-

LIST OF MAJOR AIRLINES

	Reservations	Flight Information
ON-LINE		
Air France	524 8145	769 6662
Air India	521 4321/4	769 6201
Air Lanka	525 2171	769 7183
Air Nauru	722 1036	
Air New Zealand	845 8063	524 9041
Alitalia	523 7047	769 6448
All Nippon Airways	810 7100	769 8606
British Airways	868 0303, 368 9255	868 0768, 769 8571
Canadian Airline	868 3123	769 7113
Asiana Airlines	5238585	7697782
Cathay Pacific	747 1888	747-1234
China Airlines	868 2299, 367 4181	769 8391
Dragonair Hong Kong	736 0202	738 3388
Garuda Indonesian	840 0000	522 9071
Gulf Air	868 0832	
Japan Airlines	523 0081, 311 3355	769 6524
KLM Royal Dutch Airlines	525 1255	522 0081
Korean Air	523 5177, 733 7111, 368 6221	769 7511
Lauda Air Hong Kong Ltd	524 6178	769 7107
Lufthansa German Airlines	868 2313	769 6560
Malaysian Airline System	521 8181	769 7967

	Reservations	Flight Information
Northwest Airlines Inc.	810 4288	769 7346
Philippine Airlines	522 7018, 369 4521	769 8111
Qantas Airways	524 2101	525 6206
Royal Brunei Airlines	747 1888	522 3799, 747 7888
Royal Nepal Airlines	369 9151/2	747 7888
Singapore Airlines	520 2233, 369 4181	769 6498
South African Airways	846 7879	868 0768
Swissair	529 3670	769 8864
Thai International	529 5601, 730 9225	
United Airlines	810 4888	769 7279
OFF-LINE		
ALIA: The Royal Jordanian Airline	861 1811	
American Airlines, Inc.	525 7081	
Kenya Airways	868 0303	868 0768
Pakistan International Airlines	366 4770	
Scandinavian Airline System	526 5978	
Trans World Airlines Inc.	525 4189	
AIRLINE GENERAL SALES AGENT		
Group Systems International (Asia) Ltd	526 5875	

po, Hunghom, Kwuntong, Tuen Mun, Tsing Yi, Hunghom (train station for China) and Tsimshatsui East. At the Outlying Districts Pier, about 500 m to the west of Star Ferry, ferries run each 30 or 60 minutes to islands such as Lantau, Lamma and Cheung Chau. A very relaxing 45-90-minute trip, except on hectic weekends and holidays, when such journeys should be avoided. The ferries stop running around 10 to midnight. Timetables are available at the piers.

HIRE CARS: Hire cars are available, but roads are very congested in Hongkong and the visitor is advised against hiring a car in the inner areas. For trips to the New Territories or the southern side of Hongkong Island, they may be worthwhile for a group of several people. Self-drive cars cost from HK$200-400 daily while a chauffeur-driven car will cost considerably more. The several car-hire companies are listed in HKTA publications.

There is no shortage of tour operators in Hongkong, so one can readily make arrangements at any hotel for trips to the different places of interest. Tours include a half-day trip around the main points of Hongkong Island, including The Peak and Aberdeen Harbour, a half-day tour through the New Territories, including a visit close to the border with China, and harbour tours. One-day trips to China, either via Macau or across the Hongkong border are available. The trip via Macau is especially good for those looking for a little more than a Chinese stamp in their passport. Prices change quickly, but an indication of costs can be obtained from the nearest HKTA office before you depart. The tourist association itself runs a number of tours, all of which are good value.

The standard of accommodation available in Hongkong is second to none anywhere in the world. Several of the territory's hotels rank as deluxe and the majority of others for tourists are well up to international levels. Almost all are air-conditioned, have private bathrooms, telephones and TV, and in most cases, refrigerators. The majority are located in the tourist shopping areas of Tsimshatsui (Kowloon), Causeway Bay and Central District (see hotel section at end of this chapter).

Hongkong receives about 5.5 million tourists a year and the hotels sometimes fully booked.

Hotel reservations should be made before arrival. The Hongkong Hotels Association does have a service at Kai Tak Airport for those who have not made bookings. If you are booking one of the higher grade hotels, it will almost always be cheaper for you to book before you arrive in Hongkong. Hotels offer a number of very good packages for intending tourists provided bookings are made before arrival.

The **Hongkong Tourist Association** (HKTA) will be able to advise if your travel agent has difficulty. There are HKTA offices in Auckland, Barcelona, Chicago, Frankfurt, London, Los Angeles, Milan, New York, Osaka, Paris, Rome, San Francisco, Singapore, Sydney, Tokyo and Toronto.

Outside the luxury and family hotels, the **YMCA** and **YWCA** have rooms. There are also a number of reasonable, simple hostels and guest-houses where rates range from US$20-50 for a single room. **Chungking Mansions**, 40 Nathan Road, Kowloon, has guest-houses of various classes (unprepossessing would be the best adjective). A variety of cheap accommodation is published in the local newspapers, some offering discount rates for weekly or monthly stays. For visitors staying a month or more, serviced apartments are available for around HK$11,000 for bedroom, lounge and small kitchen.

Note: Hongkong has changed its telephone dialling system. Prefixes for Kowloon (3), Hongkong (5) and New Territories (0) no longer apply. All telephone numbers now have seven digits. If the telephone number is still listed with a prefix, add in the prefix if six digits follow or drop it if the number already has seven digits.

Chinese food in Hongkong is available in greater variety and of a generally higher standard than almost anywhere else in the world. Hongkong's Cantonese (south Chinese) food is unrivalled anywhere, and many other types of regional Chinese cuisine can be found. There are a large number of Thai, Indian, Vietnamese, Japanese and Western-style restaurants, plus a generous serving of restaurants covering every cuisine the world has to offer. For a guide to the range of food and restaurants available in Hongkong, the HKTA publication *Dining and Nightlife* is hard to beat.

Chinese meals are better taken by a group. Cantonese food centres on chicken, pork, fish and other seafood plus rice. It tends to be juicy rather than dry, always fresh and sometimes includes ingredients that Westerners tend to consider inedible or unappetising. Anyone can enjoy crab and green vegetables, fried rice with eggs, pork and shrimps, salt-baked chicken, shark's fin and mushroom soup (with a dash of Chinese vinegar to enhance the flavour), leaving such bizarre (to the tourist) items as ducks' feet, snake soup and sea slug to the real connoisseur.

It is best to order one dish per person in the party (stick to small dishes if your party is fewer than four), accompanied by plain or fried rice and a soup. The usual condiments are soy sauce, vinegar, chili sauce and mustard. Tea is always served and beer, wine or spirits are available at most Hongkong restaurants.

A favourite way to enjoy lunch in Hongkong is to yum cha (drink tea). This means to eat the tasty local morsels known as dim sum washed down with plenty of tea. Trolleys of hot and cold food pass by tables at regular intervals and diners indicate which dishes they would like as the trolley ambles by. A tally is kept either by staff filling in a "scorecard" on the table or, in some restaurants, simply totting up the number of empty plates.

If you have a local Chinese friend to accompany you, so much the better. But you can manage alone: just about all types of dim sum are to Western taste. Spring rolls (chun gun), barbecued pork dumplings (cha siu bao), small dumplings of shrimp (ha gau) and pork (siu mai) are among the best known. Try waterchestnut jelly (ma tai go) or sweet rice pudding (sa mai bo din) for dessert.

Some of the best dim sum restaurants are found in Hongkong's Central District. For an up-market look at dim sum fare, try the **Rainbow Room** on the top floor of the **Lee Gardens Hotel** in Causeway Bay. Dim sum is from noon to 3 pm. The restaurant has a well-earned reputation for the calibre of its culinary range. The **Siu Siu** restaurant in Causeway Bay is also good. On the Kowloon side of the harbour, the unimaginatively **Chinese Restaurant** on the second floor of the **Hyatt Hotel** belies its name with some exquisite, but expensive, dim sum and other Cantonese food.

For Chiu Chow food, you could do a lot worse than the **Golden Island** restaurant in the Island Centre next to Daimaru department store in Causeway Bay. This modern restaurant still manages to retain some traditional atmosphere and the Chiu Chow duck is excellent. Costs run about HK$200 a head including a drink or two.

Cantonese food is good almost anywhere — few restaurants last more than five minutes if the food is not up to scratch. Try **Yung Kee** (32-34 Wellington St) and the **Luk Yu Tea House** (24-26 Stanley St) on Hongkong Island. Pricey but excellent is the nouvelle Cantonese cuisine of the **Sunning Unicorn** restaurant, near the **Lee Gardens Hotel**.

In Kowloon the range is endless. Try the **Shang Palace** for a lot of fun and good food. The **Juno** revolving restaurant on the 24th floor of **Wu Sang House** (655 Nathan Rd) has good food and spectacular views. **The Flower Lounge** group of restaurants has three outlets on Kowloon — all are good. The **Jade Garden** chain has restaurants on both sides of the harbour with daily recommendations which offer good value.

Peking food, characteristic of north China, is also available in Hongkong, though there are far fewer restaurants than those serving Cantonese food. Peking food tends to be crisp and light. One of the great specialities of the north is Peking duck — eaten rolled up in thin wafers of unleavened bread known as bao bing, with strips of cucumber, leek and plum sauce. If you are having Peking duck, do not order too much else as it is very filling, especially if you have soup made from the remains of the duck as a final course.

Yellow fish in wine sauce, prawns in chili sauce and beggar's chicken (a whole chicken wrapped in lotus leaves and baked in ashes until tender — order well in advance), bamboo shoots fried with green vegetables and for dessert, ba sal (candied apple cooled on the spot in iced water), are all excellent, characteristically northern dishes. Peking cuisine also boasts jiao zi (ravioli-like morsels containing meat that can be had either steamed or fried) and delicious onion bread.

What is known as Mongolian hot pot is also offered at Peking — as well as other — restaurants in the territory during the winter months: fish, squid, beef, kidney, liver, vegetables and other ingredients are prepared at your table. Dip them into a tasty broth for a minute or so before eating and at the end of the meal there is a nourishing soup left for a final course. Try the **Genghis Khan** in Luard Rd, Wanchai.

Peking restaurants of note on Hongkong island include the **New American** (177 Wanchai Rd) and the **Peking Garden** group (Excelsior Hotel shopping centre, Alexandra House in Central, Taikooshing shopping centre, as well as Star House in Kowloon). In Kowloon, the

Hongkong ablaze with lights.

Photo: HKTA

Spring Deer is popular with visitors. Service is a bit pushy — they are inclined to run off with your duck and forget about the soup given half a chance — but the food is good.

Shanghainese dishes are also available in abundance in Hongkong. The food, often diced into small fragments and cooked in rather more oil than is the case with either Cantonese or Peking-style dishes, tends to manifest many of the qualities of the other main regional types. It is rather more spicy than either northern or southern food. Recommended Shanghainese restaurants include the **Great Shanghai** restaurant (26-28 Prat Ave). For excellent Shanghainese food at a reasonable price, try the **Ning Po Residents' Association Restaurant** on the 4th Floor of Yip Fung Building in D'Aguilar St, Central. The dumplings are fabulous as is a dish of delicately cooked shrimp in vinegar. The restaurant is also known for its beancurd and vegetable dishes.

Sichuan cooking is becoming more common in Hongkong and is worth trying since its rich, spicy flavours readily become a favourite of those who really enjoy Chinese food. The **Lotus Pond** in Harbour City, Kowloon, serves excellent dishes of this style, as do the **Sichuan Lau** at 466 Lockhart Rd, Wanchai (recommended), the **Red Pepper** (7 Lam Fung Rd, Causeway Bay), and the **Cleveland** (6 Cleveland St, Causeway Bay). The **Pep'N Chili** in Blue Pool Rd, Happy Valley adjusts the spice according to customers' wishes.

Restaurants in Hongkong are often crowded during the lunch period and from 7-9:30 pm and reservations are recommended. English language menus are generally available.

Wandering in the streets of Hongkong you will notice a good many small restaurants with chickens, ducks, chunks of pork and various other items displayed in the window. The chances are no one will speak English, but you can get a long way by simply pointing.

Prices in Hongkong for Chinese food generally average around HK$100-150 per person at most middle-grade restaurants. A meal of steamed rice (*pak fan*), pork and green vegetables will only cost around HK$25-35 in the smaller restaurants. Noodles work out cheapest for the budget traveller, a good meal of noodles with meat and vegetables usually costs no more than HK$20. Meals available at the many foodstalls in Hongkong are even cheaper — hygiene is not necessarily their strongest quality.

Most Chinese will only drink tea with their meals, but those who do drink alcohol will favour beer, whisky, brandy or Chinese *shao xing* or *mao tai* (rice wines similar to Japanese sake, which are best consumed warm). Hua Diao is the most common type of *shao xing*, while Jia Fan is the best and a little more expensive. Those who do not mind a little adventure when it comes to drinking might care to try a bottle of the liqueur-like Mooikwai Lo after their meal.

In the past few years, a number of Vietnamese restaurants have opened, serving variations of prawns and spring rolls among other dishes. Some of the more popular on Hongkong island are the **Vietnam City** in Elizabeth House, Causeway Bay and **Yin Ping** (24 Cannon Street, Causeway Bay) which has a nice family atmosphere and superb eel curry. French table wine is cheap and French bread can replace rice as an accompaniment to the meal.

For Western food, the standard of food in the first-class hotels can rarely be faulted but is not cheap. Without doubt, the most under-reported, first-class restaurant in Hongkong is **Parc 27** on the 27 floor of the Park Lane Radisson in Causeway Bay. An excellent buffet and superb a la carte menu. Always ask to see the set menu for the day. It offers a wide choice and is invariably very good. Service is attentive without being obsequious. Japanese and Cantonese food is also available — the latter being cultured more to Western tastes. The **Regent Hotel** in Kowloon has two extraordinarily good restaurants: the **Steak House** with American steaks and salad; and **La Plume**, with its variations on nouvelle cuisine.

The Royal Garden's **Lalique Restaurant** has a good atmosphere with an original (very pricey) menu. Traditionalists, with good reason, still love the **Peninsula Hotel** with its famed **Gaddi's** restaurant.

The Shangri-La Hotel's **Margaux Restaurant** has unusual dishes such as delicate crayfish, veal, beef and orange cream with blueberries and chopped almonds. On the Hongkong side of the harbour, the **Mandarin Grill** has an elegant atmosphere and sizzling steaks, while upstairs **Pierrot's** has more delicate fare, such as veal cutlet on artichoke hearts. The English atmosphere in the revamped **Chinnery Bar** is recommended. The **Hilton** has several good restaurants and a fine buffet.

The **Harbour City** complex has brought some new dining venues to Tsimshatsui. In the **Marco Polo** hotel is **La Brasserie**, with a touch of France in its food and decor and the **Coffee Mill**, bringing the flavour of South America. In the same building on Canton Road is the **Prince Hotel** with its **Rib Room** for grills, a Spanish-style coffee shop and a British pub called **The Tavern**, where snacks are also served.

Of the non-hotel restaurants, **Au Trou Normand** has the reputation for providing brilliant French food. It is located at 6 Carnarvon Rd, Kowloon. Also in Kowloon is **Jimmy's Kitchen** on the 1st floor of Kowloon Centre on Ashley Rd, and the **Palm Restaurant** on 38 Lock Rd (base-

ment) for superb steaks. On the island side, **Jimmy's** is also at 1 Wyndham Street. Its older brother, **Landau's**, is in the Sun Hung Kai Centre near the Wanchai ferry pier. Great if you are pining for some traditional Western fare. Not on the menu, but available if you ask, is a starter of bacon and mushrooms on toast — delicious. Diehard basic fare diners swear by the corned beef and cabbage, though the restaurant also serves a range of fine Continental food. **Dan Ryan's** restaurant in Pacific Place (near the **Marriot** and **Conrad** hotels) has taken Hongkong by storm with true American fare, and American-size servings.

Fish and chip lovers should try **The Galley**, a bar/restaurant in the basement of Jardine House near the Star Ferry. Connoisseurs of fish and seafood Western style will be tempted by **Bentleys** in Princes Building, Central.

The **Bostonian** in the **Ramada Renaissance Hotel**, 8 Peking Rd, Kowloon, has a good range of steak and seafood. The restaurant offers a 46-oz steak free to customers who can eat the lot. Alligator fritters also grace the menu.

For more international fare, try the **Beverly Hills Delicatessen** or Italian restaurants such as **La Taverna**, or **Rigoletto**. Rather oversauced and over-priced but enjoyable is **Amigo Restaurant**, 79A Wongneichong Rd, opposite Happy Valley racecourse.

There are hundreds of fast-food restaurants, from **McDonald's** to dim sum. Visit **Food Street** and its environs, two blocks east of the Excelsior Hotel, for restaurants of all kinds. Tex-Mex food is at **Casa Mexicana** on the ground floor of the Victoria Centre, Causeway Bay.

Non-Chinese Asian food is also readily found in Hongkong. For Indian dishes the **Maharajah** has outlets on both sides of the harbour specialising in Tandoori and Mughlai food. Prices are moderate. The **Shalimar** and **Viceroy** in Causeway Bay are unpretentious but serve excellent fare. Korean food at moderate prices can be enjoyed at the **Arirang Korean Restaurant** in Happy Valley on Hongkong island and Harbour City in Tsimshatsui or the **Koreana** (Paterson St, Causeway Bay). For Indonesian food visit the **Java Rijsttafel Restaurant** in Han Hing Mansion, 38 Hankow Rd, Kowloon.

All the world's beers and liquor can be obtained in Hongkong. The beers most enjoyed locally include San Miguel (brewed in Hongkong), Lowenbrau (also brewed by San Miguel) and Carlsberg. A beer will usually cost about HK$10-15 (supermarket prices about HK$4-5 a can) and Scotch whisky HK$15-25 a shot, except in the large hotels and hostess bars where the charge is considerably higher. Excellent Chinese beer, especially the lager-like Tsingtao, is also available and cheaper.

Hongkong's nightlife falls into four main categories: drinking spots of various grades with or without music; discos, nightclubs and girlie bars. In addition, the ubiquitous Japanese *karaoke* "do-it-yourself" singing bars are mushrooming all over the city. Major hotels have supper clubs offering floor shows and sometimes a singer or dance band. Newspapers will list any special guest entertainers. Some Chinese restaurant-nightclubs feature a band (usually Filipino) and vocalists.

The Lan Kwai Fong area of Central District, at the top of D'Aguilar St — a block uphill from Queen's Rd — was spawned in the yuppie era. It has matured into a nightlife area offering the gamut of options from an excellent jazz club for serious buffs of the genre to a disco/restaurant offering some of the best hamburgers in town — with music. The area includes the **Disco Disco**, and the **California Bar and Grill**, an up-market cocktail lounge with West Coast cuisine and dining and dancing until 4 am. The **1997** restaurant and adjacent bistro is arguably the founding restaurant of the area. There are also a number of smaller restaurants, and music bars which give the area a chic-quarter aura.

Discos are very popular. In Tsimshatsui, the pack is led by the **Canton** disco which should be experienced. **Apollo 18** is in the basement of the Silvercord building across from Ocean Centre. **Hot Gossip**, in the Harbour City complex, attracts a more mature audience. The **Tropical** disco in Tsimshatsui East is popular with locals. Cover charges run about the HK$100 mark and usually include a couple of drinks. The upmarket **Downstairs** at Duddell's **Discotheque** has a pretty good restaurant service to accompany its elaborate sound and light systems.

In Kowloon, there is a loose collection of seven bars and clubs in the **New World Centre** (Salisbury Rd, Tsimshatsui) called **Bar City**. It includes a disco, and a country-and-western tavern, live bands and cabaret.

The **Godown** (Admiralty Centre) is popular, and has good food and an informal atmosphere. The **Dicken's Bar** at the Excelsior is a favourite haunt for jazz on Sunday afternoons. The **Gal-**

lery Lounge at the Park Lane Radisson has show-band style music. Among pubs and taverns on Hongkong island, look for more traditional pub fare from **Mad Dogs** in Wyndam St near Lan Kwai Fong; the **Bull and Bear** on the ground floor of Hutchison House in Central, and the **Jockey** in Swire House. In Kowloon, try **Ned Kelly's Last Stand**, best after 10.30 pm, and the **Blacksmith's Arms** in Tsimshatsui. The **China Coast Pub** at the **Regal Airport Hotel** has excellent fish and chips and a boisterous pub atmosphere. **Bonker's Bar** is not a bad spot despite its name and you should not go home without calling for at least one drink at **Bottoms Up** — a lot of good, clean, naughty fun. **Bottoms Up** welcomes couples, lonely bar-hoppers and others looking for a good time with equal enthusiasm.

More exclusive bars include the **Noon Gun Bar** in the **Excelsior** (very good); **Browns Wine Bar** in Exchange Square has an excellent range of good and vintage wines and the **Champagne Bar** at the **Grand Hyatt** serves champagne by the glass, a variety of caviar and live music in the evening. In Kowloon try **Nathan's** in the **Hyatt** or the **Tiara Lounge** at the **Shangri-La**.

Visitors should be warned that the famous Wanchai and Kowloon topless bars — not quite like they were in the days of Suzy Wong — can be tempting but also very very expensive, with their sleazy habit of assuming that any Western or Japanese customer is buying drinks for all the hostesses. Although they may well be sipping cold tea, the customer will be charged for brandy — and there is no arguing against the management when the bill is presented. Be warned. The "bar fine" for taking one of the hostesses out also is way above the going rate in Asia and does not include any favours negotiated for later.

There are also several up-market clubs, designed for the expense-account executive and almost unbelievably lavish (or garish depending on your taste). Emulating the Japanese "superclub," they are huge. **Club Bboss** and its sister operation, the **Metropolitan** in Tsimshatsui East cover 140,000 ft^2 and have about 1,500 hostesses on duty. They usually have large dance floors, a number of bands (usually Filipino) plus female singers. Decor includes upholstered ceilings, Italian marble statuary, gushing fountains and partitions of etched glass around the many VIP rooms, where groups of businessmen may settle in a cosy atmosphere with their hostesses while a clock — like a taxi meter, ticks up the cost for their company.

These places are expensive, yet fully patronised even on week nights.

Other examples are the **New Tonnochy Nightclub**, which displays its charges (and its charms) clearly and the **Club Celebrity** both in Wanchai. In Tsimshatsui are the **Club Deluxe**, the **Club de Hong Kong**, the **Club Cabaret** and the **China City** night club. None of them is for the faint-hearted without a credit card but if one wants to be parted from one's money, these upmarket establishments offer better value than the sleazy ones.

CULTURE

During January and February, the **Hongkong Arts Festival** schedules several first-rate events, and there is an **International Film Festival**, usually in April. The biennial **Asian Arts** festival generally occurs in the fourth quarter of the year.

Chinese opera can be seen at any number of venues ranging from concert halls to local playgrounds. The Hongkong Tourist Association organises performances of Chinese art forms twice a week. The show lasts an hour and is free. The offer is well worth following up to get a taste of everything Chinese from martial arts to puppet theatre.

The city's offerings of Western films are usually badly cut, not only by the censors — who cut all explicit or even semi-explicit sex but leave in all the violence — but also by managements to fit in an extra performance. The screen is dominated by Chinese martial arts films, comedies or a combination of both, though the work of some serious local directors is slowly gaining recognition.

There are a number of venues in Hongkong for the performing arts. The recently opened Hongkong Cultural Centre on the waterfront near the Star Ferry in Tsimshatsui has come in for a good share of criticism because of its architecture, but at last has provided Hongkong with a world-standard concert hall and two theatres. Complaints that the seating is too crowded are being addressed and meanwhile the centre is drawing higher quality performers than the territory has previously seen.

The **Hongkong Academy for Performing Arts** in Wanchai is an impressive training centre and has within it six fairly good venues for performances. Its next door neighbour, the **Hongkong Arts Centre**, concentrates on providing an outlet for local amateur and professional performances. It is worth attending.

The **City Hall**, near the Star Ferry on Hongkong Island, has a concert hall capable of holding 1,500 people and a theatre for drama and chamber music and is a convenient place to call in to get information about what is happening at other venues in the city.

The **Fringe Club** is housed in an old warehouse in the Central District. A 10-minute climb up the hill via Ice House St or Wyndham St. It is worth paying the HK$10 one-night membership fee for a relaxed and informal evening.

The **Queen Elizabeth Stadium** in Happy Valley and the **Academic Community Hall** in Kowloon Tong play host mainly to music groups or pop concerts.

The **Hongkong Coliseum** (which looks like an inverted pyramid) near the Hunghom railway station in Kowloon has enormous capacity and is best suited for shows or sporting events.

Shopping is still one of Hongkong's prime attractions, though you should not assume that Hongkong prices are always necessarily lower than elsewhere. They are for certain lines of goods, but the city caters for a sophisticated market of international travellers, many of whom can afford to pay a great deal for their trinkets from the East, and so prices are listed to match.

With some 5.5 million visitors annually passing through Hongkong, there are sure to be a few fools and many shopkeepers operate on the basis that you are one of them.

A hard and fast rule for shopping in Hongkong is to visit several shops and try to knock the price down progressively until you reach what is fairly obviously the market price. It is probably reasonable to say that most goods aimed at the tourist market in Hongkong have a starting price at least 25% higher than the actual selling price. One good way is to price items in the fixed-price department stores — you ultimately may find the prices cheaper and a greater variety there than in the "bargain" shops.

Less reputable shops in Hongkong still occasionally sell falsely represented goods — fake brand-named goods, for instance — though the practice is now rare. Shops carrying the emblem of the Hongkong Tourist Association (HKTA) can usually be expected to carry on their business in a proper manner. One should still bargain.

However, with goods such as watches, cameras and Hi-Fi equipment, one should always buy from a shop properly certified as an agent for a particular brand of equipment and get the manufacturer's international guarantee, not the shop's guarantee. Be warned that prices at duty-free shops at the airport are sometimes higher than in Hongkong.

The usual shopping hours are 9 am or 10 am to 7 pm or 10 pm for European-type shops and department stores. Almost all are open on Sundays and the majority of public holidays except on Christmas Day and Chinese New Year. Even then, some Chinese-style shops remain open.

Main items visitors find alluring are table linen, embroidery, silk, brocades, pewter, copper, jewellery, jade, camphor-wood chests, carpets, rugs, furniture, rattan ware, porcelain, pottery, curios, watches, cameras and electronic goods. The export of carved ivory — once a major attraction — is now barred under an international agreement to try to save the African elephant from extinction and there are penalties for attempting to export ivory illegally.

Hongkong tailors have a worldwide reputation for speed, and suits can be made in 48 hours, but you will get a much better product if you give them a week. Prices are not as competitive as was once the case. Made-to-order women's garments usually take longer to make (especially at the better shops), so off-the-peg clothing is probably a better buy. Hongkong women's wear is very fashionable and there is a good range of garments. Made-to-order shoes also are easy to come by.

The principal tourist shopping areas in both Kowloon and Hongkong Island radiate out from the Star Ferry piers on each side of the harbour. There is also good shopping in Causeway Bay and Tsimshatsui East which face each other on opposite sides of the harbour. In Central District on Hongkong Island, Connaught Rd, Des Voeux Rd, Queen's Rd, and the streets that run between them are devoted to shops, restaurants and offices. Many excellent shops are found in the arcades, and on the second or third levels. Hongkong shopping should never be confined to the ground floor — prices on higher floor shops can be cheaper because rents are lower. Wyndham, D'Aguilar and Wellington Streets are also of interest, especially for Chinese curios.

Mainland Chinese department stores are a novel feature of the Hongkong shopping scene. They can be found on both sides of the harbour, selling a wide range of items from everyday household goods to Chinese crafts. Not all their products are made in China but would-be travellers to China will usually find cheaper prices and better quality in Hongkong than they will on the mainland. Prices are fixed, as is also the case in such non-communist department stores as the Japanese-owned **Daimaru** in Causeway Bay. The better known Chinese stores are **Chinese Arts and Crafts** and **China Products**, both of which have several branches, and **Yue Hwa**.

Market-style shopping is everywhere. The best known is the "designer" market in **Stanley**, on the south side of the Island, which sells

Traditional dragon boat race.

Photo: HKTA

53

namebrand casual and sports clothes at knockdown prices. A visit can be combined with a trip on a double decker bus from Central which winds along the spectacular coast road. Great bargains can be found at the Sunday clothes market one street back towards the harbour from the main street in **North Point**. Take a tram from Central to North Point (experience the Hongkong crush). The **Ladies' Market** in Tung Choi St in Mongkok, Kowloon, is worth visiting. It is open daily from 1 pm to 11 pm — go after 7 pm when the trolley vendors have finished their regular jobs and take to the streets with a range of "over-runs." The **Temple St** market in Kowloon runs from 8-11 pm specialising in menswear, watches and electronic gadgetry. The markets can be extremely crowded and, while they are well policed, visitors should keep wallets secure against pickpockets. Do not flash around large quantities of notes when buying goods.

Markets stall holders deal exclusively in cash but almost all shops will take some form of credit card. Visa/Mastercard and American Express are the most popular, though sellers may insist on a 3-5% surcharge for accepting a card.

Clubs catering for several kinds of sporting activities can be found in Hongkong, and visitors may either be granted temporary membership on the payment of a small fee or be allowed to use the facilities, again for a fee. Most golf courses are open to visitors from Monday to Friday, with the exception of public holidays. The **Royal Hongkong Golf Club** has three 18-hole courses at Fanling in the New Territories. Contact the club secretary by telephone, confirm that the course is available and check details of transport to this course or the nine-hole course at Deep Water Bay. Or you can use the new Sports and Recreation Tour offered by the HKTA. Packages include pick-up from hotels, lunch at the club, and return to hotel. Golf clubs, badminton and squash rackets can be hired, but you must supply your own sports wear and appropriate shoes.

Squash, basketball and tennis are very popular and there are many courts in the territory, including public ones as well as private clubs. Soccer, too, has a big following and there is a professional league which plays in the winter months. Amateur cricket is played during the cooler months of the year; it can be seen each weekend at the **Hongkong Cricket Club** in Wongneichong Gap Rd. Hongkong also has a vigorous rugby football league, with games on Saturday afternoons and Wednesday nights from September to May. The Hongkong seven-a-side rugby tournament is held in March or April and offers a weekend of non-stop rugby attracting world-class teams from New Zealand to Russia and all points in between. Book early with your travel agent as seats sell out long before the event.

In the summer, Hongkong's plentiful sea comes into its own, with sailing, water-skiing, skin-diving, all having their supporters. Details of clubs can be obtained from the HKTA. Swimming is a pleasant way of escaping Hongkong's summer heat. Most hotels have pools and there are 42 public beaches throughout the territory. They tend to be crowded on weekends and often the water is far from free of pollution. Cleaner beaches can be found on the outlying islands.

Joggers, even in summer, will find morning partners in Kowloon Park, Victoria Park (in Tsimshatsui and Causeway Bay respectively) and Bowen Rd, Mid-levels, Hongkong.

For hikers, Hongkong still has many trails to take one's mind off the urban congestion. More than 70% of the territory is classified as a rural or country park. For the truly adventurous, the **MacLehose Trail** offers 100 km of hiking through some of the most scenic sections of the New Territories. It passes through eight country parks and is divided into 10 sections. Bus stops intersect the trail periodically so the hiker can choose easy or difficult routes, or plan to walk for one or several days. There are plenty of shorter walks available for the casual stroller. Be sure to take a water bottle as the heat can become severe as the day progresses.

By far the most popular "sport" in Hongkong is horse racing — or rather betting. Hongkong's racing season at **Happy Valley** and **Shatin** is from September to May. Turnover has topped the US$100 million a day mark. Racing is held most Saturday afternoons, some Sundays and on Wednesday evenings during the season. One should reach the course well before the first race to be sure of getting in. Guest tickets for admission to the members' enclosure (HK$50 and passport proof that you are a bona fide visitor) can be obtained from the **Off-Course Betting Centre**, near Star Ferry, or at the club itself on the day. The HKTA has horse-racing tours that will pick you up from the hotel, take you to the course, feed you and bring you home again. It will not, however, guarantee you a winner.

Hongkong's festivities very much revolve around the traditional Chinese lunar calendar, which means that particular events will fall on different dates from one year to the next. A number of Western events are celebrated and fall on set dates (with the exception of Easter).

January 1: New Year's Day (public holiday).

January-February: Chinese New Year (first day of the first moon — public holiday, three days). The Chinese community celebrates in a carnival atmosphere. Everyone wears his best, debts are paid, families visit one another, feasts are enjoyed and everyone is wished *Kung Hei Fat Choi* (which means good prosperity). Traditional firecrackers are banned in urban areas but on the outer islands police "look the other way" and at midnight on New Year's Eve there are barrages of exploding firecrackers which continue sporadically most of the night.

January-February: The Lantern Festival marks the end of the Chinese New Year on the 15th day after the first moon. Lanterns are hung in homes and at restaurants. In Victoria and Kowloon parks thousands of children go out with their families waving lanterns to celebrate the event.

February: Hongkong Arts Festival, lasting the first three weeks of February, brings to the territory some of the world's best theatre, concerts, dance and art. (Bookings are necessary well in advance.)

March-April: Ching Ming festival (fourth or fifth day of the third moon) is a family festival when visits are made to the graves of relatives to perform traditional rites (public holiday).

Easter (public holidays — Good Friday, Saturday and Easter Monday).

April-May: Tin Hau festival is the greatest festival of the year for Hongkong's fishing community and others connected with the sea, when they celebrate the birthday of Tin Hau (the Goddess of Heaven). There are many Tin Hau temples in Hongkong and on the surrounding islands. On the festival day the most striking celebrations are held at the Tai Miu (great temple) a little way inland at Joss House Bay. At dawn the fishermen and boat people set out for the temple in gaily bedecked junks, sampans, motor boats and a special ferry which runs to the temple on this day only. The beach and the slopes leading up to the temple are packed with people, carrying offerings. Lion dances are performed outside the temple. The Tam Kung festival held on the eighth day of the fourth moon is

also a celebration for fishing folk, paying homage to a child-god said to have had the ability to control the weather.

April or May: sees the Bun Festival on Cheung Chau island — the date being decided by "divine decree." It lasts a week during which there are religious observances, processions, Chinese opera and a fiesta atmosphere on the island. The main procession is held on the fourth day. This festival has lost some of its interest for tourists, as the giant bun towers have been scaled down since two fell over in 1978 while villagers were climbing them to get the lucky buns at the top. Climbing the towers is now prohibited.

May: Birthday of Lord Buddha is celebrated most notably at Po Lin Monastery on Lantau Island.

May-June: Tuen Ng (dragon boat) Festival on the fifth day of the fifth moon is one of the territory's most famous occasions and is traditionally associated with the drowning by suicide of the poet-statesman Chu Yuan (332-296 BC) who died in protest against the social conditions of the time. The dragon boat races held on this day perhaps symbolise attempts to rescue him. The principal race is held at Taipo (the town can be reached by the Kowloon-Sheungshui train): others are held at Aberdeen, Stanley, Tuen Mun, Shatin and Cheung Chau. The boats used are long, thin shells with a dragon's head at the bow and they carry as many as 50 rowers. Amidships a huge drum is beaten to give time. The races are a most exciting occasion (public holiday). In recent years an international race, held in Hongkong harbour off Kowloon, usually on the Sunday following the actual festival, has been introduced and attracts entries from all over the world.

July-August: The Birthday of Chinese artist-engineer Lu Pan, is held on the 13th day of the sixth moon. This patron of builders is credited with the invention of the drill, plane, shovel, saw, locks and the ladder. Homage is usually paid to Lu Pan at the commencement of major construction projects.

August: Liberation Day (last Monday of August) commemorates the territory's liberation from the Japanese in 1945 (public holiday).

August-September: Yue Lan (hungry ghost) festival on the 15th day of the seventh moon marks the day that hungry ghosts wander the world and paper money, fruit and other offerings are made to appease them.

September-October: The Mid-Autumn (moon) festival on the 15th day of the eighth moon is one of the major events of the year. Moon cakes (sweet and not particularly appealing to most foreigners) are eaten and children carry beautiful lanterns made in the shape of birds and fish. People flock to the peaks of Hongkong to view the full moon.

September-October: The Birthday of Confucius (27th day of the eighth moon) is commemorated at the Confucian temple in Causeway Bay.

October: Chung Yeung Festival on the ninth day of the ninth moon. People flock to the high places on the Island following the advice of a Han Dynasty sage that this is the way to avoid disaster.

December 25, 26: Christmas Day and Boxing Day (public holiday).

Addresses

HKTA information offices in Kowloon are located in the customs enclosure at the airport, at the Star Ferry Concourse and at Shop No. G8, Empire Centre, in Tsimshatsui East. On Hongkong side the association's headquarters are at Connaught Centre (35th floor).

Information office hours are 8 am to 6 pm Monday to Friday but the office at Empire Centre is open 9 am to 6 pm daily. (Kowloon offices); 8 am to 1 pm Saturdays; 9 am to 1 pm Sundays. A telephone information service operates during the same hours on 722 5555 and 524 4191.

Publications

A number of excellent publications on Hongkong, available free or for a small charge are available from **Hongkong Tourist Association** (HKTA) offices. Titles may change but they are extremely comprehensive and include guides to shopping, eating out, walking tours, hotels, Chinese festivals and special events, sightseeing, arts and crafts and museums, public transport and the outlying islands. Also available from the HKTA centres are fact sheets on factory outlets, hostels, campsites and other accommodation in Hongkong. The head office of the HKTA is on the 35th floor of **Jardine House** (Tel: 801 7177). Information and souvenir outlets for the HKTA are located at: **G/F Royal Garden Hotel, Shop G-2, 69 Mody Rd, Tsimshatsui East; the Star Ferry** concourse and **Shop 8** in the basement of **Jardine House**. They are open from 8-9 am to 6 pm weekdays and 8-9 am to 1 pm on Saturdays. Telephone information is

available by calling 801 7177 (multi-lingual); 801 7133 (Mandarin) or 801 7188 (Japanese). There is a shopping hotline on 801 7278.

For a deeper read on what makes Hongkong tick and some excellent maps, try the **Government Information Services** shop on the ground floor of the main **Post Office** in Central.

Wanderlust Books on the mezzanine floor at **30 Hollywood Rd,** Central specialises in travel books and can provide material on almost any country in the world. (Tel: 523 2042).

The **South China Morning Post Family Book Stores** are located on both sides of the harbour. Handy for visitors are the ones located in the **Star Ferry** concourse in Central and the **Ocean Centre** in Harbour City, Tsimshatsui.

The **Swindon Book Co.** has three outlets in Kowloon: **13-15 Lock Rd** (Tel: 311 3732); **3249 Ocean Terminal** and **64 Nathan Rd.**

Hongkong and Shanghai Bank, Tel: 822 1111; Standard Chartered Bank, Tel: 842 2333; Bank of China, Tel: 521 2626; Hang Seng Bank, Tel: 825 5111; Citibank, Tel: 807 8211; Bank of East Asia, Tel: 842 3200; Bank of America, Tel: 847 6111; Security Pacific Asia Bank Ltd, Tel: 841 1811; Shanghai Commercial Bank, Tel: 841 5415; Overseas Trust Bank, Tel: 575 6657; Nanyang Commercial Bank, Tel: 852 0888.

Major government department located in Central Government Offices, Lower Albert Rd, Hongkong. Finance, Tel: 810 2669; Economic Service, Tel: 810 2762; Banking Commission, 9/F, Queensway Government Offices, 66 Queensway, Tel: 867 2671, Tlx: 64282 COFB HX; Trade, 1, 8, 13, 14, 15/F, Ocean Centre, 5 Canton Rd, Kowloon, Tel: 737 2333, Tlx: 45126 CNDI HX; Industry, 10, 14/F, Ocean Centre, 5 Canton Rd, Kowloon, Tel: 737 2573, Tlx: 50151 INDHK HX; Constitutional Affairs, Tel: 527 0380;

DISCOVERING HONGKONG

HONGKONG ISLAND

The first, almost essential, excursion is to the **Peak**, reached either by taxi or mini-bus from the Central District of Hongkong Island or — much better — by the **Peak Tram** whose lower terminal is just a little way up Garden Rd (200 m up the hill from the Hilton Hotel). Free shuttle bus from the Star Ferry. The view from the Peak, 400 m above sea level — in clear weather, which is not always guaranteed — is one of the great sights of the world. To ride up in the late afternoon and down again after dark enables you to enjoy views of the city both by day and when lit at night. From the top, you can survey the most populous district of the Island, taking in the whole span of the harbour with its multitude of merchant vessels and, from time to time, the warships of the US, British and other navies. The panorama extends right across to Kowloon's hills from which Kowloon (nine dragons) gets its name.

From the Peak tram top station there is a spectacular 45-minute walk (on level ground) round the Peak on **Lugard Rd**, which gives a full view of Hongkong and the harbour, and also over the islands of the South China Sea out towards Macau. (Alight from the tram, walk down the 30-m corridor, turn right and take the level road to the right — not the one up the hill — to reach Lugard Rd, which is really only a path for much of the way.)

If you are feeling energetic you might walk up to the gardens at the top of the Peak, from which there is a view almost all round the island. For those unable to make the walk, which is steep, there are taxis at the Peak Tram station which will make the trip to the top. From the Peak, one can also walk through Hongkong's undisturbed countryside by taking the **Pokfulam Reservoir Rd** running southwest some 3 km down to Pokfulam Rd from where buses and taxis run either back to **Central District** or in the opposite direction to **Aberdeen**, **Deepwater Bay** and the south coast. (Buy a copy of the Hongkong Island map available at the HKTA information offices, which clearly shows Lugard and Pokfulam Reservoir roads and a great many other enjoyable walks.)

The Peak tram (one-way fare HK$8 — children HK$3) is a funicular cable car, recently modernised (still with old-style carriages) and fully automated and computerised. The tram is often crowded on the ascent, but not so busy on the descent. If you find it busy at the bottom consider taking a taxi to the top and riding the tram down.

The Peak area is traditionally the home of many of Hongkong's senior government servants and businessmen. It is often wreathed in mist during the early months of the year and gets rather cool. In summer it offers a little relief from the sticky heat below.

To relieve the congestion on the pavements in Central District, a network of elevated walkways links the whole area, and most access and exit points are by escalator. From **Jardine House** the walkways take you towards the **Macau Ferry Terminal** via the **Outlying Island** ferry terminals in one direction or across the road and through **Swire House**, **Prince's Building**, **The Landmark** and the **Mandarin Hotel** and nearby buildings without having to touch ground and cross a road — often a hazard in Hongkong.

Two of the most impressive of Hongkong's skyscrapers are both relatively new — the **Hongkong and Shanghai Bank** building and the **Bank of China Tower**, built in very contrasting but equally impressive styles. The Bank of China, designed by famous Chinese-American architect I. M. Pei, is the tallest building in the territory and to some symbolically stamps China's authority over its prodigal son.

On Sundays, some of the streets in Central are closed off to traffic and given over to strollers, who include thousands of Filipino maids having their day off. **Government House**, the residence of the British governor of Hongkong — source of executive power and representative of Queen Elizabeth — is located on Upper Albert Rd, a right-hand turn from Garden Rd. You cannot enter, but the police guard will not object if you stand at the gate and peer inside. Across the road are the **Zoological and Botanical Gardens** (with good aviaries) from which one has a better view of Government House. In the early morning Chinese enthusiasts come to practise their graceful art of *tai chi chuan* (shadow-boxing).

Virtually all the 18th-century buildings in Hongkong have made way for modern blocks, with the old **Supreme Court** building (now used by the Legislative Council) opposite the war memorial, and **St John's Cathedral** two of the few old buildings still remaining.

Along **Queen's Rd** in a westerly direction (to the left as you face the harbour) the streets soon assume a much more Chinese character, and the many open-fronted shops offer an exciting picture of Chinese exotica. Climbing any of the steep, narrow, staircase streets that lead up the hillside from Queen's Rd will lead you to tiny stalls and shops selling a jumble of merchandise. Of special interest are the curio shops to be found in **Ladder St** and **Hollywood Rd**, which lie up the hill from Queen's Rd, approximately 1.2 km west of Central District. The **Man**

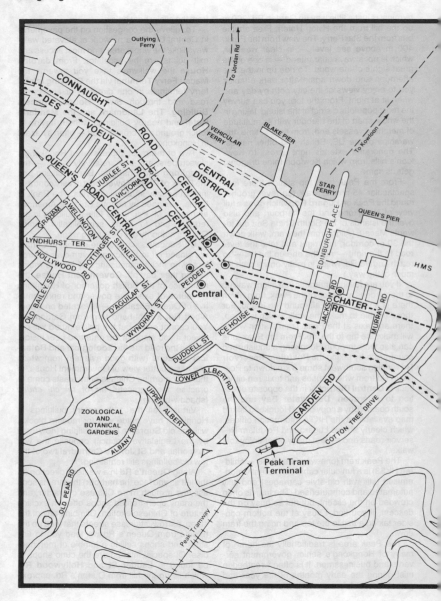

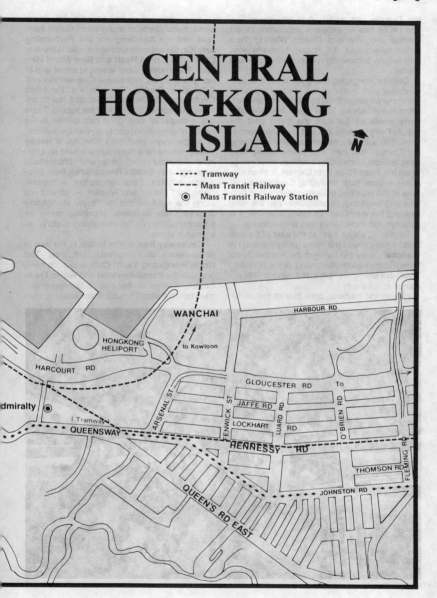

CENTRAL HONGKONG ISLAND

N

```
···· Tramway
---- Mass Transit Railway
⊙  Mass Transit Railway Station
```

WANCHAI

HARBOUR RD

HONGKONG
HELIPORT

to Kowloon

HARCOURT   RD

Admiralty

GLOUCESTER   RD   To

JAFFE RD

(Tramway)

QUEENSWAY

LOCKHART

FENWICK ST

ARSENAL ST

LUARD RD

RD

O'BRIEN RD

HENNESSY   RD

THOMSON RD

FLEMING RD

JOHNSTON RD

QUEEN'S RD EAST

Mo Temple can be found in Hollywood Rd. The HKTA has an excellent publication called *Central and Western District Walking Tour* which take about 3.5 hours. It charts you, with written commentary, through the new and the old.

Despite Hongkong being the world's largest container port, many of the territory's imports still come off cargo ships by lighter and are then unloaded on shore. Stroll down from the Star Ferry westward (or take the tram) past the Macau Ferry terminal and see the lighter-men at work. You will see junks and smaller craft flying the Chinese flag (red with yellow stars): they have brought foodstuffs, cement or other goods down the Pearl River from Canton. It often surprises visitors how freely the Cantonese (natives of the province of Guangdong, which borders on Hongkong) circulate between the territory and the mainland. To them, however, it is quite natural, especially if they are seafarers.

Beginning about 1 km to the east of Central District (take any of the trams going that way) is **Wanchai** , once the home of the fictional Suzie Wong (at the now modernised Luk Kwok Hotel). There are still "girlie" bars, but there is little romance about them.

Nearer the harbour, take one of the pedestrian overpasses to the **Arts Centre**, which presents hundreds of recitals and shows each year and the **Academy for the Performing Arts**. On the opposite side of the road to the Arts Centre, the **Grand Hyatt** and **New World Harbour View** hotels stand watch at either end of Hongkong's very impressive **Convention and Exhibition Centre**. Go into the Exhibition Centre and take the escalators up a few floors. The views across the harbour are superb. There are a couple of very good restaurants in the centre offering good food to go with the outlook.

A little way inland from Wanchai is **Happy Valley**, where race meetings are held on alternate Saturday afternoons and Wednesday evenings with **Shatin Racecourse** from September to May. Four cemeteries — Parsee, Catholic, Colonial and Muslim — spread out along the road behind the **Royal Hongkong Jockey Club Building**, providing some interesting sidelights on Hongkong history, inscribed in stone.

Causeway Bay, a little further to the east is an excellent shopping/restaurant area. **The Royal Hongkong Yacht Club** is located here, opposite the **Excelsior Hotel** and **World Trade Centre**. Further to the east is densely-populated **North Point**. To reach these areas by tram

Racing — Hongkong's obsession.

Photo: HK Jockey Club

(ride on the upper deck), you travel along a main road lined almost all the way with shops and restaurants bustling with crowds from early morning to late at night. Going east from Central District, one passes successively through the suburbs of Wanchai, Causeway Bay, North Point and **Quarry Bay** to **Shaukiwan**.

Mini-buses also make the journey through these suburbs. High on the hills above these residential areas can be seen some remaining squatters' shacks.

Hongkong is not particularly well provided with museums, but Chinese antiquities can be seen at the **Fung Ping Shan** museum at **Hongkong University** on Bonham Rd, almost 3 km to the west of Central. It is open daily except Sundays and public holidays from 9.30 am to 6 pm. Admission free. The **City Hall** near the Star Ferry has a small but interesting ceramics collection.

The **Flagstaff House Museum of Tea Ware** in Cotton Tree Drive offers a rare opportunity to view one of the few specialised collections of its kind in the world. Formed mainly of tea wares of Chinese origin, this impressive collection features pieces from the Six Dynasties to contemporary work.

Flagstaff House itself is an interesting setting for the Museum, and has its own distinct place in the history of Hongkong. Dating from 1844, it was the home of the Commander of the British Forces. It has been restored as much as possible to its former 19th century glory and is the oldest domestic Western-style building in the territory. Opening hours are 10 am to 5 pm daily (except Wednesdays), and admission is free.

On the far (south) side of the Island, and rapidly disappearing under the weight of new high-rise apartment blocks, is the fishing centre of **Aberdeen** (20 minutes by taxi, mini-bus or bus from Central District), which is worth a visit for its picturesque harbour jammed with fishing junks. A Chinese meal on board the famous **Jumbo** floating restaurant is a feature of most organised tours. **Apleichau Island**, which forms the outer barrier of the harbour, is worth visiting to see junks being made. A bridge leads to the island.

Ocean Park is located on a picturesque site at Brick Hill near Aberdeen. Its major attractions include an oceanarium, water gardens, wave tank, Ocean Theatre, dolphins and whales, an impressive aviary and greenhouse plus the usual funfair attractions including a rather fearsome roller-coaster ride called The Dragon which includes a complete loop-the-loop. Rather impressive is an attraction called the **Middle Kingdom**, a collection of re-created temples, shrines and pavilions covering 13 dynasties of Chinese history. The attraction is brought alive by demonstrations of ancients crafts, traditional dancing, lion dances and acrobatics.

Admission to the park is HK$120 for adults, HK$60 for children. There is an Ocean Park Citybus which leaves from the Admiralty MTR station to the park and return for HK$12 (adults) and HK$8 for children. Open from 10 am to 6 pm on weekdays and 9 am–6 pm Sundays and public holidays. Admission to the adjoining **Water World**, a swimming experience with giant slides, winding rivers and assorted swimming pools is HK$50, HK$35 for children. Open from 10 am to 5 pm daily (10 pm in the summer season).

Strung out along Hongkong Island's southern side are a number of beaches. The water is not the cleanest in the world. **Repulse Bay** is the largest and most crowded beach (HK$30-40 by taxi from Central District), and there are adequate refreshment facilities in the area. **South Bay** lies a little further on and has a smaller, quieter beach which can be reached by mini-bus from Repulse Bay. Immediately to the west of Repulse Bay at **Deepwater Bay** is another good beach. To the southeast 3 km away is the **Stanley Peninsula**, site of the civilian internment camp during the Japanese occupation and now an expensive housing suburb. The peninsula can be reached from Central District by bus and there is a small beach on the west coast.

Almost half an hour further on from Stanley, following the circuitous coastal road, are the beaches of **Shek O** and **Big Wave Bay** on the east coast of Hongkong Island. You can do a little modest surf-riding at **Big Wave Bay** when conditions are right. There is lifeguard supervision. At most of the other frequented beaches the sea is usually very calm. Big Wave Bay is difficult to reach unless you have your own car, though there is a bus service to Shek O from Shaukiwan.

Hongkong's hills and reservoir areas are an escape from the trauma of downtown; you wander in such fresh and green countryside that you begin to doubt that you are in Hongkong at all. Roads and trails lead beside streams and lakes where you can enjoy the fine views and even see butterflies, for there are some exquisite specimens about.

The Island's centre for walking is **Tai Tam**

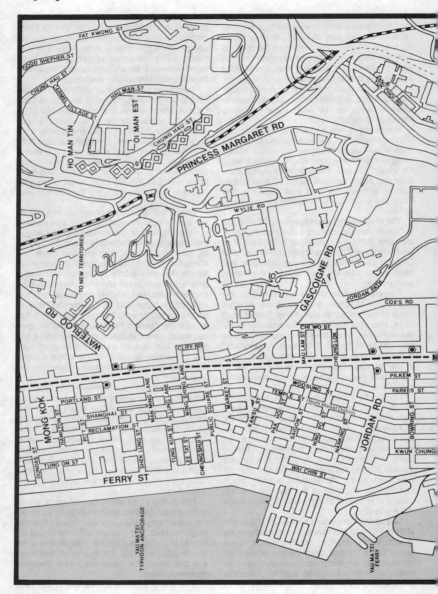

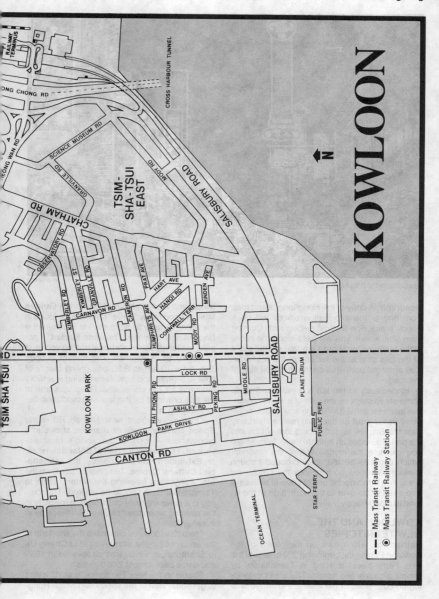

KOWLOON

N

- - - Mass Transit Railway
- ⊙ Mass Transit Railway Station

Kowloon at night: bars without bras.

Photo: HKTA

Reservoir. A copy of the Hongkong Island map from one of the information offices will be a handy precaution against getting lost. Coming from Shaukiwan, you will pass along the shore of the reservoir for about 1 km; you should alight at the bus stop at the far end of the reservoir. You enter the park area on the reservoir side of the road.

Immediately to the left is a path leading up some steep steps by the side of a water culvert; this leads for some 3 km to the southwest, eventually coming out on the main road a short way past the Stanley turnoff. Going straight on into the park you cross an embankment, from where you can see the myriad fish of the reservoir which come to be fed; then proceed through pleasant wooded country into the catchment area. You may choose any of several pathways and even cross over to the north side of the Island to reach Happy Valley.

KOWLOON AND THE NEW TERRITORIES

Nathan Rd, which runs up the centre of the Kowloon Peninsula, beginning 200 m east of the Star Ferry piers, is lined in Tsimshatsui by shops, arcades and hotels. The areas extending on both sides of the road are crowded with shops and restaurants making up the **Golden Mile**. A good many "girlie" bars can be found in the area. **Temple St** night market in Yaumati is fascinatingly Chinese. The **Jade Market**, a popular visitor attraction and local trading venue, is in **Kansu St** in Yaumati. The market is open daily from 10 am to 3:30 pm, giving plenty of time to browse and buy. Jade buying is a tricky business for the uninitiated. Read up some of the tips provided by the tourist association before leaping in.

On the waterfront near Nathan Rd is the **Space Museum**, with its dramatic shows in a planetarium — one of the world's most advanced. There is also a **Hall of Solar Sciences**, an **Exhibition Hall** and, nearby, the **Tsimshatsui Cultural Centre**. The promenade from the Star Ferry area following the waters' edge to Tsimshatsui East should be walked. The journey is a pleasant half-hour's stroll, especially in the evening when the heat is not so fierce as in the afternoon.

From Kowloon you can make the short trip to the ancient Chinese monument at **Li Cheng Uk** in Shamshuipo, which was discovered in 1955 and dates back almost 2,000 years.

Shatin, in the New Territories, is worth a visit to get some idea of the speed with which Hongkong is developing: What was once a simple village on the edge of mud flats has become a city of 700,000 people. Shatin can be easily reached by train, via the MTR or from the Kowloon station at **Hung Hom**.

Shatin is also the site of Hongkong's second racecourse, built on about 250 acres of reclaimed land of a shallow bay at Tide Cove. The complex can hold up to 40,000 spectators. In the centre of the track is an 8-ha bird sanctuary and park which is open daily except Mondays and race days. Adjoining the racecourse is the **Jubilee Sports Centre**.

From the town you can see the **Amah Rock** — shaped like a woman with a baby on her back. On top of one of the hills above Shatin is the **Ten Thousand Buddhas** monastery (actually 12,800 Buddhas).

The Chinese frontier is separated from the New Territories by a border area for which a special permit is needed. You can only visit the border railway station at **Lowu** if you are actually travelling to China but this has become increasingly easy, with a direct bus service as well as the railway. Tourists can now get a visa to visit China within one to two days.

Those not going to China can see over the border from vantage points on high ground (such as **Lokmachau**), from which a small town and a number of pill-boxes can be seen.

Far more impressive is the **Sung Dynasty Village**, opened in 1979, with tours leaving from all major hotels. The 60,000-m^2 village follows the plan of the Sung Dynasty (AD 960-1279), perhaps the greatest epoch for the arts in China. The tours include shows, food and a vivid reconstruction of the era. Tickets cost between HK$180-200 to join a group for a guided tour.

THE OUTLYING ISLANDS

Much of the New Territories is made up of islands — some 235 in all, many uninhabited — and a visit to several of them allows a glimpse of the more traditional side of Chinese life. A launch or junk picnic to the islands is an ideal way to spend a day, but for the average visitor to Hongkong it will be more convenient to go by one of the regular ferries.

Ferries to the outer islands leave from the pier marked **Outlying Districts** on Connaught Rd waterfront, Hongkong Island, 500 m west of the Star Ferry piers. Timetables are posted at the piers. A round-trip will take usually more than two hours.

Peng Chau and **Cheung Chau** are both small islands with densely populated villages. Be prepared for narrow street, dirt and smells; and do not go on Sundays when the ferries are extremely crowded.

Lantau Island is twice the size of Hongkong Island and is gaining increasing importance, though it is still relatively unpopulated. Popular Silvermine Bay at the eastern end of the Island is linked with Hongkong by a frequent ferry service. From the town, a bus service runs to **Po Lin** (Precious Lotus) Monastery via Shek Pik, the site of a vast reservoir. The Island abounds in fascinating walks and uncluttered beaches. There is a country parks information booth outside the ferry pier entrance.

The monastery stands on a plateau dotted with small pagodas that house the remains of former abbots. A large and ornate temple has been overshadowed by the world's tallest outdoor bronze Buddha, perched on the crest of the hills that split the Island. It is 34 m high and weighs some 250 tonnes. You can spend a night in the monastery guest dormitory. Take a rubber mattress, if you do not like hard boards, and a sleeping bag or blanket in winter. Meals are provided in the refectory — vegetarian only — but quite tasty with bean curd cleverly prepared to resemble meat, poultry and eggs.

Beer and soft drinks can be bought in the grounds. Visitors should respect what remains of the monastery's tranquillity and enjoy washing out of doors in the cold water of a stone pool at dawn, when the smell of incense fills the air from the billowing incense-burner in the courtyard. Visitors often rise before dawn and walk to the top of Lantau Peak to watch the sunrise.

Tai O, the so-called capital of Lantau, is connected with Silvermine Bay by road and a regular bus service runs between them. It is a grubby and noisy — but thoroughly authentic — town, separated by a creek which you cross by boat.

The shadow of progress hangs over Lantau, however, with plans for its northern coast to be the site of Hongkong's second airport, with roads and tunnels linking it to Kowloon. This is some years in the future, but see Lantau unspoiled while you can.

Off the west coast of Hongkong Island is **Lamma** Island, a favourite place for visitors and Hongkongers alike to visit for an evening fish meal at one of the many restaurants at **Sok Yu Wan**, reached by ferry from Central. The island, which unlike Lantau, has no roads, has many beautiful hill walks, but many of the island's views have been spoiled by a massive three-stack power station at the northern end.

HOTEL GUIDE

Hotel address	Phone	Fax	Telex	Cable	〰	🍴	🍵
A (US$200+) **B** (US$150-199) **C** (US$100-149) **D** (US$50-99)							
HONGKONG ISLAND							
A							
Conrad Pacific Place, 88 Queensway, HK	521 3838	521 3888	69678	CONRAHX	▲	▲	▲
Grand Hyatt Hong Kong 1 Harbour Rd, Wanchai	861 1234	861 1677	68434		▲	▲	▲
HK Hilton 2 Queen's Rd, Central	523 3111	845 2590	73355	HILTELS	▲	▲	▲
Mandarin Oriental 5 Connaught Rd, Central	522 0111	810 6190	73653	MANDARIN	▲	▲	▲
Victoria 200 Connaught Rd, Central	540 7288	858 3398	86608	HOTELVC	▲	▲	▲
B							
Furama Kempinski HK 1 Connaught Rd, Central	525 5111	868 1768	73081	FURAM	▲	▲	▲
New World Harbour View 1 Harbour Rd, Wanchai	866 2288	866 3388	68967	NWHVHTL	▲	▲	▲
Park Lane Radisson HK 310 Gloucester Rd, Causeway Bay	890 3355	576 7853	75343	PARKLANE	▲	▲	▲
C							
Evergreen 31-39 Hennessy Rd, Wanchai	866 9111	861 3121	70727	EVGNHHK	▲	▲	▲
Excelsior Hotel Gloucester Rd, Causeway Bay	894 8888	895 6459	74550	CONVENTION		▲	▲
Grand Plaza 2 Kornhill Rd, Quarry Bay	886 0011	886 1738	67645	GRANDPLAZA	▲	▲	▲
Lee Gardens Hysan Ave, Causeway Bay	895 3311	576 9775	75601	LEEGARDENS		▲	▲
Eastin Valley Hotel 1A Wang Tak St, Happy Valley	574 9922	838 1622	84323	EAHTL HX		▲	▲
China Harbour View 189 Gloucester Rd, Wanchai	838 2222	838 0136	67361			▲	▲
China Merchants Hotel 160-161 Connaught Rd West, Western	559 6888	559 0038	66701	8383		▲	▲
City Garden 231 Electric Rd, North Point	887 2888	887 1111	69128		▲	▲	▲

Hotel address	Phone	Fax	Telex	Cable	〜〜〜	🍴	🍽
HONGKONG ISLAND – *Cont'd*							
C							
Luk Kwok 72 Gloucester Rd, Wanchai	866 2166	866 2622	69628	LUKOKHTL		▲	▲
Ramada Inn HK 61-73 Lockhart Rd, Wanchai	861 1000	865 6023	82590	RAMADAINN		▲	▲
D							
Emerald 152 Connaught Rd West, Western	546 8111	559 0255	84847	EMERALDHTL		▲	▲
Harbour 116-122 Gloucester Rd, Wanchai	574 8211	572 2185	73947	HARBOHOTEL		▲	▲
Harbour View Int. 4 Harbour Rd, Wanchai	520 1111	865 6063	61073	FLAMINGOHV		▲	▲
New Harbour 41-49 Hennessy Rd, Wanchai	861 1166	865 6111	65641	NEHARBOHTL		▲	▲
Caravelle 84 Morrison Hill Rd, Happy Valley	575 4455	832 5881	65793	CARAHOTEL		▲	▲
KOWLOON							
A							
Kowloon Shangri-La 64 Mody Rd, Tsimshatsui East	721 2111	723 8686	36718		▲	▲	▲
Nikko HK 72 Mody Rd, Tsimshatsui East	739 1111	311 3122	31302	NIKHOTEL	▲	▲	▲
Peninsula Salisbury Rd, Tsimshatsui	366 6251	722 4170	43821	PENHOTE		▲	▲
Ramada Renaissance 8 Peking Rd, Tsimshatsui	311 3311	311 6611	45243		▲	▲	▲
Regent Salisbury Rd, Tsimshatsui	721 1211	739 4546	37134	REGENTEL	▲	▲	▲
B							
Holiday Inn Harbour View 70 Mody Rd, Tsimshatsui East	721 5161	369 5672	38670	INNVIEW	▲	▲	▲
Hyatt Regency 67 Nathan Rd, Tsimshatsui	311 1234	739 8701	43127	HYATT		▲	▲
Miramar 130 Nathan Rd, Tsimshatsui	368 1111	369 1788	44661	MIRAMAR	▲	▲	▲
Omni The Hongkong Harbour City, Kowloon	736 0088	736 0011	43838	OMNIHK		▲	▲

Hotel address	Phone	Fax	Telex	Cable	≋	▮▮	◗▮
KOWLOON – *Cont'd*							
B							
Royal Garden 69 Mody Rd, Tsimshatsui East	721 5215	369 9976	39539	ROYALHOTEL		▲	▲
Sheraton Hongkong Hotel & Towers 20 Nathan Rd, Tsimshatsui	369 1111	739 8707	45813	SHERATON	▲	▲	▲
Holiday Inn Golden Mile 50 Nathan Rd, Tsimshatsui	369 3111	369 8016	56332	HOLIDAYINN	▲	▲	▲
New World 22 Salisbury Rd, Tsimshatsui	369 4111	369 9387	35860	NWHOTEL	▲	▲	▲
Marco Polo Harbour City, Tsimshatsui	736 0888	736 0022	40077	OMNIMP	▲	▲	▲
Omni Prince Harbour City, Tsimshatsui	736 1888	736 0066	50950	HTLPRINZHK	▲	▲	▲
Regal Airport 30-38 Sa Po Rd, Kowloon City	718 0333	718 4111	49050	HORMA		▲	▲
Regal Meriden 71 Mody Rd, Tsimshatsui East	722 1818	723 6413	40955	HOMRO		▲	▲
C							
Ambassador 26 Nathan Rd, Tsimshatsui	366 6321	369 0663	43840	AMHOCOKL		▲	▲
Park 61-65 Chatham Rd, Tsimshatsui	366 1371	739 7259	45740	PARKHOTEL		▲	▲
Empress 17-19 Chatham Rd, Tsimshatsui	366 0211	721 8168	44871	EMPHOTEL		▲	▲
Fortuna 351-361 Nathan Rd, Yamati	385 1011	780 0011	44897	HOTELFORTUNA		▲	▲
Grand 14 Carnarvon Rd, Tsimshatsui	366 9331	723 7840	44838	GRANDEL		▲	▲
Grand Tower 627 Nathan Rd, Mongkok	789 0011	789 0945	31602	GRANDTOWER		▲	▲
Guangdong 18 Prat Ave, Tsimshatsui	739 3311	721 1137	49067	GDHITSTHK		▲	▲
Imperial 30-34 Nathan Rd, Tsimshatsui	366 2201	311 2360	55893	IMPEHO		▲	▲
International 33 Cameron Rd, Tsimshatsui	366 3381	369 5381	34749	INTERHOUSE		▲	▲
Kowloon 19-21 Nathan Rd, Tsimshatsui	369 8698	369 8698	47604	KLNHOTELHK		▲	▲

Hotel address	Phone	Fax	Telex	Cable	〰	🍴	🍜
KOWLOON – *Cont'd*							
C							
Metropole 75 Waterloo Rd, Mongkok	761 1711	761 0769	45063		▲	▲	▲
Nathan 378 Nathan Rd, Yamati	388 5141	770 4262	31037	HOTENATHAN		▲	▲
New Astor 11 Carnarvon Rd, Tsimshatsui	366 7261	711 7122	52222	NAHOTEL		▲	▲
Ramada Inn Kowloon 73-75 Chatham Rd South, Tsimshatsui	311 1100	311 6000	44582	RINNKLN		▲	▲
Royal Pacific Hotel & Towers 33 Canton Rd, Tsimshatsui	736 1188	736 1212	44111			▲	▲
Windsor 39-43A Kimberley Rd, Tsimshatsui	739 5665	311 5101	44419	WINDSORHTL		▲	▲
D							
Bangkok Royal 2-12 Pikem St, Jordan	735 9181	730 2209	52999	BKKHOTEL		▲	▲
King's 473-473A Nathan Rd, Yamati	780 1261			KINGSHOTEL		▲	▲
Shamrock 223 Nathan Rd, Yamati	735 2271	736 7354	50561	ROCKTEL		▲	▲
NEW TERRITORIES							
C							
Regal Riverside Tai Chung Kiu Rd, Shatin	649 7878	637 4748	30013	RERIVHOTEL	▲	▲	▲
Royal Park 8 Pak Hok Ting St, Shatin	601 2111	601 3666	45776	ROYALPARK	▲	▲	▲
OUTLYING ISLANDS							
D							
Warwick Cheung Chau, East Bay	981 0081	981 9174	67790		▲	▲	▲

INDONESIA

The largest country in Southeast Asia, Indonesia is a sprawling archipelago consisting of some 13,600 islands straddling the equator south of the Asian mainland, north and west of Australia. With a population of 180 million people, Indonesia is the fifth-largest country in the world.

Indonesia presents a tableau of cultures woven together by a colourful history of conquest, trade and empire. Travelling east from the capital, Jakarta, takes the visitor from a modern Muslim society to one steeped in tradition, a significant part of which still clings to the Hindu Buddhist or animist past.

Jakarta, the nation's capital is fast becoming a sprawl of modern high-rise blocks, towering above a receding sea of red-tiled housing in urban villages, or "kampongs." By day the city screeches and groans with traffic sweltering in the brilliant sunshine and high humidity. Now a centre of government, business and industry, the city spreads over 656 km² and has a population of over 8 million.

Jakarta's rapid growth reflects Indonesia's remarkable economic development from the late 1980s.

To the east lies Jogyakarta, regarded by many as the cultural heart of Java. With a still functioning court life and a sultan who acts as the city's governor, traditions are actively preserved. Nearby are the historical treasures of Borobudur and Prambanan. Further east lies Surabaya, Indonesia's second city with its stately Dutch-built avenues and a charming rural hinterland. On the eastern tip of Java lies Bali, and beyond that the islands of Lombok, Sumba, Flores and others forming a chain all the way to Indonesia's eastern extremity, Irian Jaya. To the west of Jakarta lies the huge island of Sumatra.

To the north and east lie Kalimantan (Borneo), Sulawesi and the Maluku Islands (the Moluccas) — a vast area that the visitor cannot hope to explore fully. However, significant progress in transportation throughout the country means that many of these areas are just a two-hour scheduled flight from Jakarta.

Although fossil remains of very early man have been discovered in Java, most of the present mixed population of Indonesia originated from relatively recent migrations — probably in several waves from the Asian mainland during the first and second millennia BC.

By the early centuries AD several developed kingdoms throughout the archipelago were emerging as influential powers in the region. In the 7th century the Hindu kingdom of Sriwijaya around the contemporary town of Palembang on the eastern coast of Sumatra dominated seaborne trade in the straits of Malacca.

Sriwijaya's golden era was later usurped by the kingdoms of Java, which were developing strength based on command over a rich rice-growing society governed by imported Hindu-Buddhist culture. It was during this period that the massive architectural marvels at Borobudur and Prambanan were erected.

Intermarriage, wars of succession and shifts of capital cloud the picture hopelessly from this time until the succumbing of the last Hindu-Javanese kingdom of Majapahit to Islam in the 14th century. However, evidence of these pre-Islamic times in Indonesia is amply shown by the important status of the Ramayana and Mahabarata epic dramas in the

◁ *Borobudur.*
Photo: Nancy Nash

71

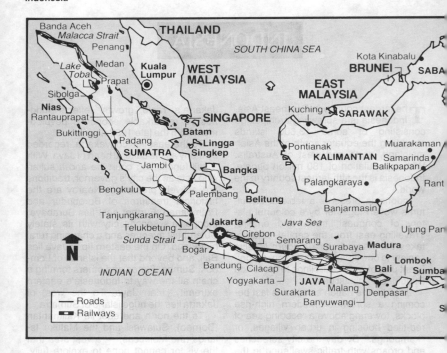

cultural life of the contemporary Javanese people. The wayang leather puppet shows dramatising the old Hindu epics reach down to the lowest level of Javanese village society and are not just vestigial elements of court life.

The first European influences were imported by the Portuguese who came in search of spices to the islands of Eastern Indonesia in the 16th century. Portuguese dominance was replaced 100 years later by the Dutch, who began a slow subjugation of Java and other islands. The process was not completed until the early years of this century with the conquest of Aceh and southern regions of Java.

Dutch colonial efforts concentrated on Java, where they harnessed the population to produce sugar and coffee for export to Europe. The oppressive way in which the Javanese were forced to cultivate cash crops became a model of colonial exploitation. There were frequent rebellions, but no mass nationalist movement for

independence until the early years of the 20th century.

By this time, the Dutch had introduced a school system and begun to send Indonesian graduates to Holland. As elsewhere in Southeast Asia, a new generation of indigenous intellectuals formed the core of the nascent independence movement. They might have been crushed by the Dutch had it not been for the Japanese occupation of the country in 1942.

Under the Japanese, Indonesian nationalists were allowed to organise and on August 17, 1945, independence was declared. Sukarno became president of the new republic which immediately had to contend with the returning Dutch. After a short war, during which British troops were also involved as Holland's allies, a UN-brokered agreement resulted in the formation of a unitary independent state in 1950.

Sukarno initially installed a full constitutional democracy, but the collapse in disunity of one government after another led him to impose

what he called "Guided Democracy" in 1959. Parliament lost its power and the state began to intervene in the economy and the judiciary. Meanwhile, the army was facing rebellion in several outlying regions, including a move by Muslim communities in Sulawesi and west Java to establish an Islamic state.

With unity restored and Indonesia's area expanded to include West Irian after another war with the Dutch in 1962, Sukarno began to face opposition to his policies, particularly that of fostering close links with the communist party at home and abroad. Frustrated by Sukarno's belligerent policies towards the west and a pointless confrontation with Malaysia in 1963, the military became more and more opposed to Sukarno. An abortive communist uprising in 1965 proved to be their cue to topple Sukarno. The army's counter-move against the communists effectively wiped out the party and three years later forced Sukarno out of office.

The new military government led by Gen.

Suharto, who became president in 1968, set a more conservative political course for the country and launched economic policies which headed off the country's decline into poverty and bankruptcy. Relations with the West improved greatly while diplomatic ties with China were frozen.

Suharto has ruled Indonesia for more than a quarter of a century, steering a course which has resulted in undeniable improvements in the welfare of the people. Shrewd policies of birth control and a drive to achieve self-sufficiency in rice have earned Suharto plaudits around the world. But recent years have seen Suharto and his government come under pressure to liberalise the economy after a disastrous fall in oil prices exposed the country's dangerous reliance on oil and the state sector. Political pressures have also become apparent as the country's successful growth has generated demands for more popular participation in government.

Indonesia

Jakarta is served by many international airlines. Overseas carriers such as Qantas, SIA, MAS, and Cathay Pacific also have direct flights to Bali from Australia, Singapore, Kuala Lumpur and Hongkong. Other cities served by international flights include Medan in North Sumatra, Solo in Central Java, and Surabaya in East Java. Merpati Nusanta Airlines operates an international flight from Kupang in Nusa Tenggara Timur to Darwin in Australia.

Examples of one-way fares to Jakarta from: Singapore — US$185, Kuala Lumpur — US$157, Hongkong — US$434.

Indonesia's three main gateways are Sukarno-Hatta International Airport, Cenkareng airport in Jakarta, Polonia airport in Medan and Ngurah Rai Airport in Bali. There are direct flights from Singapore, Penang and Kuala Lumpur to Medan and from Singapore to Surabaya. Direct services to Bali are available with KLM from Amsterdam, Qantas from Sydney and Melbourne, Cathay Pacific from Hongkong and Continental Airlines from Guam.

A limited number of passenger ships on regular trans-Pacific and round-the-world schedules call at Jakarta with frequent connections from other Asian ports, especially Singapore. Pelni Lines (Pelayaran Nasional Indonesia, P. N.), with offices at 50 Telok Blangah Rd, 02002 Citiport Centre, Singapore (Tel: 2726811-2715159-2718685) provide the most frequent services to Indonesian ports, including Jambi, Palembang, Panjang (all in Sumatra), Pontianak (Kalimantan) and Jakarta. Cruise ships now regularly call at Indonesian ports and there are also a number of ferries which ply several times daily between Singapore and Batam Island.

An exit permit is required only for residents or visitors staying for a period of more than six months, with a tax of Rps 250,000 levied upon leaving the country. An airport tax of Rps 9,000 is charged to all passengers for international travel and Rps 3,000 for internal flights.

All travellers to Indonesia must be in possession of a passport valid for at least six months on arrival with proof of onward or return passage. Visas have been waived for nationals of 31 countries for visits of no more than two months. Visas are not required for nationals of Australia, Austria, Belgium, Brunei, Canada, Denmark, Finland, France, Greece, Iceland, Ireland, Italy, Japan, Lichtenstein, Luxembourg, Malaysia, Malta, The Netherlands, New Zealand, Norway, Philippines, Singapore, South Korea, Spain, Sweden, Switzerland, Taiwan, Thailand, United Kingdom, US and Germany.

Visa-free entry is through the air and sea ports of Jakarta, Bali, Medan, Manado, Biak, Ambon, Surabaya, Batam; the seaports of Semarang, Jakarta, Bali, Pontianak, Balikpapan, Tanjung Pinang and Kupang.

The two-month tourist visa is not extendable. Visa-free entry is also allowed for registered delegates attending an officially approved conference.

For nationals of other countries not specified above, tourist visas can be obtained from any Indonesian embassy or consulate on payment of a visa fee. Two photographs are generally required.

Citizens of South Africa and Israel must obtain special travel affidavits from Indonesian diplomatic missions, since these passports are not recognised by Indonesia.

Holders of certificates of identity (CI) from Hongkong can obtain visas for group travel comprising a minimum of five people from the Consulate-General of Indonesia in Hongkong for visits not exceeding 30 days. Both arrival and departure must be in groups and travel and accommodation organised by a tour operator. Port of entry is permitted only through Sukarno-Hatta International Airport of Jakarta, Ngurah Rai, Bali and Polonia, Medan.

Tourists and those with special permits are now allowed to visit the country's newest province, the former Portuguese colony of East Timor. Some districts of East Timor however remain off-limits. Travel restrictions have also been lifted on most parts of Irian Jaya, the second-newest province.

International certificates for smallpox and cholera are no longer required. However, typhoid, paratyphoid and cholera inoculations are strongly recommended. So are malaria pills, including those for choloroquin-resistant mosquitoe areas. Yellow fever inoculation is required of those arriving within six days of leaving or transiting an infected area. Vaccination against hepatitis B is also recommended.

Show of puppets. ▷
Photo: Mary Fennessy

Indonesia

The following are admitted duty-free for each visitor on entry: a maximum of two litres of alcoholic beverages, 200 cigarettes or 50 cigars or 100 grams of tobacco and a reasonable amount of perfume per adult. Cars, photographic equipment, typewriters, and tape-recorders are allowed provided they are re-exported. TV sets, radios, narcotics, arms and ammunition, printed matter in Chinese characters and Chinese medicines are all prohibited. Prior official approval is necessary to carry transceivers. Movie films and video cassettes must be censored by the Film Censor Board. Fresh fruit, plants and animals must have quarantine permits. Antiques in reasonable amounts can be exported.

A written customs declaration is required on entry and baggage is usually searched both on arrival and departure.

The rupiah is the unit of currency, exchanging (at the time of going to the press) at around Rps 1,903:US$1. There are notes in denominations of 100, 500, 1,000, 5,000 and 10,000 rupiahs and coins of 5, 10, 25, 50, and 100 rupiahs in circulation.

Unlimited amounts of foreign currency and travellers' cheques are allowed to be imported and exported, but no more than Rps 50,000 of Indonesian currency may be taken in or out. Large amounts of foreign currency in banknotes should be declared on arrival to prevent any possibility of being interrogated on departure, but usually no currency declaration is required on leaving.

Provided exchange documents can be produced, all unspent rupiahs may be reconverted on leaving the country.

Most major foreign currencies can be readily changed in main city banks, bureaux de change and in some of the larger hotels.

There is a bank at Jakarta, Medan and Denpasar airports and most major regional airports.

Rates of exchange are better at the banks than in hotels or bureaux de change. Some banks will not accept travellers' cheques. Cash is still the preferred transaction, though credit cards such as Visa, Mastercharge and Amex are now widely accepted in larger hotels, restaurants, department stores, supermarkets and travel agencies. Some retailers charge an extra 3-5% on some credit card transactions. Banking hours are from 8 am to 1 pm and 2 pm to 4 pm Monday to Friday and from 8 am until 1 pm on Saturday.

The official language is Bahasa Indonesia, a version of Malay. Although it is spoken widely, there are still many areas — especially in the outlying islands — where regional languages and dialects are still spoken exclusively. On the main island of Java, the Javanese language coexists with Bahasa Indonesia, which does likewise with the Balinese language on Bali. English is the most common second language in the country, followed by Dutch. Amongst the Chinese population, one or more of the Southern Chinese dialects are spoken and sometimes Mandarin. The Indonesian language uses the Roman script and alphabet, so reading signs is rarely a problem.

There is a wide selection of good local phrasebooks available at most bookstores or department stores. Gramedia bookstores offer the largest variety of phrasebooks, particularly the Kamus Lengkap editions (in many languages) or *Short and Easy Conversation* and *How To Master the Indonesian Language*. Prices vary but they generally cost around Rps 5,000 each.

The Indonesian archipelago is spread over three time zones. Western Indonesia Standard Time is GMT plus seven hours, covering the islands of Sumatra, Java-Madura, West and Central Kalimantan. Central Indonesia Standard Time is GMT plus eight hours for East and South Kalimantan, Sulawesi, Bali and Nusatenggara. East Indonesia Standard Time is GMT plus nine hours for Maluku and Irian Jaya.

Indonesia is distinctly tropical. Straddling the equator, the country remains hot throughout the year, with day temperatures above 80°F (26-33°C). But the heat is rarely extreme. The humidity is usually high at all times, ranging from a minimum of 69% to a maximum of 95%. Temperatures at night vary considerably. While Jakarta remains warm, the temperature in Bandung can drop as low as 10°C. Jogjakarta, Bali and parts of east Java can be pleasantly cool in the evening. Generally the two seasons in Indonesia are well defined by heavy tropical downpours in the wet season and high humidity in the dry season. The east monsoon from June to September brings dry weather while the west monsoon from December to March is moisture-laden, maritime masses bringing rain. Thunderstorms are frequent during the rainy season and the heaviest downfall is recorded in December and January. The average rainfall in the whole country is 102 cm (40 inches).

Dress is normally informal in Indonesia. Light clothing (with a few extra pairs of underclothes and shirts) is all that is required for travel. In the mountain country a sweater is sometimes necessary in the evening, though temperatures can also reach freezing-point on slopes exceeding 3,000 m. Day attire for men is shirt and long pants, with jacket and tie for formal occasions. Long-sleeved batik shirts are acceptable for evening functions. For ladies, dresses or blouses and long pants are appropriate. Shorts, tank tops, low cut clothing should be used only on the beach or at sports facilities.

Government offices in Indonesia are open from 8 am until 3 pm Monday to Thursday, 8 am until 11:30 am on Friday, and 8 am until 2 pm on Saturday.

Commercial offices and businesses are usually open from 8 am until 4:30 pm or from 9 am to 5 pm, with a one-hour lunch break. Some open on Saturday mornings. The post offices follow government hours.

Most foreign banks are open 8 am to 3 pm Monday to Friday and until 12.30 pm on Saturday. Local banks are open from 8 pm to 1 pm and from 2 pm to 4 pm daily.

The Pasar Baru shopping centre, close to the Borobudur Hotel, is open from 9 am to 8 pm Monday to Saturday. Most of the shops in Block M at Kebayoran Baru are open from 9 am to 10 pm. Sarinah, the large department store in Jalan Thamrin and Block M, is open from 9 am to 10 pm and from 10 am until 6 pm on Sunday. Smaller shops keep irregular hours, but usually open early in the morning and close late at night. In some provincial towns shops close in the afternoon and reopen at 5-6 pm.

Restaurants are usually open until about 11 pm. Smaller street stalls stay open later. Nightclubs stay open until 1-2 am on weekdays, and until 3 am on Saturday and Sunday. On religious and some public holidays night clubs are closed.

Air transportation is the easiest and most comfortable means of travel in Indonesia. Regular air services link all provincial cities to Jakarta daily. Flights are operated by Garuda Indonesia, Merpati Nusantara Airlines, Bouraq, Sempati and Mandala Airlines.

Garuda Indonesia (the national carrier) operates exclusively on international routes. But Garuda and Merpati Nusantara share domestic routes, servicing 33 Indonesian cities, including all the provincial capitals. Garuda/Merpati also have several flights daily from Jakarta to commercial and tourist destinations such as Medan, Bali, Ujung Pandang, Manado and Yogyakarta. Shuttle flights to Surabaya and Semarang run several times a day.

For visitors Garuda Indonesia has introduced Visit Indonesia Air Passes which offer special fares on its domestic flights. The passes are sold in conjunction with travel on Garuda from Europe, US, Australia and Japan, and have to be purchased outside Indonesia.

Sample one-way fares from Jakarta are as follows:

Yogyakarta:	Rps 83,000
Denpasar (Bali):	Rps 125,000
Medan:	Rps 192,000
Ujung Pandang:	Rps 188,000
Dili (E. Timor):	Rps 283,000
Padang:	Rps 138,000
Surabaya:	Rps 103,000

One-way fares from Denpasar (Bali) to:

Yogyakarta:	Rps 67,000
Dili:	Rps 158,000
Biak:	Rps 300,000

SHIPPING: Sea transport is the economic lifeline of the nation, both in the mass movement of people and in trade. On Java the main harbours are at Jakarta (Tanjung Priok) and Surabaya. From those two ports, ships ply to all corners of the archipelago.

Pelni, the state-owned shipping line at Jl Pintu Air 1 Jakarta, (tel: 358398), serves all the main Indonesian ports from Banada Aceh in the western tip of the country to Jayapura in Irian Jaya. The ships are by no means cruise vessels but they can accommodate between 1,000 to 1,500 passengers with air-conditioned cabins in all four classes. The first-class cabins have their own private bathrooms. The ships operate on a regular schedule, all touching Tanjung Priok harbour.

Sailing frequencies vary, but there is usually a service every week or two to most important ports. Pelni, for example, sails weekly to Medan, Padang, Ujung Pandang and Tanjung Pinang.

The MV Explorer, a 40-passenger cruise liner, offers a 12-day tour of the Dhores of Celebes and a four-day cruise from Manado to Bunaken and the northern island of Talisei. Most cruises are between Bali and Kupang (West Timor), Ujung Pandang and Manado and from Jakarta to the Sunda Straits on wildlife and volcano tours. There are also many regular schedule cruises to the Spice Islands.

Pelni one-way first-class fares from Jakarta:

Padang:	Rps 76,500
Ujung Pandang:	Rps 131,000
Jayapura:	Rps 340,000

TAXIS: Metred taxis are available in Jakarta, Surabaya, Bandung, Solo and Semarang and Medan. Fares are generally low. A 10-km ride costs about US$2.50. Transport from Soekarno-Hatta International Airport to an hotel in central Jakarta (about 23 km) costs US$10, including airport surcharge and fee for the toll road. At all major airports, taxis have fixed rates and vouchers are sold at the transport desk in terminal buildings. It is advisable to avoid touts who offer taxi service.

The airport authorities operate buses to four points in the city to include various terminals such as Gambir Railway Station, Blok M and Rawamangun. The fare is Rps 3,000 per passenger, including luggage. Buses are air-conditioned, spacious and clean. They run every 30 minutes approximately.

In Jakarta taxis are in abundance but make sure they operate with metres. Flag fall is Rps 600. Taxi rentals by the hour are also available by a number of taxi companies such as Bluebird (Tel: 325607). The rent is Rps 5,000 per hour for a minimum of two hours. Some companies also offer taxi rentals on a daily or weekly basis, usually with a driver. In Indonesia all registered taxis and hired cars have yellow number plates. There are black plates for private cars and red for government-owned vehicles.

BUSES IN JAKARTA: Non air-conditioned buses cost Rps 250 irrespective of the distance. Air-conditioned buses operate every 30 minutes from Blok M to Bekasi with various stops along the route. The fare is Rps 750 per passenger. Although cheap and frequent, these city buses are almost always overcrowded. They run along fixed routes and their destinations are displayed on the front of each bus.

MICROLET/OPLET/BEMOS: These are small buses which can carry 10 passengers and ply certain routes. (Bemos in Jakarta are smaller

vehicles which can seat seven passengers.) Fares depend on the distance and they stop whenever requested.

BECAKS: These pedal trishaws are now operating only in the suburbs of Jakarta and Surabaya. In other Javanese towns, the becaks are still a popular and convenient means of transport. They are also available in Ujung Pandang (South Sulawesi) and in some cities in Sumatra. For most inner city journeys a fare of between Rps 300-500 will suffice.

HIRE CARS: It is difficult to rent a car without a chauffeur on a daily basis, though Avis Car rental office at 25, Jl Diponegoro Jakarta, (Tel: 341964, 349206) do so for about Rps 150,000 per day with unlimited mileage. Hertz (offices in the Jakarta Hyatt and Mandarin Hotels) only hire out cars with a driver at about Rps 210,000 per day. National car rental at Kartika Plaza Hotel, 10, Jl Thamrin Jakarta, (Tel: 332006, 322849) hires cars with or without driver. To rent a car to drive around the city is not only expensive but can be quite tiring. Elsewhere, prices may still be quite high, though negotiable, depending on area and types of cars. Prices are more reasonable in Bali where a day's rental is around Rps 110,000 for a chauffeur-driven car or Rps 50-90,000 without driver.

TRAINS: Train services are available only throughout Java and part of Sumatra, around Padang, West Sumatra, Medan in North Sumatra and some railroads in South Sumatra and Lampung.

Several trains run between Jakarta and Surabaya. The best of the rail services is provided by the daily Bima train between Jakarta and Surabaya in East Java, passing through Yogyakarta and Solo. The train is air-conditioned and has sleeping berths and a dining car. Leaving Kota Railway Station in Jakarta at 4 pm daily, the train reaches Yogyakarta at 1:15 am and Solo at 2:43 am and Surabaya Kota at 7:40 am. The train leaves Surabaya Subang at 4:10 pm reaching Jakarta at 7:03 pm. Fares are Rps 27,000 (sleeper) and Rps 22,500 (first-class). Between Jakarta and Yogyakarta, the fare is Rps 21,000 (sleeper) and Rps 17,000 (first-class).

The other express train is the Mutiara Utara, which runs daily from Jakarta Kota Station to Surabaya, bypassing Yogyakarta. The train has reclining seats only and the fare is Rps 25,000 (first-class) and Rps 22,000 (second-class). The train leaves Jakarta at 4:30 pm and arrives at Surabaya Pasartu at 5:45 am. The Senja night train leaves Jakarta Gambir Station at 5:35

pm and reaches Yogyakarta at 3:28 am and Solo at 4:52 am. The fare is Rps 15,000 (first-class) and Rps 11,000 (second-class). The Parahyangan offers numerous services daily to Bandung with departures from Gambir Station at 5:39, 9:49, 11:24, 13:53, 15:29 and 18:50. The trip takes about four hours. Fares are Rps 8,000 (first-class) and Rps 6,000 (second-class).

Trains serving the west leave Jakarta Tanah Abang station twice daily with connecting ferry services across the Sunda Straits and rail again to Palembang in Sumatra. The whole journey can take up to 30 hours.

There are non-express services from East of Surabaya and central Java to Bali. However, air or express buses are quicker and much more comfortable.

The Cirebon Express leaves at 10:14 am and arrives in Cirebon approximately three-and-a-half hours later. The fare is Rps 5,000.

Railway fares are very low and therefore all trains are overcrowded. Advance bookings for individuals can be made only one or two days ahead of travel. Train timetables do tend to change often, so always check with your travel agent or directly at the station.

COACHES: Express coaches linking the large towns and local buses serving the countryside surrounding the towns operate throughout Indonesia. One of the popular services is the Bali–Java–Banda Aceh (the most northwestern point of Sumatra) route. These long-haul buses are fully air-conditioned, equipped with TV sets and video programmes. Other widely used routes are from Yogyakarta and Surabaya to Bali. Fares vary between Rps 7,000 to Rps 8,500 depending on the bus company and whether the bus is air-conditioned. The Medan (east coast of North Sumatra) to Bukittinggi (west coast of Padang) route, some 730 km, is also another popular route. The fare is Rps 17,000 and the whole journey can take up to 18 hours, depending on the weather and road conditions.

Elsewhere throughout Indonesia buses are the most common method of travel, bearing in mind that floods in the wet season often result in cancelled services. The Palembang-Padang route is one to avoid in the wet season.

Bus fares over short distances are low. For example, Yogyakarta to Solo (65 km) is Rps 1,500 with air-conditioning and toilet facilities.

With a number of toll roads open in both urban and inter-urban areas, travelling overland can be most pleasant. The Jakarta-Bogor-Ciawi toll has halved the travelling time to the Bogor

Botanic gardens and to the mountain resorts of south Jakarta. Other toll roads leading to the beach resorts in the west coast of Java are also very comfortable.

With the deregulation of the economy, all sectors of the tourism industry are seeing a growth — including travel agencies and tour operators. All hotels in Indonesia catering for foreign visitors have branches of tourist agencies on the premises. There are many overland tours. One that is gaining popularity is the Sumatra overland tour, lasting for seven or nine days. The tour departs from Medan, with overnights at Brastagi, Prapat, Padang Sidenmpuan, Bukittinggi before ending in Padang. In Jakarta there are half-day bus tours of the city, ranging from US$25 to US$50 per person, depending on the number of people interested. There are a number of pick-up points from the large hotels. Tours to faraway places tend to be expensive. However, a three-day/two-night diving tour on the Thousand Island is in the region of US$200 per person for a minimum of two persons, inclusive of accommodation and meals.

There are well over 900 travel agencies and tour operators thoughout Indonesia, the majority with head offices in Jakarta and Bali. The leading ones with representatives in major towns offer inbound, outbound and domestic travel services, hotel reservations, travel document handling, national domestic airlines agents, safari/wildlife/adventures/marine life, air and overland transportation and IATA agency protection.

They include:

Vayatour, 38 Jl. Batutulis, Jakarta 10120. Tel: 3800202; Telex: 46200-41566 VAYA JKT, and 124A, Jl Hayam Wuruk, P. O. Box. 113 Denpasar. Tel: 24449, 23747, 23958; Telex: 35182 VAYA DPR.

Pacto Ltd, 8, Jl. Surabaya, Jakarta. Tel: 348634; Telex: 46128 PACTO IA, and Jl. Tanjungsari, Sanur (or) P. O. Box. 52 DPS-Denpasar. Tel: 88277/8/9; Telex: 35110 PACTOBALI.

Natrabu, 29A Jl. H. Agus Salim, Jakarta 10340. Tel: 331728, 332386, 322450, 321844; Telex: 44520 NATRABU IA. FAX: 322386, and 78, Jl. Kecubung, Denpasar. Tel: 25448/9-23452-24925; Telex: 35144 NATRABU DPR.

Tunas Indonesia, 70 Jl. Abdul Muis, Jakarta 10160. Tel: 3416851, 355167/8; Telex:

AIRLINES

Cathay Pacific, 3rd floor, Hotel Borobudur Inter-Continental Jl. Lapangan Banteng Selatan. Tel: 3806660, 370108; ext: 76087.

China Airlines, Wisma Dharmala Sakti M.1.floor, Jl. Jend Sudirman 32a. Tel: 588005, 588285, 588304.

Czechoslovak Airlines (C. S. A.), Wisata International Hotel, Jl. M. H. Thamrin. Tel: 325530, 320408; ext: 135, 136.

Garuda Indonesia, (H. O.), Danareksa Bldg, 11th floor, 13 Jl. Merdeka Selatan. Tel: 3801901, 3806276.

Garuda Indonesia (sales), Wisma Dharmala sakti, Jl. Jend Sudirman 32. Tel: 588707/8, 588797.

Japan Airlines (JAL), Mid Plaza Bldg, Jl. Jend Sudirman Kav 10-11. Tel: 5703883, 5703189.

KLM Royal Dutch Airlines, Hotel Indonesia, Jl. M. H. Thamrin. Tel: 320708, 322008; ext: 740/742.

Korean Airlines, Wisma Metropolitan 11 Ground floor, Jl. Jend Sudirman. Tel: 5780236/257/258/262.

Lufthansa, Panin Centre Bldg, 2nd floor, Jl. Jend Sudirman 1. Tel: 710241/251.

Malaysian Airlines System, Hotel Indonesia, Ground Floor, Jl. M. H. Thamrin. Tel: 320909 (4 lines).

Philippines Airlines, Hotel Borobudur Inter-Continental, Jl. Lapangan Banteng Selatan. Tel: 370108; ext: 2310/2312/2236.

Qantas, BDN Bldg, Jl. M. H. Thamrin. Tel: 327707, 326707, 327538, 4266707.

Royal Brunei Airlines, Bali Arcade, Room 8, Hotel Indonesia, Jl. M. H. Thamrin. Tel: 327214, 327265, 330272.

Saudia, Wisma Bumi Putera, Ground floor, Jl. Jend Sudirman No. 75. Tel: 5780873, 5780615, 5780628.

Singapore Airlines, Chase plaza, Ground floor, Jl. Jend Sudirman Kav. 21. Tel: 584021, 584011.

Swiss-Air, Borobudur Inter-Continental Hotel, Jl. Lapangan Banteng Selatan. Tel: 378006, 373608.

Thai International Airlines, BDN Bldg, Jl. M. H. Thamrin. Tel: 320607 (7 lines).

UTA, Jaya Bldg, Jl. M. H. Thamrin. Tel: 323609; RSVP phones: 323507 (3 lines).

UTA, Summitmas Tower, Jl. Jend Sudirman. Kav. 61. Phones: 5202262/3.

Air India, Hotel Sari Pacific Jl. M. H. Thamrin. Tel: 325534, 325470.

British Airways, Wisma Metropolitan 1, 10th floor, Jl. Jend Sudirman. Tel: 5782460 (4 lines).

Sabena Belgian World Airlines, Borobudur Inter-Continental Hotel, Jl. Lapangan Banteng Selatan. Tel: 372039, 371915.

SAS, S. Widjojo Centre, Jl. Jend Sudirman No. 57. Tel: 584110.

Aeroflot Soviet Airlines, c/o Garuda Indonesia office.

GENERAL SALES AGENTS

Air Canada/Air New Zealand/Finnair, PT Aviamas Megabuana, Chase Plaza, Ground floor, Jl. Jend Sudirman Kav 21. Tel: 588185.

Alitalia, Amaran International Courier, Wisma Metropolitan 11, Ground floor, Jl. Jend Sudirman. Tel: 5781710 (Hunting).

American Airlines, PT Aerojasa Perkasa, BDN Bldg, Jl. M. H. Thamrin 5. Tel: 325600, 325728, 325792.

Canadian Pacific, Iwata Tours and Travel, Wisma Kosgoro, 5th floor, Jl. M. H. Thamrin 53. Tel: 324742, 336521, 336397.

Delta Airlines, Tirta Amerta Jati Ltd, Hotel Indonesia, Jl. M. H. Thamrin. Tel: 320008; ext: 149.

Air Mauritius/Hawaiian Airlines/Royal Brunei Airlines, PT Duta Cardindo, Jl. Hasyim Ashari 33 B. Tel: 345332, 367852.

Northwest Orient/Pakistan International Airlines, PT Belco, Oriental Bldg, Jl. M. H. Thamrin. Tel: 320558, 326439.

Pan American Airways/United Airlines, PT Samudra Indonesia Dirgantara, Borobudur Inter-Continental Hotel, Jl. Lapangan Banteng Selatan. Tel: 361707.

Trans World Airlines, PT Ayuberga, Wisma Bumiputra 4th, Jl. Jend Sudirman Kav 75. Tel: 5781428.

46542 TUNAS IA, and Jl. Semawang-Sanur, Denpasar. Tel: 88056, 88581; Telex: 35238 DPR.

Vista Express, Central Cikini Bldg, Jl. Cikini Raya, Jakarta 10330. Tel: 321945, 336100; Telex: 61516 VITOUR IA. Fax: 3100004, and Bali Beach Hotel Arcade, Sanur (or) P. O. Box 258 Denpasar. Tel: 8511; ext: 579; Telex: 35133, 35129 HBB.

Agaphos, 16 Jl. Gajah Mada, Jakarta 10130. Tel: 351333, 359659, 351332; Fax: 8091652.

Anta Express, 88 Jl. Hayam Wuruk, Jakarta 11160. Tel: 655908 (15 lines); Fax: 6597487.

Apexindo Express Tours, Hotel Borobudur Inter-Continental, Jl Lapangan Banteng Selatan, Jakarta 104140. Tel: 376598, 376524, 370108; Fax: 6298651.

The Grand Greenfield, 7 Jl. Falatehan Raya, Jakarta. Tel: 7392127, 7392341; Fax: 370121.

Optimism in the future growth of tourism in Indonesia has generated new interest in hotel and resort development. In keeping with the government's desire to increase non-oil revenues, more hotels are being built and improved. Jakarta, Bali, Surabaya, Bandung and Yogyakarta in particular offer first-class accommodation. By the same token, there are many lower-grade hotels which would cater well for the budget traveller.

While Indonesia has developed its own hotel chains such as Hotel Indonesia International Corp., PT Natour, PT Aerowisata, PT Patra Jasa, and The Sahid Hotel group, international hotel chains are also growing rapidly. Well established in Indonesia are the Hyatt International, Hilton International, Pan Pacific, Mandarin Oriental, Club Med, Sol Hotels, Oberoi, Regent, Sheraton, Meridien and Holiday Inn.

The top-grade hotels in Jakarta are: **Borobudur Inter-Continental, Grand Hyatt, Hyatt Aryaduta, Jakarta Hilton, Mandarin Oriental, Sahid Jaya** and **Sari Pacific** — all five-star hotels. All three and two-star hotels in Jakarta have air-conditioned rooms, attached bathrooms with hot and cold running water, telephones in the rooms, restaurants, bar and room service. Most of the three-star category have swimming pools, nightclubs and shopping arcades. Most of the one-star hotel have air-conditioned rooms and restaurants.

The top-class hotels are virtually always full. Make sure a reservation is made well in advance and if it is in a first-class hotel it is worthwhile booking through the hotel's central reservation agency. It saves time and beats the frustation of waiting to get a line to call out.

A word of caution: getting messages out of even the best hotels is sometimes a problem.

UPCOUNTRY

Other provinces such as West and Central Java are also experiencing a boom in hotel development, and Bali has experienced the highest rate of hotel growth.

In Bandung (West Java) the most exciting development is the preservation of two old hotels in art deco style — **The Grand Hotel Preanger** and the **Savoy Homann. Hotel Papandayan** also offers top rate accommodation. Further on the west coast there is the **Samudra Beach Hotel** at Pelabuhan Ratu.

In central Java, Yogyakarta has a number of fine hotels such as the **Ambarrukmo Palace, Garuda Hotel** and the **Mutiara**. For the traveller who is trying to save, the guesthouse **Petit Mas** is highly recommended. Other tourist areas like north and west Sumatra, north and south Sulawesi, now have all the comforts of starrated hotels.

The choice of accommodation in Bali, whether on the beach resorts or in the mountains, is almost infinite. Despite the upsurge in occupancy rate, Bali retains its image of unique first-class hotels. The **Nusa Dua Beach Hotel** is known for its architecture and excellent service. Others, such as the **Bali Sol, Putri Bali** and **Sanur Beach Hotel**, all provide competitive service.

Most hotels in major towns have air-conditioned rooms, but many are still equipped with Asian-style bathrooms, known in Indonesia as "Bak Mandi" — a tank or built-in corner in which water is stored for dipping. Nonetheless, they are clean and decent. Mosquitoes are a problem even in some of the better hotels and it is important to carry mosquito repellent and to take anti-malaria tablets.

Notable among the cheap accommodation in Indonesia are the losmen (literally rooms to let), which are extremely comfortable. Rates per person per night are usually no more than Rps 10,000. In Jakarta, Jalan Jaksa is a popular road for this type of accommodation.

Worthy of special note are the detached bungalow-style hotels which make up much of the accommodation on Bali. Most are set in pleasant garden surroundings on or near to beaches, and provide closer contact with the

Village market in Bali.

charms of Bali than would be possible in conventional-type establishments. **La Taverna Hotel** on Sanur beach is one example of this marvellous setting.

Indonesian cuisine certainly merits a place in the international good-food ratings, though rather more for bold, rich flavour and heavy-handed spicing than for delicacy or elegance. The fact that in Jakarta some of the best food will be served to you at a rough wooden table in tent-like stalls on the roadside is evidence that the roots of Indonesian cooking are among the ordinary people.

Over the centuries there has been much culinary influence from India, and to a lesser extent from China. But Indonesia is a rich, lush land, and the eating habits of its people have responded more to the influence of coconuts growing in abundance and fish from the coastal waters, than to the habits of foreigners. So, as you stroll in Jakarta after dusk, you can take your pick in savouring the multiple choices of "nasi padang" (spicy curries with rice) or satay with peanut or soya sauce (chunks of meat on a wooded skewer repeatedly soaked in strong sauces and grilled over a low charcoal fire). Plain fried rice in Indonesia rises above itself as

"nasi goreng" to be almost the national dish — rice fried in coconut oil, with eggs, meat, tomato, cucumber and chillies.

In Jakarta there is a profusion of restaurants of all types, from the ethnic Indonesian to country specialities. Most foreign cuisines are available and the most popular is Japanese. Many hotels in their promotion campaigns, highlight authentic foreign cuisine in their regular food festivals. For the adventurous the marketplace is where there are many dishes to choose from. Those with a delicate stomach should note that it is not always safe to buy food or drink by the roadside or from passing vendors.

Other popular cuisine are the West Sumatran foods served in Padang Restaurants, the "Kurings" of West Java for their specialities in Sundanese cooking, the Makasar (South Sulawesi) grilled fish, the Tapanuli specialities — which often include dogmeat, fruit bats (a delicacy in North Sulawesi) and even snake meat. Chinese restaurants are at almost every corner of the road and many have adapted to the local tastes to compete well in the small stalls of food markets.

One Indonesian dish which must be eaten in a restaurant to savour its full flavour is the "rijstafel." Rice is the base, to which is added meats, fish, eggs and vegetables relished with different curries, sweet fruit sauces, morsels of fresh fruit, marvellously tasty dried fish, dried coconut, nuts and crisps, all served separately. It is a full meal on its own and you choose what you like as you go along.

Good thick Indonesian coffee, served with the grounds is normally available in small cafes or stalls. However, for the connoisseur, a good Balinese or Timorese blend would not go amiss. Many restaurants serve hot or cold tea (sometimes very sweet) as part of their welcome. It is of high quality and most refreshing. However, watch out for the "teh es" (ice tea). The ice is usually made from boiling water, but whether or not it has been properly boiled, and for how long, is open to question.

As the food business expands to meet the local market, many restaurants around Jakarta are also specialising exclusively in Western cuisine. **La Bastille** in Menteng offers the best available in French cuisine and **Cafe de Paris** on Jalan Capt. Tendean is a good and inexpensive restaurant.

Most of the top restaurants are in the major hotels — **Borobudur, Hilton, Hyatt Aryaduta, Sari Pacific** and **Mandarin**. Equally the nightclubs, such as the **Casablanca**, the **Nirwana**, and the **Oasis** all offer excellent suppers. Oasis is a little expensive, but very elegant, serving both Indonesian and European cuisine. It is specially known for its rijstafel served by a bevy of waitresses attired in Indonesian "Kain and Kebaya." The restaurant was built by a Dutch planter in the art deco style as his private house.

For good, inexpensive Japanese food try **Sushi** restaurant on the 4th floor of Ratu Plaza Shopping Centre, Kikugawa, on Jl. Kebon Binatang 3/13. Just around the corner is **Art and Curio** where they serve good Indonesian and European dishes. While waiting for the food to arrive, you can browse around the antique shop.

For a choice of Indonesian dishes, the **Satay House Senayan**, which has branches all over the city, offers a good selection at moderate prices. **Natrabu** on Jl. Sabang prides itself on its swift service of Padanese food. Others worth visiting include **Sari Kuring** (West Java seafood) on Jl. Batu Ceper and **Silang Monas**.

Of the Chinese restaurants, the best are **Happy Valley**, **Summer Palace** and **Dynasty**. Less prestigious, but excellent value for money, are those of the **Bakmi Gajah Mada**.

For other varieties of cuisine try the **Copper Chimney** on Jalan Antara, which specialises in Indian food, or **Kings** on Jalan Veteran for its South Indian specialities. **Paregu** restaurant in Blok M is best for Vietnamese food and the

Korea Garden can be recommended for Korean food. Next door the hungry visitor will find good English and Indian pub grub at the **George and Dragon**. Both restaurants are on Jalan Teluk Betung.

Foodstalls have sprung up in several locations; a popular one is at **Pasar Seni** (the art market) in the Ancol amusement park. On a slightly higher scale, **Pasaraya Sarinah** department store at Blok M and **Pujasera** on Jalan Jend Sudirman cater for a sit-down meal and food can be ordered from any stall.

Bintang, Anker and San Miguel are the three main locally brewed beers, and they can all be recommended.

It is worth mentioning that fresh seafood along the west coast (towards Pelabuhan Ratu) is unbeatable. Lobsters, prawns, tuna and squid cost virtually nothing.

In Denpasar, Kuta and Sanur on Bali there is an assortment of restaurants — Italian, Chinese, seafood in addition to the various regional cuisines. Being Hindus, the Balinese do not eat beef; the local favourites remain roast suckling pig and duck. Smoked fish has recently being introduced in many restaurants at very reasonable prices.

One of the best known restaurants for seafood is **Poppies** in Kuta. A short walk along the beach from the Bali Beach Inter-Continental, you will find the beach market, a seafood restaurant facing the beach with stalls along the back where you can buy a variety of tasty snacks. Also on the Sanur side, a few minutes' walk across the street from the Bali Hyatt, the **Telaga Naga** serves excellent Sichuan and Cantonese food. The **Penjor**, also in Sanur, offers many regional dishes. **Pertamina Cottages** in Kuta, provide the best Japanese cuisine, though many hotels highlight Japanese specialities on their coffee shop menu. Good pizza or fettuchine are served at **La Taverna** and **Trattoria da Marco**, both in Sanur.

For the cocktail enthusiast, **TJ**'s in Kuta (not far from Poppies) offers mighty pitchers of daiquiris and margaritas. TJ's is also an excellent Mexican restaurant. In Ubud — home for many Balinese artists and fast becoming the mountain resort of Bali — the **Lotus Cafe** is very popular for its Italian dishes.

For the budget-minded there are many foodstalls along the Kuta-Legian street offering set menus printed out on blackboards. Also in Kuta, some of the tiny alleys lead to what one would describe as the local pubs. There local liquor (often made out of rice) is consumed until the early hours of the morning. Imported liquor and beer are usually available only at the bigger hotels and supermarkets and tend to be rather expensive.

Bali is the great entertainment centre of Indonesia. Virtually every day of the year, in one village or another, there is a traditional festival and visitors are usually welcome. Cremation ceremonies may even be viewed from close quarters provided eager camera enthusiasts do not intrude rudely in the proceedings.

Exhibitions of **Balinese dancing** can be seen on most evenings, either in the villages themselves or at one of the hotel theatres. Some of the larger hotels will also have dinner music and other entertainment in the main dining room. Good jazz, cabarets, or sing-a-long music are also performed by local entertainers in many restaurants.

Yogyakarta is also the home of some of Indonesia's traditional forms of entertainment. A performance of the **wayang kulit shadow puppets**, complete with gamelan orchestra accompaniment, can be seen most evenings at the outdoor theatre adjoining the **Ambarrukmo Palace Hotel**.

The **People's Amusement Park**, open every evening, offers a number of performances for very little cost. The shows include drama, music, puppets etc. Just 17 km east of Yogyakarta, at the **Prambanan Temple**, reputed to be the biggest and most beautiful Hindu temple in Indonesia, the **Ramayana Ballet** is performed during full moon evenings.

For typical Western-style entertainment, Jakarta is the city to visit. The best hotels have live entertainment each night and some even hire overseas bands to perform regularly. Discotheques feature in many big hotels too. **Pitstop** (below the Sari Pacific hotel) is a favourite jaunt. For those who can last until the early morning hours, **Jaya Pub** on Jl. Thamrin or **Tanamur** in Jalan Tanah Abang Timur should prove the ideal spots.

The focal point of cultural activities in Jakarta is the **Jakarta Arts Centre**, known as the Taman Ismail Marzuki, at Jl. Cikini Raya. TIM is said to be the largest of its kind in Southeast Asia. There are regular classical and modern performances, from recitals, exhibitions and puppet shows to Javanese operas.

Western and Indonesian films are shown at several city theatres.

Shopping in Indonesia has reached an incredible dimension in the last 10 years. There is a large variety of goods entering the market to suit everyone. While the emphasis is still on art and handicrafts, manufactured goods made in Indonesia are drawing more attention for their quality and competitive prices, in comparison to the traditional shopping destinations in the region.

Indonesia has a growing number of modern shopping plazas and malls in the major cities. With favourable exchange rates, a visitor should get more for his or her money. Products manufactured locally cover everything from electronics goods to sports gear, though there are also the porcelain and other pottery articles that have been exported to Indonesia over past centuries from China and elsewhere on the Asian mainland. A number of antique shops in the capital sell such pieces. Jalan Majapahit has a number of these shops. In addition to the traditional fabrics from different parts of Indonesia, there is also a wide range of garments which has been created and developed to meet the tastes of the changing fashion world.

Batik, Ikat, Tenun (hand-painted, hand-woven, tie-and-dye) have spread over different parts of the country and more are finding their way from remote areas to population centres. The Sumba blankets, the songkets of Sumatra, the silks of South Sulawesi and the jumputan (tie-and-dye) of Palembang are all available in Jakarta.

Traditional wood carving of Bali, the primitive arts of Irian Jaya, Nias and E. Kalimantan, plus Asmat carvings, are now all in great demand. **Lake Toba** in North Sumatra is a well-known centre for Nias' handicraft. Wood products in modern and traditional designs are widely available. Replicas of antique pieces can be made to suit any given design. Rattan, bamboo and reed-weaving have long been on the international market. Some of the most unique pieces are the rattan baskets from Lombok. Paintings and other works of art abound in Indonesia. Many galleries in Bali, Yogyakarta and Jakarta stock the works of famous Indonesian artists. **Neka gallery** in Ubud sells quality pieces. There are more in Jakarta, such as **Djody, Oet's, Hadiprana, Duta** and the **Pasar Seni** in Ancol. Mass-produced canvases and batik paintings are also available in many towns such as **Jl. Suropati** in Jakarta and **Jl. Malioboro** in Yogyakarta.

Cultured and baroque pearls have also found their way on to the international market. Most of the cultured farms are in the eastern part of Indonesia. Gold of 20 or 22 carats is never too expensive; it is sold in small jewellery shops in shopping centres and even in some markets. **Cikini market** has a number of gold shops. For more sophisticated designs **Ratu Plaza** shopping centre provides a selection of establishments to choose from.

The land of silverwork cannot be missed in Celuk, Bali or Kota Gede in Yogyakarta. Other metals such as bronze, brass and tin are readily available. **Jl. Surabaya flea market** and **Pasar Seni** are both well stocked with brassware. Lacquerware, once a speciality of Palembang (in red and black), is now found in other areas such as south Sulawesi. Leatherware has also spread to produce other than the traditional puppets. **Cibaduyut** village in Bandung is now well known for its shoe industry. The jeans industry is also in the heart of Bandung and **Jl. Champelas** is lined with these shops.

Yogyakarta, has the largest selection of batik material and the **Malioboro Road** is lined with shops selling a whole range of handicrafts. If you feel inclined to watch the batik makers at work, there are a number of factories in **Jl. Winotosastro**.

Jakarta offers by far the widest selection of many of the regional handicrafts. **Sarinah Pasaraya** department store in Blok M and on Jl. Thamrin devotes a whole floor to textiles and crafts. Other shopping complexes have arisen in different parts of the city. The biggest is the **Plaza Indonesia**, though many of these shops are specialising in imported goods only. Others are **Ratu Plaza** for exclusive jewellery and fabrics. In **Kebayoran Baru**, Melawai Plaza and Aldiron Plaza have several small shops selling jewellery, garments, souvenirs and gifts. Downtown, **Gajah Mada Plaza, Glodok Plaza, Harco, Hayam Wuruk Plaza** are all filled with electronic goods. The Pasars (markets) can be fun places to spend a morning. Bargaining is necessary. There is a number of them, but **Pasar Baru, Pasar Pagi Pasar Tanah Abang** and **Pasar Senen** are the recommended ones.

Soccer, badminton, tennis and swimming are among the most popular sports in Indonesia. There are a number of public swimming pools and most of the better hotels have good pools. Among the best are the **Borobudur** and the **Hil-**

ton, which also offer good facilities for tennis, squash and fitness workouts, and even have jogging tracks. The **Mandarin Hotel** also has a comprehensive fitness centre. There are also a few tennis courts around the city. The main ones are in the **Senayan** sports complex and just by the **National Monument** (Monas) and the **Pondok Indah Country Club**.

For the avid golfer Jakarta has several good public courses which welcome visitors. Members of private clubs can bring guests to play at any time. There are more than 60 golf courses in Indonesia. Of special note is the course in the mountains past Bedugul (1,300 m above sea level) just 56 km from Denpasar at the **Bali Handara Country Club**. This course has been rated among the top 50 golf courses of the world by *Golf* magazine. The club also offers other sports facilities and bungalow-type accommodation.

Off Jl. Warung Buncit, on Jl. Loka Indah, there is **P. T. Kemang Sport and Recreation Centre**, a driving range, complete with restaurant, beauty salon and shops. Opening hours are from 6 am until 9 pm. tel: 7995925 and 7995839.

Traditional spectator sports include bull races, bull fights, rowing and unique ram fights, all of which are held during special festivities.

Muslims' religious observances dominate the holiday calendar in Indonesia. Dates of particular occasions vary from one year to the next, falling about 10 days earlier each successive year. Bali presents its own delightfully crowded calendar of events. There is something virtually every day of the year and it is advisable to consult the publication of the Directorate-General of Tourism's Indonesia Calendar of Events for details. In Yogyakarta the **Ramayana Ballet Festival** takes place over four nights during each full moon from May to October. If possible, one should try to time the trip to allow a visit to this festival.

January 1: New Year's Day.

Variable: Idhul Adha is the Muslim Day of Sacrifice. Muslims go to the mosque and on pilgrimage to Mecca (public holiday).

January-February: Chinese New Year, celebrated in Jakarta's Chinatown, is a gay and noisy festival among the Chinese population.

Variable: Maulid Nabi Muhammad, the birthday of Muhammad (public holiday).

March-April: Wafat Isa Almasih, Christian

Good Friday (public holiday).

Nyepi: is the most important holiday in Bali. It is a lunar year event and falls around March. Complete silence is observed and no chores are allowed for the whole day.

Variable: Idul Fitr marks the ending of the fasting month of Ramadan (two public holidays).

May: Kenaikan Isa Almasih, the resurrection of Christ (public holiday).

May: Waicak commemorates the Lord Buddha's birth, death and enlightenment. Buddhists all over Indonesia and those from abroad attend ceremonies at Borobudur and Prambanan Temples near Yogyakarta (public holiday).

August 17: Proklamasi Kemerdekaan (Independence Day) marks the anniversary of Indonesian independence declared in 1945 (public holiday).

Variable: Mi'raj Nabih Muhammad celebrates the ascension of the prophet Muhammad (public holiday).

December 25: Natal Hari Pertama (Christmas: public holiday).

Addresses

The Directorate-General of Tourism (DGT) is in Jakarta and is administered under the Department of Tourism, Post and Telecommunications, which has offices in all the main tourist destination areas.

The offices are known as **Kanwil Depparpostel**, or Regional Office of Tourism, Post and Telecommunications. Each of the 27 provinces of Indonesia also has its own tourist offices which can be identified by the abbreviation **DIPARDA** (provincial tourist service) or **BAPPARDA** (provincial tourist agency). These offices can assist in providing DGT's own publication, *Indonesia's Travel Planner*, other useful travel booklets and a map.

DISCOVERING INDONESIA

JAKARTA

The capital, Jakarta, seems at pains to hide itself in a maze of winding streets that pass through nondescript residential and shopping areas, with only here and there densities of buildings that suggest a city. Such wide expanses of untidy parkland as the **Medan Merdeka** (Freedom Park) with its towering monument, and the **Banteng Square**, fragment the city and the visitor feels to be forever walking vast distances.

The city has expanded greatly since the days when it was called Batavia; the population is now more than 8 million, swollen with Indonesians from all the distant islands attracted by the delights and possible job opportunities of the metropolis.

Very roughly, the city lies along a north-south axis, running from the old Dutch quarter near the sea, through the main centre of the newer part of town and further south to the modern, detached residential suburb of Kebayoran Baru. The harbour of **Tanjung Priok** lies six miles to the northeast, easily accessible by bus or taxi.

Merdeka Square is the city's most central landmark. The monument, with its golden flame at the top, can be seen from most points. It is an ideal spot from which to begin discovering the city's interesting places. Jalan Merdeka Utara runs along the northern side of the park and there can be found the **Merdeka Palace**, the former official residence of the Dutch governor-general. It has to be viewed from the opposite side of the road, since it is protected by armed guards who allow no one to go near it.

Just several hundred yards from the palace is the **National Museum** (Gedung Gajah) on Jalan Merdeka Barat, running along the western side of the park. It contains an excellent collection: Hindu-Javanese stone sculpture from the fifth to the 14th century; bronze objects from the same period; an ethnographic collection representative of major cultural areas in Indonesia; ceramic pieces imported from the Asian mainland, some from as early as the Chinese Sung dynasty; a small pre-history collection; a splendid treasure-room displaying gold and other precious jewellery. The museum is closed on Monday but open on other days from 8 am until 2 pm in the afternoon, except on Friday and Saturday, when it closes at 11 am. On Sunday it closes at 3 pm. English-language guided tours are available at 9:30 am on Tuesdays, Wednesdays and Thursdays; French tours at 9 am on Wednesdays, and Japanese tours on Tuesdays at 9 am. Nearby is the old town hall built in 1710, now occupied by the military.

From the northeast corner of Medan Merdeka can be seen the massive bulk of the **National Mosque**. A short distance further on is the old **Catholic Cathedral** standing alongside Banteng Square, where the central statue on high depicts a West Irian man breaking his chain of colonial subjugation. The **Borobudur Hotel** rises some dozen storeys next to the square. A

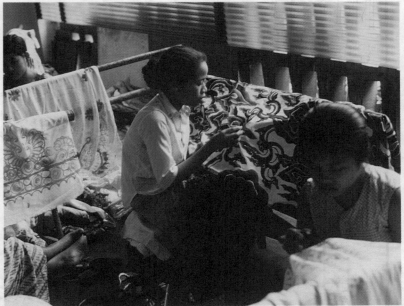

Making a batik print.

Photo: Nayan Chanda

further short walk to the north and across Jalan Dr Sutomo with its canal will bring you to Pasar Baru, one of the **interesting markets** in the city. Late in the afternoon is the best time to visit it and sample some of the dishes from the foodstalls in the area.

Beginning again from Merdeka Square, this time from the fountain at the street intersection at the southwest corner, you can head south through what is the most developed area of the city. The main street is called Jalan Thamrin and contains the Sarina Department Store, some embassy buildings, banks and a number of the city's better hotels. The helpful **Visitor Information Centre** (tel: 354094 or 364093) is in the movie theatre building next to Sarinah.

If you head west from the Presidential Palace along Jalan Merdeka Utara, you will come to Jalan Majapahit at the T-junction; a turn right will take you past several **antique shops**. Other antique shops can be found along Jalan Surabaya, Jalan Kebon Sirih Timur, Blok M, and Ciputat. Jalan Surabaya is worth a special visit.

From Jalan Majapahit northwards will take you to Jalan Gajah Mada on the opposite side Jalan Hayam Wuruk. These two **main business streets** are heavily congested during the day. Further north is the **Glodok** area or "Chinatown." The **National Archives** building in Jalan Gajah Mada is old and beautifully preserved. It was originally built as a country house. Heading straight north will take you to **old Jakarta**. Here is the **Fatahillah Museum** (Museum Kota) with its rich collections of furniture, porcelain and stoneware. Also in this area are the **Museum of Fine Arts** (Balai Seni Rupa) and the **Wayang Museum**, with a collection of puppets from all over Indonesia. Wayang performances are held here from time to time.

Visit the port of **Sunda Kelapa**, not very far from this area. Here vessels from the world's largest great commercial sailing fleet can be seen. These Buginese sailing ships are still travelling to and from Ujung Pandang (Makasar) just as they did in Joseph Conrad's time. Hire a water-taxi and explore the waterfront. While you are in the area, a visit to the **Maritime Museum**

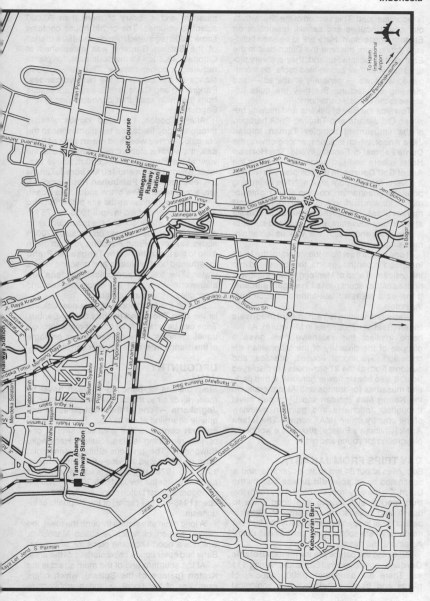

To Halim
International
Airport

Jalan Perdanakusuma

Jalan Pemuda

Golf Course

Jl. Bekasi Timur

Jalan Raya Jend Ahmad Yani

Jatinegara
Railway
Station

Jl. Jatinegara Timur

Jl. Jatinegara Barat

Jalan Raya May Jen Panjaitan

Jalan Raya Let Jen Sutoyo

Jl. Raya Matraman

Jalan Otto Iskandar Dinata

Jalan Dewi Sartika

To Bogor

Pramuka

Jl. Salemba

Kramat

Jl. Raya Kramat

Proklamasi Jl.

Jl. Prokiamasi

Jl. Dr Saharjo Jl. Prof Supomo Sh

Jalan Raya Let Jen Haryono MT

Jalan Sultan Agung

Jl. Cikini Raya

Jl. Diponegoro

Jl. Latuharhari

Jl. Rangkayo Rasuna Said

Merdeka Timur Menteng Raya

Jl. Prof Moh Yamin S H

Jl. Imam Bonjol

Jl. Sutan Syahrir

Railway Station

Jl. Kebon Sirih

Merdeka Selatan

H Agus Salim

Moh Husni Thamrin

Jl. K H Wahid Hasyim

Jen. Gatot Subroto

Jl. Kapten Tendean

Tanah Abang
Railway Station

Jalan Raya

Jalan Raya

Raya Let Jend S Parman

Kebayoran Baru

89

is recommended. This section of the city, with its old, quaint houses and canals, resembles an Eastern Amsterdam. Here are to be seen buildings dating from the time the Dutch built in the East as they built in Holland: they are very picturesque with their brown-tiled roofs, diamond-paned windows — generally shuttered — and pleasing architecture. But they are quite unsuited to the tropical conditions.

Towards the Bay of Jakarta and midway between Old Jakarta and Tanjung Priok harbour, is the amusement complex **Taman Impian Jaya Ancol**, which includes, among others, the **Dunia Fantasi** or Fantasy World. The **Horison Hotel** is here and just across the street is the **Ancol Golf Course**. In the complex you will find a drive-in theatre, pool area with five swimming pools, an oceanarium, bowling alley, nightclub, marina for windsurfing and yachting, and an **art market** (Pasar Seni), where you can see artists at work, buy souvenirs, eat at the food stalls, or just browse and watch the various entertainments.

If one heads east from the vicinity of the Hotel Indonesia in central Jakarta, the roads lead into the residential area of Menteng where the lovely houses of the recent past sit in elegant gardens. It makes a pleasant late-afternoon stroll from the hotels.

Also worth visiting is **Taman Mini Indonesia Indah** (Beautiful Indonesia in Miniature). As the name implies, this extensive park gives a glimpse of the diversity of the Indonesian archipelago. Traditional houses, dresses, and customs from all the 27 provinces are displayed here. It also boasts flower gardens, a bird park, and museums for stamps and Asmat crafts. In the **Keong Mas** (golden snail) you can travel throughout Indonesia and gain an overview of the country on an IMAX screen. The **Istana Anak** (Children's Palace) provides a wonderful playground for young and old.

DAY TRIPS FROM JAKARTA

Bogor lies about 64 km south of Jakarta, and is dominated by its **splendid palace** built by the Dutch. On the way from the capital (by road) the **fruit market** at Cibinong is a good place to pause and take some refreshment. Bogor's palace is set in spacious and beautifully laid-out gardens, where spotted deer can be seen roaming among the trees.

Adjoining the palace are the famous **Botanic Gardens**, conceived in 1827 and covering 111 ha. There are altogether 10,000 species of plants and trees, a herbarium, a zoological

museum and a library of more than 60,000 scientific volumes. The orchid house contains some 3,000 registered hybrids. In 1860 a branch of the Botanic Gardens was established at Cibodas, 43.2 km to the southeast, for plants requiring a colder climate. This other garden stands on the slopes of the **twin volcanoes**, Pangrango and Gede, and is easily accessible from the main road that connects Bogor with Bandung.

After Cibodas, the road climbs steadily through paddy fields and tea plantations to the bungalow-dotted **weekend resort area of Puncak**. It's worth a stop for refreshments and the view at the Puncak Pass, 1,600 m above sea-level. Beyond Bogor and 180 km from Jakarta is the resort centre of **Pelabuhan Ratu**, which offers a magnificent view of the south Java Coast.

Bandung, famous as the site of the first Afro Asian Conference held in April 1955, is 175 km from Jakarta, via Bogor and the mountain resort of Cianjur. The town stands on a plateau 700 m above sea-level. From Bandung you can make a trip to the top of the nearby **Tangkuban Prahu** (overturned boat) **volcano** and descend into its crater. The town's **zoological gardens** are also worth visiting to see birds, snakes and crocodiles in their natural habitat.

Just off the north shore of Java near Jakarta lie the **One Thousand Islands** (Pulau Seribu). Trips can be arranged by boat or plane through travel agencies; there are bungalows on some of the islands where the traveller can stay.

UPCOUNTRY JAVA

From Jakarta or Bandung you can travel by road, rail or air to the central Javanese town of **Jogjakarta** — one of the most pleasant and quietly charming spots in Asia. The town is the **cultural centre** for the area and seat of one of the remaining sultan, Sultan Hamengku Buwono X. The previous Sultan, Hamengku Buwono IX, served as vice-president between 1973 and 1978. Jogja, as it is usually called, is also known for the revolt (1825-30) of Prince Diponegoro against Dutch colonial rule, and it was later (1946-50) the capital of the Republic of Indonesia.

A long main street runs through the town, the central portion of which is called Malioboro, which is a good shopping place for silverwork, Batik and other curios characteristic of the area.

At the southern end of the main street is the **Kraton (palace of the Sultan)**, which offers examples of traditional Javanese architecture

Javanese court retainers.
Photo: Michael Vatikiotis

and decoration. The pavilions in the Kraton proper include the Prabayeksa in which the sacred weapons and gem-studded symbols of royalty are kept, and next to it the **Golden Pavilion** in which prominent quests were formerly received. The glass pavilion next door, called Bangsal Manis (the sweet), was used for state banquets. Permits to visit the palace are available at the entrance of the Kraton.

Every evening from 8 pm to 1 am at the People's Amusement Park there is an interesting programme, including dance and drama performances. It is an excellent spot to join the local people. The main theatres charge a small admission fee but other entertainment is free.

Most of the hotels can also arrange for a performance of wayang kulit (shadow plays).

Restaurants in Jogjakarta include **Colombo**, serving Chinese and Indonesian dishes (25 Malioboro); **Kaping**, Chinese and Indonesian (3 Jalan Suyatmajan — a small street off Malioboro); and in the main street itself are several foodstalls selling tasty lumpia chicken and vegetable rolls for Rps 150 each.

Also of interest nearby are the **old fortress** of Diponegoro at Tegalejo; the ruined (but now restored) fortress of Hamengku Buwono I, built in 1761 and now called **Tamansari**; the **silverware manufacturing** centre of Kola Gede, four miles east of Jogja where also are buried the first kings of Mataram (from whom the Sultans of Jogjakarta are descended); and the **royal tombs** of imogiri, 19.2 km to the southeast.

The drive to the coastal village of **Parangtritis**, 27.2 km south of Jogja, offers excellent views of the countryside. If you go by bus you must walk the last two or three miles (or take a pony-cart) from the village of Kretek. The bus fare is about Rps 500. Parangtritis, a centre for the cult of Nyai Loro Kidul (the Goddess of the South), is a freshwater swimming pool close to the beach, and a hot spring about a mile to the east.

Kaliurang, about 27 km north of Jogja and 1,060 m up on the slopes of the active Merapi volcano, is an ideal spot for relaxation. There are cheap bungalows available, swimming pools and a 57-m waterfall.

But the neighbourhood of Jogjakarta is notable above all for its wealth of architectural remains of Java's middle Javanese or classical period (eighth and ninth centuries), when the influence of Indian traditions — especially the religious — were most closely felt. There are numerous sites from this and later periods spread widely over central Java; an interesting group of buildings is located on the **Dieng Plateau** some distance north via Magelang and Wonosobo.

The most famous are those of **Borobudur** and **Prambanan**. Borobudur, a Mahayana Buddhist stupa-temple (the name perhaps meaning monastery of accumulated virtue), is about 40 km to the northeast of Jogjakarta. If you go by bus, go first to the town of Muntilan, and there change to the local bus that passes Borobudur.

The four-hour round-trip by car from the Amburrukmo Hotel will cost around Rps 20,000 subject to negotiation. The building, stone terraces mounted on an early mound, rises 43 m above the surrounding rice fields. Probably built under the dynasty of the Sailendras (Kings of the Mountain) around 800 AD, it was much defaced by the Muslims and was in ruins until restored by the Dutch. It was also threatened with damage owing to poor foundations, but the government of Indonesia, with aid from Unesco and private donations, undertook a major renovation programme to restore the Borobudur monument to its original grandeur and the work was completed in mid-1983.

The stupa consists of six square terraces which are in turn surmounted by three circular terraces. The stupa is symbolic of the Mahayana Buddhist cosmological view of the universe: the lower level (now hidden under a supporting bank of earth) depicts man's phenomenal place in the world, bound by rebirth under the Law of Cause and Effect, owing to his unceasing attachment to desire; the higher square terraces have highly artistic bas-relief carvings depicting the life of Gautama (the Buddha) and of Bodhisatvas (those beings of high virtue destined for Buddhahood). There are also niches containing Buddha images. The uppermost square terrace is transitional, passing to the three circular terraces bearing 72 latticed dagoba arranged concentrically around the central one. Here are depicted representations of the formless states reached by Buddhas after they have detached themselves over incredibly long periods of time from the human pressures that bind mortals to the wheel of life. The whole structure might be viewed as a massive example in beautiful carved stone of the Buddhist way that man should follow if he hopes to progress to Nirvana.

About 3 km before Borobudur is the **Candi Mendut** stone structure containing a large, finely finished Buddha seated between two Bodhisatvas.

About 16 km northeast of Jogja on the Surakarta (Solo) road is the **Prambanan** group of temples — mainly Hindu, but featuring some Buddha images. The buildings were probably constructed in the second half of the ninth century under the Mataram Dynasty. By bus the fare is only Rps 300. The compound has a square inner court enclosed by a wall. Within this court are eight stone shrines: three in a row along the west side facing east, another row of three on the east, facing west, and two rather smaller ones between them. The three westerly temples are dedicated to the Hindu Trinity — Brahma (the southernmost of the three), Siva (the largest central temple 53 m high) and Vishnu (on the north).

The large temple of Siva has four rooms. In the central one is an image of Siva (the king was considered to be an incarnation of the God and on his death was honoured in that form). The southern room contains Bhatara Guru, and the west room the elephant-headed son of Siva, Ganesh.

The temple complex at Prambanan is often alternatively called Candi Larajonggrang, after the statue of the cursed maiden to be found in the north room. Her nose is missing — perhaps knocked off by some irate follower — but her breasts and belly are worn shiny black from the fond caresses of the centuries, and she is a most disturbing presence.

From May-October each year (during the dry season) the **Ramayana Ballet Festival** is held over four nights at each full moon at the Prambanan temple on a specially prepared stage, where the floodlit temple forms a backdrop to the fabulous dancing. The whole epic is danced over each festival period by dancers from the dance academies in Jogjakarta and Surakarta, and accompanied by gamelan orchestras. The event is of special note and any visitor should make an attempt to visit Jogjakarta during one of the monthly festivals.

In the neighbourhood of the Prambanan group are the Buddhist **Kalasan Sewu** and **Plaosan temples**.

The best small books offering interesting descriptions of these temples can be bought at the sites. They are written by R. Soekmono.

From Prambanan the road continues north to **Surakarta** (Solo) about 72 km from Jogja. The kraton of the Susuhunan of Surakarta is larger than that of Jogjakarta. The first part of it is now an art gallery, also broadcasting enchanting music. The court dances, bedoyo and serimpi, are still taught and most of the dancers for the Ramayana Ballet Festival come from this area. An interesting spot in the town is the **Sriwedani Amusement Park**, which has a zoological garden, a theatre for wayang orang (live classical dance), restaurants and curio shops. Free dance performances are held on Sunday morning.

It is still possible for travellers to be lodged in the **Mangkunegaran Palace** at Surakarta, which is a more complete kraton than that of the Susuhunan.

Some 120 km north of Jogja, via Magelang, is the port of **Semarang**. The Pasar Johar market can be found next to the public square, and other places of interest are the great mosque and the main shopping street, Jalan Bojong.

Surabaya, to the east, the second port of Indonesia, is a naval base as well as the centre of sea connections with the eastern islands. Some 48 km south of Surabaya are the hill resorts of **Prigen** and **Tretes**. Tretes is largely patronised by noisy holidaymakers from Surabaya (especially at weekends and on school holidays); it has several swimming pools, hotels and bungalows. There are a number of interesting temples between Tretes and Surabaya. Malang, about 90 km south of Surabaya, stands on a plateau some 440 m up in a countryside of temples and waterfalls.

Worthwest of Malang and near Batu is another pleasant mountain resort, **Selecta**, which has cheap bungalows and a swimming pool in a setting where alpine and tropical plants grow side by side.

From Surabaya's Tanjung Perak port, it is just half an hour by ferry to the town of **Kamal** on Madura Island.

Pamekasan, the capital of Madura, is about 100 km to the east by road. There is a large hotel at Pamekasan and a showroom for local arts and crafts near the public square.

A few miles to the south of the town, there is an **eternal fire**, which is best seen at night. Madura is above all famous for its traditional **bull races** (kerapan), which are held first at village and district level and later culminate in the **Great Kerapan** held annually in the Pamekasan stadium at the beginning of September. The rider stands on a large wooden pole slung between two yoked beasts, with the rear end trailing along the ground.

BALI

The singular character of Bali has always enchanted visitors. Alone of the Indonesian Islands, Bali succeeded in preserving its Hinduism against the advance of Islam. This island of 5,620 km^2 has more than 20,000 temples scattered among the terraced rice-fields, in the cemeteries, in the markets, on the beaches, in the caves and among the roots of venerable trees. Perhaps more so than in any other country, the spirit world dominates the lives of Bali's people.

Bali can be reached by ferry from Ketapang (several kilometres north of Banjuangi) in eastern Java. The ferry crosses every hour to Gilimanuk on Bali, from where it is still another three hours by bus to the capital Denpasar. The fare is Rps 2,000 per person. If you miss the last ferry across the Bali Strait, you can stay in the hotel at Banyuwangi for the night.

Sanur Beach, Bali's main tourist centre, lies 10 km to the east of Denpasar. In the vicinity are the majority of the island's premier hotels, old and new. There are other hotels at Nusa Dua (a quieter area of Bali), in Denpasar itself and to the southwest at Kuta Beach near the airport.

Denpasar, the capital of Bali, in the south of the island, is liveliest in the evening and a stroll among the foodstalls gives the visitor a chance to mingle with the local people at the roadside market. The town museum has a good collection of cultural pieces from various periods in Balinese history. Bali's splendid countryside and wealth of temples are beyond the town, often several hours' drive away. It needs careful planning to see the greatest number of famous sites on a day's outing. The island's villagers are generally friendly and visitors can join in the crowds to watch the popular cockfights or observe a ritualistic cremation ceremony.

From nearby villages a number of interesting temples can be visited, some with distinctive scenic views. Many of these villages can be visited in a half-day by car, or better still by Jeep. Many roads are in poor condition but Bali is worth suffering a few bumps. It is advisable to ask the car hire firm for a list of bridges closed for repairs. Villages include **Celuk** (noted for its silverware), **Mas** (woodcarving) and **Ubud**, 24 km north of Denpasar, the cradle of the legong, the finest of the Balinese dances, and of Balinese dancing and music in general. It is also a centre of **Balinese painting** with a large colony of artists, both native and foreign. The town's small museum traces the development of the district's artists over recent decades. Close to the nearby village of Bedulu is the **Goa Gaja** (Elephant Cave), whose stone carvings date from the 11th century. West of these villages (but one must take a separate road from Denpasar) is the **Monkey Forest** at Sangeh, home of hundreds of spirit monkeys which are not averse to biting visitors and snatching cameras. Be careful. They can be vicious.

To the northeast of Denpasar are the two **holy volcanoes** of Gunung Agung and Mount Batur, each some 64 km from the capital. A very full day (by car) will enable you to visit both mountains and stop at the main sites along the way. Mount Batur (1,900 m) can be reached via Celuk, Mas and Ubud; visitors should stop at Gunung Kawi, where there are ancient **burial towers** hewn from the rocky hillside, and also visit the **holy Tirta Empul Spring** at Tampaksiring. The village of Penelokan stands on the edge of the Batur **volcanic crater**, offering a fine view of **Lake Batur**, which is actually in the crater. You can see where new lava has recently flowed from the small internal volcanic outlet. On the far side of the lake (reached by horse and boat) is the village of **Trunyan**, where the Bali Aga, among the island's earliest inhabitants, live. Here stands the island's **largest statue**, the Ratu Gede Pancerning Jagat, patron guardian of Trunyan.

North of Panelokan are the mountain towns of Batur, Kintamani (where there is a hotel) and Penulisan, from where the road descends onto the northern district capital of **Singaraja**.

Returning south from Penelokan by the more easterly of the two roads leading from the town, one reaches the town of Bangli and its important **temple of Pura Kehen**.

You must continue well south from Bangli to gain access to the road heading east through Klukung (where the interesting **Kerta Gosa Hall of Justice** can be visited) to make the ascent to the **Besakih**, the most holy of all Bali's temples, more than 1,000 m up on the slopes of Gunung Agung volcano.

North of Denpasar, along the road leading directly to Singaraja, are the interesting villages of **Mengwi** (with its neolithic stone thrones and impressive Taman Ayun temple) and, in the mountains, **Bedugul** on Lake Bratan.

Those wishing to travel by local bus about

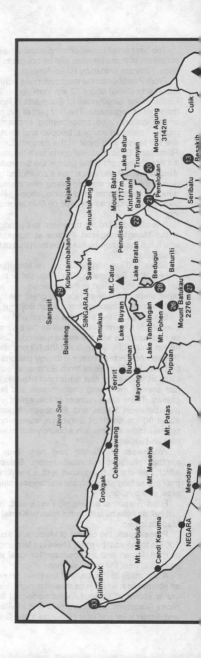

BALI

JAVA

INDIAN OCEAN

Bali Strait

Lombok Strait

Padang Bai

KLUNGKUNG

GIANYAR

Bali Sea

Nusa Lembongan

NUSA PENIDA

Toyapekeh

Kusambe

Gelgel

Pejeng

Bedulu

Mas

Celuk

Batubulan

Sanur

DENPASAR

Airport

Mengwi

Kediri

Kapal

Lukluk

Sempidi

Pliatan

Kuta

BUKIT BADUNG

Benoa

Tanah Lot

Ulu Watu

NUSA DUA

1 Denpasar Museum and Market
2 Batubulan Stone Carvers
3 Celuk Gold and Silver works
4 Mas Wood Carvers
5 Ubud Art Centre and Museum of Paintings
6 Bedulu Elephant Cave (Goa Gajah)
7 Pejeng Centre of early Balinese Dynasties
8 Pliatan Dance Group
9 Sangeh Monkey Forest
10 Gunung Kawi Hindu — Balinese Sanctuary
11 Yeh Puluh Ruins
12 Klungkung Court of Justice

13 Besakih Mother Temple
14 Kusambe Fishing Village
15 Bat Cave (Goa Lawah)
16 Padang Bai (Ferry to Lombok)
17 Tenganan Village of the Bali Aga
18 Tirta Gangga old Bathing Place
19 Ujung Water Palace
20 Trunyan Village of Bali Aga
21 Batur Temple and Volcanic Lake
22 Kintamani Mountain Village
23 Tampaksiring Tirta Empul Spring
24 Mengwi Temple Taman Ayun

25 Tanah Lot Temple
26 Batukau The Coconut Shell Mountain
27 Batukau Temple
28 Bedugul Mountain Village
29 Sangsit Temple
30 Sanur Beach Area
31 Kuta Beach Area
32 Ulu Watu Temple
33 Gilimanuk (Ferry to Java)
34 Nusa Dua Resort

the island can do so very cheaply; the fare to Klukung from Denpasar, for example, is just Rps 750. Motorcycles for hire are plentiful at around US$10 per day.

Performances of Bali's marvellous **dances** can be seen at many of the larger hotels (for example, the Bali Beach Hotel has a fine outdoor theatre), though it is better, if you have the time, to visit one of the villages that specialise in dance performances. In most cases unaffected by the corrupting influence of being exposed to mass audiences, Bali's dances are among the world's most intriguing entertainments.

From Padang Bai on the southeast coast of Bali you can take the ferry to Ampenan, the port for the town of Mataram on the neighbouring island of **Lombok** to the east. Lombok displays a mixture of Balinese and local culture. There are several hotels on the island. Further east is the small island of **Kolombo** where the famous **Komoda Dragon** can be seen, one of the world's largest lizards that grows up to 3 m long.

THE OUTLYING ISLANDS
SUMATRA

Medan, the island's chief city, lies far to the north on the east coast, almost opposite West Malaysia's island of Penang. It is a centre for rubber production but of no great tourist interest other than being a gateway to the pleasant highlands. Belawan Deli, 22.4 km away, is the port town of Medan. **Berastagi**, further south, a popular resort with several hotels, is noted for its volcano and hot springs.

From Medan, it is 176 km (about six hours by road) to Prapat on the beautiful **Lake Toba**. The lake is more than 1,000 m above sea-level and contains the densely populated island of **Samosir**. The cool surrounding countryside is covered with tobacco, rubber and oil-palm plantations. This is the region of the **Bataks**, whose architecture is distinguished by huge roofs which overhang the houses, often with elaborately carved gables. Swimming, boating and fishing are some of the pleasures of this peaceful hill area.

The adventurer can take the bus all the way from Medan, via Prapat and the west coast harbour town of Sibolga, to **Bukittinggi**. The trip takes 28 hours, and only local food is available on the way. Bukittinggi (High Hill) lies between a towering volcano and an equally grand mountain.

From there it is only a few hours by bus or narrow-gauge train down to the main port city of **Padang** — capital of the Minangkabau region.

The Minangkabaus are famous for their houses and rice barns with high roofs rising to a peak at each end, and are noted for their commercial ability. If you take the ship from Padang to Jakarta, you will anchor for a few hours off the west-coast town of **Bengkulu** (Bencoolen), where Sir Stamford Raffles (founder of Singapore) was once governor, and where there is a memorial to British rule in Fort Marlborough. The place is also famous for the Rafflesia, the largest flower in the world which blossoms only every five years.

Palembang in the southeast, now only a sad reminder of its past great days as capital of the Srivijaya Kingdom, is a centre for the great Sumatran oilfields across the Musi River at Plaju and Sungei Gerong. The old traditions manage to survive insofar as the region produces fine woven fabrics and has unique dances.

SULAWESI (CELEBES)

Ujung Pandang (once known as Makassar) is the main southern city on the island, and home for the seafaring Bugis. It is noted for crab, lobster and fish grilled over an open fire. A road runs northwards to **Rantepao** (280 km), a region famous for the splendid architectural woodcarving of the South Torajas and for the local burial sites.

The Minahasas of **Manado** in the far north are distinguished from the other peoples of Sulawesi by their light skins and by their almost universal adoption of Christianity. Every village has its church and school, and Dutch is spoken to some extent. It is Indonesia's most Westernised region.

There are regular air connections, as well as ship routes to many of the outlying spots in **Kalimantan** (Indonesian Borneo) and to the eastern islands and **West Irian**. Only local-style hotels can be expected in most places, but for the traveller with the Lord Jim spirit, a journey to the outer islands on an Indonesian steamer might be just the thing.

TIMOR

East Timor, once under Portuguese rule, is now open to travellers. It had been a closed province since the bloody civil war and subsequent Indonesian invasion of 1975. In mid-1976 a group of two dozen local leaders opted unanimously for incorporation into Indonesia and two months later President Suharto signed a decree formally declaring the territory Indonesia's 27th province.

HOTEL GUIDE

Hotel address	Phone	Fax	Telex	Cable	~~~~	🍴	🍽
A (US$100-160) **B** (US$40-100) **C** (US$30-90) **D** (US$10-25)							
BALI ISLAND — Phone code 0361							
BEDUGUL **C**							
Bali Handara Country Club Jl. Raya Sanur 131, P. O. Box 324, Denpasar	28866		35241		▲	▲	
DENPASAR **C**							
Bali Hotel Jl. Veteran 3 **D**	25681/5		35166 BALI HOTEL		▲	▲	▲
Denpasar Hotel Jl. Diponegoro 117A	26336					▲	
Pamecutan Hotel Jl. Thamrin No. 2	23491					▲	▲
KUTA BEACH **A**							
Bali Oberoi Kuta Beach P. O. Box 351	51061/5		35125 HOTEL DPR		▲	▲	▲
Pertamina Cottages Kuta Beach P. O. Box 121 **C**	51161		35131 PPRRCOT BALI		▲	▲	▲
Kuta Beach Hotel Jl. Pantai Kuta, P. O. Box 393	51361		35166 KUBEHOT		▲	▲	▲
Bali Intan Cottages Jl. Melasti 1	51770		35200 BINCO DPS				

Hotel address	Phone	Fax	Telex	Cable	〰	🍴	🍽
KUTA BEACH – *Cont'd* **C**							
Kartika Plaza Beach Hotel Jl. Kartika, P. O. Box 84	51067/9		35142 KAZA BALI				
Legian Beach Hotel Jl. Melasti, P. O. Box 308	5711/5		35324 LEBE HOTEL				
NUSA DUA **A**							
Nusa Dua Beach Hotel Nusa Dua, P. O. Box 1028	71210		35206		▲	▲	▲
Bali Sol Nusa Dua, P. O. Box 1048 **B**	71510		35237		▲	▲	▲
Putri Bali Nusa Dua, P. O. Box 1 **D**	71020		35247 NUSABALI		▲	▲	▲
Bualu Hotel Nusa Dua, P. O. Box 217	71310/5		35231				
SANUR BEACH **A**							
Bali Beach Intercontinental Jl. Raya Sanur, P. O. Box 275 **B**	85117		35129 INHOTELCOR		▲	▲	▲
Bali Hyatt Bali Beach	8271/7		35127 BALIHYATT		▲	▲	▲
La Taverna P. O. Box 40	8497		35163 LATAVERNA		▲	▲	▲
Tanjung Sari P. O. Box 25	88441		35157 TANSARI		▲	▲	▲
Sanur Beach & Seaside Bungalows P. O. Box 279	8011/5		35135 AEROPACIFIC		▲	▲	▲

Hotel address	Phone	Fax	Telex	Cable	〰	🍴	🍽
SANUR BEACH – *Cont'd* **C**							
Segara Village Jl. Segara Ayu			35143 SEGARA AYU		▲	▲	▲
Santrian Beach P. O. Box 55	8181/2				▲	▲	▲
Sindhu Beach Hotel P. O. Box 181	88351/2		35166 SINDHU MOT		▲	▲	▲
Gazebo Cottages Jl. Tanjung Sari	8300		35182 VAYA DPR		▲	▲	▲
W. JAVA							
BANDUNG – Phone code 022 **A**							
Grand Hotel Preanger Jl. Asia Afrika 81	440371/5	430034	28570 GHP BDO		▲	▲	▲
Papandayan Hotel Jl. Gatot Suroto 83, P. O. Box 34 **C**	430788/799	430998	28681 PADHI IA		▲	▲	▲
Savoy Homann Hotel Jl. Asia Afrika, P. O. Box 9	432244	431583	28425 HOMANN IA		▲	▲	▲
Panghegar Hotel Jl. Merdeka 2, P. O. Box 56	432295/7		28276 PANGHEGAR BD		▲	▲	▲
Kumala Panghegar Jl. Asia Afrika 140, P. O. Box 507	52141, 50664, 438856		28176 PANGHEGAR BD		▲	▲	▲
Hotel Istana Jl. Lembong	433025, 432757				▲	▲	▲
CIREBON **C**							
Patra Jasa Motel Jl. Tuparev 11	3792/3, 3005/6					▲	▲

Hotel address	Phone	Fax	Telex	Cable	〰	🍴	🍲

W. SUMATRA — Phone code 0752

BUKITTINGI

C

Hotel address	Phone	Fax	Telex	Cable	〰	🍴	🍲
Dymen's International Jl. Nawawi	22781, 21015				▲	▲	▲

D

Hotel address	Phone	Fax	Telex	Cable	〰	🍴	🍲
Denai Hotel Jl. Rivai 5	21460					▲	▲
Minang Hotel Jl. Panorama 20	21120					▲	▲

PADANG

D

Hotel address	Phone	Fax	Telex	Cable	〰	🍴	🍲
Mariani Int'l Hotel Jl. Bundo Kandung 35	25410				▲	▲	▲
Muara Hotel Jl. Gereja 34	25600, 21850				▲	▲	▲

WEST COAST JAVA

CARITA BEACH LABUHAN

D

Hotel address	Phone	Fax	Telex	Cable	〰	🍴	🍲
Carita Krakatau Beach	325308					▲	▲

PELABUHAN RATU

B

Hotel address	Phone	Fax	Telex	Cable	〰	🍴	🍲
Samudra Beach Hotel	23		45274		▲	▲	▲

Hotel address	Phone	Fax	Telex	Cable	〰	🍴	🍽
E. JAVA							
SURABAYA							
B							
Hyatt Bumi Jl. Jend. Basuki Raachmat, P. O. Box 5130	470875, 470525		31391 HYATTBUMI		▲	▲	▲
C							
Elmi Hotel Jl. Panglima Sudirman	471570/8, 45291		31431		▲	▲	▲
Mirama Hotel Jl. Raya Darmo 72-74, P. O. Box 232	69501/9		31485 MIRAMA SBY		▲	▲	▲
C. JAVA							
SEMARANG							
C							
Patrajasa Hotel Jl. Sisingamangaraja	27371-9		22286 PATRA SM		▲	▲	▲
SOLO (*JAVA*)							
D							
Kusuma Sahid Prince Jl. Sugiyopranoto 22	6356/8, 7022		22274 SKPH SOLO		▲	▲	▲
C							
Cakra Hotel Jl. Brigjen Slamet Riyadi	5487					▲	▲
JAKARTA — Phone code 6222							
A							
Borobudur Inter Continental	370108	359741	44150 BODO JKT		▲	▲	▲
Jakarta Hilton Jl. Jend., Gatot Sobroto, P. O. Box 3315	587991, 583051	583091	46673		▲	▲	▲

Hotel address	Phone	Fax	Telex	Cable	〰	🍴	🥣
JAKARTA – *Cont'd* **A**							
Mandarin Oriental Jl. M. H. Thamrin	321307	324669	61755		▲	▲	
Sari Pacific Hotel Jl. M. H. Thamrin 6, P. O. Box 3138	323707	323650	44514 SARIPA IA		▲	▲	▲
Sahid Jaya Hotel Jl. Jend. Sudirman 86, P. O. Box 41	587031	583168	46331		▲	▲	▲
Hyatt Aryaduta Jl. Prapatan 44-46 **B**	376008	349836	46220		▲	▲	▲
Hotel Indonesia Jl. M. H. Thamrin	320008	321508	46220 HIPA JKT		▲	▲	▲
President Hotel Jl. M. H. Thamrin	320508	333631	61401 PREHO JKT		▲	▲	▲
Kartika Chandra Jl. Gatot Subroto, P. O. Box 85 **C**	510808	5204238	46470 KACHA IA		▲	▲	▲
Wisata International Jl. M. H. Thamrin	320308					▲	▲
Kartika Plaza Jl. M. H. Thamrin	311008		44574		▲	▲	▲
YOGYKARTA (*JAVA*) – Phone code 0274 **B**							
Ambarrukmo Palace Jl. Adisucipto	88488, 88984		02511 APH YOGYA		▲	▲	▲
Garuda Hotel Jl. Malioboro **C**	86457, 86353		25174		▲	▲	▲
Mutiara Hotel Jl. Malioboro	4531, 5173				▲	▲	▲
Sriwedari Hotel Jl. Adisucipto	88288				▲	▲	▲

Hotel address	Phone	Fax	Telex	Cable	〰	🍴	🍽
YOGYKARTA (*JAVA*) – *Cont'd*							
D							
Petit Mas Jl. Dagen 39	2896				▲	▲	▲

NORTH SUMATRA — Phone code 061

MEDAN							
B							
Danau Toba International Jl. Imam Bonjol	327000	27020	51167 HDTI		▲	▲	▲
Tiara Hotel Jl. Cut Mutia	516000		51721 GRYA IA		▲	▲	▲
C							
Polonia Hotel Jl. Jend. Sudirman	325300, 325700		51376 POTEL		▲	▲	▲
Dahrma Deli Jl. Balai Kota 2	327011		51362		▲	▲	▲
D							
Pardede International Jl. Ir. H. Judanda 14	323866		514438		▲	▲	▲

LAKA TOBA — Phone code 0625

PARAPAT							
C							
Natour Hotel Parapat Jl. Marihat 1	41021, 41081				▲	▲	▲
D							
Danau Toba International Jl. Pulau Samosir	41583, 41719				▲	▲	▲
Astari Hotel Jl. Pulau Samosir	41219					▲	▲

Hotel address	Phone	Fax	Telex	Cable	≈	🍽	🍲

S. SUMATRA — Phone code 0711

PALEMBANG

C

Swarna Dwipa Hotel
Jl. Tasik 2, P. O. Box 198 — Phone: 28322 (4 lines) — ▲ ▲ ▲

Hotel address	Phone	Fax	Telex	Cable	≈	🍽	🍲
Swarna Dwipa Hotel Jl. Tasik 2, P. O. Box 198	28322 (4 lines)				▲	▲	▲

N. SULAWESI — Phone code 0431

MANADO

C

Hotel address	Phone	Fax	Telex	Cable	≈	🍽	🍲
Kawanua City Hotel Jl. Sam Ratulangi 1	52222		74132 KCHMO		▲	▲	▲

D

Hotel address	Phone	Fax	Telex	Cable	≈	🍽	🍲
Garden Hotel Jl. WR Supratman 1	51688				▲	▲	▲

S. SULAWESI — Phone code 0411

UJUNG PANDANG

B

Hotel address	Phone	Fax	Telex	Cable	≈	🍽	🍲
Makasar Golden Hotel Jl. Pasar Ikan 52	22208/9, 22232					▲	▲
Marannu City Hotel Jl. St Hasanuddin 3-5	5087, 218211					▲	▲

C

Hotel address	Phone	Fax	Telex	Cable	≈	🍽	🍲
Raodah International Jl. Khairil Anwar 28	7055/65/75					▲	▲

TANAH TORAJA

C

Hotel address	Phone	Fax	Telex	Cable	≈	🍽	🍲
Toraja Cottage Desa Bolu, Paku	84146, 84831		46621 HB IA		▲	▲	▲

Hotel address	Phone	Fax	Telex	Cable	〰	🍽	🍵
WEST NUSA TENGGARA — Phone code 0364							
WEST NUSA							
MATARAM **C**							
Senggigi Beach Hotel Batu Layar, Mataram	23430		35340		▲	▲	▲
E. KALIMANTAN							
SAMARINDA **D**							
Mesra International Jl. Pahlawan 1, Samarinda	21011		38144 MESRA IA		▲	▲	▲
BALIKPAPAN **D**							
Hotel Mirama Jl. Mayjend. Sutoyo 11/A16, Balikpapan	22960		37189 MIRA IA			▲	▲

LAOS

Laos, once known as the land of a million elephants, is a beautiful, friendly, slow-moving country with so much charm that it is a tragedy that more people have not been able to see it. The reason, of course, was the Indochina War, followed by the communist victory in December 1975. Tourism received low priority from the new government.

Laos is a traditional Buddhist, largely agrarian society with some of the most gentle and friendly people in Asia. From the late 1980s the government, in an attempt to attract hard currency, began allowing more tourists into the country, raising hopes that Laos was returning to the tourist trade, if only in a limited way.

Laos' known history dates from the 13th century when the Thai peoples (represented today by the Shan of northern Burma, the Thai of Thailand and the lowland Lao from Laos) came south from China's Yunnan province under pressure from the armies of Kublai Khan, who had conquered much of China. Laos was first unified in 1353 by Fa Ngum, a Lao prince who had grown up in the Khmer court of Angkor and returned to his country with a contingent of Cambodian soldiers.

Fa Ngum established his capital around the northern town of Luang Prabang and brought together several scattered Lao fiefdoms into the Kingdom of Lane Xang, or kingdom of a million elephants. Later, at the expense of neighbouring Cambodia and Thailand, he expanded his kingdom so that by the 14th and 15th centuries Lane Xang was a powerful and prosperous nation.

Internal dissension during the 17th century resulted in the kingdom being divided into three parts — the kingdom of Luang Prabang in the north, Vientiane in the centre, and Champassak in the south. Each state had its own royal rulers. So weakened, most of the country fell under Thai suzerainty in 1828, while the Vietnamese controlled the mountain territory in the northeast.

The French took control of the country in 1893, incorporating it into French Indochina with Vietnam and Cambodia. Despite several armed revolts, Laos continued as a French colony until the Japanese occupation during World War II. On October 12, 1945 the nationalist Lao Issara (Free Lao) movement proclaimed the independence of Laos, but the French army again quickly seized control.

In response to nationalist pressures, France granted Laos formal independence within the French Union in July 1949. Meanwhile, pro-communist Lao Issara remnants regrouped in the mountains of the northeast in the early 1950s and joined with the Viet Minh forces from Vietnam in a military effort to drive the French from Indochina.

The Geneva Accords in 1954, after the defeat of the French at Dien Bien Phu, granted full independence to Laos and called for free elections to establish a new Lao government. But when the pro-communist Lao Patriotic Front (Pathet Lao) gained 13 seats in the national assembly elections in 1958, the US supported a rightwing faction in sabotaging the coalition government.

Fighting broke out and the Patriotic Front and neutralist forces quickly gained control of large portions of the mountainous countryside. Another attempt at a ceasefire and a coalition government of the Right, Centre, and Left failed after the Geneva Conference of 1962.

With the US and Thailand supporting the Vientiane side and Vietnam, the Soviet Union, and China supporting the Patriotic Front, poor, underdeveloped Laos took on exaggerated geopolitical prominence. Full-scale American

◁ *Ong Tu temple in Vientiane.*
Photo: Jim Page

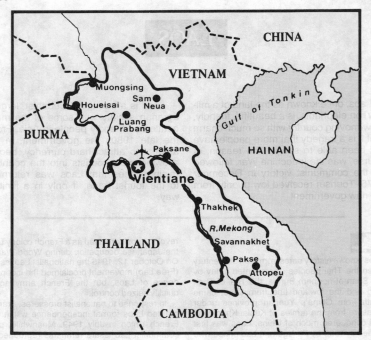

bombing began in 1964 in the communist-held areas of the northeast and along the Ho Chi Minh Trail, which was used by North Vietnam to supply its war against US-backed South Vietnam. The bombing eventually displaced a quarter of Laos' rural population.

The war continued until the signing of the Vientiane Accords in 1973 and the formation of a coalition government the following year. With the American withdrawal from Indochina in 1975, the communist Patriotic Front gained control of the government and proclaimed the formation of the Lao People's Democratic Republic on 2 December. Thirty years of war left Laos battle-scarred, underdeveloped, without a transport network, and economically dependent on foreign aid and imports.

The country's new rulers moved quickly to launch Laos down the path to socialism, setting up farm cooperatives, nationalising industry, and forcing private traders out of business. But production fell in most sectors and roughly 10% of the country's population fled as refugees to

neighbouring Thailand. Laos strengthened its ties to the Soviet Union and supported Vietnam's invasion of Cambodia in late 1978, a move which damaged its relations with both China and Thailand.

In 1986 the country's communist party abandoned its doctrinaire socialist goals, replacing cooperatives with family farms, offering unproductive industries to private entrepreneurs, and courting foreign capitalists and Western aid donors to help develop Laos' backward economy. Vientiane also took steps to improve its relations with Thailand, China and the US.

Landlocked Laos, with an area of 236,600 km², has borders with China, Vietnam, Cambodia, Thailand and Burma. More than two-thirds of the country consists of rugged mountains and dense jungles, home for the Lao Theung (Highland Lao) and Lao Suong (Mountaintop Lao, including the Hmong and Yao) ethnic groups. The Mekong River valley is inhabited by the Lao Luom (Lowland Lao) who make up roughly half of the country's population.

Laos' population is estimated at 4 million, about 90% of whom are engaged in subsistence agriculture. Lowland Lao culture reflects a deep Buddhist influence, while the other ethnic groups practise animism.

Vientiane, the capital, can be reached by air from Bangkok via **Thai International** and **Lao Aviation** every day except Wednesdays. **Air Vietnam** and **Lao Aviation** connect Hanoi and Vientiane on Tuesdays and Thursdays. The two airlines also fly to Ho Chi Minh City on Sundays and Thursdays, while **Lao Aviation** flies to Phnom Penh on Wednesdays and Fridays. **Aeroflot** connects Vientiane to Moscow via Rangoon once a week.

Normally the Lao Government insists that foreigners not resident in Laos arrive in the country by air. But if special permission is obtained, a pleasant way of travelling to Laos from Thailand is by train.

Trains to Nong Khai, across from the Lao border town of Tha Deua, leave Bangkok several times daily and take about 12 hours. The most comfortable way to travel is by first class sleeper. From the Nong Khai train station take a samlor (three-wheeled pedal trishaw) to the Mekong River customs and immigration office.

There a visitor can take a small boat, which costs about Thai Baht 30 (US$1.20), across the Mekong River. After checking through Lao immigration take a taxi the remaining 30 km to Vientiane. Taxis cost about Baht 150. Visitors should be prepared to bargain for transport on both sides of the border. Buses, costing Kip 200, run every 45 minutes from Tha Deua to Vientiane's Morning Market.

Air-conditioned tour buses leave Bangkok several times daily for Nong Khai, but the incidence of serious highway accidents is high. There is also a car ferry across the Mekong between Nong Khai and Thanaleng, near Tha Deua. Special permission, which is normally difficult to get, is required to bring a car in or out of Laos.

The Mekong River crossing between Nong Khai and Tha Deua is open every day, except Sunday, between 8-11:30 am and 2-4:30 pm.

A Lao entry visa is required to enter Laos and can be obtained from Lao embassies in Bangkok, Hanoi, Jakarta, New Delhi, Peking, Paris, Canberra or Washington. Visa costs vary between embassies from about US$12-35 and are normally issued for a 15-day period.

Allow at least four to five weeks for a visa application to be processed by the Lao Government. When applying for visas, official visitors should present a letter of invitation at Lao embassies to authenticate their application. In mid-1990 Laos was granting visas to tour groups who made advance arrangements through the Lao Tourism Office, but individual tourist visas were difficult to obtain.

Transit visas are required to stop in Vientiane en route to Hanoi, Ho Chi Minh City, Phnom Penh, Rangoon or Bangkok. Double transit visas are required if you plan to return via Vientiane.

Vaccinations against cholera, typhoid, tetanus, rabies, and hepatitis are advised, while some health officials advise visitors travelling upcountry to take anti-malaria medicine. Avoid drinking unboiled water and uncooked vegetables and meat.

Laos has no strict regulations at present on how much a traveller can bring into Laos duty-free, though an unusual quantity of cigarettes, alcohol, cameras or electronic equipment might raise the suspicion of customs officials. Currency declarations by visitors are not normally required.

The official exchange rate in 1991 was Kip 700=US$1. Visitors can usually get a slightly higher black market rate in private shops. Traveller's cheques are accepted at the state bank as well as by Lao Aviation and most hotels, but a 1% surcharge is levied. Credit cards cannot be used in Laos.

The national language is Lao, a tonal language closely related to Thai, which is understood by Lao along the Mekong River. English and French are used as second languages in most government offices. Russian is spoken by Lao who have been educated in the Soviet Union. Minority tribal languages are spoken in the mountain regions.

Laos

Vientiane lies in the tropical monsoon belt and has about five months of heavy rainfall, from May to September, with an average of 25-30 cm inches per month. The remainder of the year is dry. A very hot period immediately precedes the monsoon, with temperatures rising as high as 38-40°C (100°F). The coolest months are November, December and January, when temperatures average around 21°C (70°F) but can drop as low as 5°C (41°F). In the mountains the temperatures may drop to near freezing during the winter months.

Light tropical clothing is best all year around, with some slighty warmer things for the nights of November to January. In the mountains woollens are required during the coldest months.

Government office hours are from about 8 am-12:00 noon and from 2-5 pm Monday to Friday. Appointments should be scheduled early in the day. Many state employees leave early for "moonlighting" jobs because government salaries are too low to feed their families. On Saturdays government offices are open from about 8-11:00 am, but they often have only a skeleton staff.

Banks are open from 8:30 am-4:30 pm Monday to Friday and 8:30 am to 12 noon on Saturdays.

Shops and markets are open from about 6:30 am to sundown, while nightclubs as well as restaurants and bars catering to foreigners are open until about 11:30 pm.

VIENTIANE

FROM THE AIRPORT: Taxi fares for the 5-km trip to the hotels in Vientiane cost about US$5, depending on the availability of cars and the number of arriving passengers. Passengers should negotiate the price with drivers, who usually request payment in Thai baht or US dollars. Newcomers to Laos may want to seek assistance from Lao Aviation ground service staff in obtaining transport from the airport. Sometimes Lao Aviation will provide a bus for groups from the airport, but this must be arranged in advance.

TAXIS: Taxis in Vientiane operate in much the same way as buses. They run along the main roads (making occasional detours for passengers), picking up and dropping off passengers as they go. A taxi can be rented for a whole day for about US$20. Ask your hotel staff to assist in bargaining for the price of taxi fares.

BUSES: Buses charging Kip 50-100 operate over set routes on the main roads of Vientiane and its suburbs, though little attention is paid to existing schedules. Buses depart from the Morning Market on Lane Xang Avenue about once every 45 minutes and travel along Samsenthai and Luang Prabang roads to the Sii Khai Market (near the airport), north to Done Noun (near Dong Dok) and east to Tha Deua.

SAMLORS: Three-wheeled pedal trishaws as well as motor-driven samlors and "tuk tuks" ply the streets of Vientiane (and many of Laos' major towns). Be sure to bargain for your fare in advance.

UPCOUNTRY

Land travel more than about 6 km outside of Vientiane is proscribed for foreigners. Although checkpoints in the countryside are irregular, most official guests or residents are accompanied by a government representative when they travel outside these limits. Occasionally vehicles in the countryside are stopped or shot at by bandits or anti-government guerillas.

Lao Aviation has regularly scheduled flights to Luang Prabang, Xieng Khouang, Luang Nam Tha and Oudomsai in the north, Houei Sai in the west, and Thakkek, Savannakhet, Pakse, and Saravane in the south, but these flights are often cancelled at the last minute.

Large 6-8 tonne transport trucks provide bus services to the larger cities in the south and north, while smaller pick-up trucks and regular buses carry passengers to the larger villages on the Vientiane Plain.

Transport boats also carry Lao passengers to points along the Mekong River, but foreigners are not normally granted authorisation to travel more than a short distance on the river.

Tour groups should get in touch with the **Lao Tourism Office** (Tel: 3254 or 2998) on Sethatirath Rd near the water fountain.

The **Lane Xang** (Tel: 3267) is the most modern hotel in Vientiane. Single rooms begin at US$36 per night. Reservations can be made by cabling Lanxotel Vientiane.

The **Ekalat** (Tel: 2881), formerly the Imperial and located near the That Dam stupa, was recently refurbished by a Vietnamese company. Single air-conditioned rooms with hot water cost US$22.

In mid-1990 a Thai company was reconstructing the former headquarters of the 555 Tobacco Co., near Vientiane's radio station, into the **Ambassador Hotel**. Some modern rooms, beginning at US$25 per night, are already available for use in one of the buildings.

Other hotels, all of which offer rooms for less than US$20 per night, include the **Santiphab** (Tel: 2489/3305) and the **Vientiane** (Tel: 3685) on Luang Prabang Rd en route to the airport, the **Inter** or **Lao Chaleun** (Tel: 2514) on the Mekong River, the **Anou** (Tel: 3571/3324) in the downtown area, and the **Muang Lao** (Tel: 2278) on the road to Tha Deua.

The **Vieng Vilay** (formerly the Constellation), a favourite with journalists during the Vietnam War, has been torn down and a new building was being constructed in mid-1990.

In **Luang Prabang**, visitors can stay at the **Mitaphab** on a hill overlooking the city, or the cheaper **Phousi** near the city's pagodas, and former royal palace.

Eating in Vientiane is simple and quite good. Most private restaurants closed shortly after the communist victory in 1975, but new ones have opened in recent years thanks to the economic reforms which again allow private enterprise. The availability of French dishes make Vientiane restaurants distinctive in Asia.

Uniquely Lao dishes are generally hard to find at restaurants in Vientiane. Adventurous visitors can find Lao sticky rice, which you make into a ball with your fingers for dipping into chilly sauce or eating with green papaya salad or barbecued chicken, at small street stalls in the vicinity of the theatres on Haeng Buon and Anou streets as well as along the Mekong River.

Pa Phao Restaurant (Tel: 3059), near the State Bank's tennis courts off Nong Bone Rd, specialises in Lao food for foreigners. The **Mekong** at Km 4 on Tha Deua Rd also serves Lao and European food.

Excellent French food is served at **Le Sureya** (Tel: 4411), opposite the Lao Aviation office, the **Nam Phou** (Tel: 4723) near the water fountain but closed for reconstruction in mid-1990, and **Sabaidi** (Tel: 5760), near the That Luang stupa. Other restaurants serving Western food are the **Arawan** (Tel: 3977) on Samsenthai Rd, the state-run **Lane Xang Hotel** (US dollar payment only), and the **Ekalat** and **Santiphap** hotels.

The **Sa Loong Xay**, across from the Lane Xang Hotel, has live traditional Lao music, and serves a variety of Western and Asian dishes. **Ban Phim** on Luang Prabang Rd on the way to the airport is a trustworthy alternative, but for steak a visitor might try the **Inter Hotel** near the Mekong River or **Ban Tavan** (Tel: 2737) on Khum Borom St near the Lao-Soviet Cultural Centre. Western food is also available at the **Australian Embassy Recreation Club** on Tha Deua Rd, but for members and their guests only.

The **Dao Vien** (Tel: 2330), meaning "Vientiane's star," on Haeng Boun St, serves Chinese food, but the quality of the meals has deteriorated since it was taken over by the government. An Indian restaurant offering some vegetarian dishes has opened opposite the Vieng Vilay Hotel on Samsenthai.

Several small Vietnamese restaurants near the Vieng Vilay Hotel as well as in the theatre area serve simple Vietnamese meals, including spring rolls, sour fish soup and Vietnamese noodle soup. The best known Vietnamese restaurant is the **Nang Viengsavanh** on Haeng Boun St. The streets around the theatres also have a variety of small, popular stalls selling cheap meals of fried rice or noodles, spicy Thai food and Asian sweets.

Breakfast is served at all the major hotels. Coffee and croissants are available at **Santisouk** (Tel: 3926), formerly known as La Pagode, near the National Stadium.

Lao vodka (lao lao), a rather potent variation of Japanese sake, can be found at many small stalls and in the local markets. Imported soft drinks, beer, wine, and other alcoholic drinks are usually available at restaurants and bars catering to foreigners.

Most of the dozen nightclubs opened in Vientiane during the past few years offer drinks and simple Asian dishes along with live rock music. The most popular nightclubs among Lao patrons are the **Vieng Latri Mai** (operated by Vientiane municipality) on Lane Xang Ave near the Morning Market, the **Lane Xang** close to the Dong Palan Market, and **Nok Kaeo Latri Mai** on the road to the airport.

Sporting activities in Vientiane are limited. Tennis is available at the **Vientiane Tennis Club** (Tel: 3370), and visitors introduced by members can play squash or swim at the **Australian Embassy Recreation Club** overlooking the Mekong River.

Thanks to recent economic reforms, more imported consumer goods and Lao handicraft items are again available in Lao markets. Beautiful hand-woven silk for a sin (Lao skirt) and elaborately embroidered skirt borders (often made with gold and silver thread) are available in the **Morning Market** on Lane Xang Ave. Other attractive, traditionally woven, dyed or embroidered cloth from different parts of the country are also available in the market.

Lao handicrafts such as cloth, baskets, pottery and the khene (musical bamboo pipes) are available at the **Handicraft Centre** on Luang Prabang Rd, the **House of Dolls** on Phon Kheng Rd, the **Inpeng Boutique** near the Vieng Vilay Hotel, as well as in the boutiques in the Lane Xang Hotel and the airport departure lounge.

Jewellery shops on Samsenthai Rd and in the Morning Market will produce almost any design of gold or silver necklace, bracelet, or Lao skirt belt within a few days. Tailors near the Vieng Vilay hotel still sew smart-looking Lao-style shirts.

Many Lao Buddhist festivals fall on different dates from one year to the next, depending on the lunar calendar. Other holidays, marking more contemporary political events, fall on the same date each year. Many political holidays are celebrated with ceremonies at the That Luang Square.

In the listing below, only the months are given for events with variable dates. Various ethnic groups celebrate religious and cultural holidays other than the lowland Lao, but they are not detailed in the listing.

January 6: Lao Patriotic Front (Neo Lao Haksat) Day.

January 20: People's Liberation Army Day.

February: Wat Phou Festival held at the an-

cient Wat Phou Pagoda, near Champassak in southern Laos.

Makha Buja is observed in Lao pagodas in commemoration of the first sermon preached by Buddha.

March 8: International Women's Day.

March 22: Lao People's Revolutionary Party Day.

April 13, 14, 15: Pee May (Lao New Year) is observed by pouring holy water on the Buddhist statues in pagodas. On the streets, people drench each other with water. Make sure to wear your old clothes and join in the fun. You may want to leave your camera at home to avoid the risk of having it ruined. Pee May is also the time for a baci, a ceremony including the chanting of an animist blessing by a village "priest" and tying cotton strings around the wrists of one's family members and friends to wish them good health, prosperity and longevity.

May 1: International Labour Day.

May: Visakha Buja. The most important of the annual Lao Buddhist celebrations commemorating the birth, enlightenment and the passing into Nirvana of Buddha. (Each event is believed to have taken place on the same day of the year.) Candle processions in the evening make three clockwise circuits around the pagoda.

Boun Bang Fai, the traditional rocket festival, is held just before the rainy season to fertilise the clouds. If it is not celebrated properly, many Lao farmers believe that drought will follow. The firing of home-made rockets, music and folk dancing are the main features of this fertility festival.

June 1: International Children's Day.

July: Boun Khao Watsa. The Buddhist equivalent of Lent begins and lasts through the rainy season. Practising Buddhists are expected to lead a more devout life during this time and monks keep themselves more to their pagodas for study and meditation.

August 13: Celebration of the first conference founding the Lao Issara (Free Lao) movement in 1945.

August 23: Commemoration of the people's uprising to "liberate" Vientiane from the US-backed government.

September: Boun Khao Padabdin — a memorial day observed by the Lao people in memory of their departed relatives. Food is offered to their spirits at pagodas or their tombs.

Boun Khao Salak is a festival in which Buddhists take a bamboo basket filled with food and other gifts to monks, who "pass" them on to the believer's departed parents or relatives. The names of the worshippers are drawn from a bowl to determine the order in which they present their offerings to a monk or an image of Buddha.

October 12: Celebration of the Declaration of Independence from France in 1945.

Boun Ok Watsa: The end of Buddhist Lent is marked with a religious ceremony at each pagoda in the morning during which Buddhists offer food to the monks. In the evening, the people light candles in front of their houses, take part in candle processions and launch tiny boats made of banana leaves bearing flowers and burning candles.

Boun Song Hua: Boat races along the Mekong, sometimes with competition between Thai and Lao teams, mark the end of the rainy season.

November: The That Luang Festival, which attracts tens of thousands of people, begins with religious ceremonies in which devout Buddhists give food to monks. During the first night of the festival a procession of people solemnly march around the stupa carrying candles and "money" trees, before monks end the evening with a fireworks display. The festival is accompanied by a fair which attracts exhibitions of traditional handicrafts and products from each province of the country.

December 2: Date of the founding of the Lao People's Democratic Republic in 1975.

The **Bank of Foreign Trade** (Tel: 2646/3646) is on Pangkham Street (near the Lane Xang Hotel).

The **Joint Development Bank,** a joint venture with a Thai company, is across from the Morning Market on Lane Xang Ave.

DISCOVERING LAOS

VIENTIANE
Vientiane, the city of sandalwood, has always been more of a rural Asian town than a bustling capital city. The traffic jams of Bangkok are unknown, and cows and chickens regularly roam the city's streets.

MAJOR AIRLINES
Lao Aviation (Tel: 2093/2094) makes reservations and sells tickets for the Lao airline, Thai International and Air Vietnam. The Lao Aviation office is on Pangkham St (near the Lane Xang Hotel) in Vientiane.

The **Aeroflot** office (Tel: 3501) is on Samsenthai St, next to the Ekalat Hotel.

TOURIST AUTHORITIES
The **Lao Tourism Office** (Tel: 3254 or 2998) is on Sethathirat Rd (near Vientiane's water fountain).

EMBASSIES
Australia: Nehru St (near Independence Monument). Tel: 2477. **Bulgaria:** Nong Bone Rd. Tel: 3236. **Burma:** (Myanmar), Sokpaluang Rd (off Tha Deua Rd). Tel: 2789. **Cambodia:** Sophanethong Neua Rd. Tel: 2750/4527. **China, People's Republic:** Sokpaluang Rd (off Tha Deua Rd). Tel: 3494. **Cuba:** Sophanethong Neua Rd. Tel: 3150. **Czechoslovakia:** Tha Deua Rd. Tel: 2705/4423. **France:** Sethathirat Rd (across from Mohosot Hospital). Tel: 2642/2377/4423.

Germany: Nehru Rd (near Independence Monument). Tel: 2024. **Hungary:** That Luang Rd (near That Luang). Tel: 2205/3111. **India:** That Luang Rd (near the Ministry of Commerce and Tourism). Tel: 2255. **Indonesia:** Phon Kheng Rd (near Independence Monument). Tel: 2370/2373. **Japan:** Si Sung Won Rd (near That Luang). Tel: 2584. **Korea, Democratic Republic:** Wat Nak Village. Tel: 3727. **Malaysia:** That Luang Rd (near That Luang). Tel: 2662. **Mongolia:** Tha Deua Rd. Tel: 3666. **Poland:** Nong Bone Rd (near That Luang). Tel: 2456. **Soviet Union:** Tha Deua Rd (across from the Australian Embassy Recreation Club). Tel: 5012. **Sweden:** Tel: 2922/5729. **Thailand:** Phon Kheng Rd (near Independence Monument). Tel: 2508/2765. **US:** Near the Morning Market. Tel: 2357/2220/3570. **Vietnam:** That Luang Rd (near Independence Monument). Tel: 5578.

CHAMBER OF COMMERCE
The Chamber of Commerce, established in early 1990, is in the Ministry of Commerce and Tourism (Tel: 5157).

Chilis for sale.

The **Morning Market,** which sells primarily cloth, electronic equipment, handicrafts and consumer goods, and the **Nong Douang Market,** which sells mostly food and household products, are good to visit early in the morning for their atmosphere and education about the Lao way of life. Sunsets on the Mekong River are beautiful. Except for the theatre areas, the streets of Vientiane are quiet and almost deserted by 8 pm.

Buddhist pagodas provide some of the most interesting sights. **Wat Phra Keo** was built in 1563 to house the Emerald Buddha now possessed by the Thais. Wat Phra Keo, which lies between **Hor Kang Palace,** the former king's Vientiane residence, has been converted into a museum housing a collection of beautiful Buddhas.

Along the Mekong River 2 km east of the Lane Xang Hotel, is **Wat That Khao,** built in traditional Vientiane style with thick masonry walls and a serpent along the edge of the roof. **Wat Sisaket,** built in the early 19th century at the corner of Lane Xang Avenue and Sethathirat Street, shows Burmese influence in its square compact design with a small stupa on top. Formerly, each new government was sworn in at this pagoda.

Among Vientiane's 30-odd pagodas, **Wat Ong Tu** (corner of Sethathirat and Anou streets), **Wat Phiavat** (a kilometre east of the Lane Xang Hotel), and **Wat Sii Muang** (at the eastern junction of Sethathirat and Samsenthai streets) are some of the most interesting. The Lao always remove their shoes before entering a holy place.

On the northeastern edge of Vientiane stands the **That Luang,** a golden stupa sitting on a pyramid surrounded by 30 smaller spires, built by King Sethathirat in 1566 and restored in 1929 and 1976. Before the communist takeover in 1975, the That Luang was a major focus of pilgrimages from all over Laos and northeastern Thailand.

In the centre of the city, opposite the Ekalat Hotel, is the **That Dam,** a black stupa which, according to Lao legend, houses a sleeping dragon which will rise up in anger if Thailand threatens Vientiane.

At the end of Lane Xang Avenue stands **Independence Monument,** a massive arch sometimes called the "vertical runway" because it was built under the former regime with concrete provided by a US aid project for Vientiane's airport.

A **revolutionary museum** detailing the Lao communist victories over France and the US, has been established on Samsenthai St near the National Stadium. A **war memorial** for soldiers from the communist side killed during both wars has been erected near the That Luang.

Travel more than 6 km outside of Vientiane without special government authorisation is off-limits for foreign residents and visitors. Some foreigners arrange to take day trips to the **Nam Ngum Dam,** about 90 km northeast of Vientiane.

UPCOUNTRY

Luang Prabang, the former royal and religious capital of Laos, is at the junction of the Nam Khan and Mekong Rivers, 350 km north of Vientiane and 335 m above sea level. The city is surrounded by lush, forested hills and valleys. Once virtually closed to tourists, Luang Prabang is now more accessible through organised tours from Vientiane.

The city derives its name from the **Pra Bang**, or Gold Buddha — palladium of the former Lao kingdom — which was brought to Fa Ngum, the first Lao king, by a priest from Angkor in Cam-

Novice monk cleaning a temple wall in Vientiane.

Photo: Jean Leo Dugast — The Stock House

bodia. The Pra Bang is believed to have originated in Sri Lanka and to have been, even at that time, at least 500 years old.

A hill called the **Phousi** rises in the centre of Luang Prabang and its peak provides an outstanding view of the area in clear weather. At the tip is the **That Chomsi** with a golden pyramid surrounded by nine ritual umbrellas, the former emblem of royalty. It is thought to have been built on the ruins of an old temple and was restored by King Sri Savang Vong in 1962.

The former **Royal Palace** lies between the Phousi and the Mekong, and next to it is **Wat May Souvanna Phoumakam,** founded in 1821 and completed in 1891. Its front walls are adorned with gilt reliefs showing the royal court and village life of Laos. Previously, this pagoda housed the Pra Bang.

Wat Xieng Thong, built in 1561, demonstrates northern Lao architectural style, with its steep roof sweeping down almost to the ground on either side. It is here that Lao kings were invested and crowned in the past.

Wat Pa Ke, which was restored in 1852, is sometimes known as the Dutch pagoda because of the gold frescoes on two doors depicting visitors from the Netherlands during the 17th and 18th centuries. Other interesting pagodas include **Wat Aphay, Wat May, Wat Manorom**, with its 12-tonne Buddha from the 14th century, **Wat Visoum** and the **That Mak Mo** which is adjacent.

Visitors can also arrange to take a 20-km trip up the Mekong to the 400-year-old cave temples of **Tham Ting,** which house hundreds of carved wooden Buddhist statues.

Wat Phou, the crumbling ruins of an ancient temple built by Cambodian kings late in the 5th century, is about two-and-a-half hours from the southern city of Pakse. Today much of the temple complex lies in ruins and many of its statues have lost their heads and limbs. Vegetation is rapidly encroaching, causing further destruction.

Few foreigners have visited the temple in recent years. UNESCO and the UN Development Programme have begun the painstaking process of renovating the temple and building a museum in nearby Champassak to house some of Wat Phou's more valuable artifacts.

MACAU

Macau, consisting of a total of 15.5 km² (including the islands of Taipa and Coloane), is a Portuguese colonial outpost built on a peninsula on the south China coast. It is a "living museum," traditionally a leisurely place steeped in memories of great days when East met West and fought for territory amid its fortresses and chapels.

But while much of the sleepy image engendered by the old Macau is being shaken off as modernisation continues apace, it retains an old-world charm and tranquillity. Visitors to the Orient have viewed Macau as an almost compulsory side-trip from Hongkong.

Now, gearing up to take its place in modern Asia — and due to be handed back to China in 1999 — the enclave is transforming itself into a vibrant, go-ahead tourist venue in its own right. While huge investments in deluxe hotels and other attractions are already providing competition to Hongkong, the Macanese are determined to preserve the cobbled streets, terraced houses and old churches that create its air of graciousness.

For weary travellers seeking complete peace, Macau is arguably as near ideal as can be found anywhere in Asia, though the two annual bursts of noise, the Macau Grand Prix motor race and Chinese New Year, might drive visitors to the nearby islands of Taipa and Coloane.

These are accessible via a bridge and causeway. A new 3,900-m bridge under construction between Macau and Taipa will connect to a road system linked with a new airport and port now being developed on this island. With Macau's romantic atmosphere of the past retained, it is still possible for the visitor to relax, to stroll without playing life-or-death games with the traffic, to study the territory's event-packed history or to test a private gambling system in the famed casinos.

Officially styled City of The Name of God, There Is None Other More Loyal, Macau is the oldest European outpost in the East. It was founded in 1557, apparently by agreement with the neighbouring Guangdong (China) province authorities. But no official treaty has ever been found. Macau was an early centre of missionary activity, becoming the seat of a bishopric of China and Japan created in 1575.

In its first century, Macau grew rich on trade with China and Japan, but later went into a long decline, mainly because Japan closed its doors to foreign merchants. The Portuguese also had to deal with commercial and piratical competition from Dutch and other European adventurers.

As more and more Westerners were attracted to the lucrative China trade, Macau became the summer residence for the British (and sometimes US) taipans (big traders) who retreated from their factories in Canton to wait for the next trading season.

In 1845 Macau was declared a free port. Tonnage dues, import duties and ground rent previously paid to the Chinese authorities in Guangdong province were abolished. This situation was consolidated by Governor Joao Ferreira do Amaral when he arrived in 1846. He expelled the Chinese customs officials from the city and declared it a free port — a status which is still maintained today. (Governor Amaral was later set upon by angry local farmers near the border because of his harsh rule. He was dragged from his horse and beheaded.)

◁ *The facade of Sao Paulo, all that is left after an 1835 fire.*
Photo: Richard Breeze

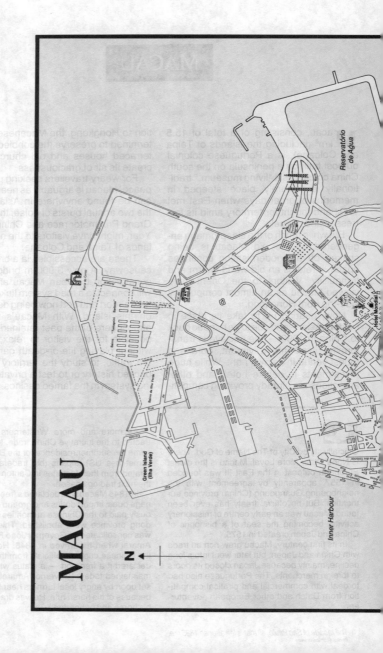

On December 1, 1887, a Treaty of Amity and Commerce was signed between Portugal and China, and Macau acquired official Chinese recognition under Portuguese rule. Portugal undertook in return "never to alienate Macau and its dependencies without agreement with China."

During World War II Macau was neutral and in 1951 was proclaimed an overseas province of Portugal. In the winter of 1966-67 riots triggered by the Cultural Revolution in China badly shook the Portuguese authorities, but calm later returned.

The change of government in Portugal following the bloodless military coup on April 25, 1974 and its subsequent decolonisation programme for the Portuguese African territories did not at first affect the status quo of Macau — a Chinese territory with a Portuguese administration and a community of, at that time, 400,000, of which 97% were Chinese. (The present population is about 460,000.)

However, in 1984 the Legislative Assembly was dissolved by Portugal at the request of the governor, Vasco Almeida e Costa, and new electoral laws were introduced with a view to making the assembly more democratically representative. In June 1986 Peking and Lisbon opened talks on returning Macau to Chinese sovereignty. Macau's future administration is expected to be similar to that of Hongkong, which will revert to Chinese sovereignty in 1997 but retain a large degree of autonomy.

Macau lies some 64 km west-south-west of the British territory of Hongkong across the mouth of the Pearl River. Tourism, gambling and export trade (principally textile goods) provide a large part of Macau's revenue.

Macau is reached by way of Hongkong. Ferries, hydrofoils, jetfoils, hoverferries, jetcats, high-speed ferries and even helicopter shuttles. Timetables for most of these services are published daily in all major newspapers. The hydrofoils take from 65-75 minutes; jetfoils about 55 minutes; jetcats 70 minutes or so; and the high-speed ferries about 90 minutes. Helicopters, usually making five round trips a day, take about 20 minutes for each leg. Most waterborne craft leave Hongkong Island from wharves at Shun Tak Centre, 200 Connaught Rd Central. The helicopter pad is also at the centre. Hoverferries, which take just over one hour, leave from Tsimshatsui in Kowloon, and a limited daylight jetfoil and hydrofoil service operates from the same pier.

Buying ferry tickets is a simple process. Except at weekends and during public holidays you can usually obtain them on the spot at the wharf. Otherwise they are on sale at Ticketmate offices in Hongkong's Exchange Square and various Mass Transit Railway (MTR) stations. In addition you can book jetfoils by phone (859 5696) using Visa, Diners, MasterCard and American Express cards. For hydrofoils you can use American Express (call Hongkong 523 2136). Bookings can be made up to 28 days in advance.

Hydrofoil fare is HK$62 weekdays, HK$72 weekends and public holidays. Jetfoil fares, depending on the deck favoured, day and time of day, range from HK$72-92. The night service (6:30 pm to 1:30 am) is HK$108. Weekday ferry charges are HK$54 first class, HK$43 tourist and HK$30 economy. At weekends and on public holidays the charges are HK$66, HK$56 and HK$45, respectively. The hoverferry costs HK$55 weekdays, HK$68 at weekends and public holidays and HK$80 at night. Rates for the jetcat are HK$72 weekdays, HK$78 at weekends and public holidays. Helicopter flights cost HK$830 weekdays and HK$930 weekends and public holidays. Bookings can be made through (HK) 859 3359 and, in Macau, 572983.

Departure tax for the trip from Hongkong to Macau was fixed at HK$22 from October 1990.

Visitors need a passport or other valid travel document. Nationals of the following countries do not require a visa: Britain, US, the Philippines, Japan, Australia, Canada, Singapore, South Korea, Luxembourg, Republic of Ireland, New Zealand, Malaysia, Thailand, Brazil, Austria, Belgium, Denmark, Spain, France, Greece, Italy, Norway, the Netherlands, Switzerland, Germany and Sweden (up to six months' stay). Hongkong residents and other British Commonwealth subjects can stay for up to 20 days, other nationalities up to three days. Nationals of countries that do not have diplomatic relations with Portugal must obtain their visa from an overseas Portuguese consulate.

Others can get them on arrival. For an individual traveller the cost is HK$145 and for a child under 12 years, HK$72.50. For a family including children under 18, the cost is HK$290. Members of a bona fide tour group each have to pay HK$72.50. Note: if travel arrangements are made through an agent, visa processing is handled by the Macau tour operator.

The authorities in Macau seem to assume that all health documents have been checked upon arrival in Hongkong. Hence the only time that you will need to produce valid certificates for smallpox and cholera vaccinations upon arrival in Macau is if there is an outbreak of either disease in Hongkong.

Weapons, explosives and drugs are forbidden imports. Note that Hongkong customs regulations allow local residents only one bottle of wine and 100 cigarettes. Others can bring in a litre of liquor and 200 cigarettes. There are no export duties on articles purchased in Macau.

The Macau pataca is the legal currency and is roughly at par with the Hongkong dollar. Exchange rates with the US dollar and other currencies vary from day to day. The pataca is divided into 100 avos. Notes of 5, 10, 50, 100 and 500 Patacas and coins of 1 and 5 Patacas and 10, 20 and 50 avos are in circulation.

There are no import or export restrictions on currency. The Hongkong dollar circulates freely in Macau, but the pataca is not acceptable in Hongkong or elsewhere. Exchange facilities are available at the wharf.

The southern Chinese dialect, Cantonese, is most widely spoken. Putonghua, or Mandarin, the official Chinese national language, is also used. Officials speak Portuguese and some English, French and Spanish. The visitor can manage well enough with English.

Weather is sub-tropical — warm to hot, average maximum temperatures in excess of 28°C (82°F) from June to September, with high humidity from April to October, when most of the annual rainfall occurs. The cool sea breezes make the hot months more pleasant in Macau than in Hongkong. Winter months are much cooler and the average temperature drops

below 20°C (67°F), with the humidity down to a comfortably low level. The weather is at its best in November and December, though it stays cool right through the winter until early April.

Lightweight clothing is suitable except during the cooler months, when woollens are advisable.

Government offices are open from 9 am to 5 pm Monday to Friday and from 9 am to 1 pm on Saturday, though government-run information counters, at the arrival pier, for instance, are open until 6 pm every day. Banks generally work from 9 am to 5 pm Monday to Friday and 9 am to 1 pm on Saturday, though there are some small variations.

Because there is so much nightlife generated by the round-the-clock casinos, most shops are open until 10 pm.

TAXIS: Macau has almost 600 taxis. Flagfall is Patacas 5.50 for the first 1,500 m, then 70 avos for every subsequent 250 m. There is a Patacas 5 surcharge to Taipa, and Patacas 10 to Coloane (no surcharge on the return trip). Make sure that the meter is used for very short journeys. If you want to negotiate your own rate for special purposes — such as hiring the vehicle to explore Macau — bargain with the driver. When doing this, make sure that the driver understands that the price agreed is in patacas and includes all passengers in the taxi. Not all taxi drivers speak English, so carry with you a bilingual map available from the Department of Tourism. Taxi fares on the islands of Taipa and Coloane are the same as in Macau.

PEDICABS: A gentle way to see Macau is to hire a pedicab and to proceed slowly around the sights. You should negotiate the fare before setting off. The average is Patacas 10 for a short trip and 30-40 for about one hour's sightseeing. Pedicab men understand some English and know what the tourist usually wants to see.

BUSES: Public buses run from 7 am until midnight, and the fare on all city routes is Patacas 1.50. Bus service No.3 runs between the ferry pier and the centre of the city. Several buses serve the islands, including open-top double-deckers in summer. Fares are Patacas 2 to

Taipa, Patacas 2.30 to Coloane and Patacas 3 to Hac Sa Beach. A convenient pick-up point in Macau is outside the Hotel Lisboa.

MINI-MOKES: These open-topped jeep-like vehicles are one of the most popular forms of tourist transportation available in Macau (Macau Mokes Ltd, Avis Mokes Ltd), though as an alternative you can hire a saloon car. Mini-mokes can be hired for about HK$280 on weekdays and HK$320 at weekends and public holidays. There are also special whole-weekend prices and a midweek special deal. You need a valid driver's licence.

BICYCLES: Bicycles for Macau peninsula can be hired for a few patacas per hour one block from the Hotel Lisboa on Ave Dom Noao IV. On Taipa island the village has two or three bicycle-renting establishments. Pedalling down the causeway to Coloane is a delightful experience. The **Hyatt Regency** and **Mandarin Oriental** hotels also have bikes for hire, but the cost is a little higher. Bicycles are not permitted across the bridge linking Macau with Taipa.

A wide variety of tours are run by several operators. These include Able (Tel: Macau 89798, Hongkong 545 9993); Asia (Macau 82687, HK 548 8806); China Travel Service (Macau 88922, HK 540 6333), especially for one-day trips to China; Estoril (Macau 573614, HK 559 1028); Hi-No-De Caravela (Macau 338338, HK 368 6181-2); H. Nolasco (Macau 76463); International (Macau 86522, HK 541 2100), the pioneers in one-to-five-day trips to China; Lotus (Macau 81765); Macau Tours (Macau 85555, HK 542 2338); MBC Tours (Macau 86462); Sintra (Macau 86394, HK 540 8028); South China (Macau 87211, HK 544 9053); TKW (Macau 591122, HK 723 7771); Wing On (Macau 77701). All these agencies can arrange overnight or day tours of Macau and, if the tour is booked in Hongkong, will arrange your transfers from the hotel to the ferry wharf in Hongkong as well as tickets and visas.

In the past Macau was criticised for its lack of good hotels. But no longer. Of the newer hotels, the **Pousada de Sao Tiago** — picturesquely built into the old Barra Fortress — has to be the most charming. The **Hyatt Regency** is now well established across the bridge in Taipa (there is

a regular shuttle service), and the **Mandarin Oriental** sits at the edge of the Outer Harbour, close to the **Presidente**. Behind it on the hill is the **Royal Hotel**, which faces Vasco da Gama Park. The elaborate **Lisboa's** odd architecture makes it one of the more startling local sights. Smaller, but equally modern, are the **Metropole** and the **Matsuya**.

The **Bela Vista**, at present undergoing refurbishment, is in colonial style and boasts an astonishing history. Budget travellers might try the **Hoi Pan, Tai Fat, Universal** or the 160-room **Central**, which has been renovated and is good value. Of higher standard is the **Pousada de Coloane** on Coloane Island. It offers clean, modern facilities while preserving the simple style of quiet Portuguese country living overlooking a small beach.

Macau is generally cheaper than Hongkong, and this is reflected in the room rates at most of the hotels and pousadas (inns). Booking inquiries from Hongkong can be directed to the Macau Tourist Information Bureau, Ticketmate and the hotel's Hongkong offices, or you can telephone the hotel direct. It is essential to book accommodation in advance for weekends and holidays.

To the traveller who has become a little jaded by a surfeit of Chinese food in Hongkong, Macau beckons as an oasis. Most of the Western food available is Portuguese in the simple country style. Typical ingredients to accompany meats, poultry and fish are tomatoes, potatoes and tihy, delicious black olives. Many dishes are stewed. Even lobster can be prepared this way and is surprisingly good. Seafood is excellent and generally much cheaper than in Hongkong restaurants. Some specialities such as "African chicken" — grilled and coated with an exotic blend of spices — have an intriguing influence that can be traced to the Portuguese colonies in Africa. Preserved cod and fresh sardines, both imported from Portugal, are other outstanding local dishes. The cod comes in many forms, including deep-fried fish cakes which make an excellent starter, or fish stew with vegetables. The sardines — most of the year frozen but in season flown out fresh — are grilled and three or four with plenty of lemon juice can hardly be bettered for fish-lovers. Roast quails are another local standard.

A favourite is **Henri's Gallery** at 4 Ave da Republica, with tables by the roadside where you can order huge spicy prawns, African chicken or a delicious fondue. Sunday lunch at the **Solmar**, 11 Rue da Praia Grande, is popular, though the food is good any time of the week. For pure Portuguese food, one must try the Sunday lunch buffet at **Pousada de Coloane**.

At 69 Ave Sidonio Pais is **Riquexo**, a strange little place on a balcony in a building basement, overlooking Park'n Shop grocery store. Open from 11 am to 3 pm only, it is worth sampling, though you are advised to get there early. The home cooking is Macanese style and the atmosphere informal. You can go to **Belo's** afterwards for an almond souffle (45 Ave Almeida Ribiero).

On the outer islands, one should visit **Pinocchio's**, 4 Rua do Sol, Taipa, for its roast quail and chilli crab, as well as the fine wines. Although Pinocchio's has lost its open-air charm and has become perhaps too popular — booking a table ahead is essential at weekends — it is still one of the finest Portugese restaurants and well worth the journey by taxi.

The hotel restaurants vary. The Lisboa's **A Galera** has Portuguese food in an elegant setting. While the Pousada de Sao Tiago's **Grill Fortaleza** cuisine might be considered high-priced, it can be enjoyed in a priceless setting. Its coffee shop food, meanwhile, is superbly prepared and inexpensive. The Mandarin Oriental has a good **Grill Room** and the more locally inspired **Cafe Girassol**, while the Hyatt Regency has the excellent **Afonso** and **Flamingo** restaurants. The Pousada de Coloane has, besides its Sunday buffet, excellent lunches and dinners, and good wines. The Presidente has a fine Korean restaurant and the **Royal** a first-class Cantonese dining room.

Non-European or non-Chinese restaurants tend to have a short life in Macau, though there are a number of Thai, Burmese and Indonesian restaurants around. By the Leal Senado in the Largo do Senado is the **Long Kei** Chinese restaurant. Birds' nest soup or pigeon in a great many styles, and dozens of other delights, give the place a good reputation. Roast pigeon is the house speciality at the **Fat Siu Lau** restaurant on Rua da Felicidade, one of the town's oldest eating houses. Here the styles of South China and Portugal have blended in a way typical of Macau itself. The **Lee Hong Kee**, 35 Rua da Caldeira, and the popular **Pun Kai**, 44 Rua da Praia Grande, are other excellent Chinese restaurants. Chinese food prices are moderate. Also noted for their good food are **A Lorcha, Balichao, Bara Nova** and the **Restaurant Portugues**. Popular on Taipa island are the **Galo** and **Mocambique**, and on Coloane island **Fernando's** and the **1999** eateries.

Portuguese wines, both red and white, are very good and, by Hongkong standards, very cheap. Table wines range from the light, slightly fizzy, white *vino verde*, through the rich, heavy Dao red, to many varieties of Port (including the unusual white Port). All are free of import duty.

On the whole, with wine, a meal will cost 40% less in Macau than in Hongkong.

The Barrier Gate to China.

The evening entertainment operates around the seven casinos. The **Casino do Lisboa**, taking up two floors of the Lisboa Hotel, is a gambling extravaganza, offering such international games as roulette, blackjack, boule, chemin-de-fer, craps and keno, row upon row of slot machines and the Chinese games — fan tan and dai sui (the big and the small). The casino in the Mandarin Oriental is elegant and less hectic, open from noon to 4 am.

The **Macau Palace**, like a Mississippi steamer gone Oriental, is moored in the inner harbour near the opposite end of the Avenida de Almeida Ribeiro from the Lisboa. It has a casino over two of its floors, as well as a restaurant, nightclub and bar. It is open 24 hours a day.

The **Crazy Paris Show** at the Lisboa features a dozen or so girls from Europe in a pretty classy, revue-style show once described as "a little naughty, a little nice." There are two shows on weekdays at 8:30 and 10 pm. On Saturdays and public holidays the shows are at 8:30, 10 and 11:30 pm. Tickets are Patacas 90 Monday to Friday, and Patacas 100 on Saturday, Sunday and public holidays. No one under 18 is allowed in. Tickets are available at the wharf in Macau, the Hotel Lisboa and Hotel Sintra, and at the theatre itself one hour before show time.

For those who want something a little raunchier, there are several Bangkok-style nightclubs. There are also Thai and Filipina masseuses available in many of the hotels.

The Hotel Presidente has the **Skylight Discotheque** (and a cabaret) which is open from 9:30 pm to 4 am. A modest, minimum charge is levied. The **Royal Discotheque** at the Royal, open from 10 pm to 3 am, also has a minimum charge. **The Mikado's** (Lisboa) entrance charge includes two drinks. Over at the Jai Alai Palace, the **Ritz Night Club** on the top floor is open from 11 am to midnight, and becomes a nightclub on Tuesdays, Thursdays and Saturdays.

Away in the back streets of the town (Rua de Cinco de Outubro, for example) are charming antique shops selling the cultural remains of a China that no longer exists, as well as historical curios from a colonial period dying but not quite dead. And if you are prepared to search the general merchandise shops, Macau is still enough of a real Chinese city to have available the interesting chinaware and carved wooden furniture that local people use in their daily lives. Many such objects retain the characteristics of the great artistic tradition of old China.

The Macau Grand Prix is the highlight of the sporting calendar. It is held in late November, the event attracts the world's Formula 3 drivers and several of Europe's racing teams.

Greyhound-racing is highly popular in the town, with events held four nights a week at the canidrome. Horse-racing on Taipa is also popular, though it has yet to achieve the scale and quality of its Hongkong counterpart. Long the host for marathon foot races, Macau is now the venue each December for a race on the official international marathon circuit.

Chinese and many Western (Christian) festivals are linked to the lunar and church calendars. Consequently their dates vary from one year to the next. Other religious occasions and events marking Portuguese political events fall on fixed dates.

January-February: New Year's Day (public holiday); Chinese New Year's Day (public holiday); Lantern Festival.

March-April: Procession of Our Lord of Passos; Feast of the God Toutei; Commemoration of the death of Dr Sun Yat-sen; Easter (public holiday); Ching Ming Festival (public holiday); Anniversary of the Portuguese Revolution (public holiday); A-Ma Festival.

May-June: Labourers' Day (public holiday); Procession of Our Lady of Fatima; Feast of the Bathing of Lord Buddha; Corpus Christi (public holiday); Camoes Day and Portuguese Communities Day (public holiday); Dragon Boat Festival (public holiday); Feast of St Anthony of Lisbon; Feast of St John the Baptist, Patron Saint (public holiday).

July-August: Feast of Battle of July 13 (holiday only on the islands); Feast of Maidens; Feast of the Assumption of Our Lady (public holiday); Festival of the Hungry Ghosts.

September-October: Mid-Autumn Festival (public holiday); Confucius Day; Republic Day (public holiday); Festival of Ancestors — Chung Yeung (public holiday); International Fireworks Display Contest; International Music Festival.

November-December: All Saints Day/All Souls Day (public holiday); Macau Grand Prix; Restoration of Independence (public holiday); Feast of the Immaculate Conception (public holiday); Winter Solstice; Christmas (public holiday).

Addresses

The **Department of Tourism** is at 11 Largo do Senado, Macau, Tel: 315566. A number of useful publications are available. There is also an information office in the arrival terminal.

The **Macau Tourist Information Bureau** in Hongkong is in Rm 305, Shun Tak Centre, 200 Connaught Rd Central, Tel: 540 8180. Hotel and tour bookings can be arranged through the office and general information can be obtained. Information about Macau can also be obtained from the following offices:

Australia: Macau Tourist Information Bureau, 449 Darling St, Balmain, Sydney, N.S.W. 2041. Tel: (02) 555 7548, (008) 252 488; Fax: (02) 555 7559.

Britain: Macau Tourist Information Bureau, 6 Sherlock Mews, Paddington St, London W1M 3RH. Tel: (071) 224 3390; Fax: (071) 224 0601; Telex: 28955 MEDINT G.

France: Portuguese National Tourist Office, 7 Rue Scribe, 75009 Paris. Tel: 742 55 77; Telex: 220550 PORUGURIF; Cable: PORTUGALIA.

Germany: Portuguese National Tourist Office, Kaiserstr 66-IV, 6000 Frankfurt-Main. Tel: 0611 234094/97; Telex: 4-13976; Cable: PORTUGA.

Japan: Macau Tourist Information Bureau, 4th Floor, Toho Twin Tower Bldg, 5-2 Yurakucho 1-chome, Chiyoda-ku, Tokyo 100. Tel: (03) 501 5022/5023; Fax: (03) 3502 1248.

North America: Macau Tourist Information Bureau, 3133 Lake Hollywood Drive, P. O. Box 1860, Los Angeles, California 90078. Tel: (213) 851 3684, (800) 331 7150; Fax: (213) 851 3684. Macau Tourist Information Bureau, Suite 316, 704 Greenwich Ave, New York, NY 10011. Tel: (212) 206 6828; Fax (212) 924 0882. Macau Tourist Information Bureau, 630 Green Bay Rd/P. O. Box 350, Kenilworth, Illinois 60043-0350. Tel: (708) 251 6421; Fax: (708) 256 8542. Macau Tourist Information Bureau, P. O. Box 22188, Honolulu, Hawaii 96922. Tel: (808) 588 7613; Macau Tourist Information Bureau, Suite 305, 1530 West 8th Ave, Vancouver, BC, Canada V6J 1T5. Tel: (604) 736 1095; Fax: (604) 736 7761. Macau Tourist Information Bureau, 5059 Yonge St, Toronto, Ontario, Canada M2N 5P2. Tel: (416) 733 8768; Fax: (416) 221 5227.

Portugal: Macau Tourism Representative, Avendia 5 de Outubro 115-5th Floor, 1000 Lisbon. Tel: 769864/6; Telex: 64291 GOMACP.

Singapore: Macau Tourist Information Bureau, 11-01A Pil Building, 140 Cecil St, Singapore 0106. Tel: 2250022; Telex: 29024 MBURO; Fax: (65) 2238585.

Thailand: Macau Tourist Information Bureau, 150/5 Sukhumvit 20, Bangkok 10110, or GPO Box 1534, Bangkok 10501. Tel: 258 1975, 239 7834; Fax: (662) 258 1975.

Publications

Maps and various brochures are available from either the information office in Hongkong at Shun Tak Centre, or from the Tourism Department and main hotels in Macau. This literature is free. The Macau Tourism Department publishes brochures on restaurants and places of interest, either free or at nominal prices. The most up-to-date guide book, *Macau* by Shann Davies, is a useful guide for first-time and frequent visitors alike. The best history of Macau is the now out-of-print *Golden Guide to Hongkong and Macau* by P. H. M. Jones. Prof. C. R. Boxer's *Fidalgos in the Far East* has been re-issued and his *Macau Three Hundred Years Ago* has been reprinted under the title *Seventeenth Century Macau*. Other histories have been written by Father Teixeira and Austin Coates, the latter's *Macau Narrative* having enjoyed critical acclaim. Also on some shelves is a book by C. A. Montalto de Jesus called *Historic Macau*. A photographic study with impressions of modern Macau and an anecdotal history written by Harry Rolnick, *Macau, a Glimpse of Glory*, is available through the Department of Tourism and most bookshops. *Viva Macau* by Shann Davies, published by Macmillan, tells the story of a single day in the enclave through an imaginative text and pictures.

DISCOVERING MACAU

From the wharf on the outer harbour you can take a taxi or a bus to the central area where most of the hotels are. First, you will see the **Mandarin Oriental Hotel** and the pits for the Macau Grand Prix, and later the odd-wedding cake-looking **Lisboa Hotel**, next to which stands the statue of **Governor Ferreira do Amaral**.

Around the corner from the harbour is the

The Lisboa Hotel.

Photo: Garry Marchant

Rua da Praia Grande, which runs as a broad and pleasant tree-lined avenue along the water's edge. Macau's main commercial street, the **Avenida Almeida Ribeiro**, cuts across the peninsula from the Praia Grande to the inner harbour, right by the **Macau Palace** casino and fishing port.

In the centre of town a square, the **Largo do Leal Senado**, adjoins the Avenida Almeida Ribeiro and here may be found the imposing **Leal Senado** (Loyal Senate) Building — the town hall. The square is also the location of the Macau Government's Information and Services Department. The Senado acquired its epithet in 1809, having sent a warship to the aid of the Portuguese court that had fled to Brazil from the armies of Napoleon.

The present building is said to have been built in 1784 on the site of a previous Senate building. The facade was added in the 1870s and a complete restoration effected a few years ago. Inside is a beautiful courtyard and art gallery. A staircase leads up to the Council Chamber and library, which boasts some splendidly carved woodwork. The library has an interesting collection of old books, some dating from around the 16th century.

At the northeastern end of the Largo do Leal Senado stands the fine **Church of St Dominic**, most of which probably dates from the 17th century. To gain admission, ring the bell to the right of the facade. The streets behind the church are especially picturesque and along them can be found a number of shops selling antiques and other items of historic and cultural interest, along with a great deal of fascinating old junk.

The morning market here is quite picturesque. On the Largo also stands the **Santa Casa da Misericordia** (Holy House of Mercy), a branch of a charitable institution founded in 1498. The Macau branch owes its origin to Dom Belchior Carneiro, first Bishop of China and Japan. His skull is preserved in a glass case in a council room on the first floor.

From beside the Leal Senado, the Rua Central leads to the **Church of St Augustine**, the largest in the territory and an excellent example of the baroque style. The present building dates from 1814 and the facade from 1873. The restrained plaster-work of the interior is particularly fine. Across the lane is the **Teatro Dom Pedro V**, which is part of the premises of the Club de Macau. If you ring the bell of the club's door, one of the staff will be happy to show you the delightful little theatre. A few yards along the same way is the **Church of St Lawrence**, with its baroque interior and crystal chandeliers. Down the slope beyond is an old residential district, the most typical and photogenic in town.

Immediately behind St Lawrence's is the **Seminary of St Joseph**, which possesses a church built from 1746-58, with a facade situated at the top of a flight of stairs. From St Lawrence's a narrow street descends to the Praia Grande, emerging beside the pink stuccoed **Government House**. From the Praia Grande, along towards the end of the peninsula, a road leads up to Penha Hill, where stands a chapel and the Bishop's residence. The Penha provides a view of the town and the inner harbour.

A walk around the end of the peninsula — past the walls of the old Fortress of Barra, now the hotel **Pousada de Sao Tiago**, and the area of the naval dockyard storage sheds — brings one to the **Ma Kok Miu Chinese Temple**, sacred to a sea-goddess known as A Ma, from whom the province's name seems to have been derived. The shrine, said to be more than 600 years old, is built of rock quarried from the outcrop nearby, where you can see a brightly painted carving of the ship said to have carried the goddess. The oldest section is the lower pavilion to the right of the entrance. Close to the fortress is a small but comprehensively stocked Maritime Museum.

On the western side of the peninsula (the area north of the Avenida Almeida Ribeiro) are the **Camoes Gardens**, overlooking the inner harbour and the hills of China beyond, with clusters of simple village houses, watchtowers and fields. The view of China from the gardens is far more revealing than that obtained from Hongkong's New Territories. The gardens contain the grotto dedicated to Portugal's great national poet, Camoes, who is supposed — on fairly flimsy evidence — to have lived in Macau about the year of its foundation. The nearby old **Protestant Cemetery** with its weather-beaten grave stones also provides extremely interesting testimony to the past.

Macau's most celebrated attraction is the great facade of **Sao Paulo**, which is all that remains of St Paul's collegiate church. It was built between 1601 and 1673 by Catholic Japanese artisans under the direction of Italian Jesuits. The church, which originally stood behind the facade, was burned down in 1835, but what remains is an impressive example of Italian-influenced baroque architecture, and the carvings show a fascinating combination of Western and Oriental motifs. You will need binoculars to study the fine details at the top of the facade.

Overlooking Sao Paulo from the hill nearby is the fort of **Sao Paulo do Monte**, built about 1620 and displaying many old cannons. There is a good view from the fort.

High upon Guia Hill are a fort — built about 1637 — a chapel and the **Guia** lighthouse, first lit in 1865 and the oldest of its kind on the China coast.

The **Porta do Cerco** (Barrier Gate), separating Macau from China, stands in the very north of the town. However, the Barrier Gate no longer has the mystery of the past. More and more daytrippers to Macau extend their journey by an extra day with a side trip through the Barrier Gate into China. Most travel agents can arrange this, though it costs a few hundred patacas. The trip includes visits to a commune or school, a market town, the home of Sun Yat-sen (founder of modern China), a few museums and lunch. Or one can continue the trip to embrace Canton, returning to Macau down through Hongkong. One of the better Hongkong travel agents for this is **International Tourism**, Tel: Macau 86522, HK 541 2100.

Some distance south of the gate is the interesting, labyrinthine temple of **Kun Iam Tong**, dedicated to the goddess Kwan Yin. There are fine Buddha statues in the temple and the main hall possesses a carving of the Goddess of Mercy herself. In the temple grounds is the stone table on which was signed the first treaty between China and the US in 1844. This temple is also popularly supposed to have been sacred to Marco Polo. On the way back to the Leal Senado are the monuments that commemorate a remarkable victory over the Dutch fleet, which attacked Macau in 1622, and Vasco da Gama, discoverer of the sea route to India.

In two of the colonial-style mansions in Avenida de Conselheiro Ferreira de Almeida are the **Archives**, and new **National Library** containing letters, books and manuscripts pertaining to Portugal's exploration and Macau's relations with Europe, China, Japan and Southeast Asia. These come from a wide variety of sources — government, civic, ecclesiastical and private — and the most valuable are now on micro-film.

Across the picturesque bridge from Macau is **Taipa**, whose best-known attractions are the **race-track** and the **University of East Asia**. Also on Taipa is a delightful old church (**Our Lady of Carmel**); a new **folk museum**; some wooded areas worth exploration and two temples.

Across the causeway is the island of **Coloane**, which has junk-building yards, two pine-shaded beaches of middling quality and an interesting old church built early in the 20th century, outside of which is a memorial to the Portuguese military who rescued some kidnapped children from pirates. In the church are the bones of Japanese martyrs who died in the 17th century and a (bone) relic of St Francis Xavier. Nearby is an old temple with a large model boat carved from whalebone. The **Pousada de Coloane** on the way to **Hac Sa Beach** is a pleasant small hotel. Other attractions are the comparatively new **aviary** and **park** off the West Rd, and a comprehensive **sports centre** at Hac Sa.

HOTEL GUIDE

Hotel address	Phone	Fax	Telex	Cable	≈	🍴	🍽
A (US$100-140) **B** (US$75-99)	**C** (US$50-74)	**D** (Less than US$50)					
A							
Lisboa Avenida da Amizade	377-666 HK 540-8180	567-193	88203 HOTEL		▲	▲	▲
Mandarin Oriental Avenida da Amizade	567-888 HK 548-7676		88588 MACEX	ORIENTAL	▲	▲	▲
Pousada Ritz Rua da Boa Vista	339-955 HK 739-6993	317-826	88316 RITZM		▲	▲	▲
Pousada da Sao Tiago Avenida da Republica	378-111 HK 810-8332	552-170	88376 TIAGO		▲	▲	▲
B							
Beverley Plaza Avenida do Dr Rodrigues	337-755	308-878	88345 HTLBP			▲	▲
Mondial Rua da Antonio Basto	566-866 HK 540-8180		88363 TAYTC	MONDIAL	▲	▲	▲
Presidente Avenida da Amizade	553-888 HK 526-6873	552-735	88440 HPM		▲	▲	▲
Royal Estrada da Vitoria	552-222	563-008	88514 ROYAL		▲	▲	▲
C							
Guia Estrada do Eng Trigo	513-888	559-822	88736 GUIA			▲	▲
Matsuya Calcada de Sao Francisco	577-000	568-080				▲	▲
Metropole 63 Rua de Praia Grande	388-166 HK 833-9298	330-890	88356 CTS	METROPOLE		▲	▲
Sintra Avenida Dom Joao IV	85-111	567-769	88234 SINTRA	HOTEL SINTRA	▲	▲	▲
D							
Central Avenida Almeida Ribeiro	77-700						▲

Hotel address	Phone	Fax	Telex	Cable	〰	🍴	🍲
TAIPA **D**							
Hyatt Regency Taipa Island	321-234 HK 770-9303		88512 HYMAC		▲	▲	▲
COLOANE **B**							
Pousada de Coloane Pria da Cheoc Van	328-143 HK 730-1166	328-251	88251 MBC		▲	▲	▲

MALAYSIA

Rapid changes over the past decade have made Malaysia an easy country in which to travel. Whatever obstacles and pitfalls involving immigration, customs and the rest of officialdom there may be, there is still less red tape in Malaysia than in most countries in the region. It is best to tour the country at a gentle pace, choosing specific destinations in advance, rather than try to do everything in one go.

In Peninsular Malaysia, the population is a thorough mix of Malays, Chinese and Indians, while in West Malaysia Kadazans and Chinese dominate Sabah and Dayaks and Chinese dominate Sarawak. The people as a whole have forgotten their colonial past and welcome visitors quickly and easily. Although Bahasa Malaysia (Malay) is the national language, English is widely spoken and most business can easily be conducted in it.

The country's capital, Kuala Lumpur (known locally as KL) is a fascinating place. Its buildings are an interesting mixture of East and West, modern high-rise blocks interpersed with some fine surviving colonial architecture and the domes of mosques, an easily visible sign of the country's concern with its Muslim religion. During the day the capital is as busy as any other Asian capital city, but it is in the early evening around dusk when the city shows its other face. As the sun goes down and the reddish twilight glows on the Moorish architecture of the British-built railway station, this is the time to walk around the small shops and pleasant arcades, exploring the streets and meeting the people.

To the northwest there is Penang, with old-fashioned streets, winding lanes and tree-lined suburban avenues in the town (Georgetown) and the coastal road winding through the villages of the tear-drop shaped island. There are also superb views from the top of Penang Hill.

To the south, Malacca is another charming old town steeped in history. Here the visitor can wander around ruins and remains of the settlements established by the several colonial masters the country has known — Portuguese, Dutch and English.

The east coast of Peninsular Malaysia is one of the great attractions, with beautiful beaches and unspoilt countryside. Fishing boats will ferry tourists to some of the outlying islands, which boast idyllic scenery and clean beaches. On the east coast too, visitors can see spectacular performances of huge kites in the air and witness the annual visits of giant turtles weighing as much as a tonne, laying about a hundred eggs at a time in the sand.

The states of Sabah and Sarawak lie in the South China Sea, on the western side of the island of Borneo. Kota Kinabalu in Sabah is worth more than a passing look, for it is the starting point for a trip up Mount Kinabalu and a tour of the Kinabalu National Park. In Sarawak, Kuching is one of the few places in Asia which can still stir colonial memories.

That Malaysia was one of the earliest sites inhabited by man is shown by the interesting discoveries at the Niah limestone caves in Sarawak, where relics dating back as far as 50,000 years have been discovered. In Penin-

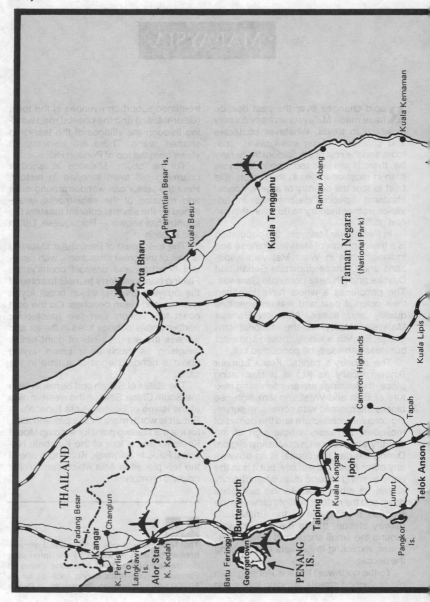

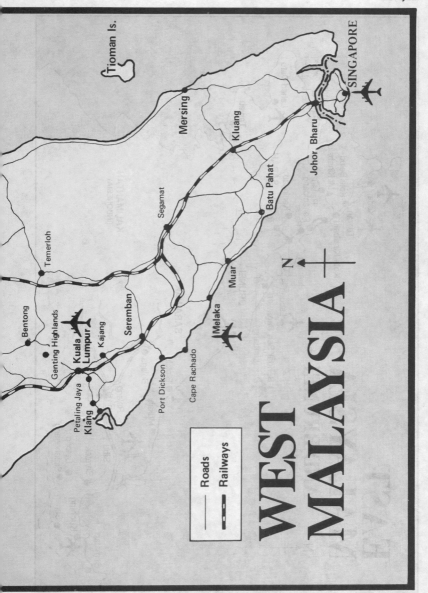

WEST MALAYSIA

Roads
Railways

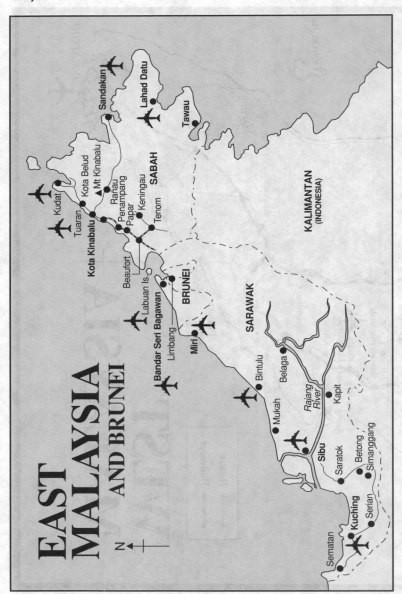

sular Malaysia, the mountain aboriginal peoples attest to the land's occupation prior to the arrival of the Malays.

The early kingdom of Funan, based in the area of today's Cambodia extended its influence over the Malay Peninsula in the early centuries. Later, around the seventh century, the Sumatra-based Sri Vijayan Empire dominated many of the lands surrounding the South China Sea, including the Malay peninsula. Sri Vijaya's hegemony was replaced by that of Majapahit in the second half of the 13th century. It was the Sri Vijayan prince, Parameswara, fleeing from the forces of Majapahit around 1403, who was to establish a new kingdom at Malacca which was introduced to Islam in the early 15th century and where, by 1498, the new faith was well-established and the kingdom counted much of the peninsula as well as certain parts of Sumatra in its domain.

The Portuguese came to Malacca in 1509 and by 1511 had taken over by force and were to rule until displaced by the Dutch in 1641. The English became a power in the area in the late 18th century, establishing trading posts on Penang Island in 1786 and in Singapore in 1819. Malacca was ceded to the British in 1824.

The several other Malay states, each under their own sultan signed agreements with the British and in 1895 Perak, Selangor, Negri Sembilan and Pahang states formed a loose union known as the Federated Malay States. Johor, along with the states transferred from Thai control in 1909 (Kelantan, Trengganu, Perlis and Kedah), existed under less direct British control and were known as the Unfederated Malay States. It was during the period of British rule that a good many Chinese and Indians migrated to Malaya to seek employment.

The Japanese occupied the country from the time of their invasion in 1942 until September 1945. The states formed into the Malay Union after the war and then in 1948 into the Federation of Malaya.

In June 1948, a state of emergency was declared to cope with a communist insurgency: it was not lifted until 1960. The first national elections, convincingly won by the Alliance, were held in 1955 and under the Alliance leader, Tunku Abdul Rahman, the country achieved independence — known as Merdeka in the national language, Bahasa Malaysia (Malay) — on August 31, 1957.

Sabah was ruled by the British North Borneo Company — which turned the territory into a substantial rubber producer — from 1882 until the Japanese occupation. Sarawak, as a result of successive concessions by the sultans of Brunei, came to be ruled by the "White Rajahs" of the Brooke family from the 1840s until 1942. Both were British colonies from the end of the war until 1963.

Malaya joined with Singapore, Sarawak and Sabah in 1963 to form the Federation of Malaysia but Singapore left the Federation in 1965.

Racial antagonism between the Malays and Chinese brought about serious clashes in 1969, and parliamentary rule was suspended until February 1971.

Rigorous efforts to redress the economic imbalance between the races followed and the Malays have now begun to acquire a larger share of the economy.

During 1972, Malaysia moved away from its previous close ties with the Western world and initiated contacts with the communist world, its foreign policy aimed at making Southeast Asia a zone of peace, freedom and neutrality. Diplomatic ties between Malaysia and the People's Republic of China were forged in 1974 during a visit to Peking by the late Malaysian prime minister Tun Abdul Razak, who died in 1976 and was succeeded by the late Tun (then Datuk) Hussein Onn whose policies helped reduce racial tension.

When Tun Hussein resigned as prime minister in 1981, he was succeeded by Datuk Seri Mahathir Mohamad who won a landslide election victory in 1986.

According to the Department of Statistics, the population of Malaysia in late 1990 was estimated to be 17.9 million, with 75% of them living in Peninsular Malaysia.

Many international and Asian regional airlines operate into Kuala Lumpur, including the national carrier, **Malaysian Airline System (MAS)**, **Garuda**, **Singapore Airlines**, **Cathay Pacific**, **British Airways**, **Lufthansa** and **Aerofloat** to name a few.

Singapore to the south and Bangkok to the north handle a great deal of international air traffic and it is a simple matter to reach Peninsular Malaysia from these points. Domestic MAS flights are available to the main cities of every state. On a number of these sectors, the airlines provide special economy tourist flights. In the East Malaysian states of Sabah and Sarawak,

Malaysian Airlines Rural Service serve many isolated towns and villages.

Another domestic air service within Peninsular Malaysia is the **Pelangi Air** which operates a network covering Kuala Lumpur, Ipoh, Penang, Alor Setar, Langkawi, Malacca, Taman Negara, Tioman Island, Kuantan and Kuala Trengganu.

The **Malayan Railways (KTM)** operates two main lines, one from Singapore through Kuala Lumpur and Butterworth which meets the Thai railways at the border, and the other from the town of Gemas up to the northeastern part of the peninsula near Kota Baru also meeting the Thai railways at the border.

Visitors to Malaysia must have a valid passport or other travel document recognised by the Malaysian Government, valid for at least six months beyond the period of stay allowed in

Malaysia. For holders of a national passport not recognised by Malaysia, a Document in Lieu of Passport can be obtained from the nearest Malaysian mission abroad.

No visas are required for citizens of the following countries: Republic of Ireland and all Commonwealth countries except India. For stays not exceeding three months, no visas are required for citizens of Austria, Belgium, Denmark, Finland, France, Iceland, Italy, Japan, Luxembourg, Norway, South Korea, Sweden, Tunisia, US and Germany. For US citizens, a visa is only required for the purpose of local employment.

Nationals of Vietnam, Israel and South Africa are not allowed to enter Malaysia. Nationals of the Republic of China are allowed in on a government-to-government basis only. Chinese residents of Taiwan must have a Certificate of Identity in lieu of an international passport as Malaysia does not recognise a Taiwan passport.

EMBASSIES AND COMMISSIONS IN KUALA LUMPUR

Argentina	2550176	**North Korea**	9847110
Australian High Commission	2423122	**South Korea**	9842177
Austrian Embassy	2484277	**Kuwait**	9846004
Austrian Trade Commission	2614724	**Libya**	2432112
Bangladesh High Commission	2423271	**Netherlands**	2431143
Belgium	2485733	**New Zealand High Commission**	2486422
Brazil	254820	**Norway**	2430144
British High Commission	2482122	**Oman**	4575011
Brunei High Commission	2612828	**Pakistan**	2418877
Myanmar	2423863	**Palestine**	4561411
Canadian High Commission	2612000	**Papua New Guinea**	
Chile	2616203	**High Commission**	4574202
People's Republic of China	4239939	**Philippines**	2484233
Czechoslovakia	2427185	**Poland**	4576733
Denmark	2416088	**Romania**	2423172
Egypt	4568184	**Saudi Arabia**	4579433
Fiji High Commission	2428470	**Singapore High Commission**	2616277
Finland	2611088	**Soviet Union**	4567252
France	2484122	**Spain**	2484868
Germany	4562894	**Sri Lanka High Commission**	2423094
Indian High Commission	2617000	**Sweden**	2485981
Indonesia	9842011	**Switzerland**	2480622
Iran	2433575	**Turkey**	2986455
Iraq	2480555	**US**	2489011
Ireland	2985111	**Vietnam**	2484036
Italy	4565122	**Yugoslavia**	4564561
Japan	2438044		

A valid vaccination certificate is required for visitors who, within the preceding 10 days, have been in or visited any country in the yellow fever endemic zone such as countries in Central America and Central Africa. Any visitor who fails to have a valid vaccination certificate will be put under quarantine for a maximum period of six days upon arrival in Malaysia.

Although there have been periodic reports of cholera, it is by no means endemic but visitors are advised to eat only freshly prepared food.

Travellers to Malaysia staying for a period of not less than 72 hours enjoy customs exemption on the following items: Wine, spirits/malt liquor not exceeding 1 litre, tobacco not exceeding 225 grams, food items not exceeding M$75 in value, souvenirs to a total value not exceeding M$200, cosmetics and soap not exceeding M$200, 1 unit of portable electrically and/or battery operated appliance for personal use. A 50% tax will be levied on items that exceed the above limits.

Used portable personal effects excluding household goods are exempted from all custom duties.

Visitors must declare to customs or the plant quarantine inspector any plant or parts of a plant or animals in their possession.

An export licence from the Director of Museums is necessary for the export of antiques and historical objects. No licence is required if these items were originally imported and declared to customs.

The Malaysian currency is ringgit but is usually written with a $ sign. It comes in denominations of 1,000, 500, 100, 50, 20, 10 and 1 notes. Coins of M$10, M$5, M$1, 50 cents, 20 cents, 10 cents, 5 cents and 1 cent are in circulation.

There is no restriction as to how much money a tourist can bring into or take out of Malaysia. A traveller may freely import or export any amount of foreign or Malaysian currency notes on his arrival at or departure from Malaysia. There is no restriction on the import or export of foreign currency notes and other travellers' payment media. Tourists are not required to convert their foreign currency when entering Malaysia.

Money and travellers' cheques may be freely exchanged at banks, authorised money changers and hotels, with money changers offering the lowest rates. For visitors to the country it would be best to change your money and traveller's cheques at the money changers in town rather than at the airport exchange counters. There are several money changers in Leboh Ampang in Kuala Lumpur as well as in major shopping complexes.

In Penang, the money changers can be found in Pitt Street and also in major shopping complexes.

Most international credit or charge cards such as American Express, Visa, MasterCard and Diners Club are accepted by major establishments in the larger towns. Credit cards can be used for a wide range of goods and services in hotels, department stores and restaurants, but in the country cash is needed.

Bahasa Malaysia or Malay is the national language, though English is widely spoken throughout the country. There are several local phrase books for those who wish to speak in Malay. A good buy would be the *Malay Phrase Book For Tourists* costing M$7.70. Another is *Speak Malay* which costs M$13.30. These books are available at most leading bookshops in Kuala Lumpur, such as the Times Bookshop in the Weld, the MPH bookshop and the Berita Book Centre both in the Bukit Bintang Plaza.

The climate on the lowland coastal areas is warm throughout the year. Temperatures range from 21°C to 32°C with conditions in the hills cooler particularly in the evenings. The east coast of Peninsular Malaysia and Sabah and Sarawak experience heavy rainfalls during the months of November to February. For the west coast states of Peninsular Malaysia, the wet months are usually April, May and October.

Cool, lightweight summer clothing is ideal with only medium weight woollens required at night in cooler highland areas. For formal and semi-formal occasions, batik shirts and dresses are accepted. Jackets for men are only necessary for very formal occasions. Women are not encouraged to wear shorts, miniskirts or off the shoulder or even sleeveless garments, as it offends Muslim practice, especially in rural areas.

When entering a mosque, visitors should remove their shoes and wash their feet. Women are advised to cover their heads with a scarf if possible.

GOVERNMENT OFFICES

In Johor, Kedah Perlis, Kelantan and Trengganu, government offices open from 8 am to 12:45 pm and 2 pm to 4:15 pm on Saturdays through to Wednesdays, from 8 am to 12:45 pm on Thursdays and close on Fridays.

Government offices in other states are open as follows:

Monday to Thursday	8:00 am to 12:45 pm
	2:00 pm to 4:15 pm
Friday	8:00 am to 12:45 pm
	2:45 pm to 4:15 pm
Saturday	8:00 am to 12:45 pm

BANKS

Banking hours are as follows: In Kedah, Perlis, Kelantan and Trengganu banks open from 10 am to 3 pm on Saturdays to Wednesdays (including Sundays) and from 9:30 am to 11:30 am on Thursdays and close on Fridays.

In other states, banks are open Monday to Friday, 10 am to 3 pm and Saturdays 9:30 am to 11:30 am.

Private firms and offices:
Mondays to Fridays 8:30-9 am to 5-5:30 pm.
Saturdays 8:30-9 am to 12:30-1 pm.

SHOPPING CENTRES

Mondays to Saturdays 10 am to 10 pm and most major department stores remain open on Sunday.

Shops 9:00 am to 7:00 pm.

Liquor can be purchased from sundry shops and supermarkets. However, there is a restriction on the time for purchase. At some shops, liquor cannot be purchased after 6 pm. At others it is after 9 pm. This depends on the locality of the shop. Liquor at pubs and bars can be purchased until midnight on weekdays and until 2 am on weekends. Beer can be purchased at any time.

KUALA LUMPUR

TAXIS: You can hail taxis in the capital by the roadside or hire them from your hotel for a slight extra charge. Taxis are fitted with metres which start at M$1 for the first 2 km and 10 M cents for

each subsequent 200 m, inclusive of air-conditioning charges. Between midnight and 6 am, a surcharge of 50% applies. For phone bookings, an extra M$1 is charged.

For airport taxis, travel vouchers are available at the airport counters. Rates are fixed at M$15.60, M$17.60 and M$18.40 depending on which part of the city you are heading for.

Privately run companies operate bus services within the city as well as long inter-urban routes linking the city with neighbouring towns. Fares vary from as little as 20 M cents up to M$1.50.

Mini-buses charge a flat rate of 50 M cents irrespective of the distance travelled.

The main bus terminals are: Klang bus terminal at Jalan Sultan Mohammed for buses around Kuala Lumpur and Selangor, Pudu Raya bus terminal at Jalan Pudu for long-distance buses heading north and south including Singapore, Putra bus terminal at Jalan Putra for outstation buses to the east coast only, Pekeliling bus terminal at Jalan Tun Razak also for buses to the east coast only and the Mara bus terminal at Jalan Tunku for outstation buses to the south.

Both self-drive and chauffeur-driven cars can be hired in Malaysia. **Avis**, **Hertz** and **Sintat** are among the many companies which offer a rent-it-here, leave-it-there service in Penang, Kuala Lumpur, Kuantan, Johor Baru and Singapore. Different car rental companies offer different rates.

UPCOUNTRY

SELF-DRIVE: In Peninsular Malaysia it has become increasingly hazardous driving on the roads, particularly in urban centres. Although the roads are good, the volume of traffic has increased dramatically in the past few years and traffic manners are extremely bad.

Communications between states have improved tremendously with the construction of new highways which also shortens travel time. Driving on the Kuala Lumpur–Seremban Expressway and the Seremban–Ayer Keroh Expressway will bring you to the states of Negeri Sembilan and Malacca. The Karak Highway reduces travel time to Pahang, Kelantan and Trengganu.

TAXIS: Share-taxis (those taking a full load of four passengers) run between main Malaysian towns. The fares are higher than the bus fares, but the trips are quicker and more comfortable. The taxis leave from established depots in the towns.

Sample fares: From Kuala Lumpur to Kuantan: M$25 per person; to Malacca M$13 per person, to Penang M$40, to Ipoh M$20, to Kota Baru and Kuala Trengganu M$45.

Sample fares of long-distance buses: Kuala Lumpur to Kuala Trengganu M$20, to Kuantan M$11, to Malacca M$6.50 to Ipoh M$8.50 and to Johor Baru M$15.20.

TRAINS: Rail services run on the main west coast line Singapore-Seremban–Kuala Lumpur-Ipoh-Butterworth, and on an east coast line that branches off the former at Gemas in the south and runs through the central mountain country via Kuala Lipis to Tumpat (a little north of Kota Baru). Both lines continue into Thailand in the north.

AIR: The national carrier, Malaysian Airline System (MAS) flies to the main towns of both Peninsular Malaysia and Sabah and Sarawak and also to a large number of smaller towns, especially in the two Borneo states. Sample fares on MAS flights one way from Kuala Lumpur: to Kuala Trengganu M$123 (first class), M$86 (economy); to Kuantan M$87 (first), M$61 (economy); to Alor Setar M$134 (first), M$94 (economy); to Ipoh M$79 (first), M$55 (economy); to Kota Baru M$123 (first), M$86 (economy); Penang M$123 (first), M$86 (economy); Johor Baru M$110 (first), M$77 (economy); to Kuching M$329 (first), M$231 (economy); and to Kota Kinabalu M$540 (first) M$380 (economy).

Cheap fares are available on the night tourist flights from Kuala Lumpur to Penang, Kuching and Kota Kinabalu arriving at the respective destinations after midnight. The one way fares are: to Penang M$87 (first), M$61 (economy); to Kuching M$231 (first), M$162 (economy); and to Kota Kinabalu M$378 (first), M$266 (economy).

A good many tour companies operate in Malaysia. Hotels usually provide brochures from one or another of these organisations. They list where, what and how much. The leading travel bureaus are:

Kuala Lumpur

Angkasa Travel Service, 1/F, Angkasaraya Bldg, Jalan Ampang, 50450 K. L. Tel: 248-6566.

Enesty Travel & Tours, G/F, Wisma Merlin, Jalan Sultan Ismail, 50250 K. L. Tel: 2426891.

Kris Travel Tours, 1/F, K. L. Plaza, Jalan Bukit Bintang, 55100 K. L. Tel: 2417500.

Mytravel & Tours, 2/F, Wisma HLA, Jalan Raja Chulan, 50200 K. L. Tel: 2425177.

Vistasia Tours & Travel, 2/F, Wisma Central, Jalan Ampang, 50450 Kuala Lumpur. Tel: 2611946.

Wing Onn Travel, 2/F, Sungai Wang Plaza, Jalan Bukit Bintang, 55100 K. L. Tel: 2432800.

Penang

Harpers Tours, Suite 603, Penang Plaza, Burmah Rd, 10050 Penang. Tel: 362315.

South East Asia Travel, Jalan Sri Bahari, 10050 Penang. Tel: 633471.

Sabah

Bakti Tours & Travel, Aked Hyatt Kota Kinabalu, 88000 Kota Kinabalu. Tel: 240834.

Borneo Wildlife, Block L, Lot 4, Sinsuran Komplek, 88000 Kota Kinabalu. Tel: 213-668.

Coral Island Cruises, Wisma Sabah, 88000 Kota Kinabalu. Tel: 223490.

Sarawak

FTC Trading & Tours, 42 Jalan Padungan, 93100 Kuching. Tel: 254878.

AIRLINES IN KUALA LUMPUR

	Tel		Tel
Aeroflot Soviet Airlines	2610231	Korean Airlines	2428311
Air India	2420166	Lufthansa German Airlines	2614666
British Airways	2426177	Philippine Airlines	2429040
Cathay Pacific	2383377	Qantas Airways	2389133
China Airlines	2427344	Royal Jordanian	2487500
Czechoslovak Airlines	2380176	SAS Scandanavian Airlines	2426044
Garuda Indonesia Airways	2410811	Singapore Airlines	2923122
Japan Air Lines	2611722	UTA French Airlines	2326952
KLM-Royal Dutch Airlines	2427011	United Airlines	2611433
Malaysian Airlines System	2610555	Yugoslav Airlines	2419245

Kuala Lumpur's ornate railway station.

Photo: Veronica Garbutt

Inter-Continental Travel Centre, Jalan Satok, 93760 Kuching. Tel: 422796.

Malacca

Aquarius Travels & Tours, Madonna Bldg, Jalan Laksamana, 75000 Malacca. Tel: 231876.

Pahang

Cherating Getaways Travel & Tours, Sdn Bhd G/F, Cherating Holiday Villa, 26080 Kuantan. Tel: 503833.

Hotel accommodation in Malaysia is of a high standard, especially as a result of the extensive expansion programme carried out over the past few years, notably in KL and Penang. Not only are there hotels of international standards such as the **Hilton**, **Shangri-La**, and **Hyatt** to suit the more affluent; in the capital at least, there is a wide choice of moderate places to suit the budget traveller. Many of the larger hotels have business centres to cater to the needs of travelling businessmen. These centres are well equipped with the standard fax and telex facilities, and experienced secretaries. There

are health centres at the larger hotels, and most hotels have supper clubs, discotheques and bars with live entertainment shows. A government tax of 5% is levied on room rates and 10% for service charge.

Upcountry there are luxury resorts in many places on the east and west coasts and in the central highlands. For the budget traveller there are old-fashioned guest houses which, if minimal in facilities, are clean and honestly run.

Malaysia is a veritable paradise for food lovers. The different peoples that make up its multi-racial community each have their individual foods and cooking styles, so one can eat with great variety around the country. You can eat in the comfort of well-decorated, air-conditioned restaurants or rub shoulders with the local people by trying out delicious local cuisine at street stalls. Restaurants cater for a wide variety of tastes and include Malay, Chinese, Indian, Japanese, Thai and Korean food. Cooking and eating at the open-air stalls is a distinctive Malaysian experience and a variety of all the local cuisines is available.

Malay food (along with that of Indonesia, which is closely related) is largely restricted to its home territory of Southeast Asia. Being the food of Islamic people no pork is used. Strict Muslims insist on only eating at restaurants which guarantee their food is *halal* — prepared in religiously approved conditions. The rich and spicy flavours vary from state to state. It makes ample use of seafood and meat, coconut and many other indigenous fruits and, of course, rice. Although a generous amount of chilli is used in some Malay cuisine, the food is rarely too spicy for even those unused to it.

The best known of the Malay dishes is *satay* which is spicy skewered pieces of chicken or beef, marinated and then barbecued over a charcoal fire. They are best enjoyed with peanut sauce and eaten with sliced cucumber, onions and steamed rice (*ketupat*) which comes wrapped in coconut leaves.

Rendang is another Malay dish which may be found with very slight variations throughout Peninsular Malaysia. It consists of meats prepared in spices and coconut milk. It is served with rice and can be accompanied by other dishes of fish, meat and vegetables.

Nasi Padang, named for the town of Padang in Sumatra, literally means rice served Padang-style. The steamed rice is served with portions of rendang, spiced fish, prawns and vegetables. The dishes are usually all placed on display and customers select the ones they fancy and are charged only for what they take.

Soto, a very good soup that originates in Java, is widely available in Malaysia. To a basic chicken stock are added rice, chicken pieces, bean sprouts, onions and celery.

Laksa is another type of soup, rather spicier than soto, made of fine noodles and fish stock. Unlike Chinese laksa, no meat is used. Penang laksa is rather hotter than the variation in Johor, where the bite of the chilli is largely removed with generous use of coconut milk.

Nasi lemak is another delicious Malay food. Mostly eaten for breakfast, nasi lemak is rice cooked in coconut milk and served with spicy anchovies, eggs and garnished with peanuts and cucumbers.

Chinese food can mean anything from shark's fin and abalone at an upmarket restaurant to a road-side "chicken-rice" stall. Most of the various provincial styles are available — Cantonese, Peking, Sichuan, Hokkien, Teochew, Hakka and Hainanese. Particular favourites, apart from the universally known Cantonese *dim sum* and Peking duck, are the Hokkien noodle dishes, especially fried mee, Teochew porridge — a rice broth served with salted vegetables, salted eggs and salted fish — and *yong tau fu* which is stuffed beancurd and vegetables, Hakka-style. Another popular Chinese meal is the "steam boat." A pot of boiling water is placed in the centre of the table on top of a small stove. Raw meat, fish and vegetables are dipped in the water until cooked, leaving a good broth for the end of the meal.

Char Kuey Teow or fried flat noodles made from rice flour is another popular Chinese dish. These white noodles are flattened into strips and then cut into thin slices and fried with meat, prawns, cockles and eggs.

Indian cuisine, from northern tandoori dishes and Moghul-inspired curries to southern *dosai* and *murtabak* is widely available. To savour the true Indian delights, try eating the various curries and vegetables with rice using your fingers on a banana leaf. Be sure to ask for papadam, a crisp cracker, and pickles.

Thirst quenchers : after a hearty meal, try "*teh tarik*" which is tea prepared with a special milk and found in mostly Malay and Indian restaurants and stalls. The prepared tea is then transferred from one mug to the other by several "long pulls" to bring out the froth before finally being served.

The *sirap bandung* is another popular drink served mostly in Malay stalls and restaurants. This pink drink is made of rock sugar and red colouring. Condensed milk is then added along with a few cubes of ice before serving.

The *air batu campur* or "ABC" is a mound of ice shavings coated with either brown sugar or red syrup and heaped with colourful jelly cubes, red beans, sweet corn and Chinese black jelly.

Malay food varies according to the state from which it originates. In KL, one of the most popular restaurants is the **Yazmin** at Jalan Kia Peng. Diners are entertained daily with cultural shows incorporating traditional Malaysian folk dances and music. Northern Malay food at moderate prices is available at the **Rasa Utara** in Bukit Bintang. The **Matic Sri Saloma** at the Malaysian Information Tourist Complex in Jalan Ampang is a new restaurant serving commendable Malay food. Also worth a visit is the **Bunga Raya Restaurant** at the Putra World Trade Centre. The floating restaurant, **Nelayan** at Lake Titiwangsa serves buffet-style Malay food. The hawker centre at Kia Peng also serves Malay food along with Chinese and Thai food.

Hawker stalls serving Malay food can also be found at the Campbell Complex in Jalan Dang Wangi, the Medan Mara at Jalan Semaran and the Central Market.

For Nyonya — Straits cuisine essentially from Penang and Malacca — the **Dondang Sayang** at the Weld Supermarket in Jalan Raja Chulan is highly recommended as is the **Bon Ton** in Jalan Ampang. Another restaurant that serves Nyonya food is the **Nyonya Heritage** in Jalan Bukit Bintang.

For Thai food, the **Cili Padi** at the Mall is recommended as is the Sri **Chengmai** at Jalan Perak (behind the Equatorial hotel). Japanese and Korean restaurants too have made their mark in the city. The **Chikuyo-tei** in See Hoy Chan Plaza and the **Hoshigaoka** restaurant at the Mall in Jalan Putra both serve excellent Japanese food. Korean cuisine is available at the **Koryo-Won** in Antarabangsa Complex.

KL also boasts a wide variety of Indian restaurants. The **Omar Khayam** in Medan Tunku, **Bangles** in Jalan Tunku Abdul Rahman and the **Aladin** in Jalan Telawi, Bangsar, serve northern Indian cuisine. **Shiraz** in Medan Tunku serves an excellent mixture of north and south Indian food. The **Devi Annapoorna** also in Medan Tunku serves strictly vegetarian food. The **Hamid Shah** in Jalan Tengah specialises in **Indian-Muslim** food. Smaller Indian restaurants can be found in Leboh Ampang, Jalan Tun Sambanthan and Jalan Masjid India.

For those who like Chinese food there is plenty of choice. The **Chef** or **Rasa Sayang** in Naga Ria complex, Jalan Imbi is reputed to serve the best Peking duck. Another one of their specialities is **Beggar's Chicken**, cooked in Chinese herbs wrapped in clay before baking. The **Sze Chuan** in Jalan Sultan Ismail is worth a visit for their Sichuan smoked duck as is the **Misan** at the Holiday Inn City Centre. For those who enjoy seafood, head for the **Rainbow Palace** in Campbell Complex, Jalan Dang Wangi, and savour king prawns cooked in special sauce. Other restaurants serving commendable Chinese food are the **Happy Valley Seafood Restaurant** in Menara Promet, Jalan Sultan Ismail, the **Hakka Restaurant** in Jalan Bukit Bintang, the **Teochew Restaurant** in Jalan Changkat Thambi Dollah, the **Marco Polo** in Jalan Raja Chulan or the **Kum Leng** in Jalan Pudu.

The less pricey restaurants and hawker stalls can be found at the lower ground floor of Imbi Plaza, KL Plaza, Kota Raya Complex and Sungai Wang Complex.

Night life is not as tame as it used to be, but there is still nothing to match the sort of raunchy entertainment — if that is the word — offered in neighbouring Bangkok. Kuala Lumpur offers a wide choice of places for entertainment ranging from venues for cultural shows to the most active Western-style bars and discotheques. Hotels such as the **Shangri-La**, **Hilton**, **Holiday Inn**, **Parkroyal**, **Federal**, **Equatorial** and the **Saujana** provide good bands and vocalists, local and foreign. For those who want to dance the night away, there are numerous discotheques complete with laser beams and the latest sound techniques. The more popular discos are the **Tin Mine** at the Hilton hotel, **Faces** on Jalan Ampang, **Scandals** at the Kuala Lumpur Plaza, **Sapphire** at the Yow Chuan Plaza, **Factory** at the junction of Jalan Sultan Ismail and Jalan Ampang, **Miami** in Jalan Conlay and **Piccadilly** in Damansara Jaya.

For those who prefer a slower evening, there are some good bars and lounges which offer jazz, country and western and rock music. **Blue Moon** at the Equatorial, **7th Avenue** at Apera ULG and **Betelnut** in Jalan Pinang all offer golden oldies. The **Longhorn** in Damansara Utama, **Cee Jay's** in Lorong P. Ramlee and **Silverado** in Jalan Kia Peng offer country and western music. The **Ship** in Damansara Utama, **Bull's Head** in the Central Market and the **Traffic Lights** in Jalan Sultan Ismail all offer a wide variety of music. For those who enjoy jazz, head for the **Riverbank** at the Central Market or **All That Jazz** at section 19 in Petaling Jaya. **The Hard Rock Cafe** in Taman Tun Ismail offers what its name suggests.

Lately, karaoke "sing it yourself" lounges have become very popular. **The Karaoke Evergreen Lounge** in Kuala Lumpur Plaza and the **Ritz Karaoke** in Nagaria Complex are just two of several such spots for this sort of entertainment.

For those who enjoy traditional arts, there are several cultural show venues in Kuala Lumpur. The **Central Market**, the **Sulaiman Court**, the **City Hall Auditorium** and the **Malay Theatre Restaurant** all feature cultural shows.

From huge department stores to colourful bazaars shopping in KL is a unique experience. Local handicraft items from the east coast and Sabah and Sarawak are all to be found in the capital.

The major shopping centres in KL are situated along **Jalan Tunku Abdul Rahman**, **Jalan Raja Chulan**, **Jalan Petaling**, **Jalan Bukit Bintang** and **Jalan Ampang**. Most prices are fixed and department stores and shopping complexes display price tags, but you may bargain at the smaller retail outlets and roadside stalls.

Along **Jalan Chow Kit**, watch out for woven *mengkuang* (pandanus leaves plaited into bags, hats, etc.). Small shops situated along the byways and lanes off Jalan Tunku Abdul Rahman sell many made-to-order products at very reasonable prices. For genuine Indian saris, go to **Jalan Masjid India**. For pewter the best outlet is **Selangor Pewter** at 231, Jalan Tunku Abdul Rahman, which has a worldwide reputation for quality. Along Jalan Tun Perak is the showroom of **Batik Malaysia**, where a wide range of batik and songket fabrics are available. If you are short of time and want everything under one roof, go to **Karyaneka**, the Malaysian Handicraft Centre at Jalan Raja Chulan or **Infokraft** in the Sultan Abdul Samad Building in Jalan Sultan Hishamuddin.

Dozens of shops and boutiques selling everything from household utensils to jewellery, fashion wear and fabrics can be found in the **Bukit Bintang Plaza**, **Sungai Wang Plaza**, The **KL Plaza**, **The Mall**, **The Weld**, **City Square**, **Kota Raya Complex**, **Ampang Park** and **Yow Chuan Plaza**. The **Central Market** is renowned for its comprehensive array of traditional ware such as handicraft and batik.

For jewellery, **P. H. Hendry** in Jalan Tunku Abdul Rahman has long been established as a leading jeweller as is **K. M. Oli** in Yow Chuan Plaza. Smaller shops can be found in Lebuh Ampang.

The cosmopolitan city of Penang has always been a favourite shopping place for tourists. Shops in **Jalan Penang**, **Lebuh Campbell**, **Lebuh Pitt**, **Lebuh Chulia** and **Lebuh Pantai** all cater for a variety of tastes.

The **Chowrasta** market is a typical bazaar for local items. The **KOMTAR** building too, houses various shops and boutiques which is worth a visit.

Tourists wishing to buy precious stones are strongly advised to purchase them only from established outlets. Be very wary of road-side vendors selling "precious stones" as they are very often fakes.

Storch Borthers in Wisma Stephens, **Sena H** in Hotel Shangri-La, **Selberan** in Kuala Lumpur Plaza, **La Putri** in Ampang shopping complex and **De Silva** in Kuala Lumpur Plaza are all very reputable outlets and sell precious and semi-precious stones.

Spectator sports in Malaysia include soccer, rugby, hockey, cricket, badminton and horse-racing which is held throughout the year, with meetings on weekends and public holidays; race weekends rotate between KL, Ipoh, Penang and the neighbouring country of Singapore.

Game hunting is still permitted under certain limitations: details can be obtained by writing to the Director-General, Wild Life and National Park Department, Block K 20, Government Bldg, Jalan Duta, Kuala Lumpur. Inland fishing requires a licence.

There are a number of golf courses across the country and permission to play (on the payment of green fees) is usually granted by the club secretary. Sets of clubs can be hired at the larger establishments.

Traditional Malay sports have been given a boost in the country since independence in 1957. One of them is sepak raga which is elevated to an international level when Malaysia meets neighbouring Indonesia, Thailand, Singapore or the Philippines. Using what closely resembles a badminton court with a high net, youths lob, drive and smash a light rattan ball using principally their feet. The rest of the body, except the forearms and hands, is also used. Scoring rules resemble those of badminton. Main gasing (top spinning) is a popular pastime, even with adults, as is main wau (kite flying).

Silat (Malay martial art) is a fighting technique with or without weapons. Unarmed demonstrations of the movements are as graceful as ballet performances and are a common sight at weddings and other feasts. The sport is very popular in rural areas.

Addresses

Kuala Lumpur

Malaysian Futures Clearing Corp., 4/F, Citypoint, Dayabumi Complex, Jalan Sultan Hishamuddin, 50050 Kuala Lumpur. Tel: 2936611; Fax: 2748370.

The Kuala Lumpur Commodity Exchange, 4/F, Citypoint, Dayabumi Complex, Jalan Sultan Hishamuddin, 50050 Kuala Lumpur. Tel: 2936822; Fax: 2742215.

The Kuala Lumpur Stock Exchange, 3 & 4/F, Block A, Bukit Naga Complex, Off Jalan Semantan, Damansara Heights, 50490 Kuala Lumpur. Tel: 2546433; Fax: 2557463.

Associated Chinese Chamber of Commerce & Industry of Malaysia, G/F, Selangor Chinese Assembly Hall, 1 Jalan Maharajalela, 50150 Kuala Lumpur. Tel: 2380278; Fax: 2383670.

Associated Indian Chamber of Commerce & Industry, 116, 1/F, Jalan Tunku Abdul Rahman, 50100 Kuala Lumpur. Tel: 2924817; Fax: 2911670.

Federation of Malaysian Manufacturers, 17/F, Wisma Sime Darby, Jalan Raja Laut, 50350 Kuala Lumpur. Tel: 2931244; Fax: 2935105.

Malay Chamber of Commerce & Industry Malaysia, 17/F, Tower Block, Plaza Pekeliling, Jalan Tun Razak, 50400 Kuala Lumpur. Tel: 4427664; Fax: 4414502.

Malaysian International Chamber of Commerce & Industry, 10/F, Wisma Damansara, Jalan Semantan, 50490 Kuala Lumpur. Tel: 2541690; Fax: 2554946.

National Chamber of Commerce & Industry Malaysia, 17/F, Plaza Pekeliling, Jalan Tun Razak, 50400 Kuala Lumpur. Tel: 4429871; Fax: 4416043.

Tourist Development Corp. of Malaysia, 24-27/F, Menara Dato Onn, Putra World Trade Centre, Jalan Tun Ismail, 50480 Kuala Lumpur. Tel: 2935188.

Johor

Tourist Development Corp., Rm 1-3, 2/F, Tun Abdul Razak Complex, Jalan Ah Fook, 80000 Johor Bahru. Tel: 223590.

State Tourist Promotion Office, Sultan Ibrahim Bldg, Jalan Bukit Timbalan, 80000 Johor Bahru. Tel: 241957.

Kelantan

Kelantan Tourist Association, D149 Jalan Bayam, 15200 Kota Bahru, Kelantan. Tel: 794207.

Malacca

Malacca Tourist Information Centre, Jalan Kota, 75000 Malacca. Tel: 236538.

Perak

Perak Tourist Information Centre, Jalan Dewan, 30000 Ipoh, Perak. Tel: 532800.

Pahang

Pahang Tourist Information Centre, Teruntum Complex, Jalan Mahkota, 25000 Kuantan, Pahang. Tel: 505566.

Penang

Tourist Development Corp., Jalan Tun Syed Sheh Barakbah, 10200 Penang. Tel: 620066.

Sabah

Tourist Development Corp., G/F, Wisma Wing On Life, Lorong Sagunting, 88000 Kota Kinabalu, Sabah. Tel: 211698.

Sarawak

Tourist Development Corp., 4/F AIA Bldg, Jalan Song Thian Cheok, 93100 Kuching, Sarawak. Tel: 246575.

At any Tourist Developement Corp. office and Information Centre, visitors will be able to get brochures on the various states in Malaysia. The larger bookshops and hotels too stock up very good guide books.

Malaysia's crowded festival calendar reflects the multi-cultural character of the country: Malay, Chinese, Indian, Kadazan, Dayak and Western holidays (among others) are all celebrated.

Most occasions are determined by the lunar calendar and fall at different times each year. In Malaysia, when a holiday falls on a Sunday, the following Monday is a public holiday.

January: January 1, New Year's Day (a public holiday except in the states of Johor, Kedah, Kelantan, Perlis and Trengganu).

January-February: Chinese New Year. National public holiday. On the eve of this festival, Chinese families hold reunion dinners followed by the firing of fireworks to ward off evil spirits. Lion and dragon dances are held to welcome the New Year and **ang pows** (a gift of money in red packets) are given by married couples and elders to the young and unmarried.

Taipusam: Public holiday in Penang, Negri Sembilan, Perak and Selangor. Hindu celebration of Lord Subramaniam's birth, marked by rites of penitence. Devotees carry kavadis, or wooden frames decorated with flowers. Some have long needles stuck into their backs and chests, or skewers pushed through their tongues and cheeks.

March: Awal Ramadan. Public holiday in Johor. The first day of the fasting month for Muslims.

April: Hari Raya Puasa. National public holiday. The end of the fasting month. Muslims usher the day by performing prayers in mosques and feasting at home.

Good Friday: State holiday in Sabah and Sarawak.

May: May 1 Labour Day. Public holiday.

Wesak Day. National public holiday. Commemorate the birth, enlightenment and Nirvana of Lord Buddha. Buddhists go to temples throughout the country offering incense, josssticks and prayers.

May 30: Holiday in Sabah and Federal Territory of Labuan. Harvest Festival in Sabah is celebrated to mark the end of the harvest season. The colourful celebrations include the traditional Kadazan dance, the **Sumazau**. Much of the merry-making arises from drinking of tapai (rice wine).

June: June 1 and 2, state holiday in Sarawak. Dayak festival celebrates the end of a successful harvest. For the Dayaks of Sarawak, this is a major festival celebrated with much drinking of rice wine and dancing especially the Dayak warrior dance.

First Wednesday in June: National public holiday. Birthday of His Majesty The Yang di-Pertuan Agung.

The feast of San Pedro (St Peter), patron saint of fishermen, in celebrated at the Portuguese settlement in Malacca. The traditional blessing of fishing boats, which are colourfully decorated for the festival, is held and prayers are offered for a good season. Not a public or state holiday.

July: Hari Raya Haji. National public holiday. Marks the 10th day of Zulhijjah, the 12th month of the Islamic calendar when pilgrims perform their Haj in Mecca. Prayers are held and goats and cows are sacrificed and the meat distributed to the poor.

Maal Hijrah (formerly called Awal Muharram). National public holiday. Marks the beginning of the Muslim calendar.

Turtle festival, held in Trengganu to celebrate the annual return of the giant leatherback turtles who come to lay their eggs on the beach. Not a holiday.

August: August 12, National Day marking the independence from British rule. National public holiday. Parades, concerts and firework displays are held.

October: Birthday of Prophet Muhammad (National public holiday).

October-November: Deepavali. Public holiday except in Sabah and Sarawak. The Hindu festival of lights. Hindu homes are decorated with little flames on small silver platters. In some homes, the womenfolk draw intricate designs called Kolam on the floors.

December: December 25, Christmas Day. National public holiday.

Malayan Banking Bhd, 100 Jalan Tun Perak, 50050 Kuala Lumpur. Tel: 2308833; Fax: 2304027.

Bank Bumiputra Malaysia Bhd, Menara Bumiputra, Jalan Melaka, 50100 Kuala Lumpur. Tel: 2981011; Fax: 2934667.

United Malayan Banking Corp., Bangunan UMBC, Jalan Sultan Sulaiman, 50000 Kuala Lumpur. Tel: 2309866; Fax: 2322627.

Public Bank Bhd, Bangunan Public Bank, Jalan Sultan Sulaiman, 50000 Kuala Lumpur. Tel: 2741766; Fax: 2742179.

The Hongkong and Shanghai Banking Corp., Leboh Ampang, 50100 Kuala Lumpur. Tel: 2300744; Fax: 2301146.

Standard Chartered Bank, Jalan Ampang, 50450 Kuala Lumpur. Tel: 2326555; Fax : 2383295.

DISCOVERING MALAYSIA

KUALA LUMPUR

Named after its site at the junction of the Kelang and Gombak rivers, Kuala Lumpur (muddy estuary) dates from 1859 as a settlement of Chinese tin miners. With high-rise buildings creeping closer to the Lake Gardens, the city today is far more than a river junction town. Kuala Lumpur is not just the capital city of the country but is the heart and soul of the country and is a major tourist destination in its own right.

The city centre lies astride the Kelang river. Situated at the junction of the Kelang and Gombak rivers is the **Masjid Jame (Jame Mosque)**. Built in traditional Arabian style, complete with intricately designed domes and minarets, the mosque nestles within a grove of coconut palms. The old section is in the south with its collection of Chinese-type shops spilling over onto the streets. It merges to the north with the newer section where there are many banks and commercial offices. But the growth is no longer confined to the central region. Many high-rise buildings are appearing further away from the centre.

From Masjid Jame proceeding south and across the Gombak river is the **Sultan Abdul Samad Building** which is elaborately Moorish in design. Built in 1894-97, this impressive structure stands with its 41-m clocktower amid curving arches and domes and currently houses offices and courts of the Malaysian judiciary. Across from this building is the **Merdeka**

Penang bridge: world's third longest.

Photo: Veronica Garbutt

Square located on what used to be known as the Selangor Club Padang (field).

On the other side of the square is the very British Selangor Club. From the club, it is a pleasant walk of about 3.5 km to the **Muzium Negara** on Jalan Damansara. The museum, provides an excellent introduction to Malaysian culture. Two murals of Italian mosaic tiles flank the main entrance, depicting the history and customs of the Malaysians. Still south of the city is the **Railway Station**. Built in 1911, the building with its domes, arches and pillars reflects a Moorish style of architecture.

The Malayan Railways Headquarters Building opposite is also of Islamic design. Next to this is the old colonial building which was once the Majestic Hotel. It is now the **National Art Gallery** and contains a permanent collection by Malaysian artists. A short walk from the Railway Station will bring you to the **Masjid Negara** (National Mosque), one of the largest mosques in Southeast Asia. Surrounded by green lawns and ornamented with pools and fountains, it is built in traditional Muslim decorative style. A 73-m-high minaret rises from the centre of the pool and the mosque is crowned by an unusual shell-shaped dome. Visitors may enter this mosque, though shoes must be removed and women wear must be covered — a covering garment is provided by the attendants.

Roughly 1 km from the mosque is the **Central Market**, a former wet-market and now an arts and crafts centre. It is renowned for its comprehensive array of traditional ware such as handicraft and batik and its excellent food outlets which include an authentic English pub.

From Masjid Jame, heading southeast will bring you to the old section of the town. At the junction of Jalan Maharajalela and Jalan Stadium is the interesting old **Chan See Shu Yuen Temple**. Erected in 1906 and of typical Chinese design, this temple is made up of courtyards and pavilions and surrounded by sculptures depicting the Taoist faith. Immediately behind this temple is the Chinwoo Stadium and up a small hill nearby is the Stadium Merdeka and the indoor Stadium Negara. In this old section of the town is also the **Sri Mahamariaman Temple**, a Hindu temple which boasts a very elaborate decorative scheme which incorporates gold, precious stones and a mixture of clay and attractive tiles. Built in 1873, it is one of the largest and most ornate of such temples in Malaysia. Kuala Lumpur's Chinatown is just around the corner in Jalan Petaling where one can buy almost anything from herbs and medicines to cheap designer watches and clothes. At night this stretch of the road is closed to traffic and becomes one long street market.

Southwest of Masjid Jame is Brickfields

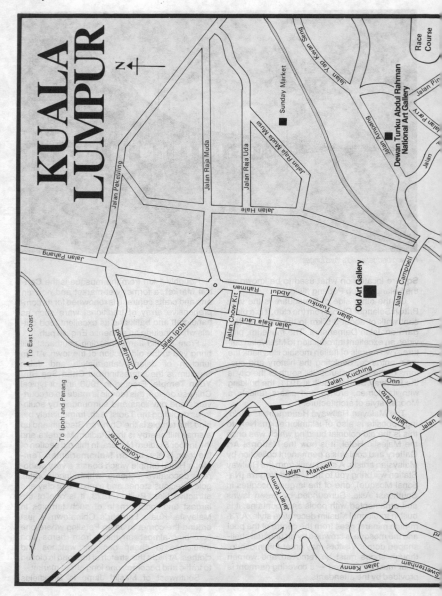

KUALA LUMPUR

N

To East Coast

To Ipoh and Penang

Jalan Pekeliling

Jalan Pahang

Jalan Raja Muda

Jalan Raja Uda

Jalan Raja Muda Musa

Jalan Hale

Sunday Market

Jalan Yap Kwan Seng

Dewan Tunku Abdul Rahman
National Art Gallery

Race
Course

Jalan Pin

Jalan Par V

Jalan Ampang

Jalan

Circular Road

Jalan Ipoh

Jalan Chow Kit

Jalan Tuanku Abdul Rahman

Jalan Raja Laut

Old Art Gallery

Jalan Campbell

Kolam Ayer

Jalan Kuching

Onn

Dato

Jalan

Jalan Maxwell

Jalan Kenny

Jalan Swettenham

Jalan Kenny

148

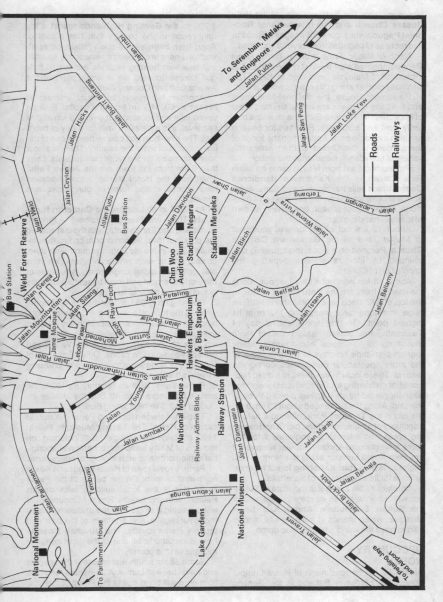

where in Jalan Tun Sambanthan are the **Holy Rosary Church** and the **International Buddhist Pagoda** which contains images of Buddha and replicas of pagodas from several countries.

North of Masjid Jame is Jalan Tunku Abdul Rahman, named after the first prime minister of independent Malaysia, who died in 1990. The Saturday market along this road is worth a visit.

Parliament House, the National Monument and the Lake Gardens are all situated West of Masjid Jame. The lake Gardens include a butterfly farm and deer park. Facilities for boating are also available here. Located on the fringe of the gardens is the Orchid Garden where the variety of orchids will mesmerise the visitor.

Proceeding East from Masjid Jame on Jalan Raja Chulan is the **Karyaneka Handicraft Centre** which sells traditional handicrafts. Apart from a showroom, the centre comprises 14 traditional Malay houses, each one selling its own respective handicrafts.

About 12 km out of city centre, southeast of Masjid Jame is the **Getsamani Catholic Church**. Perched on a slope, this church is surrounded by life-size statues depicting the cruxifiction of Christ.

About 13 km north of Kuala Lumpur, along the road to Ipoh, are the **Batu Caves** where, at the top of 272 steps, is a Hindu shrine within a huge limestone cave measuring 112 m at its highest point. On the Hindu festival day of Taipusam the caves are crowded with thousands of devotees and tourists. Many tourists plan their holidays to witness some of the more spectacular ceremonies during the festival. These include devotees in a deep hypnotic trance bearing a kavadi, which is a wooden alter supported by steel spikes pierced through the skin. Along the same road about 23 km from the city is the **Templer Park**, offering a natural sanctuary of jungle, waterfalls, picnic and camping areas and interesting jungle treks for the more adventurous. Another popular reserve 22 km from Kuala Lumpur along the North-South Highway is the **Lipur Kanching** forest reserve, famous for its seven levels of waterfalls.

South of Kuala Lumpur is the state of Selangor with Shah Alam as its state capital, site of the **Sultan Salahuddin Abdul Aziz Shah Mosque**, which stands in a 15-ha site, and is said to have the world's largest blue dome.

UPCOUNTRY
NORTH

Almost 52 km by road north of Kuala Lumpur across the border in Pahang is the Genting Highlands. Set in the finest mountain country at 1,700 m, the **Genting Highlands resort** is the only resort in the country that has a casino. Apart from international-class hotels, other attractions here are a theatre restaurant, an artificial lake with boating facilities and an 18-hole golf course located on a lower plain at the Awana Golf and Country Club.

Another hill resort of equal interest is **Fraser's Hill**, 105 km from the capital. Built on seven hills and located just over 1.5 km above sea level, it is a pleasant spot for a day or two's rest. The nine-hole golf course here is one of the few public courses in the country. There is also a sports complex for the health enthusiasts. Less than 5 km from the town are the **Jeriau Falls**. Apart from the **Hotel Merlin**, accommodation here comes in the form of bungalows and chalets.

At 1,524-m altitude are the **Cameron Highlands**. There are three districts here — Ringlet, Brinchang and Tanah Rata, with the last-named the principal town. Accommodation facilities include hotels in the old English country-inn style, chalets and government resthouses. One may play golf, walk along jungle paths, see some of the world's largest and most beautiful butterflies or just relax in the cool fresh air.

North again — 65 km from the town of Tapah, which is the turn-off point for the Cameron Highlands on the main north-south highway — is the town of Ipoh, capital of Perak state. Approaching through the surrounding Kinta Valley, you will see open-cast tin mines. Only 6 km north of Ipoh, in the huge limestone caves of **Gunung Tasek** is the Buddhist temple.

Perak Tong. Built as recently as 1926, the temple has more than 40 Buddha statues including a 12.8-m-high sitting Buddha.

Taiping, between Ipoh and Penang is the old capital of Perak. The Taiping Museum, built in 1883, contains interesting exhibits including collections of Malay weapons, ornaments, aboriginal implements and archaeological specimens.

Perak's royal town of Kuala Kangsar is 48 km northwest of Ipoh. On the banks of the Perak River stands the local sultan's **Iskandariah Palace**, with the nearby Royal Museum. Built without using a single nail, the museum houses the royal regalia, and artefacts of the past and present Perak royalty. **The Ubudiah Mosque** here is reputed to be one of the most beautiful mosques in the country.

Some 88 km southwest of Ipoh is the seaport and naval base of Lumut. A 30-minute ferry ride from here will bring you to the Pangkor Islands, which sport three resorts — Puteri Dewi Beach, Coral Bay and Pasir Bogak Beach. Water sports facilities are aplenty at these resorts. The Coral Bay is especially well known for its swimming, snorkelling and diving.

Further north up the west coast of the Malayan peninsula is Butterworth and adjacent — across a mile of water spanned by the world's third-longest bridge — **Penang**. First established as a British trading post in 1786 this "Pearl of the Orient" — possibly the first of several places now claiming that title — is one of the major commercial and trading centres in Malaysia. The island bustles with all the activity of a metropolitan city and is famed for its picturesque beaches.

Fort Cornwallis marks the spot where Francis Light, the founder of Penang, landed. The present structure dates from 1810. **St George's Church** in Farquhar Street was built in 1818 and is the oldest Anglican Church in Southeast Asia. It features lofty spires and white columns rising from a marble floor. Along Pitt St is the **Kuan Yin (Goddess of Mercy) Temple** built in 1800 by the first Chinese settlers on the island. The temple's roof is carved with ornamental dragons. Also in Pitt St is the oldest of the places of worship — the **Kapitan Kling**

Tanjong Huma
Muka Head
Tanjong Bungah
P. Tikus
Tanjong Tokong
1 2 3 4 5 6 7
Batu Feringgi
Telok Bahang
Tanjong Kalok
Western Hill
Waterfall Gardens
GEORGETOWN
Penang Hill
Kg. Pantai
Ferry to Butterworth
Race Course
AYER ITAM
Sungai Pinang
Jelutong
Kg. Batu Uban
Balik Pulau
S. Nibong
Ginting
S. Ara
P. Betong
Tanjong Masari
Bagan
P. Betong
Telok Kumbar
Bayan Lepas
P. Jerejak
Airport
P. Aman
Gertak Sanggul
Tanjong Gertak Sanggul
Kg. Telok Tempoyak Besar
P. Rimau
P. Kendi
PENANG
N

1 Bayview Hotel
2 Casuarina Beach Hotel
3 Holiday Inn
4 Lone Pine Hotel
5 Golden Sands Hotel
6 Palm Beach Hotel
7 Rasa Sayang Hotel

Mosque of Indian-Moorish architecture, built in 1786.

Situated in Lorong Burmah is the **Wat Chayamangkalaram**, a magnificent Buddhist temple which houses the world's third-largest reclining Buddha, measuring 33 m.

A visit to the Snake Temple is a must. Probably the only one of its kind in the world. Venomous pit vipers coil around the altars and other parts of the temple but never seem to strike.

For a panoramic view of the island, a visit to **Penang Hill** is recommended. The journey to the 821-m summit by funicular railway is not to be missed. Ayer Hitam, at the foot of Penang Hill, is the site of the **Kek Lok Si Temple**, the largest Buddhist temple in Malaysia and one of the finest in Southeast Asia, reflecting Chinese, Thai and Burmese influence.

Another place of interest is the Butterfly Farm in Teluk Bahang, claimed to be the world's first tropical live butterfly farm. For beach lovers, head to **Batu Ferringgi** in the extreme north of Penang and its main resort.

The **Langkawi** group of islands, further north, off the coast of Kedah state, is a formation of 99 islands, most of them uninhabited. The attractions include scuba-diving, boating, golf, tennis, trekking, and bird and butterfly watching. The clear waters off the island are rich with coral and marine life. Access to Langkawi is by plane from Kuala Lumpur or Penang and also by ferry from Kuala Kedah. It can also be reached from Singapore.

SOUTH

Just 150 km south of Kuala Lumpur is **Malacca**, one of the oldest towns in the country. This historic state was founded in 1403 and had been colonised by the Portuguese, the Dutch and the British until (then) Malaya obtained its independence in 1957. Each rule left its mark in the architecture of the various historical buildings that still stand to this day.

One of the major tourist attractions is the old Portuguese fortress **A Farmosa**. This fort was built in 1511 to protect the Portuguese from other invaders. During the Dutch attack it was badly damaged and in 1670 the Dutch renamed it as the "Voc" after repairing it. In 1807 the walls were demolished by the British when they occupied the then Dutch settlement.

During the reign of the Portuguese, Christianity became prevalent with the visit of St Francis Xavier. The leading Catholic church was built in 1521. Originally known as Duarte Coelho, the Dutch renamed the church **St Paul's**. In 1753 the Dutch converted St Paul's Hill into a burial ground. Huge tombstones with Latin and Portuguese inscriptions can still be found. The open grave in St Paul was where St Francis Xavier was buried before his body was moved to Goa.

The Church of St Peter dating from 1710 is now the **Church of the Portuguese Mission**. This is the only church in Malaysia which contains a life-size alabaster statue of "The Dead Lord Before The Resurrection." The other significant old church in the town, the **Christ Church** next to the Stadthuys (town hall), is a fine example of Dutch architecture. The handmade pews here are more than 200 years old. The brass bible rest dates from 1773. Still visible on the church floor are tombstones in Armenian script.

The **Stadthuys** is the oldest example of Dutch architecture in the East, dating from between 1641 and 1660. It now houses government offices. The town's museum, housed in a lovely 300-year-old Dutch building, displays articles (clothing, weapons and coins, etc) from the different periods of Malacca's history. St John's Fort, to the east of the town, gives a good view of the surrounding area. **The Bukit Cina** (Hill of the Chinese) is said to be the settlement of the first Chinese to arrive in the area. They came to the country as part of the entourage of Princess Hang Li Poh, who was given as a bride to Sultan Mansur Shah (1459-88). The only private museum in Malaysia, **Baba Nyonya Heritage** is at Jalan Tun Tan Cheng Lock. **Jalan Hang Jebat**, formerly known as Jonker St, is the place to visit for antiques.

About 3 km from the town centre at Ujong Pasir is the **Portuguese Settlement**, were authentic Portuguese food can be found and local cultural shows are performed every Saturday night in the Portuguese Square.

Just 15 km out of Malacca town is the Mini Malaysia cultural village in **Air Keroh**, where the various states of Malaysia are represented by 13 state houses. These houses also contain works of art and culture. Next to Mini Malaysia is the **Air Keroh Country Resort**. Set amid a splendid green environment, the country club has one of Asia's best 18-hole golf courses.

South of Malacca, the road passes through pleasant coconut palm groves and traditional Malay houses. The towns of Muar and Batu Pahat are passed en route to **Johor Baru** on the southernmost tip of the Malay Peninsula, next to

Trengganu fishing village.

Photo: Tourist Development Corp.

Singapore. Johor Baru is the administrative and royal capital of the state of Johor. The town's notable buildings include the government offices on a commanding hill overlooking the causeway and providing a panaromic view of Singapore island and the surrounding seas. The **Istana Besar** (Principal Palace) in Jalan Tun Dr Ismail was built in 1866. The beautiful gardens of the Istana cover 53 ha, providing an excellent relaxing place for picnics. Near the Istana Besar overlooking the Straits of Johor is the **Sultan Abu Bakar Mosque** built in 1900.

About 56 km north of Johor Baru is a 32-m waterfall known as the **Kota Tinggi** waterfall. A popular spot for local and foreign visitors, it has several Swiss-type chalets for visitors wishing to spend the night. **Desaru**, the "Village of Casuarinas," approximately 96 km northeast of Johor Baru, has more than 25 km of unspoilt beaches. It offers all kinds of sports from snorkelling, swimming and canoeing to jungle trekking.

There are several off-shore tourist resort islands in Johor and the better known ones are **Pulau Rawa, Pulau Sibu Besar** and **Pulau Besar**. All are ideal places for snorkelling, scuba diving and other sea sports. Accommodation is available in chalets. For more information contact the Tourist Centre in Mersing at 07-791204.

EAST COAST

The east coast of Peninsular Malaysia is a Malay stronghold; the Chinese and Indians have encroached very little. Here the markets are effectively run by the Malay women while on the west coast business is still a Chinese concern.

The people of the east coast are more conservative than those in the more outward looking states along the Straits of Malacca; the Muslim faith is stronger and the traditional Malay village customs are largely retained. The settled areas are mainly in the coastal regions, though there are pockets of settlements in the less rugged inland valleys. In the north of Kelantan state, next to the Thai border, there is a noticeable Thai-Buddhist element.

It is easy to fly from KL and Penang to the state capitals of **Kuantan, Kuala Trengganu** and **Kota Baru**. There is also a good road from KL to Kuantan, although the coastal roads from Kuantan north can be poor in the monsoon season.

Kuantan is the capital of Pahang, the largest state in Peninsular Malaysia and the original home of cottage industries such as batik and silver-making. Only 5 km from Kuantan is **Teluk Chempedak**, an excellent beach for activities like sailing, surfing, skiing and sunbathing. About 15 km north of Kuantan is the **Balok**

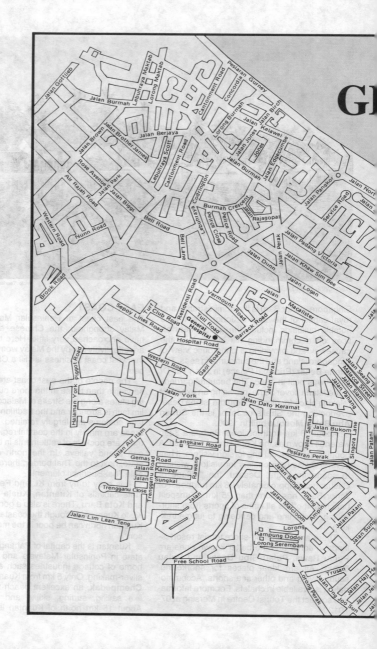

G

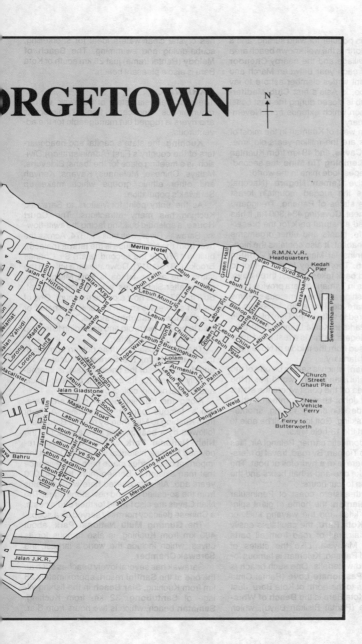

beach, which is popular for wind surfing, and a further 32 km north is the well known beach area of **Cherating** village and the nearby **Chendor Beach**, where each year between March and September giant turtles clamber ashore to lay eggs. Here, too, is Asia's first **Club Mediterranee**. The club is closed during the east coast monsoon season which extends from November to mid-January.

About 25 km west of Kuantan in the midst of tropical forests are the million-years-old limestone **Charah Caves**, and 49 km from Kuantan is the **Sungei Lembing Tin Mine**, the second-largest and deepest lode mine in the world.

The extensive **Taman Negara** (National Park) straddles the rugged mountain forest land where the states of Pahang, Trengganu and Kelantan meet. Covering 434,300 ha, it has been designated a natural park for the preservation of wildlife, plants and other organisms in their natural habitat. It also contains the highest peak in Peninsular Malaysia, the 2,190-m **Gunung Tahan**. The journey from the foot to the summit and back takes at least three days. The many rivers in Taman Negara provide pleasant spots for fishing and the numerous streams and waterfalls are ideal for a dip. Intending visitors are required to write to the Dept of Wildlife and National Parks in Kuala Lumpur before visiting Taman Negara as this is a restricted area. The park is closed from the middle of November to the middle of January.

Pulau Tioman, which is said to be one of the ten most beautiful islands in the world, lies in the South China Sea off the coast where the states of Pahang and Johor share a common border. Facilities include skin-diving, fishing, snorkelling and water skiing. Golf lovers will be able to enjoy a game at the 18-hole links.

Malaysia's domestic carrier, Pelangi Air, flies daily from KL to Tioman. By road, travel to Mersing and from there take a hydrofoil or boat. The hydrofoil will take one-and-a-half hours and the boat trip lasts up to four hours.

On the north-eastern coast of Peninsular Malaysia is **Kelantan**, the home of giant spinning tops and kites and the wayang kulit, or shadow play. **Kota Baru**, the capital, is easily accessible by air, rail or road from all parts of Peninsular Malaysia. Like the states of Trengganu and Pahang, Kelantan is famous for its beaches and waterfalls. One such beach is the **Beach of Passionate Love** (Pantai Cinta Berahi), 10 kms to the north of Kota Baru. Just 58 km east of Kota Baru is the **Beach of Whispering Breeze** (Pantai Bisikan Bayu), which

has crystal clear waters ideal for snorkelling, scuba-diving and swimming. The **Beach of Melody** (Pantai Irama) just 25 km south of Kota Baru is also a pleasant beach.

SARAWAK

The east Malaysian state of Sarawak, with its mountainous landscape, tropical rainforests and rivers is rugged but manageable for the adventurous.

Kuching, the state's capital and headquarters of the country's First (Administration) Division, is a meeting place for the Ibans, Bidayuhs, Malays, Chinese, Melanaus, Kayans, Kenyah and other ethnic groups which make up Sarawak's population.

As the entry point for visitors to Sarawak, Kuching has many attractions. The **Court House**, a splendid building facing the swift-flowing Sarawak River, was built in 1874. Across the river from the courthouse is the **Istana** (palace), built in 1870 by the second rajah, Sir Charles Brooke (1870-1917). Downstream a little on the same side as the Istana is **Fort Margherita**, named after Sir Charles' wife, Ranee Margaret. Built in 1878, it is now a police museum. One of the fort's towers is known as "bilik antu pala," or the **chamber of laughing skulls**. The skulls are said to be 200 years old and according to legend they emit human laughter.

The state mosque with its golden dome is in the heart of town. The **Sarawak Museum**, reputed to be one of the finest in Asia, is internationally known for its excellent archaeological and natural history collections.

Along the Kuching-Serian road are Sarawak's famous pepper plantations. A flight from Kuching to Miri, then by road to Batu Niah, followed by a boat trip will take a visitor to the **Niah National Park**, which has caves renowned for their historical wonders. One of the important discoveries made here was evidence that man existed in Borneo more than 40,000 years ago. Also discovered here were remains from the so-called old and new stone ages. The Niah Caves are also famed for their bird's nests, a Chinese delicacy normally served as a soup.

The **Gunung Mulu National Park**, about 480 km from Kuching, is also famous for its caves, which include the world's largest, the **Sarawak Chamber**.

Sarawak has several lovely beaches such as the one at the **Santini** resort, approximately 28 km from Kuching, **Siar Beach** in the fishing village of **Santubong**, 32 km from Kuching, **Sematan** beach, which is two hours from Siar, and the **Penyok** and **Bandong** beaches, 4 km north of Santubong.

A major attraction in Sarawak is the **Iban longhouses** — community dwellings constructed of ironwood, roofed with palm leaves and standing on stilts, mainly along river-banks. They may be seen by taking a trip upstream along the Sarawak River.

SABAH

Sabah, also in east Malaysia, is known as the Land Below The Wind. It is endowed with jungles and mountains and has one of the world's largest rainforests. Its colourful native culture and natural attractions have made tourism a major revenue earner of this state.

The state's capital, **Kota Kinabalu**, is a relatively new town equipped with the latest facilities and amenities of modern living. The city's gold-domed **state mosque** is three miles from town in the direction of the airport. The **Sabah Museum** offers a rich collection of artefacts reflecting Sabah's cultural and anthropological history, including a collection of tools used by the early men of Borneo. Also displayed are some of Sabah's unique animals, birds, reptiles and fish. At Gaya Street on Sunday mornings there is an **open air market** known as "Tamu." The natives of Sabah gather to buy and sell their handicrafts, traditional wares and food items or barter their farm produce.

A mile from the town centre is the **Tanjung Aru Beach** lined with palm and casuarina trees along its soft fine sand. Half an hour's drive from Kota Kinabalu is the picturesque **Mengkabong Water Village**, where the houses are built on stilts over the sea.

One of the most popular marine parks in Malaysia is the **Tuanku Abdul Rahman National Park**, comprising five islands. The islands — Gaya, Sapi, Mamutik, Manken and Suluk — are 10-25 minutes away from Kota Kinabalu by speedboat. Coral formations and colourful marine life teem in the clear waters surrounding the islands, especially Mamutik and Suluk where rare corals can be found.

Just 77 km from Kota Kinabalu lies **Kota Belud**, home of Bajau horsemen. On festive days Bajau cowboys — skilled horsemen noted for their flamboyant dress — parade on horses. One of the biggest and most colourful tamus — open air markets — is found here where the Bajaus and Kadazans gather to buy and sell their local goods.

The **Kinabalu National Park**, 93 km from Kota Kinabalu, was conceived as a World War II memorial in honour of the men who died in what is known as the "death march." The march, which took 11 months, began in September 1944 when the Japanese moved 2,400 Allied prisoners of war to the foothills of Mt Kinabalu. The park is now a paradise for nature lovers and bird watchers. It is also the home of the world's largest flower, the Rafflesia, a reddish orange flower with large petals.

Towering majestically 4,101 m above the park, South-east Asia's highest peak, **Mt Kinabalu**, is regarded by the Kadazan people as the resting place of the dead. Its craggy, saw-tooth summit jutting above the steaming jungle clouds is an awe-inspiring sight.

It is possible, with transport arranged to and from the base camp, to leave Kota Kinabalu, climb the mountain and be back in Kota Kinabalu in two hectic days. If, on the other hand, you are dependent on public transport to and from the mountain, you must allow four days for the excursion: day one from Kota Kinabalu by Landrover to the national park headquarters at the foot of the mountain where you can stay overnight; day two climb to 3,600 m and spend the night in one of the huts; day three rise very early and make the final ascent to enjoy the best view and return to the park headquarters and stay overnight; day four take the Landrover back to Kota Kinabalu.

Tambunan, 80 km from Kota Kinabalu, is a hidden valley known for its rows and rows of green terraced paddy fields and rolling scrub-covered hills. The villages of **Keranan, Tibabar** and **Sunsuron** have concrete monuments containing human skulls — reminders of the area's head-hunting era.

To the southeast of Sabah is **Semporna**, a town where the famous giant-sized Sabah pearls are found. At the oyster farm here, one can buy quality pearls and oyster shells at bargain prices. Semporna also boasts beautiful coral reefs and 30 km off the coast is Malaysia's only oceanic island, **Pulau Sipadan**, which has one of the best diving sites in Southeast Asia, offering sparkling blue waters which afford views of fascinating underwater scenery and marine life.

About 386 km from Kota Kinabalu is **Sandakan** and 24 km from Sandakan is the **Sepilok Forest Reserve**, where rare plants, animals and birds have taken sanctuary. In this reserve is the world-famous **Sepilok Orang Utan Sanctuary**. The orang utans, rescued from captivity, are cared for here before being sent back to the forest.

HOTEL GUIDE

Hotel address	Phone	Fax	Telex	Cable	≋	🍴	🍹
A (US$100-280) **B** (US$60-80) **C** (US$40-60)							
ALOR STAR (*KEDAH*)							
D							
Grand Continental Jalan Sultan, Badlishah, 05000 Alor Star, Kedah	735263	735161	MA42448 GCHKDH			▲	▲
CAMERON HIGHLANDS (*PAHANG*)							
C							
Strawberry Park 39007 Tanah Rata, Cameron Highlands, Pahang	941166	941949	MA44507 SPMCH		▲	▲	▲
D							
Ye Olde Smokehouse 39007 Tanah Rata, Cameron Highlands, Pahang	941214	941214				▲	▲
DUNGUN (*TRENGGANU*)							
D							
Tanjung Jara Beach Hotel 8th Mile, Off Dungun, 23009 Dungun, Trengganu	841801	842635	MA51449 JARA		▲	▲	▲
FRASER'S HILL (*PAHANG*)							
D							
Merlin Inn Fraser's Hill, 49000 Pahang	382300	382284			▲	▲	▲
GENTING HIGHLANDS (*PAHANG*)							
C							
Awana Golf Course 69000 Genting, Highlands, Pahang	2113015	2113535	MA26009 AWANA		▲	▲	▲
Genting Hotel 69000 Genting, Highlands, Pahang	2112345	2616611	MA32324 GHTP		▲	▲	▲

Hotel address	Phone	Fax	Telex	Cable	〜	🍴	🍲
IPOH (*PERAK*)							
B							
Royal Casuarina Jalan Gopeng, 20250 IPOH, Perak	505555	508177	MA44573 ROCAS		▲	▲	▲
JOHOR BHARU							
C							
Holiday Inn Jalan Dato, Sulaiman, 80990 Johor Bharu	323800	318884	MA60790 HOLJB		▲	▲	▲
D							
Merlin Inn Jalan Bukit, Meldrum, 80300 Johor Bharu	228587	248919	MA60028 MIJB			▲	▲
KOCHING (*SARAWAK*)							
C							
Hilton Jalan Tunku Abdul Rahman, 93748 Kuching	248200	428984	MA70184 HILKCH		▲	▲	▲
D							
Holiday Inn Jalan Tunku Abdul Rahman, 93748 Kuching	423111	426169	MA70086 HOLIN	HOLIDAYINN	▲	▲	▲
KOTA BHARU (*KELANTAN*)							
D							
Perdana Jalan Mahmud, 15200 Kota Bharu	785000	747621	MA53143 HODANA	HODANA	▲	▲	▲
Murni Jalan Dato Pati, 15000 Kota Bharu	782399	747255				▲	▲

Hotel address	Phone	Fax	Telex	Cable	〰	🍴	🍷
KOTA KINABALU (*SABAH*)							
A							
Tanjung Aru Beach Hotel 88999 Kota Kinabalu	58711	217155	MA80752 TABHOT	ARUHOTEL	▲	▲	▲
B							
Hyatt Kinabalu Jalan Datuk, Salleh Sulong, 88994 Kota Kinabalu	221234	225972	MA80036 HYATTKK		▲	▲	▲
KOTA TINGGI (*JONOR*)							
B							
Desaru View Tanjung Penawar, 81907 Kota Tinggi	821221	821237	MA60626 DSRVIEW		▲	▲	▲
KUALA LUMPUR							
A							
Shangri-La Jalan Sultan Ismail, 50250 Kuala Lumpur	2322388	2301514	MA30021 SHNGKL		▲	▲	▲
Regent Jalan Bukit Bintang, 55100 Kuala Lumpur	2418000	2430535	MA33912 REGKL		▲	▲	▲
Kuala Lumpur Hilton Jalan Sultan Ismail, 50250 Kuala Lumpur	2422122	2438069	MA30495 HILTELS	HILTELS	▲	▲	▲
Parkroyal (former Regent) Jalan Sultan Ismail, 50250 Kuala Lumpur	2425588	2415524	MA32489 ROYAL	ROYHOTEL	▲	▲	▲
Pan Pacific Jalan Putra, 50246 Kuala Lumpur	4425555	4417236	MA33706 PPHTKL	PANPACKUL	▲	▲	▲
Ming Court Jalan Ampang, 50450 Kuala Lumpur	2618888	2612393	MA32621 MINGKL		▲	▲	▲
Micasa Hotel Apartments 3688 Jalan Razak, 50400 Kuala Lumpur	2618833	2611186	MA21362	MICASA	▲	▲	▲
B							
Melia (former Prince) Jalan Imbi, 50100 Kuala Lumpur	2428333	2439479	MA211117 HMELIA		▲	▲	▲
C							
Holiday Inn On The Park Jalan Pinang, 50450 Kuala Lumpur	2481066	2435930	MA30239 HOLINN	HOLIDAY INN	▲	▲	▲

Hotel address	Phone	Fax	Telex	Cable	≋	❙❙	◥
KUALA LUMPUR – *Cont'd*							
C							
Grand Continental Jalan Raja Laut, 50350 Kuala Lumpur	2939333	2939732	MA28200 GCONTI		▲	▲	▲
Equatorial Jalan Sultan Ismail, 50250 Kuala Lumpur	2617777	2617920	MA30263 EQATOR	EQUATORIAL	▲	▲	▲
Federal Jalan Bukit Bintang, 55100 Kuala Lumpur	2489166	2438381	MA30429 FEDTEL	FEDEROTEL	▲	▲	▲
D							
Merlin Jalan Sultan Ismail, 50250 Kuala Lumpur	2480033	2426917	MA30487 FABMER	MERLINKUALA LUMPUR	▲	▲	▲
Plaza Jalan Raja Laut, 50350 Kuala Lumpur	2982255	2920959	MA30987 PLAZA	PLAZA		▲	▲
KUALA TRENGGANU (*TRENGGANU* **)**							
D							
Pantai Primula Jalan Persinggahan, 20904 Kuala, Trengganu	622100	633360	MA50403 PANTAI	PANMOTEL	▲	▲	▲
KWANTAN (*PAHANG* **)**							
A							
Holiday Villages 29th Mile, Jalan Kuantan/Kemaman, 25710 Kuantan	513133	503624	MA51443 CMHVM		▲	▲	▲
For reservations: Club Mediterranee, 1/F MAS Bldg, Jalan Sultan Ismail, 50250 Kuala Lumpur	2614599	2617229	MA31404 MAKLCLUB				
C							
Hyatt Kuantan Teluk Chempedak, 25050 Kuantan	525211	507577	MA50252 HTTKN		▲	▲	▲
D							
Merlin Inn Resort Teluk Chempedak, 25050 Kuantan	522388	503001	MA50285 KINMER		▲	▲	▲
Cherating Holiday Villa Cherating, 26080 Kuantan	508900	507078	MA50339 CHVILLA		▲	▲	▲

Hotel address	Phone	Fax	Telex	Cable	≋	🍴	🍽
MALACCA D							
Ramada Renaissance Jalan Bendahara, 75100 Malacca	248888	249269	MA62966 RAMADA	RAMADARENA	▲	▲	▲
Malacca Village Resort Air Keroh, 75450 Malacca	323600	325955	MA62854 MVRBIH			▲	▲
City Bayview Jalan Bendahara, 75100 Malacca	239888	236699	MA62420 CBVIEW		▲	▲	▲
PENANG A							
Penang Mutiara Beach Resort Jalan Teluk Bahang, 11050 Penang	812828	812829	MA40829 PMBR		▲	▲	▲
Rasa Sayang Batu Ferringhi, 11100 Penang	811811	811984	MA40065 RASTEL	RASAYANG	▲	▲	▲
B							
Ferringhi Beach Batu Ferringhi, 11100 Penang	805999	805100	MA40634 FERTEL		▲	▲	▲
Shangrila Inn Magazine Rd, 10300 Penang	622622	626526	MA40878 SHNGPG		▲	▲	▲
C							
Equatorial Jalan Bukit, Jambul, 11900 Bayan Lepas, Penang	838000	848000	MA40665 EQAPIN		▲	▲	▲
City Bayview Farquhar St, 10200 Penang	363161	634124	MA40322 CBVIEW		▲	▲	▲
D							
Eastern & Oriental Farquhar St, 10200 Penang	635322	634833	MA40270 EANDO		▲	▲	▲
Ming Court Macalister Rd, 10400 Penang	368588	367257	MA40092 MINGPG		▲	▲	▲
PETALING JAYA B							
Holiday Villa Jalan SS12/1, 47300 Petaling Jaya	7338788	7337449	MA36762 HVC		▲	▲	▲

Hotel address	Phone	Fax	Telex	Cable	≈	🍴	🍽
PETALING JAYA – *Cont'd*							
C							
Hyatt Saujana Subang Airport Highway, 46710 Petaling Jaya	7461188	7462789	MA37903 HYTSJN		▲	▲	▲
Petaling Jaya Hilton 2 Jalan Barat, 46200 Petaling Jaya	7559122	7553909	MA36008 PJHLTN		▲	▲	▲
PULAU LANGKAWI (*KEDAH*)							
C							
Pelangi Beach Resort Cenang Beach, 07000 Pulau, Langkwai, Kedah	911001	911122	MA42189 PBRL		▲	▲	▲
D							
Langkawi Island Resort Dato' Syed Omar Beach, Kuah, 07000 Pulau Langkawi	788209	788414	MA42044 LCC		▲	▲	▲
PULAU PANGKOR (*PERAK*)							
A							
Pan Pacific Resort Teluk Belanga, 32300 Pangkor	951091	951052	MA44309 BAYVIL		▲	▲	▲
PULAU TIOMAN							
A							
Tioman Island Resort 86800 Pulau Tioman, Pahang	445445	445718	MA50279 TIOMAN		▲	▲	▲
RANAU (*SABAH*)							
D							
Hotel Perkasa Mt Kinabalu Kundasang, 89309 Ranau	889511	889101	MA80316 KIPALS		▲	▲	▲

PAPUA NEW GUINEA

Papua New Guinea is unique. The contact of many of its people with outsiders came only recently, and then peripherally. The variety, traditions and lifestyle of its people — who speak more than 700 different languages — fascinate the visitor first; then the terrain makes a remarkable secondary impression with its mountain ranges, which reach 4,000 m, coral reefs and palm-fringed, white-sand beaches.

Papua New Guineans see themselves as people of the Pacific, rather than of Asia. About 80% of them live in villages even though the towns offer comprehensive shopping facilities. The capital, Port Moresby, faces a fine bay and its national institutions — especially the imaginative new museum and parliament building — are eye-catching, but it is most unlike the rest of the country, which can be reached only by plane or boat. Papua New Guinea is not a cheap country to visit or travel in. It is a country wealthy in natural resources, in copper, gold, coffee, cocoa, copra, oil-palm, timber and fish. Its people are not poor but they are friendly, open and polite. They are too proud to accept tips for the hospitality which is their tradition. Papua New Guinea is a parliamentary democracy, a nation determined to develop — but to develop its own, uniquely Melanesian way.

Virtually all Papua New Guineans are Melanesians who probably moved to the New Guinea island and the scattered tropical off-islands about 50,000 years ago. Traces of highland settlements at least 8,000 years old have been found. The people lived, for the most part in small warring clans and tribes, in the valleys, on the mountain ridges, on the coastal plains and the islands, in a largely unchanging lifestyle until contact with Europeans.

The first recorded European sighting of New Guinea island was by two Portuguese explorers. Another explorer, Jorge de Meneses, landed at the north-west corner and named the island Ilhas dos Papuas. In 1824 the Netherlands and Britain agreed to the Dutch claim on the western half of the island, now the Indonesian province of Irian Jaya. Later in the 19th century Britain made increasing landings in the eastern half — the present Papua New Guinea — and the Germans also entered the picture by claiming the north of the country. In 1906 the southern half — British New Guinea — was renamed Papua and handed to Australia to administer. In 1920 the League of Nations handed German New Guinea to Australia as a mandated territory.

The United Nations inherited this mandate until Papua New Guinea became independent from Australia on September 16, 1975.

Papua New Guinea was a major theatre of World War II when the turning point was Australia's last-ditch defence of Port Moresby against the Japanese push along the Kokoda Trail. Sir Michael Somare, who was elected chief minister in 1972, led the country into independence from Australia in 1975 and remained prime minister until losing his parliamentary majority to Sir Julius Chan in 1980. Somare regained the prime ministership at the next election in 1982, only to lose it again in parliament in 1985 — this time to highlander Paias Wingti. Wingti kept power following the 1987 election, but lost it the following year to Somare's successor as leader of the Pangu Party, Rabbie Namaliu. Namaliu immediately faced the country's biggest crisis — the rebellion on Bougainville island which first closed the copper mine that produced 40% of PNG's export income, then in May 1990 led to a unilateral declaration of independence.

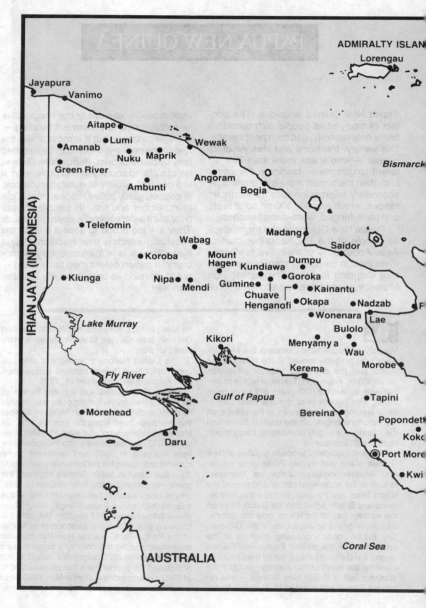

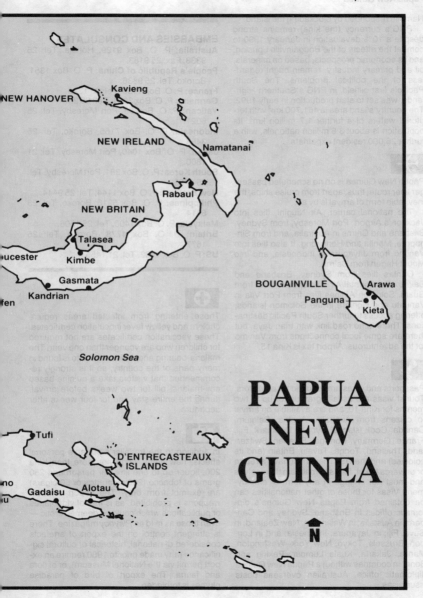

Namaliu responded by blockading the island.

PNG's currency (the kina) remains strong despite a 10% devaluation in January 1990 to combat the effects of the Bougainville uprising, and its economic prospects, based on minerals, oil and primary industry, remain bright regardless of the political problems. The South Pacific's first oilfield, in PNG's Southern Highlands, was set to start production in early 1992. The country's land area is 461,700 km^2 with territorial waters of a further 1.7 million km^2. Its population is about 3.6 million nationals, with a further 26,000 resident expatriates.

Papua New Guinea is on no scheduled passenger liner route; thus, apart from cruise ships, the inevitable form of arrival is by air.

The national carrier, Air Niugini, flies into Jackson's Airport, Port Moresby, from Sydney, Brisbane and Cairns in Australia, and from Singapore, Manila and Hongkong. It also flies into Vanimo from Jayapura in Indonesia, and into Mount Hagen from Cairns.

Qantas flies from Sydney, Brisbane and Cairns. Continental/Air Micronesia flies from Guam. Solomon Airlines flies from Port Vila in Vanuatu and Honiara in the Solomon Islands, offering access to further South Pacific destinations. There is no road link with Irian Jaya, but there are some local connections from Vanimo for the adventurous. Airport tax is Kina 15.

Passports and visas are required by all visitors. Tourist visas are usually granted for up to two months for Kina 10, and are available on arrival to citizens from Australia, Austria, Belgium, Canada, Cook Islands, Cyprus, Denmark, Fiji, France, Germany, Portugal, Sweden, Switzerland, Thailand, Tonga, Tuvalu, Britain (and its colonies) and the US. They must have a return or onwards ticket, funds to maintain themselves and must not engage in any form of employment. Visas for those of other nationalities can be obtained from Papua New Guinea's diplomatic offices in Brisbane, Sydney and Canberra in Austalia; in Wellington, New Zealand; in Suva, Fiji; in Jayapura, Indonesia; and in London, Brussels, Tokyo, New York, Washington, Manila, Jakarta, Kuala Lumpur, Peking and Bonn. In countries without a Papua New Guinea diplomatic office, Australian overseas posts issue visas.

EMBASSIES AND CONSULATES

Australia: P. O. Box 9129, Hohola. Tel: 25 9333; Fax: 25 9183.

People's Republic of China: P. O. Box 1351, Boroko. Tel: 25 9836.

France: P. O. Box 1155. Tel: 25 1323.

Germany: P. O. Box 3631. Tel: 25 2971.

Vatican: P. O. Box 98, Port Moresby. Tel: 25 6021.

Indonesia: P. O. Box 7165, Boroko. Tel: 25 3455.

Japan: P. O. Box 1040, Port Moresby. Tel: 21 1800.

South Korea: P. O. Box 381, Port Moresby. Tel: 25 4755.

New Zealand: P. O. Box 1144. Tel: 25 9444.

Philippines: P. O. Box 5916, Boroko. Tel: 25 6414.

Malaysia: P. O. Box 1400. Tel: 25 1506.

Britain: P. O. Box 4778, Boroko. Tel: 25 1677.

US: P. O. Box 1492. Tel: 21 1455.

Those entering from infected areas require cholera and yellow fever inoculation certificates. These vaccination certificates are not required for children who are younger than one year. The malaria-bearing anopheles mosquito is found in many parts of the country, so it is strongly recommended that visitors take a quinine-based anti-malarial pill for two weeks before arrival, during the entire stay and for four weeks after departure.

In addition to the traveller's portable personal effects, new items worth not more than Kina 200, liquor up to one litre per person and 250 grams of tobacco (200 cigarettes or 50 cigars) are exempt from duty. The import of most weapons is prohibited, as is that of videotapes or publications which could be deemed erotic — even those as mild as *Playboy* magazine. There is stringent control on the export of artefacts considered of national, historical or cultural significance (any made prior to 1960 require an export permit via the National Museum), or of flora and fauna. The export of bird of paradise plumes is forbidden.

The unit of currency is the kina which is divided into 100 toea. In March 1991 the rate of exchange was Kina 1:95 US cents. Notes in denominations of Kina 50, 20, 10, 5 and 2 and coins of Kina 1 (with a hole in the centre) and of 50, 20, 10, 5, 2 and 1 toea are in circulation. There are no restrictions on importing foreign currency. However, the export of kina is restricted to a maximum of Kina 200 in notes and Kina 5 in coins. Non-residents may take out the amounts of foreign currency they brought into the country. Foreign currency is not normally accepted for the purchase of goods or services, but all banks and major hotels will accept traveller's cheques and exchange currency. American Express is the most widely accepted credit card, and with, to a lesser extent, Visa and Diner's Club are acceptable at major hotels, stores and artefact shops. But the visitor should not depend on credit card purchases beyond meeting hotel, air ticket and car hire bills.

There are three official languages — English, Pidgin and Hiri Motu. English is widely understood, since it is the language of instruction in schools. In addition there are 700 local dialects. A Pidgin phrase-book is a useful aid to communication because the language is a lot more complicated than a simple variation on English.

Temperatures vary little throughout the year, and the average daily coastal range is between 21°C and 32°C. In highland areas the temperature varies with altitude and at night can be cool, or even really cold. Humidity is high, ranging on the coast between 70-88%.

The average rainfall is 2,500 mm, but in some areas it can be double that. Only Port Moresby — in the rainshadow of the Owen Stanley mountain range — has clearly distinct wet and dry seasons. There are two prevailing winds — the southeast or tradewind from May to October, and the northwest or monsoon from December to March.

Light, easily washable clothing, with light jumpers, is recommended if the traveller is visiting the highlands. Ties are rarely seen and never de rigueur, though many hotels and restaurants rule out thongs or sandals, shorts and T-shirts. While informality is otherwise fine, suggestive or revealing Western fashions are frowned upon, especially in rural areas.

Government offices work from 7:45 am to 5 pm from Monday to Friday. Commercial firms work until 4:30 or 5 pm. Stores normally open from 8:30 am to 5 pm, Monday to Friday and 8 am to 12 noon on Saturday. Markets — selling mainly fresh foodstuffs — are open during daylight hours, normally 7 am to 6 pm. Banks open from 9 am to 2 pm from Monday to Thursday and from 9 am to 5 pm on Friday. Liquor licensing is a function of the 19 provincial governments, so it differs from place to place. But it is generally possible to purchase liquor from 8 am to 5 pm on weekdays, and from 8 am to 12 noon on Saturday. Public bars tend to close at 8 pm and hotel cocktail bars at midnight.

FROM PORT MORESBY AIRPORT: (8 km from the main two centres): hotel buses and tour buses are available; taxis are metered.

HIRE CARS: available from most large towns at Kina 50-75 per day, with some franchisers adding a surcharge of up to 40 toea per kilometre.

BUSES: public motor vehicles (PMVs) ranging from medium-sized buses to open utility trucks, operate inside towns and between major centres. Fares inside towns are 50 toea or less, and long-distance fares in the Highlands only a few kina. However, standards of comfort and maintenance are varied. Foreigners should also be cautious about their security, and consider a hire car if cramming many calls into a short stay. Taxis are available in only a few centres.

BOATS: a large number of cargo boats operate inside Papua New Guinea and afford an adventurous — though slow and slightly uncomfortable — way of travelling. It is difficult to book far in advance.

AIR: because of the limited road network, air travel has become more common for ordinary people in Papua New Guinea than perhaps anywhere else in the world. Air Niugini flies Fokker F28 jets and De Havilland Dash 7s between provincial centres; third-level operators serve the hundreds of smaller airstrips. Flying within the country is not cheap.

MAJOR AIRLINES

Air Niugini: P. O. Box 7186, Boroko. Tel: 27 3200; Fax: 27 3482.

Talair: P. O. Box 108, Goroka. Tel: 72 1613.

Douglas Airways: P. O. Box 1178, Boroko. Tel: 25 3499.

Nationair: P. O. Box 488, Boroko. Tel: 25 4179; Fax: 21 3986.

Qantas: P. O. Box 330, Port Moresby. Tel: 21 1200; Fax: 21 3073.

Singapore Airlines: P. O. Box 1162, Port Moresby. Tel: 21 3975.

Philippine Airlines: P. O. Box 1271. Tel: 21 1244.

Continental/Air Micronesia: P. O. Box 9208, Hohola. Tel: 25 7588; Fax: 25 1876.

Solomon Airlines: P. O. Box 7248, Boroko. Tel: 25 5724.

An increasing number of tours are now available, specialising in wildlife — the famous bird of paradise is found exclusively on the New Guinea island — traditional lifestyles, diving, etc. A number of provincial governments are also now establishing their own tourist bureaux; more details can be obtained via the National Tourist Office. The main tour operators are Melanesian Tourist Services, P. O. Box 707, Madang; Trans Niugini Tours, P. O. Box 371, Mount Hagen; Air Niugini Travel Service, P. O. Box 7186, Boroko. Other tour companies are Tribal World New Guinea, P. O. Box 86, Mount Hagen; Pacific Expeditions, P. O. Box 132, Port Moresby. The opportunity for glorious reef diving is provided by Dive Rabaul, P. O. Box 65, Rabaul; Diving Specialists of PNG, P. O. Box 337, Madang; Jais Aben Resort, P. O, Box 105, Madang; Niugini Diving Adventures, P. O. Box 707, Madang; Rabaul Dive Centre, P. O. Box 400, Rabaul; Telita Cruises, P. O. Box 303, Alotau; Tropical Diving Services, P. O. Box 1748, Port Moresby; Knight Dive Shop, P. O. Box 105, Lorengau; Walindi Diving, P. O. Box 4, Kimbe; and New Guinea Diving, P. O. Box 320, Lae.

Accommodation in Papua New Guinea is expensive. In most centres there are reasona-

bly well-appointed hotels, though more intermediate-level accommodation is gradually becoming available. De luxe tourist lodges include **Ambua Lodge** in the Southern Highlands and **Karawari Lodge** in the upper Sepik. The government is encouraging the establishment of clean, comfortable **village-style guesthouses** run by Papua New Guinea nationals. The longest established of these is the Kofure Village Guesthouse, whose address is c/o Post Office, Tufi, Oro province. Others include the Kaiap Orchid Lodge at Wabag, Krangket Island Lodge off Madang and Kaibola Lodge on Kiriwina island.

Port Moresby is not quite a gastronomic delight, yet eating establishments are growing in number and variety. Like a number of other towns in Papua New Guinea, Port Moresby, has several reasonable-quality Chinese restaurants, the best being the **Kwangtung Village** (Cantonese, some Szechuan, noted for its crab and fish). The **Daikoku** is the only Japanese restaurant, offering beef and seafood tepanyaki. The **Seoul House** provides traditional Korean cuisine, and the best European restaurant is the **Galley**, next to the Aviat Club. The **Kokoda Trail Motel** on the Sogeri plateau above Port Moresby serves tender kebabs of locally killed crocodiles. Licensing hours are strictly adhered to, both for take-away sales and in bars. The locally brewed South Pacific lager is of a high quality, and a large range of Australian and other wines and spirits from around the world are widely available. Drinkers may choose to specify the imported product in bars, instead of the reconstituted, locally bottled versions usually dispensed. Papua New Guinea's coffee — Arabica and Robusta — and teas are first rate and make ideal souvenirs.

All towns have cinemas. Port Moresby has a drive-in. Leading hotels in Port Moresby and Lae frequently provide live music in their restaurants.

Broadcast TV is widely available through satellite dish, including ABC and Channel 9 from Australia, Cable News Network from the USA, and the local station EM TV. Video is also popular. Local and Australian daily and weekly newspapers and international magazines are widely available.

Papua New Guinea offers a great variety of traditional artefacts — basketwork from the islands, carvings from the north coast, tapa cloth from northern province, woven articles from the highlands, shells and pottery from the coast. They are available in special artefact shops, in most hotel foyers and occasionally from street sellers, particularly at Port Moresby's **Boroko** shopping centre on Saturday mornings. The prices — as everywhere, including the markets — are fixed. Papua New Guineans do not haggle.

Sport of all kinds is played in Papua New Guinea. Soccer, rugby league, rugby union and Australian Rules football — the contact sports — are most popular. There are also bowls, cricket, tennis, basketball, softball, golf, squash and polo, among others. Neither Port Moresby nor Lae offers good swimming beaches, though Moresby has a public pool. There are opportunities for reef-diving, water-skiing, fishing, wind-surfing and sailing.

January 1: New Year's Day.
March-April: Good Friday and Easter Monday.
June 18: Queen Elizabeth's (official) birthday.
July 23: Remembrance Day.
September 16: Independence Day.
December 25: Christmas Day.
December 26: Boxing Day.

The Highlands Show is usually held on alternate years at Goroka and Mount Hagen in August or September.

At variable dates: other annual festivals include the Hiri Moale and the Agricultural Show (in Port Moresby, the former during the Independence anniversary, the latter over the Queen's Birthday weekend), the Frangipani and Warwagira Festivals (Rabaul), the Mabarosa Festival (Madang), the Malangan Show (Kavieng) and the Lae Agricultural Show. The Chinese New Year is most actively celebrated in Lae.

Addresses

TOURIST AUTHORITIES

National Tourist Office (a national government agency): P. O. Box 7144, Boroko. (Tel: 25 1269; Fax: 25 9447).

Madang Visitors Bureau: P. O. Box 1071, Madang.
East Sepik Tourist Bureau: P. O. Box 1074, Wewak.
Milne Bay Visitors Bureau: P. O. Box 337, Alotau.
East New Britain Tourist Bureau: P. O. Box 385, Rabaul. The Industry's coordinating body, the Tourist Association of PNG, can be contacted c/o The Manager, Islander Hotel, P. O. Box 1981, Boroko.

Publications

The Tourist Association's monthly publication is *Traveller's Times*, obtainable via P. O. Box 1982, Boroko. (Tel: 25 2500). *Papua New Guinea, A Travel Survival Kit* by Tony Wheeler (published by Lonely Planet Guides), is a helpful and down-to-earth guide. Air Niugini publishes a variety of useful brochures, and *Paradise*, an award-winning in-flight magazine. Talair also has an in-flight publication, *Insait*. The National Tourist Office produces a *Visitor's Guide*.

Agriculture Bank of Papua New Guinea, ANZ Banking Group, Bank of South Pacific, Papua New Guinea Banking Corp., Indosuez Niugini Bank, Niugini Lloyds Bank and Westpac Bank.

CHAMBERS OF COMMERCE
Papua New Guinea Chambers of Commerce and Industry: P. O. Box 1621, Port Moresby. Tel: 21 3057.
Port Moresby Chamber: P. O. Box 1764, Port Moresby. Tel: 21 3077.
Lae Chamber: P. O. Box 265, Lae. Tel: 42 2340; Fax: 42 6038.

DISCOVERING PAPUA NEW GUINEA

PORT MORESBY

The capital is a spread-out city of 180,000 people with a ridge dividing the older town on the bay from the newer inland suburbs, including the government centre at **Waigani**, where the exciting lines of the **National Museum** make it a good starting point for visitors (though it is closed on Fridays and Saturdays). Nearby is the new parliament, built in a style echoing that of

Local entertainers.

the traditional Sepik "haus tambaran" or spirit-house; debate inside is spirited, and well worth observing during sessions. A few kilometres distant is the modern **university campus**, next to the **National Botanical Gardens**, which include a remarkable orchid collection. Driving out of town towards the hills, is the **Moitaka** wildlife sanctuary, including a crocodile farm; it opens to the public on Friday afternoons. The **Varirata National Park**, on the cool **Sogeri plateau** 50 km from Port Moresby, offers walks through tropical rainforest, barbecue sites, and the occasional glimpse of birds of paradise. The **Kokoda Trail Motel** is nearby. The **Loloata Island** resort, a tropical-island hideaway reached via a ferry service, is only a few minutes' drive from Port Moresby.

UPCOUNTRY

Lae, the nation's second city, major centre for secondary industry and the port for the newly prosperous highlands, is lush compared with Port Moresby. The Highlands Highway, the nation's arterial road, winds through the fertile **Markham Valley** up to the pleasant coffee town of **Goroka** and beyond to **Mount Hagen**, the

fast-expanding frontier town of the highlands at 2,600 m. The highlands offer breathtaking views, a pleasant climate and the opportunity to meet an energetic and outgoing people whose contact with Western ways is recent. The **Balyer River wildlife sanctuary**, which can be reached from Mount Hagen, offers basic but acceptable self-catering accommodation and an opportunity to see birds of paradise; but local advice on security precautions needs to be obeyed. **Madang**, which can be reached by road from Lae or the highlands, offers the best example of relaxed Pacific style in Papua New Guinea, with its lagoon, tiny islands and north coast drive through endless coconut plantations. The huge **Sepik** river, winding down to **Wewak** at its mouth, hosts one of the country's great cultures.

The islands region — from **Milne May** in the south, up through **New Britain, New Ireland** and **Manus** — offers yet another experience, with wonderful seascapes and elegant people. **Rabaul** in East New Britain is set inside the rim of a huge underwater volcano and has a good claim to be the most beautifully situated town in the South Pacific.

HOTEL GUIDE

Hotel address	Phone	Fax	Telex	Cable	〰	🍽	☕

A (US$80 or above) **B** (US$50-80) **C** (US$30-50) **D** (US$30 or less)

AITOPE
C

Hotel address	Phone	Fax	Telex	Cable	〰	🍽	☕
Tamara PO Box 72	87 2060					▲	

ALOTAU
A

Hotel address	Phone	Fax	Telex	Cable	〰	🍽	☕
Masurina Lodge PO Box 5	61 1212	61 1286		MASURINA		▲	

AMBOIN
A

Hotel address	Phone	Fax	Telex	Cable	〰	🍽	☕
Karawari Lodge PO Box 371, Mt Hagen	52 1438	52 2470	52012	KUNDU (Mt Hagen)	▲	▲	

BENSBACH
A

Hotel address	Phone	Fax	Telex	Cable	〰	🍽	☕
Bensbach Lodge c/o Westpac Travel, PO Box 77, Port Moresby	22 0700/ 22 0749			KUNDU (Mt Hagen)		▲	

BOGIA
D

Hotel address	Phone	Fax	Telex	Cable	〰	🍽	☕
Bogia Hotel PO Box 44, Madang Province	83 4422					▲	

BULOLO
B

Hotel address	Phone	Fax	Telex	Cable	〰	🍽	☕
Pine Lodge Highland Resort PO Box 90	44 5220	44 5284	82707	PINELODGE		▲	

Hotel address	Phone	Fax	Telex	Cable	≋	🍴	🥣
DARU **B**							
Wyben Hotel PO Box 121	65 9055/ 65 9057	65 9065	65409				▲
GOROKA **A**							
Bird of Paradise PO Box 12 **C**	72 1144	72 1007	72628	BIRDPARA	▲	▲	
Hotel Goroka PO Box 759	72 2351					▲	
Minogere Lodge PO Box 2	72 2307/1009			GOROKAUNSIL		▲	
HOSKINS **C**							
Hoskins PO Hoskins West New Britain	93 5113					▲	
KAINANTU **C**							
Kainantu Lodge PO Box 31	77 1021/ 77 1020	77 1043	77632	JASCAR		▲	
KAVIENG **B**							
Kavieng PO Box 4 **D**	94 2199	94 2283	94924	HOTEL		▲	
Kavieng Club PO Box 62	94 2224	94 2106				▲	

Hotel address	Phone	Fax	Telex	Cable	〜	🍴	🍽
KEREMA **C**							
Elavo PO Box 25	68 1041						
KIETA **B**							
Davara Hotel PO Box 241, Toniva St	95 6175	95 6218	95852	DAVARA	▲	▲	
Siromba Hotel PO Box 228, Town	95 6277	95 6085	95843	KIETOL		▲	
KIMBE **C**							
Palm Lodge PO Box 32	93 5001	93 5401	93114			▲	
KIUNGA **B**							
Kiunga Guest House PO Box 20	58 1084	58 1195			▲	▲	
KUNDIAWA **B**							
Simbu Lodge PO Box 191	75 1144/ 75 1008		75605	CHIMLODGE	▲	▲	
C							
Kundiawa PO Box 12	75 1033					▲	
LAE **A**							
Lae International PO Box 2774	42 2000	42 2534	42473	LAELODE	▲	▲	

Hotel address	Phone	Fax	Telex	Cable	〰	🍴	🥣
LAE – *Cont'd* **A**							
Melanesian PO Box 756	42 3744	42 3706	44187	MELO	▲	▲	
B							
Huon Gulf PO Box 612	42 2844	42 3706	44187		▲	▲	
D							
Klinkii (OK) Lodge PO Box 192	42 6040		42468			▲	
LORENGAU **C**							
Harbourside Hotel PO Box 89	40 9093	40 9392				▲	
Lorengau Kohai PO Box 100	40 9004					▲	
LOSUIA **C**							
Kiriwina Lodge PO Box 2	61 1004					▲	
MADANG **A**							
Madang Resort PO Box 707	82 2766/ 82 2655	82 3543	82707	MELTOUR	▲	▲	
B							
Smugglers Inn PO Box 303	82744	82 2267	82722	SMUGGLERS	▲	▲	
C							
Coastwatchers PO Box 324	82 2684	82 2716			▲	▲	

Hotel address	Phone	Fax	Telex	Cable	≈	🍴	🍽
MADANG – *Cont'd*							
C							
Jais Aben Resort PO Box 105	82 3311	82 3560			▲	▲	
D							
Madang Lodge PO Box 969	82 3395	82 3292					
Malolo of Madang PO Box 413	82 3176	82 3506				▲	
MENDI							
B							
Mendi PO Box 108	59 1188	59 1243		MENDI		▲	
Mendi Riverside Lodge PO Box 50	59 1261	59 1305				▲	
MINJ							
B							
Plumes and Arrows PO Box 86, Mt Hagen	55 1555	55 1546	52070	TRIBAL		▲	
C							
Minj PO Box 13	56 5538					▲	
MOUNT HAGEN							
A							
Highlander PO Box 34	52 1355	52 1216	55108	HOTEL	▲	▲	
B							
Tribal Tops Inn PO Box 86	56 5556	55 1546	52070	TRIBAL	▲	▲	

Hotel address	Phone	Fax	Telex	Cable	〰	🍴	🍽
MOUNT HAGEN – *Cont'd*							
C							
Hagen Park PO Box 81	52 1388/ 52 1396	52 2282	52056	HAPARK		▲	
Haus Poroman PO Box 1182	52 2722/ 52 2250	52 2207				▲	
Kimininga Lodge PO Box 408	52 1865	52 2480	52008	KIMININGA		▲	
POPONDETTA							
A							
Lamington PO Box 27	29 7152/ 29 7065			LAMHOTEL		▲	
D							
Uro Guest House PO Box 2	29 7127					▲	
PORT MORESBY							
A							
Airways PO Box 1942, Boroko	25 7033	21 4759	23435			▲	
Gateway PO Box 1215, Boroko	25 3855	25 4585	23082	GATEWAY	▲	▲	
Islander PO Box 1981, Boroko	25 5955	21 3835	22288	ISLANDER	▲	▲	
Travelodge PO Box 1661, Port Moresby	21 2266	21 7534	22248	TRAVELODGE	▲	▲	
Davara PO Box 799, Port Moresby	21 2100		23236	DAVARA	▲	▲	
C							
Amber's Inn PO Box 1139, Boroko	25 5091				▲	▲	
Boroko PO Box 1033	25 6704/ 25 6677			BOROKOTEL		▲	

Hotel address	Phone	Fax	Telex	Cable	〰	🍴	🍽
PORT MORESBY – *Cont'd*							
C							
Granville PO Box 1246	25 7155	25 7672	23482			▲	
Kokoda Trail PO Box 5014, Boroko	25 3322				▲	▲	
Loloata Island Resort PO Box 5290	25 1369/ 25 1369	25 8933				▲	
Popuo PO Box 92	21 2622		22353	PAPTEL		▲	
Westside PO Box 112, Konedobu	21 7057	21 4739				▲	
RABAUL							
A							
Kulau Lodge Beach Resort PO Box 65, Kabakada	92 2115	92 2450	92930	KULAULODGE		▲	
Travelodge PO Box 449	92 2111	92 2104	92975		▲	▲	
B							
Kaivuna Resort PO Box 391, Mango Ave, Rabaul	92 1766	92 1832	92982		▲	▲	
C							
Hamamas PO Box 214	92 1999	92 1927	92927			▲	
D							
Kanai Guest House PO Box 510	92 1995	92 2776				▲	
New Britain Lodge PO Box 296	92 2247					▲	
New Guinea Club PO Box 40	92 1801					▲	

Hotel address	Phone	Fax	Telex	Cable	〰	🍴	🍜
RAMU **C**							
Ramu Sugar Lodge PO Box 2183, Lae	44 3299				▲	▲	
SAMARAI **C**							
Kinanale Guest House PO Box 88	61 2399					▲	
TABUBIL **C**							
Hotel Cloudlands PO Box 226	58 9277	58 9301			▲	▲	
TAPINI **B**							
Tapini Lodge PO Box 6036, Boroko	25 9935					▲	
TARI **A**							
Ambua Lodge PO Box 371, Mt Hagen	52 1438	52 2470	52012			▲	
TUFI **D**							
Laki Hotel PO Tufi	25 3524/ 25 4599					▲	

Hotel address	Phone	Fax	Telex	Cable	≋	▮▮	◥◤
VANIMO **B**							
Vanimo Resort PO Box 42 **D**	87 1102/ 87 1173	87 1131				▲	
Vanimo Guest House PO Box 35	87 1087		87109			▲	
WEWAK **B**							
Sepik International Beach Resort PO Box 152	86 2388	86 2701	86119			▲	
Sepik Motel PO Box 51 **C**	82 2422		86143		▲	▲	
Paradise New Wewak PO Box 20 **D**	86 2155/ 86 2554		86161			▲	
Ambunti Lodge PO Box 496, Wewak	86 2922					▲	
WUVULU ISLAND **C**							
Alaba Lodge PO Box 494, Wewak	86 2331	86 2331	86122			▲	

PHILIPPINES

Despite political instability and some weak areas of the economy, the Philippines remains an attractive bargain as a tourist destination. The country gained acceptance from travellers because of its round-the-year warm climate, comparatively low prices, breathtaking natural scenery — and its people's unique kind of hospitality, which remains as sincere.

The Philippine archipelago comprises 7,107 islands, of which only 11 main islands account for more than 95% of the country's total land area of 300,400 km². The islands are dotted with numerous white-sand beaches, exotic tropical vegetation and beautiful lakes and rivers. The population is 64 million, of whom around 10 million are concentrated in Metro-Manila.

The Filipino people have been shaped by a mixture of Malay, Spanish, American and Chinese culture and influence. The English language is widely spoken — the Philippines is the third-largest English-speaking country in the world — the inheritance of 48 years as an American colony.

There is a vast array of local dialects — around 70. Some 85% of the population is Roman Catholic, as a result of the country's more than 300 years of Spanish colonisation. The other significant religious groups are Muslims, mostly in the south, who make up 4.9% of the national population, Protestants at 3.2%, and Buddhists at 1%.

The capital of the Philippines is Manila, on the main island of Luzon. This urban centre, however, has expanded into Metro-Manila, which covers a total of 13 municipalities and four cities, home for some 10 million Filipinos. Metro-Manila boasts more than 10,000 hotel rooms, mostly first-class, mostly built in the mid-1970s for a series of major international conferences that created a short-lived tourism boom. Most of the hotels offer big discounts on room rates — up to 50% — at certain times of the year to boost occupancy.

Major regional and international conferences are mostly held at the well-equipped **Philippine International Convention Centre**, built on reclaimed land in Manila Bay and part of the cultural centre complex. Also in this complex are the **Philippine Centre for International Trade** and **Exhibitions (Philcite)**, where trade fairs are regularly held; **Philtrade Exhibits**, a permanent showcase for various Philippine industries, and several theatres.

Places in the Philippines worth visiting are so numerous that the tourist can only hope to see a few of them. They range from the fabled rice terraces of Banaue in the north to the pearl farms, guitar factories, tropical countryside and coral beaches in the south. Everywhere, the visitor experiences the warmth and friendliness of the Filipinos which make the country one of the most exciting in the world.

Visitors can walk freely in the main streets of Metro-Manila by day or night in relative safety. Just about the only hazard is the disorderly traffic, but even that can be an attraction, watching the gaily decorated jeepneys (enlarged passenger-carrying Jeeps) weaving through the traffic. A wide array of bars, restaurants and nightclubs remain open late into the night for fun-loving visitors.

◁ *The traditional Maria Clara style dress with antique gold earrings.*
Photo: Patrick Lucero

183

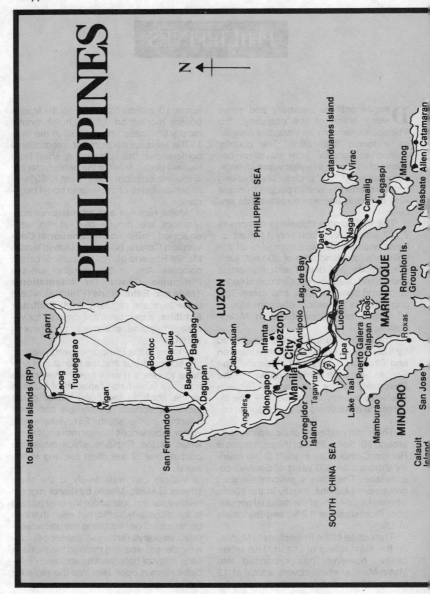

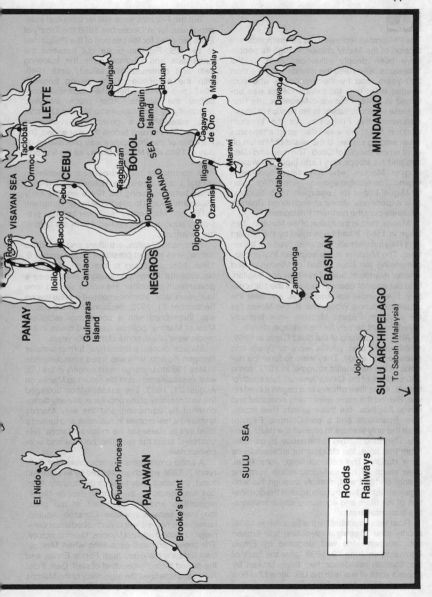

Surigao

LEYTE

Tacloban

Ormoc

Butuan

Camiguin
Island

Malaybalay

Davao

CEBU

BOHOL

BOHOL
SEA

Cagayan
de Oro

MINDANAO

Cebu

Tagbilaran

Marawi

Roxas

VISAYAN SEA

Bacolod

Dumaguete

MINDANAO

Iligan

Cotabato

Panay

Iloilo

Canlaon

NEGROS

Ozamis

Dipolog

Zamboanga

Guimaras
Island

Puerto Princesa

PALAWAN

El Nido

Brooke's Point

BASILAN

SULU ARCHIPELAGO

To Sabah (Malaysia)

Jolo

SULU SEA

Roads

Railways

The Philippines represent the northern most extension of the Malay culture, though its people have been deeply influenced both by the Spaniards, who ruled the islands for more than 300 years, and by the Americans who succeeded them until full independence was obtained in 1946. Ferdinand Magellan, the Portuguese explorer, sailing in the service of Spain, discovered the Philippines for the Western world in 1521. He was killed soon afterwards when wading ashore at the island of Mactan off what is now the city of Cebu. The man who killed him and his troops was Lapu-lapu, the warrior king of Mactan, who has since become a legend. The archipelago was annexed for Spain by Miguel Lopez de Legazpi in 1565. Successive expeditions slowly strengthened Spanish influence over the northern Philippines.

Manila, then in the hands of the Muslims, was taken in 1568. It had been ruled by the Muslim king Rajah Solaiman, who destroyed it in his retreat. The Muslims in the southern Philippines, comprising the large island of Mindanao and smaller islands of Sulu, Tawi-tawi and Basilan, held out against Spanish rule until the 19th century. Even under the Americans, and later the Japanese during World War II, the Moros (as the southern Filipino Muslims were formerly called) fought fiercely for their independence.

After the opening of the Suez Canal in 1869, ambitious Filipino youths went to Spain and elsewhere to study. They were to form the nucleus of the nationalist struggle. In 1872, some 200 soldiers of the Cavite Arsenal, just south of Manila, killed their officers and began a brief revolt. Behind the move were many educated and liberal Filipinos, but three priests (two locally born Spaniards and a part-Chinese Filipino) were the only leaders to receive the death penalty. They died martyrs to the cause, by garrotte. From that time, the struggle for independence grew rapidly. The national hero, Jose Rizal, drew much of his early inspiration from the events of 1872 and, notably through his writings, carried on the struggle against the domination of the friars and economic and administrative authoritarianism.

Rizal was executed by the Spanish in 1896, shortly after a general revolution had broken out. Independence was declared by Emilio Aguinaldo on June 12, 1898, after the back of the Spanish resistance had been broken by Spain's state of war with the US. June 12 is now celebrated as Independence Day.

But the Filipinos were still far from real independence, for in December 1898 the Treaty of Paris provided for the cession of the Philippines to the US. Fighting broke out between the Americans and Filipinos early the following year and continued sporadically until 1946, with the exception of the period between 1942 and 1945, when the Japanese controlled the islands. After much lobbying, principally by the charismatic Manuel Quezon, who established a government-in-exile in Washington but died before the war ended, the Republic of the Philippines was proclaimed on July 4, 1946 with Manuel Roxas as the first president.

A communist-inspired peasant rebellion in central Luzon under the Hukbalahaps (Huks) raged between during the 1940s and the early 1950s and sought to overthrow the government, but Ramon Magsaysay, who later became president, successfully crushed it with the help of the Americans.

Ferdinand Marcos, a brilliant and ambitious lawyer, was elected president on November 9, 1965, after switching to the then opposition Nacionalista Party, previously having been a government supporter. He won a second term four years later. Marcos imposed martial law on September 21, 1972, declaring that the nation was threatened with a communist rebellion. Most of Marcos' political foes and critics in the media were jailed, some of them for years.

Marcos' closest political rival, former senator Benigno Aquino, who was freed from detention in May 1980 to undergo heart surgery in the US, was assassinated upon his return to Manila on August 21, 1983. The assassination outraged the vast majority of the populace, already disenchanted by corruption and the way Marcos favoured a few cronies in business and turned a blind eye to abuses of the military. Marcos' rule crumbled amid the resulting political and economic crisis.

A snap presidential election called for February 7, 1986 was characterised by widespread fraud, the worst ever seen in the country. Marcos was declared the winner despite the irregularities and his opponent at the polls, the slain senator's widow Corazon Aquino, launched a non-violent civil-disobedience campaign to protest against Marcos' claim to victory. The movement was escalating when Marcos' own defence minister, Juan Ponce Enrile, and the armed forces' vice–chief of staff, Gen. Fidel Ramos, challenged the legitimacy of the Marcos government on February 22. They established their headquarters at two premier military installations, Camp Aguinaldo and Camp Crame, where they were joined within hours by thousands of civilian supporters. The putsch ended on the night of February 25 with Marcos, his close relatives (including wife Imelda) and key military advisers fleeing to the US Clark Airbase, from where they were flown to Guam and subsequently Hawaii.

Aquino was quick to proclaim herself the rightfully elected president and champion of "people power," and the military leaders accepted this. In February 1987 the Filipinos ratified a new constitution providing for a democratic republican state and a presidential form of government. Aquino then faced the difficult tasks of attempting to revitalise a negative growth economy and removing the inefficiency and corruption inherited from the Marcos regime.

Although the economy has since shown modest signs of revival, the per capita GNP in 1988 of approximately US$600 was still at the 1978 level largely owing to population growth. The Marcos-era problems — feudal attitudes, monopolies, confusing investment policies, communist insurgency, aid either clogged in the bureaucracy or disappearing into politicians' pockets, labour militancy, inflation, destruction of the environment, typhoons, overcrowded cities, electricity shortage and a general lack of law and order — have been exacerbated by six military coup attempts against Aquino to date. A devastating earthquake which killed hundreds in July 1990 did nothing to help and virtually removed the mountain resort of Baguio from the tourist map.

The Muslim secessionist conflict in the south, which peaked in 1974, came to a temporary halt in December 1976 after the Philippine Government signed the Tripoli Agreement in Libya with the Moro National Liberation Front (MNLF). But in late 1977, the ceasefire collapsed and there was renewed fighting until 1980 with the rebels who pressed for an autonomous Muslim region. Later the MNLF shifted in favour of secession.

A 1989 referendum on the issue saw most southern provinces choosing to remain outside the Autonomous Region of Muslim Mindanao. Only Maguindanao, Tawi-tawi, Sulu and Lanao del Sur voted for autonomy. But the MNLF remains a secessionist force whose avowed aim is the creation of an autonomous Muslim state in the whole of Mindanao.

On the whole, Filipinos have fewer anti-colonial complexes than many other formerly co-

lonised people. A special relationship with the Americans still exists for many Filipinos. They now present a unique blend of Malay, Chinese, Spanish and American cultures, as well as indigenous ethnic tribes, mainly in the highlands, who have preserved their distinct crafts and way of life despite the encroachment of civilisation.

Luzon and the Visayas are Christian-dominated and exhibit a large degree of Western influence in their customs and traditions. Even here, however, there are interesting diversities: the Ifugaos of the northern Luzon mountains are famed for their woodcarvings, woven fabrics, dances and musical instruments, and their centuries-old rice terraces on the face of the mountains represent a crowning achievement in Filipino ingenuity.

Basically an agricultural country, though with expanding industrial development, much of the farmland is devoted to rice, corn, sugar and coconut plantations. There are substantial exports of sugar, coconut products, bananas and abaca (Manila hemp). Copper, iron, chromite and gold are among the mineral resources exploited.

Ninoy Aquino International Airport in Manila is served by no less than 40 airlines flying daily to cities throughout the world, as well as from other Asian countries. Departure tax is P220 per passenger.

Tourists can also arrive by cruise or passenger ship and there are many inter-island cruises from Manila.

Passports are required, though in some cases other valid travel documents, complete with re-entry permits to ports of origin, are accepted. Most travellers are entitled to 21 days' stay, providing they have onward or return tickets. If they want to extend their stay up to 59 days they must apply to the Commission of Immigration and Deportation on arrival.

All visitors staying longer than 59 days must apply again for a visa extension and pay immigration fees at the **Commission of Immigration and Deportation**, Magallanes Drive, Intramuros, Metro-Manila (Tel: 407651).

Nationals of the following countries must obtain a visa from Philippine diplomatic missions overseas before travelling to the Philippines: Albania, Austria, Belgium, Cambodia, China,

Cuba, Denmark, Finland, France, Germany, India, Italy, Iran, Laos, Libya, Luxembourg, Macau, the Netherlands, North Korea, Norway, South Africa, Spain, Sweden, Syria, Taiwan, Soviet Union, Vietnam and stateless persons.

EMBASSIES AND CONSULATES

Arab Republic of Egypt (Tel: 880396); **Argentina** (Tel: 875655); **Australia** (Tel: 8177911, Fax: 8173603); **Austria** (Tel: 8179191); **Belgium** (Tel: 876571, Fax: 8172566); **Brazil** (Tel: 8167116, Fax: 8197202); **Britain** (Tel: 8167116 to 18, Fax: 8197206); **Brunei** (Tel: 8162836, Fax: 8152872); **Canada** (Tel: 8159536, Fax: 8159595); **Chile** (Tel: 8150795, Fax: 8150795); **China** (Tel: 853148); **Colombia** (Tel: 9212701); **Cuba** (Tel: 8171192); **Czechoslovakia** (Tel: 7212584, Fax: 7215484); **Denmark** (Tel: 8191906, Fax: 8175729); **Finland** (Tel: 8162105 to 09, 8151401); **France** (Tel: 8101981, 8175047); **Gabon** (Tel: 8176459); **Germany** (Tel: 864906 to 09); **India** (Tel: 872445, 873339); **Indonesia** (Tel: 855061); **Iran** (Tel: 871561); **Israel** (Tel: 885329, Fax: 8190561); **Italy** (Tel: 874531, Fax: 8171436); **Japan** (Tel: 8189011, Fax: 8171436); **Jordan** (Tel: 8185901, Fax: 8184856).

Yellow fever inoculation is required of arrivals from infected areas, except children aged under 12 months who are subject to isolation or surveillance when deemed necessary.

Personal effects are allowed duty-free provided they are re-exported on departure.

Other duty-free allowances: 400 cigarettes or 100 cigars or 500 grams of tobacco and two bottles of alcoholic drink.

For stays of less than one month, motorcycles and boats do not require bond. For longer periods, a re-export bond is required.

Cars and other vehicles that a tourist wants to bring in must be covered by an international customs declaration (*Carnet de Passage en Douane*) and a letter of commitment from the Philippine Motor Association guaranteeing the exportation of the vehicle within a year from the date of arrival, or the payment of corresponding taxes and duties thereon.

It is prohibited to bring the following items into the Philippines:

• Dynamite, gunpowder, ammunition and other explosives, firearms and weapons of war and parts thereof, except when authorised by law.

• Written or printed articles, negatives or cinematographic films, photographic materials, engravings, objects, paintings and other representations of an obscene nature.

• Written or printed articles in any form, containing any matter advocating or inciting treason, rebellion, insurrection, sedition or subversion against the government of the Philippines or forcible resistance to any law in the country.

• Equipment, machines, and contrivances used in gambling.

• Any article made of gold, silver or other precious metals, the brands or marks of which do not indicate the actual fineness of quality of the material.

The unit of currency is the peso. The exchange rate is liable to fluctuation, but in early 1991 was ₱28:US$1. Coins are of ₱1 and 2, 50, 25, 10, 5 and 1 centavo denominations, and notes of 5, 10, 20, 50, 100 and 500 pesos.

Import and export of pesos is allowed to a maximum of ₱500 (of which coins must not exceed ₱5). Foreign currencies are allowed entry in unlimited volume but amounts exceeding US$3,000 must be declared on entry.

Foreign currencies acceptable to the central bank and at exchange counters in Manila for converion to pesos are the US dollar, sterling, Deutschmark, Swiss franc, French franc, Canadian dollar, Italian lira, Dutch guilder, Japanese yen, Australian dollar and the Hongkong dollar. Exchange counters usually offer a better rate and swifter transactions than banks. Street money changers should be avoided as they invariably cheat the hapless tourist. As holds true of most parts of Asia, the best foreign currency to hold is the US dollar. Outside Manila, US dollars are widely acceptable, but the exchange rate in the capital is always better. Traveller's cheques can be cashed in major towns, but the transaction can prove time-consuming and sometimes frustrating. The rate for travellers' cheques is 5-10% lower than the rate

She sells sea shells on the seashore. ▷
Photo: Patrick Lucero

Philippines

for cash.

Purchase receipts for traveller's cheques and a passport are required. It is often difficult to encash traveller's cheques outside Manila.

Major credit cards such as **American Express**, **Visa**, **Master Card** and **Diners Club** are accepted in Manila only. Cash withdrawals by means of credit cards require the presentation of a passport. Holders of one of the major credit cards may obtain cash advances in pesos at the following addresses:

American Express, Philamlife Bldg, UN Ave/Orosa Sts, Ermita, Manila.

Visa and Master Card, Equitable Bank, UN Ave/Bocobo Sts, Ermita, Manila.

Diner's Club, Security Bank, UN Ave/Mabini Sts, Ermita, Manila.

Personal cheques are not usually honoured for payment of hotel and restaurant bills, airline tickets or shopping.

The national language is Pilipino (Tagalog). English and Spanish are widely spoken. English is spoken almost everywhere, being the medium of instruction in schools and often the language of administration. Spanish, though a considerable social asset, is now far less prevalent.

The widespread use of English in the Philippines allows the English-speaking visitor a chance to establish contact at many different social levels. The possibility of meaningful conversation with the people is one of the great attractions of the country.

The climate is typically tropical: warm to hot with high humidity. The nights are often pleasantly cool and frequent sea breezes moderate the effects of the day's heat. There are two seasons: dry and rainy. The rains come between June and November, wet days interspersed with hot, sunny days.

Before the heavy rains come, the temperature tends to be higher during the dry season from March to June, and people from Manila in particular (if they can afford it) like to get away to the beach or cool mountain resorts during this season. May to November invariably brings typhoons.

The average maximum daily temperature is a little above 30°C (85°F) dropping to an average minimum of 22°C (72°F) at night.

Light clothes of natural fibres are best for casual wear. Tropical conditions require frequent changes of clothing if you are moving around in the heat. Jackets are expected for men in some establishments in the evenings, though the Filipino barong tagalog (a lightweight, long-sleeved, embroidered shirt — traditionally made from woven banana leaf fibre — worn outside the trousers) is a sensible, acceptable substitute on such occasions. The short-sleeved type is not considered formal.

Evening wear for women is much as it is in the West. When visiting churches and mosques, it is well to remember that shorts and scanty or provocative dress is inappropriate and in Catholic churches women should cover their heads with a scarf. Although no tourist is likely to be asked to leave, they would offend local feelings if these traditions are not observed.

Government and private offices are open on weekdays from 8 am to 5 pm. Some private offices open on Saturdays from 8 am until noon, but this is generally considered a day off.

The Post Office keeps government hours. The main one in Manila is situated at Liwasang Bonifacio by the MacArthur Bridge over the Pasig River. It offers a 24-hour cable service.

Commercial banks are open from 9 am to 3 pm on weekdays only.

Most savings banks remain open late, but also on weekdays only. Most of the department stores in Quiapo and Santa Cruz districts of Manila are open from 10 am to 9 pm. The shops along Carriedo Street in Quiapo stay open until 11 pm selling general goods. The shops of Escolta and Ermita districts close rather earlier, around 7 pm. Some shops close between noon and 2 pm. Fashionable commercial centres have sprouted in the plush shopping centres of Makati, Quezon City and Greenhills districts. They cater mostly to above-average-income residents but are convenient for tourists in a rush.

Most restaurants are open until midnight, at least. Most nightclubs swing all night. Some open as early as 2 pm for those who need a little something to help their lunch go down. Bars are normally open from mid-day or even mid-morning until the early hours.

Liquor can be purchased from liquor stores and supermarkets, generally open from 10 am to 8 pm Monday to Saturday. Some stores are open on Sunday with shorter hours. Beer and local spirits are also available at *sari-sari* stores, the Philippine equivalent of "Mom and Pop" stores, which are often open in the evening until 9 pm or 10 pm.

MANILA

FROM THE AIRPORT: A limousine service offered by most tourist hotels costs approximately US$15 for the one-way journey. An airport bus shuttle service charges US$3 a passenger; it makes stops at major hotels in Makati and along Roxas Boulevard, but the service is somewhat haphazard. The taxi fare via G & S Coupon Taxi from the airport to hotels in Makati, Pasay and central Manila is approximately ₱200-300.

TAXIS: Philippine taxi fares are among the cheapest in Asia — or the world for that matter. Non-air-conditioned cabs start their flagfall at ₱2.50 for the first 500 m, with ₱1.00 for every 250 m thereafter. For air-conditioned taxis the flagdown is ₱3.50, then 1.00 for each 125 m thereafter. Tourists should be wary of the sharp taxi drivers who ask for a price — usually outrageous — for a journey and are reluctant to put their meters on.

JEEPNEYS: These are converted jeeps operating as mini-buses along set routes. To use them, you must have some idea where you are going and its relation to the destination indicated on the front and at the sides of the jeepney. The jeepneys show the name of the suburb, or a particular place (such as a park or monument), and sometimes the name of the main road which they intend to use. Fares are low, starting at ₱1.00. Jeepneys are often equipped with stereo music (as are some taxis) and radio, and are lavishly decorated with coloured streamers, masses of wing-mirrors and other ornaments especially horses, a sign of power. Foreigners always receive a warm welcome from other passengers and riding jeepneys is an interesting way of travelling, and offers the chance of talking to average Filipinos. The vehicles can be stopped by simply waving them down.

BUSES: These operate along most of the main roads in Manila and its suburbs. Destinations are shown. Like the jeepneys, they are cheap, but you must know precisely where you are going. Many buses are being replaced by those of the government-run Metro-Manila Transit Co., some of which are air-conditioned, like the Love Bus, charging ₱8.50. Long-distance buses and coaches also can be caught in Mani-

la for most parts of Luzon island.

METRORAIL: An elevated light-rail transit system in Metro-Manila, Metrorail charges a uniform rate of ₱3.50 between any points along its 15 km line along Taft Avenue from Baclaran in the south to Caloocan City in the north. There are 16 stations along the route. Tokens are required to pass through the turnstiles.

METRO TRAK: This commuter train operates from Tutuban Station to Carmona, Laguna just south of Manila. It stops at Espana, Santa Mesa, Pandacan, Paco, Vito Cruz, Buendia, Pasay Road, EDSA, FTI, Bicutan, Sucat, Alabang, Muntinlupa and San Pedro. Trains run every 30 minutes during morning and evening peak periods, otherwise hourly. Fares range from ₱1.00 to ₱6.50 according to distance.

METRO FERRY: Just next to the Manila Central Post Office beneath the MacArthur Bridge is the terminus of the Pasig River Ferry. It operates a 45 minute service to Guadalupe near Makati, costs ₱9.50 and offers an unusual view of river life with glimpses of dusty old warehouses, factories, barges and the Malacanang presidential palace and gardens en route. Photography is not permitted in the vicinity of Malacanang.

HIRE CARS: Air-conditioned cars for rent, with or without drivers, are widely available. A chauffeured car costs from ₱800.00 for three hours, and from ₱1,500.00 for a day. Fuel is not included in the rental. Car-rental agencies normally want a deposit. Many car-rental companies have representatives in hotel lobbies. Valid driving licences in the tourist's country of residence will suffice; but those staying for more than 90 days will have to get a local licence.

KALESAS: These horse-drawn rigs operate mainly in the older part of town, around the Manila City area, north of the Pasig River. Prices are subject to negotiation with the driver.

UPCOUNTRY

TRAINS: Rail services in the country leave a lot to be desired. The **Philippine National Railways** (PNR) has closed its northern passenger line because commuters have better alternatives in bus services. A programme to update and reopen the line will take some time. The southern line runs to Camalig in Albay province. From there the brave tourist can take PNR buses to Legazpi City where the view of the Mayon Volcano is spectacular. Tutuban in Manila's Tondo district serves as the railway's central station. The only other railway system in the country is on Panay island, linking Iloilo City with Roxas City. There are three services daily to Camalig

TRANSIT LOUNGE TO OVER TEN ISLAND HIDEAWAYS CEBU.

Emerald waters that beckon. Kilometric stretches of shimmering white sand that invite long, lazy strolls. Where a gentle sea wind is your only company. It's the perfect island hideaway. And there are over ten breathtaking island hideaways that await you around Cebu, the Queen City of the South.

On your way to Cebu, fly Philippine Airlines and experience the lavish pampering of our flight attendants Grace and Rosanna, whose warm smiles are the appropriate introduction to a lifelong love affair with life in the tropics.

Cebu of the Philippines.

Philippine Airlines

S H I N I N G
T H R O U G H

Philippines

at 5 am, 3 pm and 8 pm. Fares are ₱100-200 and journey time is approximately 15 hours.

BUSES: The country has a fair system of roads, especially in the Central Luzon region surrounding Manila and near the provincial capitals on the more developed islands.

On Luzon, dozens of bus companies operate, providing good and frequent services. **Philippine National Railways Bus Co.** operates reasonably new buses at lower prices than many other lines. **Pantranco-North Express** (terminus in Quezon Boulevard) and **Philippine Rabbit** are two of the biggest bus operators on the northern routes. **Batangas Laguna Tayabas Bus Co.** (BLTB) operates from Manila

as far southeast as Quezon province, while **Pantranco-South Express** and **J. B. L. Transit Co.** serve as far down as Bulan Town, near the southern tip of Luzon. BLTB is located on E. delos Santos Ave, Pasay City. It has the largest network of buses comprising economy, air-conditioned and super deluxe classes. The latter, like tourist buses, sometimes offer video movies, stereo music and snacks for passengers on long journeys.

Fares are low, being under government control. Buses operate at fixed intervals on specific routes, with busy routes serviced more frequently. Also, air-conditioned buses (sometimes with added amenities such as TV and

MAJOR AIRLINES' OFFICES
Metro-Manila
Aeroflot Soviet Airlines (SU), 837 Pasay Rd, Makati, Metro-Manila. Tel: 867-756, Fax: 817-7737.

Aerolift Philippines Corp., Grd. Flr, Chemphil Bldg, 851 Pasay Rd, Makati, Metro-Manila. Tel: 817-2361, 817-2369, 818-4223.

Air Canada (AC), Tel: 810-4461/64, Fax: 810-5131.

Air France (AF), Century Towers, Tordesillas corner, H. V. de la Costa Sts, Salcedo Village, Makati, Metro-Manila. Tel: 815-6968, 815-6970, Fax: 815-6969.

Air India (AI), Gammon Centre Bldg, Alfaro St, Salcedo Village, Makati, Metro-Manila. Tel: 815-2441, 815-1280.

Air Nuguini (PX), Pacific Bank Bldg, Ayala Ave, Makati, Metro-Manila. Tel: 819-0206, 810-1846/48, Fax: 817-9826.

Alitalia (AZ), M3 The Gallery Bldg, Amorsolo St, Makati, Metro-Manila. Tel: 854-854.

American Airlines (AA), G/F Olympia Condominium, Makati Ave, corner, Sto. Tomas St, Makati, Metro-Manila. Tel: 817-8645, 817-8575, Fax: 810-3230.

British Airways (BA), 135 Filipino Merchants Bldg, de la Rosa & Legaspi Sts, Legaspi Village, Makati, Metro-Manila. Tel: 817-4571, 817-0361, Fax: 819-0410.

Canadian Airlines Int'l (CP), Allied Bank Centre, Ayala Ave, Makati, Metro-Manila. Tel: 810-2656/59.

Cathay Pacific Airways (CX), Gammon Centre, 126 Alfaro St, Salcedo Village, Makati, Metro-Manila. Tel: 815-9401, 815-9417, Fax: 819-5610, 815-2445.

135 Ermita Centre Bldg, Roxas Blvd, Manila. Tel: 598-063/65.

China Airlines (CA), Manila Pavilion Hotel, United Nations Ave, Ermita, Tel: 590-085/89.

Continental Airlines (CO), SGV Bldg, 6760 Ayala Ave, Makati, Metro-Manila. Tel: 818-8701, Fax: 8153702.

Delta Airlines, Inc. (DL), Makati Stock Exchange Bldg, Ayala Ave, Makati, Metro-Manila. Tel: 859-215, 810-1167.

Egypt Air (MS), Windsor Tower Condominium, Legaspi St, Legaspi Village, Makati, Metro-Manila. Tel: 815-8476/79.

Flying Tigers Lines (FT), International Cargo Terminal, Ninoy Aquino Int'l Airport, Pasay City. Tel: 831-9791/94, Fax: 831-5511.

Garuda Indonesia Airlines (GA), Manila Peninsula Hotel, Ayala Ave, Makati, Metro-Manila. Tel: 862-458, 862-205.

Gulf Air (GF), Windsor Tower Bldg, 163 Legaspi St, Legaspi Village, Makati, Metro-Manila. Tel: 815-8229, 817-6909.

Japan Airlines (JL), Hotel Nikko Manila Garden, EDSA corner, A. Arnaiz St, (Pasay Rd) Makati, Metro-Manila. Tel: 810-9776/80, 810-9352/55, 810-9781, Fax: 817-1718.

KLM Royal Dutch Airlines (KL), Athenaeum Bldg, 160 Alfaro St, Salcedo Village, Makati, Metro-Manila. Tel: 815-4790, Fax: 819-5680.

video) ply these busy routes. **Sarkies Tours** (Tel: 582413) and **Sunshine Run** (Tel: 584787) have regular services to Legazpi and some other cities. Before the 1990 earthquake these included Baguio. Fares are higher than on the regular bus service.

SHIPPING: For visitors with the time it is pleasant to travel by ship between the islands. Many shipping companies ply the island routes from Manila. The yellow pages of the telephone directory provide a comprehensive guide to the shipping lines and services offered. But it is almost impossible to book a berth by telephone or to persuade a travel agency to take a booking. It is best to go to the port area and find the ship you

want by perusing the noticeboards outside the shipping offices. Then make your bookings on the spot.

Some of the coastal villages served by the steamers can hardly have changed since Conrad's day and, arriving at sunset with seemingly the entire local population on the wharf waiting to see who is aboard is well worth the effort involved.

Some ships have air-conditioned cabins, but where these are not available it is better to sleep on deck — using the camp bed and linen provided on request. Local food can be bought, though it is often of very poor quality. Take a bottle of water, chocolate and fruit.

Korean Air (KE), LPL Plaza, 124 Alfaro St, Salcedo Village, Makati, Metro-Manila. Tel: 815-8911/13, 815-9261/62.

Kuwait Airways (KU), JEG Bldg, 150 Legaspi St, Makati, Metro-Manila. Tel: 817-2778, 817-2789, 817-2795, Fax: 818-2364.

Lufthansa (LH), Legaspi Park View Condominium, Legaspi corner, Alvarado Sts, Makati, Metro-Manila. Tel: 810-4596.

Malaysian Airlines System (MH), Legaspi Towers 300, Roxas Blvd, corner, Vito Cruz St, Manila. Tel: 575-761/66, 586-893.

Northwest Airlines (NW), G/F, Athenaeum Bldg, 160 Alfaro St, Salcedo Village, Makati, Metro-Manila. Tel: 818-7341, 810-4718, Fax: 815-6455.

Olympic Airways (OA), Dona Narcisa Bldg, Paseo de Roxas, Makati, Metro-Manila. Tel: 816-2316, 816-0794.

Pacific Airways Corp., Domestic Airport Rd, Pasay City. Tel: 832-2731.

Pakistan Int'l Airways (PK), ADC Bldg, Makati, Metro-Manila. Tel: 818-3711, 818-0502.

Philippine Airlines (PR), L&S Bldg, Roxas Blvd, Manila. Tel: 521-3694, 506-120, Fax: 818-3298, 815-0418, 810-9214. Data Centre Bldg, Pasay City. Tel: 832-3166, 819-1771.

Qantas Airways (QF), Cityland Condominium, Valero corner, Cedeno Sts, Salcedo Village, Makati, Metro-Manila. Tel: 817-1631/815-1750, Fax: 882-367.

Sabena Belgian Airlines (SN), Manila Pavilion

Hotel, United Nations Ave, Ermita, Manila. Tel: 508-636.

Saudi Arabian Airlines (SV), Cougar Bldg, Valero St, Salcedo Village, Makati, Metro-Manila. Tel: 818-7866, 819-5132.

Scandinavian Airlines System, F&M Lopez Bldg, Legaspi St, Legaspi Village, Makati, Metro-Manila. Tel: 810-5050, Fax: 818-1128.

Singapore Airlines (SQ), 138 H. V. de la Costa Sts, Salcedo Village, Makati, Metro-Manila. Tel: 810-4960, 810-4951, Fax: 815-2527.

SwissAir (SR), Country Space I Bldg, Sen. Gil J. Puyat Ave Ext., Makati, Metro-Manila. Tel: 818-8521, 818-8351 Fax: 815-3350.

Thai Airways International (TG), Country Space 1 Bldg, Sen. Gil J. Puyat Ave Ext., Makati, Metro-Manila. Tel: 815-8421/27, 815-8438/40, Fax: 817-4044.

United Airlines (UA), Alpap Bldg, 140 Alfaro St, Salcedo Village, Makati, Metro-Manila. Tel: 8185421/24, 818-7321/29, Fax: 817-4162. 4/F, University Bldg, Paseo de Roxas corner, Perea Sts, Legaspi Village, Makati, Metro-Manila. Tel: 868-051 to 58.

Cebu

Philippine Airlines (PR), Capitol Ticket Office, N. Escario St. Tel: 52464.

Davao

Philippine Airlines (PR), Regina Commercial Complex, C. M. Recto St. Tel: 73785.

Zamboanga

Philippine Airlines (PR), Lantaka Hotel, N. S. Valderrosa St. Tel: 2022.

Small boats serve the smaller islands. From Zamboanga in southern Mindanao, the **Sin Hap Hing Agency**, Governor Lim St, Zamboanga City (Tel: 3421), has ships sailing through the Sulu islands as far south as Sitangkai, near Sabah. Only deck accommodation is available. The ship calls at Jolo, Siasi, Bongao and sometimes Sibutu. Ships sail every four or five days, but the conflict with Muslim rebels in this area has also brought irregular services. Check with authorities.

Ferries run between such adjacent spots as Iloilo and Bacolod (between Panay and Negros islands) and Zamboanga City and Jolo. The Zamboanga-Basilan trip is P20 first-class, P15 second class.

Information about these smaller boats is best obtained locally.

AIR: Air travel is the most convenient method of movement between the islands, with flights serving all important provincial cities. Most of the traffic is out of Manila, though Cebu's Mactan airport in the Visayas is an important centre. Examples of round trip fares from Manila on **Philippine Airlines** (PAL) are Cebu P2,660; Davao P3,456; Zamboanga P3,208; Legazpi P1,430 and Baguio P702. There is an airport tax of P15 on domestic flights originating in Manila. Lower amounts are charged at some of the other local airports.

Although PAL is the major domestic (and international) carrier operating to over 40 domestic points, new airlines now compete with the flag carrier. These include **Aerolift** (Daet, Cebu, Boracay, Bohol, Dipolog, Lubang and Busuanga) and **Pacific Airways Corp.** (Lubang, Boracay and Busuanga).

There are more than 200 licensed tour operators, many with offices in the main tourist hotels, who will arrange for any city or upcountry tours. Visitors may select from a variety of special interest tours lasting from one to 12 days. They include: camping, cruising, fishing, mountain-climbing, scuba-diving, bird and wildlife-watching and special festivals. Most of the tour operators provide air-conditioned buses or cars for the tours. One of the out-of-town tours will give the visitor a look at rural life in the Philippines.

There are also tours of Malacanang Palace, the official residence of the Philippine president, where relics of the Marcos family's ostentatious lifestyle are on display.

TRAVEL AGENTS/ TOUR OPERATORS
Metro-Manila
Anscor Travel Corp., Regina Bldg, Makati, Metro-Manila. Tel: 815-9181.

Baron Travel Corp., Pacific Bank Bldg, Ayala Ave, Makati, Metro Manila. Tel: 815-1425.

Philippine Experience, Pacific Contact, Negros Navigation Bldg, Pasay Rd, Makati, Metro Manila. Tel: 819-5485.

Rajah Tours Phil., Inc., New Physician's Tower, UN Ave, Ermita, Manila. Tel: 522-0541.

Sarkies Tours Philippines, Inc., J. P. Laurel Bldg, M. H. del Pilar St, Ermita, Manila. Tel: 597-658.

Southeast (Phil) Travel Centre, 451 Pedro Gil St, Ermita, Manila. Tel: 506-601.

Sundowner Travel Centre, 1430 A. Mabini St, Ermita, Manila. Tel: 521-2602.

Baguio
American Express PCI, Travel Service, Hyatt Terraces Hotel, Baguio City. Tel: 442-4722.

Rowan Trading, Abanao, Baguio City. Tel: 442-3341.

Bacolod
Thomas Cook, San Juan St, Bacolod City. Tel: 211-96.

Cebu
American Express PCI, Travel Service, Arcade 3, Magellan Hotel Bldg, Lahug, Cebu City. Tel: 734-98.

Amity Travel Corp., Jones Ave, Cebu City. Tel: 732-34.

Baron Travel Corp., Magellan Hotel Bldg, Lahug, Cebu City. Tel: 797-26.

Davao
Amity Travel Corp. Kalimsi Bldg, Legaspi St, Davao City. Tel: 718-83.

Amity Travel Corp. Davao Insular Inter-Continental Hotel, Lanang, Davao City. Tel: 760-51.

Iloilo
Delamar Travel and Tours, Hotel del Rio, M. H. del Pilar St, Molo, Iloilo City. Tel: 719-66.

Tourmaster Travel Service Inc., M. H. del Pilar St, Molo, Iloilo City. Tel: 737-05.

PUERTO PRINCESA
Princesa Travel & Tours Inc., Rafols Hotel, Puerto Princesa. Tel: 211-1.

Zamboanga
Tourismo Filipino Inc., NS Valderroza, Zamboanga City. Tel: 393-1.

Zamboanga Hermosa Tours Inc., San Jose, Zamboanga City. Tel: 257-2.

The range of hotels in Manila allows travellers on various budgets to find accommodation to suit their needs. The best hotels match their counterparts in other parts of Asia; some of the cheaper hotels are a little run down.

Service, though usually of a high standard, can be erratic. Filipinos are natural hosts and offer service with a genuine smile. From the excellence of the numerous top hotels to the cheap places in Santa Cruz and Quiapo, the traveller will generally find hotel staff helpful. The wide use of English helps and Filipinos will often volunteer all kinds of information even without being asked.

Most of the better hotels in Manila are scattered near the area known as Ermita, as well as the business centre of Makati. New hotels are also being built in Greenhills as well as on reclaimed land along Roxas Boulevard in Pasay. Ermita is the capital's tourist belt and lies south of the old walled city, Intramuros, and the Pasig river. Rizal Park, Manila Bay sights, tourist shopping and nightlife all lie in this area.

Government taxes run at 13.7%, service charge at 10%.

Better hotels provide transport to and from the airport. Most of the cheaper hotels, though lacking the gloss of luxury, are perfectly satisfactory for visitors who expect basic Western standards. Most rooms are air-conditioned, though many have only a shower rather than a bath.

Discounts ranging from 20-50% are available at many hotels, particularly as Manila often has more rooms than tourists. It is always worth asking.

Outside Manila, except at modern resorts, accommodation is often basic and water and electricity may be rationed. Prices are lower, but not always as low as they might be given the standard of facilities.

At home under a sultry tropical sun, the Filipino has always enjoyed many kinds of fresh seafood and plump fruit. The people refer to their own dishes as "native" — in contrast to foreign. Typical Filipino food includes suckling pigs, banana flowers and hearts of palm. Although they may not be cooked in the traditional manner over open fires, today these very dishes, along with a great many more, are popular in some of the very best Manila restaurants.

For the really adventurous gourmet there is *balut* — unhatched duck embryo eaten straight from the shell.

Some of the best native dishes are *adobo* where chicken or pork — and sometimes both — is cooked in vinegar, garlic, spices and soy sauce; *kare-kare* — beef prepared in a spicy peanut sauce and served with vegetables mixed in a sauce of shrimps cooked in pork lard; *lechon*, pork cooked so that the skin crisps, served with a liver sauce or one made from sweet and sour ingredients; *crispy pata* — pork knuckle cooked in spices, again with crisp skin; *lumpia* — spring rolls prepared with shrimp, pork or chicken mixed with the tender heart of the young coconut plant; *afritada* — beef prepared in olive oil, tomato paste and served with olives and other vegetables; and the very fine soup known as *sinigang*, slightly sour and made from one of several meats and vegetables. For dessert, *halo-halo* is a mixture of fruits, ice and coconut milk, not to mention a little sweetcorn and beans.

The Philippines' close association with first the Spanish and later the Americans, has led to a variety of dishes being modified in tastes peculiar to these two nations. Chinese cooking, too, has been an influence.

The traditional Filipino breakfast consists of fruit, followed by fried eggs with spicy beef and fried rice, then coffee or chocolate. Many of the tourist hotels serve it.

When ordering meals it is best to watch the Filipinos. Even before the food arrives, sauce dishes are brought in and people automatically reach for the vinegar bottle with hot chili, or the soy sauce which they mix with the juice from kalamansi (small green citrus fruit). Grilled items are good with crushed garlic, vinegar and chili. It's a good idea to start a meal with *sinigang*, a clear broth slightly soured with small fruit and prepared with *bangus* (milkfish) or shrimp.

Manila, as an international city, also provides a wide range of restaurants offering Asian and Western food.

For native food, the following restaurants are among the best: **Josephine**, at the Greenbelt Park in Makati, on Roxas Blvd (near the Cultural Centre area) and at Greenhills, is patronised for its fresh seafood and other Filipino dishes. Cultural shows, where diners may join in folk-dancing, are staged during dinner. The **Kamayan** chain of restaurants (on

Buffalo cart with local beauties.

Photo: Veronica Garbutt

Pasay Rd in Makati, Padre Faura in Manila, and E. delos Santos Ave, or EDSA, in Quezon City) popularised eating with the hands. **Aling Asiang**, **The Plaza** and **Via Mare**, at the Greenbelt Park in Makati, and **Gloriamaris**, at the Cultural Centre Complex, are among the more expensive places specialising in fine Filipino cuisine. Also known for excellent Filipino food are **Tito Rey** (Pasay Rd, Makati), **Kuya** (a crab and oyster restaurant at the Milelong Bldg, Amorsolo St, Makati), Leo's (Roxas Blvd), **Cafe Adriatico** and **Bistro Remedios** (Adriatico St, Ermita, Manila) and **Pinausukan** (Pasay Rd, in Makati, Roxas Blvd in Pasay and West Avenue in Quezon City). Prices are moderately high.

There is also a proliferation of simple and inexpensive restaurants serving local dishes. They can be crowded during lunchtime. Among them is **Aristocrat** which has branches in Roxas Blvd (near the Malate Church), Greenbelt in Makati, Quzon Ave (near E. delos Santos Ave) and Cubao in Quezon City, and Greenhills Commercial Centre in San Juan. **Barrio Fiesta**, which has outlets in West Avenue and Cubao in Quezon City, EDSA in Greenhills, Makati Ave and Buendia Ave in Makati, is well-known for its crispy *bata* and *kare-kare*. **Max's**, famous for its spring fried chicken, is on Scout Tuason St, and Cubao in Quezon City, Greenbelt and Quad car park in Makati, and Orosa St, in Ermita, Manila. **The Harbour View** in Luneta Park is a fine place to experience the Manila Bay sunset while munching on *pulutan* (snacks) and drinking local beer.

Spanish food is served at: **El Comedor**, M. Adriatico St in Ermita; **Muralla Calle Real** in Intramuros; **Zarzuela** on Pasay Road, Makati; **Casa Marcos**, Roxas Boulevard Extension, **Nielson Tower**, Makati Avenue, Makati, and **La Tasca** at Greenbelt, Makati.

For other European food, **Au Bon Vivant**, L. Guerrero St in Ermita and **L'Orangerie**, Zodiac St (at the EDSA end of Buendia Ave) in Makati specialise in French cuisine, while **Schwarzwalder** at Greenbelt in Makati serves German food. Italian food is good at **La Taverna**, M. Adriatico in Ermita; **Mario's** on Makati Avenue and **La Primavera**, Greenbelt Park, Legaspi St in Makati. **L'Eau Vive en Asia** on Paz Mendoza Guazon St in Pandacan is run by lay missionary workers of Donum Dei. It specialises in good French cooking with an Asian accent.

The Philippines continues to attract a sizeable number of Japanese tourists and businessmen and as a consequence several good Japanese restaurants have gained a stronghold in Metro-Manila. Among the best are: **Kimpura**, at the Makati Commercial Centre near the Hotel Inter-Continental; **Benkay** and **Gojinka** at the Manila Garden Hotel also located at the Makati Commercial Centre; **Furusato** on Roxas Blvd, near the Holiday Inn Hotel; **Aoi** at Century Park Sheraton in Manila; **Sugi** at the Greenbelt Park in Makati, and Takayama Garden at Greenhills. **Kamameshi House** has branches on Makati Ave in Makati and West Avenue in Quezon City. Others include **Mikimoto** on Roxas Boulevard and **Oshio** on Pasay Road, Makati.

Korean cuisine is available at **Korea Gardens**, Burgos St, Makati; **Korean Village**, Malate in Manila, and **Seoul** Garden on Roxas Blvd. Chinese food is best in Manila's lively Chinatown and Ongpin Street, but there are several good restaurants elsewhere in the city. These include: **Peacock Restaurant** at the Century Park Sheraton; **South Villa** at Greenbelt and Greenhills; **Kowloon House** in Makati Commercial Centre, Makati and A. Mabini St in Ermita; **Emerald Garden** on Roxas Boulevard and **Aberdeen Court** in Makati and Quezon City.

Indian food-lovers should try **Al-Shams** in A. Mabini in Ermita, and **Kashmir** on Padre Faura and Makati Ave.

New Orleans, Greenbelt Park, Makati is the Manila home of Creole and cooking with jazz, while **Rosie's Diner** on del Pilar St in Ermita does a good imitation of American fast food. Fast growing in popularity is the **Seafood Market** chain of restaurants on Jorge Bocobo and Padre Faura, Ermita; Makati Ave in Makati, and EDSA in Cubao. Diners choose from an array of fresh fish and accompaniments, in supermarket style, pay for it, then instruct a waitress how it should be cooked.

The sight of a lineup of chefs visible from the street, cooking away at their woks and pans is both enticing and mouthwatering.

Beer and mixed drinks are available throughout the Philippines, though they are expensive in certain establishments. Manila is home of one of Asia's best beers, San Miguel — though those versions of it brewed under licence elsewhere are not of such high quality. Locally made rums and gins are the basis of several exciting cocktails which, if one can judge from their names, endow one with all kinds of desirable traits. Imported wines are available at most liquor shops and supermarkets; in hotels they are expensive.

Music is the heart of Manila's night scene. Filipino musicians are famous throughout Asia, if not the world, and bands and singers are widely exported to other Asian capitals. The big hotels have cornered much of the best live music in town and you can enjoy top-rate bands and singers in just about all top-class hotels but notably at the **Calesa Bar** at the Hyatt Hotel and **Tap Room Bar** at the Manila Hotel. Those looking for dancing can head for the discos; **Euphoria** at the Inter-Continental Hotel; **Lost Horizon** at the Philippine Plaza Hotel; **Faces** on Pasay Road; **Kudos** at Makati Creekside Mall; **Subway** on Adriatico St, Ermita; **Cheek to Cheek** on Wilson St in Greenhills; **Birdland** in Quezon City and **Bistro RJ** in Makati. Popular with Filipinos, and well worth trying, are **Love City**, **Heartbeat**, **Thunderdome** and **Jealousy** — though be prepared to make the long trek to Quezon City to get away from the tourist spots of Ermita.

For "girlie" shows the higher class ones are **Jools** on Makati Ave, Makati, and **Moulin Rouge** on UN Ave in Ermita, but there are dozens of others. Apart from the nightclubs, there are a multitude of bars with hostesses, called "hospitality girls," to tempt the less inhibited male visitor. M. H. del Pilar, which boasts no less than 40 bars over a short stretch of Ermita, and Mabini which runs parallel, are the most popular bar streets. Beer costs P30-40, often two drinks for the price of one during Happy Hour. Drinks for the girls — who are normally not as aggressively mercenary as their counterparts in some other Asian capitals — cost P75-90.

The usual caution should be used in flashing money around and making sure what sort of charges one is involving oneself in. In Manila much of the entertainment is aimed exclusively

Smiles come easily to Filipinas.

Photo: Edwin Tayay

at men. Its character is determined more by what the average Filipino man expects when he goes on the town than by any special considerations of foreign tastes and locals normally far outnumber foreign visitors.

There are also a number of less boisterous bars in Makati, notably the British-style **San Mig** in Legaspi St (and in Pafre Faura, Ermita), the **Prince of Wales** in Greenbelt Park, **Billboard** on Makati Avenue and **Fire and Rain** on Pasay Road. **The Pool**, **Visions**, **Superstar** and **Firehouse**, all in or near M. H. del Pilar in Ermita are also enjoyable.

Bodega Folk Theatre on Quezon Ave offers excellent folk songs, while **The Hobbit House** in Malate district has the rather tasteless gimmick of being staffed entirely by dwarves.

Dinner theatre and fashion shows are presented at some of the best hotels in town. There was a time when fashion shows, with local film stars as models, were regular entertainment features during lunch at big hotels and restaurants but the fad has somewhat faded.

Rather more serious entertainment can be enjoyed regularly at the impressive **Cultural Centre**, on the reclaimed land complex off Roxas Blvd. Concerts featuring local and visiting orchestras, jazz musicians and ballet are held in the grand main theatre. Plays are also staged here, as well as the nearby **Folk Arts Theatre** and sometimes at **Fort Santiago** and **Puerta Real**, Intramuros.

Free concerts are held at **Luneta Park** on Sundays and at **Paco Park** on Fridays from November to June.

Manila abounds in cinemas. Many are located along Quezon Blvd and Rizal Ave in Quiapo and Santa Cruz, and in the commercial centre of Makati. The city normally receives films from Hollywood soon after they are released. The local film industry also churns out movies in Tagalog but many of these are of doubtful artistic merit. Filipino traditional dancing can be seen at several of the hotels and restaurants including the Manila Hotel's **Maynila**, the **Philippine Plaza** poolside, **Zamboanga** on Adriatico and **Pistang Pilipino** on M. H. del Pilar.

By far the best buys both in Manila and upcountry are handicrafts, some of them unique to the Philippines. There is very little point in buying imported items with the exception of Chinese porcelain, some of which was shipped to the Philippines as export ware during the Chinese Sung, Yuan, Ming and Qing dynasties. Bargain in all places as a matter of principle. Even one-price department stores can sometimes be persuaded to give a small discount. Look and compare prices before buying. The tourist shops will generally give a 10% discount without you trying too hard.

The transparent woven materials used for tablecloths, placemats and the barong tagalog shirt is an interesting and inexpensive buy. They include pina (from pineapple fibre) and jusi (from banana tree fibre or silk).

They are often heavily embroidered; this, of course, influences the price. Hand-made lace, usually produced in upcountry villages, is also a good buy. Try **Pistang Pilipino** in Ermita or one of the many branches of **Tesoros** for such items.

For shoes, women can visit the outer suburb of Marikina where there is a thriving shoe factory, and prices are low.

Handbags as well as numerous household items — both of utility and for decoration — are available made from leather, abaca (Manila hemp), wood, beads and snakeskin. Especially notable are objects made from the capiz shell which, when polished, becomes beautifully transparent.

Manila is a town of dressmakers and this is a good place to have women's wear made. Top designers are **Pitoy Moreno**, **Aureo Alonzo** and **Ben Farrales**. Also unusual are the knitted designs of **Lulu Tan Gan** and barongs by **Barge Ramos**.

The best work is of course expensive, but something inspired by the local tribal fashions would be excitingly unique back home.

Some dining and kitchen household items in kamagong or acacia woods can be pleasing. Some of the wood is not kiln-dried and therefore subject to cracking or warping when taken out of the humid local climate. Narra wood chests and furniture inlaid with bone or mother-of-pearl are local products of some character.

Antiques, especially Catholic religious figures and Chinese porcelains, are offered for sale. Many are probably recent copies. Most of the galleries exhibit mass-produced paintings.

Filipinas love to adorn themselves and spend much time buying and selling jewellery, a popular investment too. Gold, silver and diamonds are the traditional favourites but pearls are becoming very desirable. The best silver jewellery is to be found in Baguio where the guild-like

training from St Louis University has resulted in fine craftmanship. Jewelmer's south sea pearls are the world's largest (9-15 mm in diameter compared with the 2-9 mm cultured pearl) and take about seven years to mature. They come in a rainbow of natural colours with a lustrous nacre layering, guaranteeing long life. For antique jewellery try **Capricci** and for modern designs choose from **Diagem** or **Fe Panlilio**.

Cigars produced in the Philippines are of high quality — Alhambra and Tabacalera brands are among the best. Shops can arrange for the buyers name to be printed on the cigar labels.

The city's main shopping areas, many being developed with air-conditioned shopping malls, are Ermita, Makati, Cubao (Araneta Centre), Escolta, Quaipo and Santa Cruz. Shoemart and Rustan's in Makati, Cubao, Harrison Plaza and EDSA in Greenhills are comprehensive department stores.

The Philippines is strong on both spectator and participatory sports. Basketball is the national sport and matches are played regularly at the **Ninoy Aquino Memorial Stadium** in Manila (mainly at amateur level) and at the **ULTRA** sports complex (home of the only professional basketball league outside the US) in Pasig. Baseball is played at Ninoy Aquino Memorial Stadium and at the **Rodriguez Sports Centre**. Soccer matches are also held at the Ninoy Aquino Memorial Stadium and ULTRA. Local newspapers carry useful guides to sporting activities.

Horse-racing is held on Saturdays and Sundays, alternating between the two tracks — the **Philippine Racing Club** and the **San Lazaro**. There are also several golf courses. Some, like the **Muni** course that runs round the perimeter of Intramuros, are public, while others require an introduction from a member. Ask the manager of your hotel or ring the secretary of one of the clubs. Manila also has several golf driving ranges.

The great sporting attraction in Manila (and Cebu) is jai alai (pronounced hai alai). This exciting Basque game is played at the *fronton* in Taft Ave. every night of the week, except Sundays, from 4:15 pm until after midnight. The game is a little like modern squash, but a sling-like wicker basket is used to catch the fast-travelling ball and hurl it against front wall. Betting is a feature of the night's fun at the *fronton* and there is also a restaurant from where the games can be followed. No one interested in sports should miss a night of *jai alai.*

Cockfighting is legal and very popular in the Philippines, with each barrio (village) having its own cockpit. In Manila cockfights are held on Sundays at the **Paranaque Cockpit** (near the airport), the **La Loma Cockpit** (Quezon City) and the **Marikina** sports complex, in Marikina, Rizal. Fights are held between 9 am and 7 pm.

For the fisherman, the Philippines offers some excellent deep-sea sport. In the far north of Luzon, boats leave Aparri for the fishing grounds out among the **Babuyan Islands**. To the west of Luzon, off **Ilocos Sur** and **La Union** provinces, there are also fishing grounds. Fishing to the south is best in **Tayabas Bay**. The mouth of **Manila Bay** provides some fishing. Tuna, garoupa, snapper, marlin and sailfish are among those taken. Freshwater fishing can be had on **Santa Cruz Lake** and **Caliraya Lake**, where in season (May to September) duck may also be shot. Licences are required.

The Philippines' tropical waters team with fish of many varieties as well as with coral reefs, so scuba divers also enjoy activities such as underwater photography. There is a growing interest in water sports — such as hobie-cat sailing, windsurfing and water-skiing. Some local resorts offering scuba diving include: **Anilao Seasports Centre** in Batangas (Tel: Manila 801-1850); **Capt'n Greggs Dive Resort**, Puerto Galera (Tel: Manila 522-0248); **El Nido**, Palawan (Tel: Manila 818-2623); **Badian Island**, Cebu (Tel: Manila 581-835) and **Dakak** and **Dapitan**, Mindanao (Tel: Manila 721-0426).

Sports facilities in the metropolis cover most types of games and exercises. Health clubs offer saunas, jacuzzis, and massage. The Manila yacht club has reciprocal arrangements with most other clubs round the world.

Jogging is quite popular, with Roxas Blvd and Rizal Park the favourite routes. After 5 pm, Makati executives and office workers pound the pavement around the Ayala Triangle. Over in Quezon City, the Quezon Memorial Circle is a breezy and spacious trail.

Alabang Country Club, Ayala Alabang Village, Alabang, Muntinlupa, Metro-Manila (Tel: 842-3530-39). Championship swimming pool, 10-lane bowling concourse, 21-hole golf course, polo field, four indoor and four outdoor tennis courts, badminton court, squash court, softball field, basketball court, skating rink, recreation park and children's playground. Guests must be sponsored by members.

Canlubang Golf and Country Club, Canlubang, Laguna (Tel: 883402 and 883458). Two 18-hole golf course, two swimming pools (one for adults, one for children), two tennis courts (covered and uncovered), courts for racquetball, squash and badminton. Golf package rates include green fees, lunch, drinks, use of locker room facilities.

Capitol Hills Golf Club, Old Balara Road, Quezon City (Tel: 976691). Eighteen-hole championship golf course and driving range.

Celebrity Sports Plaza, Capitol Hills, Quezon City (Tel: 951061). Bowling, swimming, billiards, table and lawn tennis, shooting range, basketball, gym and sauna.

Makati Sports Club, Salcedo Village, Makati (Tel: 817-8731). Six-lane bowling alley, six covered tennis courts, swimming pool, pelota, squash, gym, sauna and massage. Guests must be sponsored by members.

Manila Golf and Country Club, Harvard Rd, Makati, (817-4948). Eighteen-hole championship golf course. Guests must be sponsored by members.

Manila Polo Club, McKinley Rd, Makati (Tel: 817-0951). Polo fields, horse riding, tennis, racquetball, squash, bowling, swimming and softball. Guests must be sponsored by members.

Manila Yacht Club, 2351 Roxas Blvd, Manila (Tel: 521-4457, 502545 and 521-4458). Marina and clubhouse, with boats for rent. Guests must present membership cards from yacht clubs or must be sponsored by a member.

Metropolitan Club, Estrella St, Makati (Tel: 859986). Pelota, tennis, bowling, swimming, and gym with sauna and massage. Guests must be sponsored by members.

Quezon City Sports Club, E. Rodriguez Senior Blvd, Quezon City (Tel: 774076 and 774071). Nine tennis courts (three covered courts), two squash courts, pelota and badminton courts, short-course swimming pool, wading pool, 10-lane tenpin bowling alley, snooker, weight rooms and saunas, masseurs, skating rink and children's playground. Guests must be sponsored by members.

Wack-Wack Golf and Country Club, Shaw Blvd, Mandaluyong (Tel: 784021). Two 18-hole championship golf course. Arrangements must be made a day before play.

Filipinos always find an excuse to hold celebrations. Local festivals are held in honour of patron saints, mythical figures and historical events. The festive days are often a strange blend of native customs and Christian festivals, topped by the supreme ability of Filipinos to have fun and extend hospitality.

There are 11 national holidays during the year, and the president customarily declares special public holidays at national, provincial and municipal levels. The list of Philippine festivals and holidays is long and includes:

January 1: New Year's Day.

January (first Sunday): Feast of the Three Kings, official end of the Christmas festivities.

January 9: Feast of the Black Nazarene in Quiapo district in Manila.

January 10: Feast of the Santo Niño de Cebu, Cebu City.

January (third Sunday): Ati-Atihan in Kalibo, Aklan. A rowdy festival with much singing and street dancing.

January (third Sunday): Sinulog in Kabankalan, Negros Occidental. Similar to the Kalibo festival, which honours the birth of Christ.

January (fourth Sunday): Dinagyang, in Iloilo City. Another version of the Mardi-Gras-style of honouring the birth of Christ.

February 11: Lourdes Feast, in Quezon City.

February 22-25: People Power Celebration. A fiesta commemorating the accession of Corazon Aquino revolution.

February (movable): Hari Raya Hadji, in the Muslim provinces.

February 24-25: Bale Zamboanga Festival, in Zamboanga City.

March 10-16: Araw ng Dabaw, in Davao City. The week-long activities coincide with the city's founding anniversary.

March-April: Easter week. On Good Friday, penitencial rituals are seen best in suburbs of Manila where many people practice self-flagellation. In certain places, such as Cainta in Rizal province, heavy crosses are carried and thorns worn on the head. In San Fernando, Pampanga, north of Manila, penitents have themselves nailed to crosses.

April 24: Magellan's Landing, in Cebu City. Commemoration of the landing in Mactan of Portuguese explorer Ferdinand Magellan in 1521.

May 1: Labour Day (public holiday).

May 6: Araw ng Kagitingan (public holiday). The nation commemorates the fall of Bataan and Corregidor to the Japanese.

June 12: Philippine Independence Day (public holiday).

June 28-30: Feast of Saints Peter and Paul, in Apalit, Pamapanga.

July 4: Philippine-American Friendship Day (public holiday).

November 1: All Saints Day (public holiday).

November 30: National Heroes Day (public holiday). Leader of the revolution Andres Bonifacio gets most attention.

December 25: Christmas Day (public holiday).

December 30: Rizal Day commemorates the death of the national hero.

Outrigger canoes known as bancas.

Photo: Garry Marchant

Addresses

TOURIST AUTHORITIES
HEAD OFFICE

Department of Tourism Bldg, T. M. Kalaw St, Rizal Park, Manila, Philippines. Telex: 401883 DEPTOUR PM, Cable: MINTOUR MANILA, Tel: 599031, Fax: 5217374.

LOCAL REGIONAL OFFICES
Luzon

Laoag Sub-office, Ilocandia Heroes Hall, Laoag City.

Angeles Regional Office, DAU Interchange, Mabalacat, Pampanga. Tel: 2243 Mabalacat.

Baguio Regional Office, Department of Tourism Complex, Gov. Pack Rd, Baguio City. Tel: 3415, 5716, 7014, 9906.

La Union sub-office, Cresta del Mar Beach Resort, Paringao, Bauang, La Union. Tel: 2411.

Legazpi Regional Office, Penaranda Park, Albay District, Legazpi City. Tel: 4492, 4026.

Cebu Regional Office, Fort San Pedro, Cebu City. Tel: 91503, 96518.

Iloilo Regional Office, Sarabai Bldg, General Luna St, Iloilo City. Tel: 78701.

Tacloban Regional Office, Children's Park, Senator Enage St, Tacloban City. Tel: 321-2048.

Mindanao

Davao Regional Office, Apo View Hotel, S. Camus St, Davao City. Tel: 74866.

Zamboanga Regional Office, Lantaka Hotel, Valderossa St, Zamboanga City. Tel: 3931.

Cagayan de Oro Regional Office, Ground Floor, Pelaez Sports Complex, Cagayan de Oro City. Tel: 3340.

OVERSEAS OFFICES
US

Chicago, Suite 111, 30 North Michigan, Chicago, Illinois 60602 USA. Telex: 206420; Cable: MINTOUR CGO; Tel: (312) 782 1707.

Los Angeles, 3460 Wilshire Blvd, Suite 1212, Los Angeles, California 90010 USA. Telex: 0677167; Cable: DEPTOUR LSA; Tel: (213) 487 4527.

New York, Philippine Centre, 556 Fifth Ave, New York, New York 10036 USA. Telex: 6801425; Cable: DEPTRPH; Tel: (212) 575 7915.

San Francisco, Philippine Consulate General, 447 Sutter St, 6th Fl., San Francisco, California 94108 USA. Telex: 470345; Cable: RCPO; Tel: (415) 433 6666.

Europe

Frankfurt, Philippine Tourist Office, Arndstrasse 19, 6000 Frankfurt/M, Germany. Telex: 4139660; Cable: DOTFO D; Tel: (069) 742574; (069) 742575.

London, Embassy of the Philippines, 199 Piccadilly, London, W1 V9 LE, Britain. Telex: 265115; Cable: PTOEPL G; Tel: 01 439 3481.

Australia

Sydney, 3rd Fl., Philippine Centre, 27-33 Wenthworth Ave, Darlinghurst, NSW 2010, Australia. Telex: DOTSYD AA 27331; Tel: 267 2675; 267 2756.

Asia

Tokyo, Embassy of the Philippines, 11-24 Nampeidai Machi, Shibuya-ku, Tokyo, Japan. Telex: DPTOUR J J22105; Tel: 464 3630/35; Fax: 4643690.

Osaka, Philippine Tourism Centre, 2nd Fl., Dainan Bldg, 2-19-23 Sinmachi, Nishi-ku, Osaka 550, Japan. Telex: 5222534; Cable: DAINAN J; Tel: 535 5071/72; Fax: 534-1780.

Hongkong, Philippine Consulate General, Public Relations Office, 1301 Hang Lung Bank Bldg, 8 Hysan Ave, Causeway Bay, Hongkong. Telex: 65452; Cable: DOTRP HX; Tel: 7903367, 5762502.

Publications

Speak Filipino, Philippine Book Co., (₱37.00).

English-Tagalog, Websters, (₱39.00).

Bagong English-Pilipino Dictionary, Philippine Book Co., (₱15.00).

English-Tagalog Visayan Vocabulary, Philippine Book Co., (₱28.00).

English-Tagalog-Ilocano, Philippine Book Co., (₱28.00).

Cockatoo's Handbook, Cockatoo Press Inc., (₱300.00).

Living in the Philippines, American Chamber of Commerce, (₱200.00).

Manila: The Traveller's Companion, Devcom IP Inc., (₱180.00).

Insight Guide: Philippines, Apa Productions, (₱380.00).

The above are available at hotel bookshops and National Bookstore which has several branches around town at Harrison Plaza; Greenbelt Arcade, Makati; Araneta Centre, Cubao; Virra Mall, Greenhills; North Edsa, Shoemart Centre, Quezon City.

English-Language Guides are available through **Guides, Inc.**, 1,300 Roxas Blvd, Pasay

Rice terraces at Banaue.

City, Metro-Manila. Tel: 5221989. Rate is now approximately ₱500.00 per day for Metro-Manila.

The Department of Tourism on the second floor, Department of Tourism building at Rizal Park (Tel: 501703) has the following publications available to visitors: *Road map of the Philippines, Philippine Travel Guide, Philippines — Diver's Paradise, Corregidor, The Philippines (Quarterly magazine), Incentive Travel Guide, Visitor's Guide to the Philippines, Fiesta Directory.*

Manila Tips (₱20) is available at hotel book shops. Other useful publications: *What's on in Manila magazine,* available free of charge in the major hotels. *Ins and Outs,* and *A-Z map book of Manila* is available at branches of National Bookstore (Rizal Avenue; Harrison Plaza; Greenbelt, Makati; Araneta Centre, Cubao and Virra Mall, Greenhills). Guidebooks are listed in the language section above.

DISCOVERING PHILIPPINES

MANILA

Quezon City, adjacent to Manila, was formerly the capital of the Philippines, but now Metro-Manila has taken over, housing the political, social and economic life of the country. It is at times a confusing place to describe for so much of Manila in fact lies in other places: Pasay City, Makati, Caloocan City and Quezon City to name the main centres. Manila has simply sprawled beyond its original boundaries and now covers 13 municipalities and four cities to produce a conurbation popularly known as Metro-Manila.

The shoreline of Manila Bay runs approximately north-south and the city spreads along it, divided into northern and southern sections by the Pasig River. Ermita, on the southern side, is in the heart of the tourist belt, though that

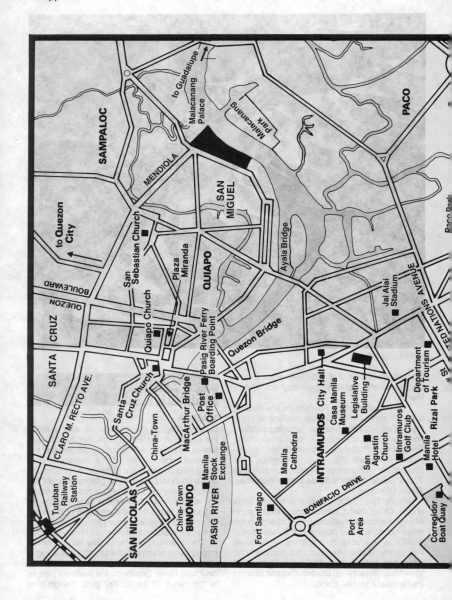

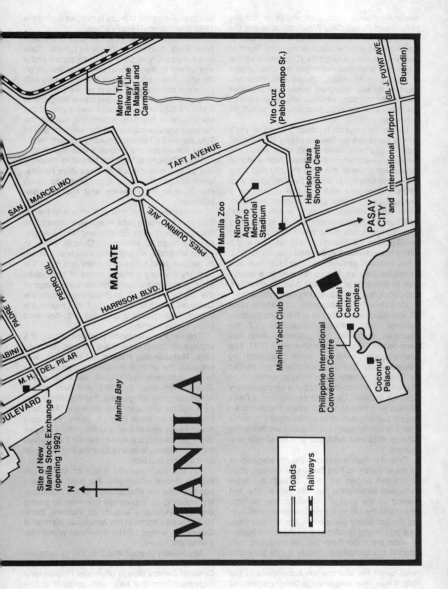

Philippines

N

Site of New
Manila Stock Exchange
(opening 1992)

MANILA

Roads
Railways

Manila Bay

BOULEVARD
M. H. DEL PILAR
MABINI
PADRE
PEDRO GIL

M. H.
M. H. DEL PILAR

SAN MARCELINO

TAFT AVENUE

PRES. QUIRINO AVE.

HARRISON BLVD.

MALATE

Manila Zoo

Ninoy
Aquino
Memorial
Stadium

Harrison Plaza
Shopping Centre

Vito Cruz
(Pablo Ocampo Sr.)

GIL J. PUYAT AVE.

(Buendin)

International Airport

PASAY CITY
and International Airport

Metro Trak
Railway Line
to Makati and
Carmona

Manila Yacht Club

Philippine International
Convention Centre

Cultural
Centre
Complex

Coconut
Palace

designated area runs southwards to include Malate and Pasay City. Within the area are the majority of the tourist hotels as well as much of the shopping and the classiest nightlife. North of the river, Quiapo and Santa Cruz make up the nucleus of what one might call the oriental part of Manila. Here shops, restaurants, theatres, apartments and churches bustle and shoulder each other for room, while all around and within the populace throngs, pressing on about its business.

Miguel de Legaspi founded the city in 1571 on the ruins left by the retreating Raja Solaiman. It originally covered an area which the Spaniards enclosed with a broad, high wall and named Intramuros; this was the city that King Philip II of Spain (for whom the Philippine was named) honoured with the title of *Insigne y Siempre Leal Ciudad* (Distinguished and Ever Loyal City). Intramuros, only a few minutes' walk from the hotel district of Ermita, is still being restored and is one of the best historical sites to see. Tours of the district run daily at 9 am and 2 pm by **Intramuros Experience** (Tel: 8195485). It has cobbled streets, baroque churches and tile-roofed houses. It was reduced to a shambles in World War II. Where historic churches and convents once stood, only ruins remain.

One church, **San Agustin**, on General Luna St, the oldest stone church in the Philippines — survives, and warrants inspection. Of the churches destroyed, the cathedral alone has been rebuilt — for the sixth time since 1581. The stained-glass windows were designed by Filipino artists. The Spanish chapel (presented by Spanish dictator Gen. Franco) contains an impressive bronze crucifix by a contemporary Spanish sculptor. Opposite San Agustin is **Casa Manila** — a museum and shops housed in an ornate building modelled on the style of a home from the rich Spanish era. It is also worth visiting **Silahis Arts and Artifacts** and **Illustrado** restaurant.

One of the seven gates to the city also serves as the entrance to **Fort Santiago**. Construction of the fort began on 1590, though the work remained incomplete for 150 years. The fort served as the seat of colonial power for both Spain and the US — the next colonial ruler. During the Japanese occupation, the fort was used as a prison and hundreds died there, particularly when the water from the nearby Pasig river flooded the dungeons. Today it is a park and contains a memorial museum to Jose Rizal (who spent his last months imprisoned in the fort). It was also used to stage lavish parties and

celebrations by the Marcos family, as during the 1982 International Film Festival.

Immediately south of Intramuros is the vast **Rizal Park**, also known locally as Luneta. Rizal met his death here before a firing squad and a monument to the national hero now stands on the spot. The park is pleasant and swarms with people in the evenings and at weekends.

One of the city's greatest travel bargains is a Manila Bay cruise. Boats leave a pier at the south side of the park waterfront, next to the Harbour View restaurant at the western end of T. M. Kalaw St. The best time to go is early morning or sunset and the charge is less than P20.

Rizal Park runs from the bay at its westerly end up to the vicinity of the **Executive House**, which houses the national museum and which stands near the **Finance and the Tourism** buildings.

Across the Quezon Bridge — one of the six that span the Pasig river — and very close to the shopping centres on Escolta and Rizal Avenue, lies the heart of Manila — Quiapo. Here, in **Plaza Miranda**, an unending variety of humanity passes at all hours of the day and night. On January 9 yearly a milling mass of half-naked male worshippers carry the life-size image of the Black Nazarene in procession from the **Quiapo Church** bordering the Plaza around the district. The church is crowded with devotees every Friday evening.

The old **Paco Cemetery**, where victims of a cholera epidemic in 1820 were buried, is now a park. **Malacanang Palace**, by the river, was originally the country house of a Spanish aristocrat. It became the official residence of the Spanish governor in 1863 and later of the American governor-general. It is the official residence of the president and while the Marcoses lived there for more than 20 years. President Aquino lives elsewhere, and the palace is open to the public who are able to see for themselves the lavish lifestyle enjoyed by the former president and his first lady.

On the southeasterly fringe of Manila lies **Makati** district, which over the past few years has become the Philippines' richest municipality, housing an impressive commercial centre and the exclusive suburb of **Forbes Park**. Makati is also home to the **American Memorial Cemetery**, where 17,186 American World War II dead are buried.

Mrs Imelda Marcos was the driving force behind two of Manila's civic projects. The majestic **Cultural Centre** stands off Roxas Blvd on land reclaimed from the bay, and contains a fine theatre in addition to a museum of Filipino and imported arts plus Imelda's former party house, the **Coconut Palace** which is now open to the public. Also of interest is the **Nayong Philipino** park near Manila airport, where villages representative of the country's principal regions sell handicrafts and other goods. For those not able to leave the capital it also gives an instant glimpse of the rural life of the Philippines.

UPCOUNTRY LUZON

A 30-minute drive south from Manila is **Tagay-tay City**, atop a ridge some 600 m above sea level. The climate is cooler than in the capital. The ridge commands a fascinating view of the **Taal** lake lying in the crater of a vast volcano, though this is sometimes obscured by the mist. Within the lake is a smaller volcano containing a small lake in its crater. This lake in turn has a very small, and sporadically active, volcano projecting from it.

Along the road to **Tagaytay**, stands the church of **Las Pinas** with a famous organ. In 1794 a Spanish priest, Fr Diego came to the Philippines to build organs. Finding neither metal nor any of the other materials normally used, he built an organ of bamboo. The instrument still stands in Las Pinas and may be heard on request.

Due east of Manila, less than an hour's drive away, is the pilgrimage town of **Antipolo**, containing a shrine to the image of Our Lady of Peace and Good Voyage, brought from Mexico in 1626. The inland body of water known as **Laguna de Bay** lies immediately southeast of the capital and beyond it again is the province of Laguna. Here, the rivers have worn steep gorges in the land, and there are rapids and waterfalls along their courses. The most interesting of these rivers is the **Pagsanjan** with falls and rapids. The town of Pagsanjan lies just two hours away from Manila. The falls on the river are reached by a trip upstream through beautiful jungle. Local boatmen handle the boats up and steer during the exciting trip down when visitors shoot the rapids. You will get wet on the river, so wear casual clothes and wrap your camera in plastic.

Los Banos (The Baths) is a small town at the foot of **Mount Makiling** on the road to **Pagsan-jan**. Hot springs flow in the area and their waters have been tapped for swimming pools and resort baths in the area. Nearby is the research station where work is carried out on various types of quick-growing rice.

The beaches at **Matabungkay** and **Na-**

sugbu, two to three hours' drive from Manila, are the best within range of the capital for a day's visit. **Punta Baluarte** is the finest resort in this area. **Nipa** huts — small wood and thatch cottages — along the beaches provide facilities for a stay of a day or more. **Noveleta** and **Tanza** in Cavite have beaches closer to Manila but they are not as fine as Matabungkay. **Puerto Azul** resort hotel complex overlooks the whole Manila Bay approach. **Balesin Island**, off Quezon province, caters mostly to rich executives with private aircraft. **Bataan**, the peninsula forming the northern arm of Manila Bay, and **Corregidor**, the island near its tip, were the scenes of the stand by the Philippine-American forces against the Japanese invasion in 1942. These two famous battlefields have now been proclaimed national shrines. They may be visited from Manila on one of the special tours that run daily by boat from the ferry terminal near the **Manila Hotel**. A new hotel built by the Tourism Department is scheduled to open in 1991.

The many day trips from Manila include: Hidden Valley Springs in Laguna on the southern slope of the extinct volcano of Mount Makiling, a 90-minute drive where several springs — hot, cold and soda — have been chanelled into specially constructed swimming pools. A series of paths leads through the jungle of fruit trees, giant ferns and wild orchids to the gurgling pools and to a natural waterfall. After a native-style lunch you can go hiking to yet another waterfall for a swim in the waters which are said to be therapeutic.

Deep in the heart of Quezon province, amid lush green fields and mountains, lies a coconut plantation which is one of the Philippines' more unusual and romantic experiences. **Villa Escudero**, the ancestral home of Conrado Escudero, is a working coconut and rice farm situated just outside the town of Laguna, some 80 km south of Manila.

The hacienda is home to an unusual museum crammed with artifacts from the Asia-Pacific region. The heart of the resort, however, is the river and a palm-fringed lake in which, on a clear day, Mount Banahaw is perfectly reflected. Jutting out into the water is a large restaurant — The Coconut Pavilion — a swimming pool and a group of native-style cottages.

A diving platform is moored in the water which teems with fish, and there are long, narrow bamboo rafts, some with seats, which can be poled up and down the river and lake.

Some 90 km south of Manila, **Taal** in Batangas province is the base for the Philippine Experience (Tel: Manila 819-5485), a community-based tourism project based on the idea that seasoned travellers' most savoured experiences occur when they can mingle with locals in their everyday environment.

Participants travel to an old house in **Barrio Casasay**, thence to adjacent **Lemery** town and barrio **Nonong Casto** along the coastline of Balayan Bay for a carabao cart ride to the beach. A visit to a nipa hut follows where housewives and teenage girls embroider local cloth in intricate patterns. A tour of Lemery market where embroidered dresses, tablecloths, napkins and barong materials can be bought comes next, capped by a ride in the local out-rigged boats known as *bancas* across the Pansipit river. Native lunch on banana leaves at an elegant Spanish-style house ends the morning.

Along the main highway north of Manila lies the garish city of **Angeles**, parasitically close to the US airbase at Clark. Sociology students interested in the influence of foreign military bases on local populations might find the place worthy of study, though for the average visitor it is only worth a passing glance on the way to northern Luzon. Similar is **Olongapo** near the US naval base at Subic Bay. Both towns cater largely to servicemen and provide a large number of raunchy bars, strictly for males.

In the far north of Luzon at **Banaue** are the breathtaking rice terraces built on the mountain face by Ifugao tribesmen. The terraces are at least 2,000 years old. Banaue's main drawback is its remoteness — which is an attraction in itself to some. It takes a full day's travel by air and road from Manila. The journey used to start from Baguio, virtually destroyed by the 1990 earthquake, from where Banaue is a 14 km drive.

For the hardy, the journey is rewarding in itself, taking you through attractive mountain scenery into a land where the tribespeople still have very little contact with outsiders. Although only one bus goes right through to Banaue, several others go to **Bontoc**, well on the way to Banaue and which has its own, though less spectacular, display of terraces one hour's walk away at Malegcong. Other attractions in the area of Bontoc are the caves at **Sagada**, where there are buried mummies belonging to the local tribes (30 minutes by car back along the road towards Baguio then turn off); and the **Mainit** hot springs where you can enjoy a soak in the soothing mineral water.

Accommodation is basic though clean. There are several hotels in Bontoc and the government has built a resort at Banaue. Midway from Baguio to Bontoc is **Mount Data Lodge**, also built by the government. It is wise to book well ahead for these places, especially in the busy tourist months between December and June. One idea to break up the long haul into the mountains is to spend a night at Mount Data. The lodge has an elevation close to 700 m, so be prepared for the night to be cold. The lodge is pleasant and the management charming.

Bontoc, like many of the villages in Luzon, is a shanty town built largely of corrugated iron. The people are the main attraction and many of the Igorots wear native costume. It is only a two-hour journey from Bontoc to Banaue and, as you approach the terraces, the valley opens out and the road drops down into warmer conditions. Then suddenly, there you are in one of the engineering wonders of the world.

The people in the barrios (villages) around Banaue and deeper into the mountains lead exceptionally primitive lives. Visits to these barrios can be arranged in Banaue. Walking through the town and in the surrounding hills, the traveller will meet near-naked tribespeople, the men carrying spears, as well as polite school-children who will greet you with "Good day, sir" in American-accented English. Elsewhere in the Philippines, the friendly call to foreigners is "Hey Joe," the American colonial era refrain.

Even further north than Banaue is the **Batanes** archipelago ("Home of the Winds") — the smallest and northernmost province in the Philippines. It consists of 10 main islands with Y'ami lying just 100 km south of Taiwan. The best time for a visit is April or May, as the area is subject to typhoons for much of the year. Philippine Airlines operates five flights weekly from Manila to **Basco**, the capital. With a population of just over 4,000 swelled by a few hundred visitors a year, Basco is one of the few "undiscovered" destinations in Asia. And it is likely to remain so as the locals do not welcome tourism development. The local architecture is unusual and one could almost be in rural Ireland, with the solid typhoon-proof structures built from grey rock with thatched roofs. The locals, called Ivatans, are a polite and hardy people, but not particularly outgoing in comparison with other Filipinos.

Luzon also offers good beaches in the north. Some of the best are in **La Union** province and at **Hundred Islands** in Lingayen Gulf, Pangasinan province. The best of the resorts along the great stretch of long beach are found at **Bauang La Union** which can be reached by bus or car.

The Hundred Islands can be reached by road from Manila via the town of **Alaminos** and then along the coast to Lucap. Looking like half-submerged ships strewn over the waters of the gulf, the Hundred Islands have good beaches, fishing, caves, and coral reefs, though the use of explosives by local fishermen has caused considerable damage to the reefs. Outboard bancas (taking up to five people) can be hired for exploring the islands. A government rest-house provides accommodation at Lucap along with small privately run resorts.

Other spots worth visiting in northern Luzon include the Spanish-style town of **Vigan** and, further north, Ferdinand Marcos' hometown of Laoag. The impressive **Fort Ilocandia Resort** hotel is recommended as is a visit to the Marcos' museum at **Sarrat**, the Malacanang Ti Amianan (Malacanang of the North) at barrio Suba.

In the extreme south of Luzon island, near the town of **Legaspi** in Albay province, is the coned **Mayon** volcano. This stately mountain rises from the plain to a height of 2,400 m. Its most destructive eruption was in 1814 when it buried the whole town of Cagsawa under lava, leaving the church steeple visible. It still erupts from time to time, but on a so-far harmless scale. Mayon is reached from Legaspi which can be reached from Manila by air, bus or a combination of train and bus. The trip takes an hour by air, eight hours by car and 18 by train and bus. **Kagayonan** is a beach resort hotel facing **Albay Gulf**, situated at the foot of Mayon and one of the most beautiful spots in the country.

About 40 km from Legaspi is the hot springs resort of **Tiwi**. The town stands in a nest of volcanic vents which provide steam under pressure (the Philippines is harnessing its steam vents to develop geothermal energy). The hot springs are chanelled into bath-houses and swimming pools. The springs have a choice between plain and sulphur-charged water in the two pools which are positioned by a picnic grove in the shade of big trees with the Mayon volcano on the horizon.

Mindoro island can be reached by a two-hour ferry ride from Batangas to Puerto Galera, the former capital of the island. This has been developed — some would say overdeveloped — as a resort area. Although Sabang beach, only a decade ago a completely unspoiled area, has been described as "Little Ermita" owing to the proliferation of bars and "honky-tonks" as the locals call them, there are still a few peaceful, beautiful spots to be found. Try **Small**

Lalaguna (fine diving), **White** or **Tamaraw Beach**.

It is possible, but slow, owing to poor roads, to cross over from Puerto Galera to **Abra de Ilog** in Mindoro Occidental, whence you can take a bus down to **Mamburao** on the west coast. Here on an idyllic spot of land an enterprising developer has built a back-to-nature style resort called **Mamburao**. There are regular flights from Manila to Mamburao, while ferries also cross over from Batangas to Abra de Ilog.

CEBU ISLAND

Cebu City, Queen of the Visayas, the islands stretching over the central Philippines, lies 560 km southeast of Manila on the island of the same name. Transport by jet aircraft — there is an excellent, frequent service — takes just one hour from Manila. Transport by ship is readily available, with departures almost daily from Manila. The city's airport is the former US Air Force field on Mactan Island.

Founded in 1565, Cebu is the oldest city in the Philippines and has many points of historical interest, though it has suffered the fate of many other Philippine cities and grown noisy, crowded and shabby in parts. There are many supermarkets and even drive-in theatres. A large hollow cross stands in its plaza, protecting an old inner cross, said to be the one planted by the explorer Magellan when he and his soldiers celebrated their first mass on the island. Nearby is the beautiful **San Agustin Church**, where rests the most ancient image in the Philippines — the Santo Nino (Holy Child) brought from Mexico more than 300 years ago.

The triangular Spanish stone **Fort San Pedro** was originally no more than a wooden stockade named San Miguel. It now houses a zoo, with ancient cannon still guarding the walls and the well-preserved watch-towers. The local tourist office in Fort San Pedro will arrange tours of the city, including a visit to the Chinese temple on the outskirts. You can also ask about scuba diving, which is excellent in Cebu.

One of the easiest and most popular excursions from Cebu City is the launch trip to **Mactan** island where Magellan met his death. A monument marks the spot. You can also drive over to Mactan, crossing the long bridge from Cebu, by taxi or hire car. The journey takes about half an hour from Cebu City. Mactan is a lovely tropical island, with get-away-from-it-all white sand beaches and clear, coral sea. If you want to stay longer than just a day on the beach,

Mock crucifixion on Guimaras Island.

Photo: Veronica Garbutt

there are a growing number of resorts sprouting along the coastline, with villas for hire, with food service and boat trips to **Santa Rosa** island or any of the other mostly uninhabited islands. **Tambuli** and **Coral Reef** are two resorts on Mactan: each is a collection of simple buildings with facilities for swimming.

The village of **Guadalupe**, just on the fringe of the city, is a garden of orchards, roses, carnations and other flowers which are grown there for sale in Cebu and Manila. Further out of town the exclusive suburb of **Beverly Hills**, has a view of the city and surrounding hills worth experiencing.

The anthropology department of the **University of San Carlos** — founded at the Collegio de San Ildefonso in 1595 — has an interesting exhibition of early Cebuanos artifacts.

For good seafood visit the town of **Talisay**, a short bus or taxi ride from Cebu City. Try also the food stalls at the nearby fishing village of **Tangki**, serving a range of fresh fish which you can eat while perhaps tossing the odd coin down to the group of young boys leaping around in the sea, waiting to dive for your money. In Talisay almost everyone owns a swimming pool — made possible by an impervious stratum of soil below the island's surface.

For sightseeing in Cebu, hire a public utility car, which with driver will cost about ₱100 per hour. For the romantic, the local horse and car-

riage (tartanilla) is a different way to see the town. Bargain over the price.

Taxis are cheaper than in Manila, as is just about everything else. You can catch mini-taxis to take you anywhere in the city centre for ₱20.

Guitars and ukeleles made in Mactan are a bargain. For those interested in jewellery, the aquamarine and pink Osmena pearls (from the inner part of the chambered Nautilus) are available, as is a wide range of shell and coral craft. Black coral jewellery is much cheaper here than in Manila.

For good eating in town try either the revolving restaurant at the **Skyview Hotel**, the restaurant at the **Magellan Hotel** or **Alavar's** on Archbishop Reyes Ave. There are a few good Chinese restaurants. Cebuanos are famous for their music, and standards are often as good as the the best in Manila. Cebuanos also enjoy a reputation among Filipinas as being among the most beautiful women in the country.

Beyond Cebu City the province boasts many attractions, particularly beaches. The town of **Moalboal** on the southwest coast is a haven for scuba diving enthusiasts and budget travellers while **Badian Island** is possibly the finest hideaway resort in the region. **Argao Beach Club** near Dalaguete some 70 km south of Cebu City offers the full range of water sports.

Cebu City is a good point from which to set off to explore the other islands since it is a communications centre for the Visayas, with many aircraft and shipping routes either beginning or terminating here.

There are flights out of Mactan to all the important towns further south and several ships a day leave the harbour. For shipping companies, however, no one can forecast sailing dates with any accuracy and it is best to check at the jetty for exact information.

Across the strait from Cebu is the island of **Bohol**, celebrated for the unusual **Chocolate Hills** — so called because of their appearance in the dry season. The ferry ride to the island takes two hours, or there is a longer journey to the main town of **Tagbilaran** in the south of the island. The island shows off its brown hills to the best effect when seen from the air, as from flights heading for **Cagayan de Oro** and **Davao** in Mindanao.

NEGROS ISLAND
Bacolod City in the province of Negros Occidental is the Philippines' sugar capital. From Manila the airfare is ₱1,432. The trip by boat, though much cheaper, takes 19 hours. Bacolod can also be reached by air from Mactan and Iloilo.

Overland from Cebu City you take the bus to **Toledo City** on the west coast of Cebu Island, then use the ferry to cross to **San Carlos** on Negros island and from there again by bus on to Bacolod. The trip is hardly cheaper than going by air, but you get to see the countryside.

Bacolod has the **San Sebastian Cathedral**, and you can visit the neighbouring hot springs at **Mambucal** or travel down to the beach at **Santa Fe** — both excursions taking about one hour from town. Another interesting trip from the city is to visit one of the many sugar plantations that surround it.

Taxis charge the usual cheap upcountry rates. From the jetty to the centre of town the jeepney fare is around ₱5. But if you take a taxi to your hotel, beware of the driver who will offer to carry your bag into the reception desk. He gets a commission for this service from the hotel on your bill. **Maxim's** combines eating facilities with its nightclub.

From Bacolod, you can fly south to the main city of Negros Oriental province, **Dumaguete**. From there you can easily continue by air or sea to Mindanao island to the south, or head for Cebu. Dumaguete's **Silliman University** has a renowned marine biology department, which might be of interest to the traveller.

For the more adventurous there are regular buses running between Bacolod and Dumaguete, both normal and express. The express bus takes eight hours for the trip, which costs around ₱60. It is an excellent way to see the great stretches of sugar cane plantation.

PANAY ISLAND
Two hours west of Bacolod by ferry or 15 minutes by air is Iloilo City on Panay island. The ferry crosses twice daily except on Sunday when it makes only one journey. There are also regular flights from Manila and ships sail from the capital frequently.

Iloilo is a pleasant enough spot, though a little dilapidated. The town is noted for its fine local fabrics. The best barong tagalog shirts use such embroidered fabrics and the town is a good place to buy one of these cool, smart garments. Ternos, the Spanish-inspired dress for Filipinas, with the butterfly sleeves, are also a good buy in Iloilo if you have time to have one made.

Iloilo has a museum with exhibits dating back to pre-Hispanic times. The baroque **Miag-ao Iloilo Church** is worth a visit. **Guimaras** island nearby boasts a handful of fine beach resorts.

From Iloilo, the only railway outside Luzon runs north to the town of **Roxas**. The railway journey offers a good view of the countryside, and you can return to Manila by air from Roxas if you wish.

Northwest of **Panay**, some three hours' drive by jeepney from **Kalibo** followed by a 15-minute sea crossing by banca, lies Boracay, an island of superlative beauty. Although still a haunt of Manila cognoscenti and foreign backpackers, this butterfly-shaped island is now moving upmarket and boasts several resorts: **Friday's**, **Pearl of the Pacific**, **Lorenzo's**, **Sandcastles** and **Boracay Beach and Yacht Club** among them. A gentle sea, a slight breeze and tall coconut palms swaying in the wind make this the almost perfect tropical paradise. By day there is boardsailing, scuba diving, tennis and horse riding. In the evenings there are gatherings at the **Beachcomber**, **Bazura** and **Sandbar** discos. Philippine Airways operates daily flights to **Kalibo**, but a faster way is to fly on **Pacific Airways** or **Aerolift** to Caticlan.

LEYTE AND SAMAR ISLAND
Leyte is best remembered as the scene of Gen. MacArthur's return to the Philippines in October 1944 to recapture the country from the Japanese.

The island is well served by sea, with ships

from Manila, Cebu, Samar and Mindanao. Air services connect it with Manila and Mactan.

Buses fan out from **Tacloban** to the outlying districts of the island, and a journey to **Ormoc City** on the west coast will prove rewarding to anyone prepared to sacrifice a little comfort for an excellent look at the countryside. The actual scene of MacArthur's landing is a red beach 16 km south of Tacloban. In the city, the hall immortalises both Magellan and MacArthur by way of a life-size mural.

The island of **Samar** is relatively undeveloped with good beaches, but wide areas should be avoided because of a serious law-and-order problem. Samar is very closely aligned to Leyte Island, the two being connected by the San Juanico bridge over the narrow San Juanico Strait. **Catbalogan**, capital and the main port of Western Samar province, is only 112 km from Tacloban and you can travel on a first-class highway up to Catbalogan.

The roads in Samar are generally in bad shape, but in the northern part new ones are being built with help from a huge Australian aid project. The road running north along the coasts from Catbalogan to **Calbayog** is kept in good order. From **Loang** on the north coast, boats connect to Manila and also to the town of **Virac** on the island of **Catanduanes**. From there one can take the short flight to Legaspi in Luzon. Catarman on the north coast is also connected to Luzon by air.

By far the most reliable way to go north from Calbayog is to hire a motorised outrigger and sail the 60 km to Allen on the northwest tip of the island. The trip will take about four hours and should not cost a great deal more than P200, though you will have to bargain. The boat never sails far from the land (or if it does, you will know you are lost in the Samar Sea) and the view of the palm-fringed shores with the mountains as a backdrop is magnificent. Allen is only a fishing village which seldom sees foreigners. However, there is a small lodging house, **La Suerte**, conveniently placed near the pier, market and bus station. Accommodation charges are less than P100. From Allen to Catarman there is a road and buses make the trip. There is also a ferry which runs to Matnog on Luzon, making the trip daily.

When travelling around the island of Samar, it is wise to check with the local police about the law-and-order situation. In recent years, the communist New People's Army has been increasingly active, particularly in northern and eastern Samar. Some areas in these parts of the island are barred to foreigners from time to time.

MINDANAO ISLAND

The large southern island of Mindanao is of great interest to the traveller. Not only does it have special attractions — such as the **Maria Cristina** waterfall and the ancient Spanish fortress port of **Zamboanga City**, with its excellent beaches and bougainvillaea-bedecked tropical greenness — but it serves as gateway to the fascinating **Sulu** group of islands which stretch down to the southernmost **Tawi-tawi** islands, a few miles away from the north coast of the East Malaysian state of Sabah. However, travellers to Western Mindanao and the Sulu, Basilan and Tawi-tawi islands should check with their embassies in Manila first to find out if the current conflict with Muslim rebels in the area allows for free movement.

Boomtown **Cagayan de Oro** lies on the north coast of Mindanao and is the centre of the region's pineapple industry. It has recently sprouted with factories producing steel, ferrochrome, sintered iron, cement flour and coconut oil. The ride into town from the airport — situated high above on a narrow plateau — offers spectacular views. In the "City of Golden Friendship" itself be sure to visit **Gaston Park**, **San Agustin Cathedral**, **Xavier University** and the **Del Monte** pineapple cannery. Many flights from Manila call at the city from where it is possible to connect with most of the other major towns on the island.

A two-hour bus ride to **Balingoan** followed by an hour's ferry trip will take you to **Camiguin**, a remote, unspoiled paradise island which has been described as "Boracay 10 years ago." For nature lovers, Camiguin's main attractions are **Hibok Hibok** volcano, **Katibasawan** waterfalls and **Salang** springs. Because accommodation is strictly Robinson Crusoe style in simple nipa huts, Camiguin is a destination for adventure travellers who can enjoy a vacation without air-conditioning and wall-to-wall carpets.

The drive from **Cagayan** to **Iligan** is pleasant, following the road along the coast. **The Maria Cristina** waterfall is only a short drive from **Iligan City**. **Marawi City** nearby is the centre of Islam in the Philippines. Its main attractions are **King Faisal Mosque** and **Institute of Islamic and Arabic Studies**, **Signal Hill**, the **Aga Khan Museum**, the **Sacred River** and **Lake Lanao**.

The city of **Davao**, on the east coast of Mindanao, is a popular resort and the area is the home of some of the most colourful tribal people in the Philippines, including the Bagobos, Manobos, Taga Kaolos, Mangguagan, Mandaya, Kulaman and Bilaan tribes. Some of these people are fast disappearing from their traditional lands as newcomers settle. Davao is a booming centre for the abaca (Manila hemp) industry. Its main attractions are the **Shrine of the Holy Infant Jesus of Prague**, **Magsaysay Park**, **Caroland Resort**, **Aldevinco Shopping Centre**, the **Buddhist Temple** and **Samal Island**. There is an 18-hole golf course and the swimming at **Talomo** and **White Beach** is good.

Mount Apo, the highest Philippine peak at 2,954 m presents a challenge to climbers. Of great interest to conservationists is the **Philippine Eagle Breeding Station** near Baracatan. To get there, board a jeepney for Toril at Aldevinco Shopping Centre in Davao. Change at Toril for a Baracatan jeepney. Alight at the terminus and walk 1-1/2 km to the camp.

Davao is connected by regular flights to Manila and Mactan, Cebu. It is also connected by road to most of the major cities in Mindanao, including Cotabato and Zamboanga. But there is some risk in travelling, not only because of the conflict with Muslim rebels, but also with communist guerillas in the area. Check with the police before travelling anywhere overland in Mindanao.

Zamboanga City is one of the most colourful, distinctly exotic places in the Philippines. It can be reached directly by air from Manila, as well as from other major provincial towns. The air fare from Manila is around ₱3,208. The city is also served by ship from Manila and Visayan ports. Small coastal steamers sail to **Pagadian** and **Cotabato** from Zamboanga every few days, and there are also boats to **Sulu** — but again, check the law-and-order situation.

Zamboanga is a small, bustling port dating back to early Spanish times. The local dialect, Chabacano, is a corruption of Spanish. The city was largely destroyed during World War II and re-building has detracted a great deal from the old Spanish atmosphere. The tropical climate allows bougainvillaea and orchids to flower in profusion — Zamboanga is known as the city of flowers. The only relic of the Spanish occupation is **Fort Pilar**, which though small is quite a fine example of military architecture; it is now a barracks. The city also has the country's oldest nine-hole golf course.

Many Filipinos like to travel to Zamboanga simply to go shopping in the barter market at the wharf. Here, because of the legal barter trade

through neighbouring Sabah and elsewhere, you can buy batik cloth made in Malaysia and Indonesia, and nearly all kinds of imported goods — chocolates, TV sets, radios, perfumes and other goods which normally carry a high duty. There is also silk from Cotabato. Brassware in ornate style can be bought, both modern and supposedly antique. You might also be lucky and pick up a Ming or Qing piece of pottery at the antique market a few steps away from the **Lantaka Hotel**. But be careful because there are a lot of fakes.

There are one or two very good beaches, particularly on the nearby **Santa Cruz** island. Here you can dive among the fish and coral in crystal-clear water. Carasagan beach, about 16 km along the coast road to the west, is only fair and may be out of bounds to foreigners because of the risk of rebel activity. The Lantaka Hotel is a charming place to stay or have a meal. You can have a drink or eat outdoors with a marvellous view of the harbour looking over to the island of **Basilan**. The local Badjaos (a water-gypsy tribe) float up to the edge of the hotel in their boats, offering shells and coral and beautiful eye-catching Sulu mats. Boats to Santa Cruz island can be arranged at the hotel.

For a look at the lush tropical countryside, you can take a hire car, taxi or tricycle cab to **Pasonanca Park**. The park has a tree-house, where you can stay for a night or two if you book well ahead. A letter to the **Officer in Charge of the Tree-House Bookings, City Hall, Zamboanga**, should do the trick. You may have to pay a few pesos for supplies. The tree-house is supposed to be for honeymooners, but as dozens of visitors pass through the house every day, serious honeymooners might be advised to look for other accommodation. There is a Muslim village called **Rio Hondo** built on stilts over the mouth of a small river on the outskirts of Zamboanga, but it is better to travel the 20 km out to the village of **Taluksangay**.

Just a two-hour trip away by ferry from Zamboanga is **Isabela** on Basilan island. This is sometimes out-of-bounds to foreigners because of the Muslim rebellion but, if you can go there, Sunday is perhaps the best day. This is when the weekly market is held. If you want to see a local plantation, either rubber, coconut, palm oil, coffee or black pepper, you should visit **Menzi's Plantation**, near the town.

In Zamboanga City, good places to eat are the Lantaka Hotel or **Alavar's**. For a night out, you might go to **Justice R. T. Lim Boulevard**, about 2 km along the coast, where you can eat grilled chicken at the local stalls and have a beer to the accompaniment of some of the world's loudest juke-boxes. Then on to one of the few nightclubs in town — which include the **Fishnet Pub House** where they have hostesses and dancing to loud music.

North of Zamboanga City, some 40 minutes by air, is **Dipolog**, provincial capital of Zamboanga del Norte. Some 25 km away by tricycle (a motorcycle with a side car) lies the sleepy town of **Dapitan** where Jose Rizal was exiled from 1892 to 1896. It is said by some to be the prettiest town in the Philippines. A short banca ride will take you to the thatched-roof style **Dakak Beach Resort** with sandy beaches, swimming pools, jacuzzis, Spanish Galleon–style bars, mango trees and air-conditioning.

Southwest of Mindanao lies **Palawan**, the oil-site of the country, which, despite exploration and drilling, is still unspoiled by too many tourists. There are fine beaches and the **Rafols Hotel** in the capital, **Puerto Princesa**, offers modern facilities. Using Puerto Princesa as a base you can reach the **Underground River National Park**, the islands of **Honda Bay** and **Tabon Caves** where, in 1962, archaeologists discovered human fossils carbon dated to 22,000 BC, the oldest trace of man in the Philippines.

Hundreds of wild animals roam free on **Calauit Island** on the northern tip of **Palawan**. Among their number are endemic creatures such as parrots, bearcats, monkeys, wild boar and leopard cats. In 1977, following a presidential decree, the island was declared a game reserve and wildlife sanctuary. There followed the importation of exotic African species including zebra, eland, giraffe, impala and topi. To visit the sanctuary permission must be obtained from the **Philippine Conservation and Resource Management Foundation** (Tel: Manila 815-2451).

The underwater world around Palawan is equally rich in wildlife — perfect diving territory. Many wartime wrecks can be found to the northest, around **Busuanga** and **Koron** islands. Puerto Princesa is the jumping-off point for the area's prime dive site, **Tubbataha Reefs**.

Near the northern tip of the main island of Palawan is **Taytay**, one of the first Spanish bases in the archipelago. Off Taytay is **Malampaya Sound**, a paradise for anglers, dubbed the "fish bowl of the Philippines." Some 50 km northwest of Taytay are the black towering cliffs of **El Nido** where swifts build their nests in nooks and crannies. Gatherers collect and ship the

nests to Manila's Chinatown where they fetch a high price as the essential ingredient of Bird's Nest soup.

A bonus of visiting these islands is staying at one or two far-flung resorts. **El Nido Ten Knots** on Miniloc island is a diver's haven, complete with snorkeling, windsurfing and the whole gamut of aquatic sports. It is popular with Japanese divers who appreciate El Nido's fabled shrimp and lobster dinners.

Some 40 minutes by banca from El Nido village lies **Pangalusian Island Resort** on a small island. A romantic resort, well known to cognoscenti who sail down from Manila, Hongkong and Singapore, Pangalusian's restaurant has been described as "the finest in the Philippines" by award-winning Swiss journalist Thomas Diethelm. Many would agree with him.

THE SULU ARCHIPELAGO

Beyond Basilan an infinite number of stepping stones — the far-flung islands of the Sulu archipelago — lead to Borneo. But note that travelling in this region can be hazardous as there is much piracy, banditry and confrontation between the MNLF and the Philippine military.

Forty minutes by air from Zamboanga lies **Jolo**, capital of Sulu province and the only place in the region where the Spanish managed to hoist their flag (some 300 years after they reached the Philippines). In 1974 Jolo town was burned to the ground when fighting broke out between Muslim and government troops.

Every day at 10 am a PAL flight departs Zamboanga for **Sanga Sanga**, some 12 km. from the Tawi Tawi capital of **Bongao**. The sight which greets arriving passengers is pure Arabian Nights: a silver dome capping a mosque with graceful minarets towering above a water village on stilts; tall people with dazzling smiles feasting on *curachas* (coconut crabs) and children frolicking in the water.

Further out into the Celebes Sea is **Sibutu** famous for its wild boar. Finally, almost at the border with Malaysia is "The Venice of the East," **Sitangkai**, a town built on stilts over a crystal-clear reef. Other Sulu islands worth visiting include **Siasi**, **Laparan**, **Simunul**, **Manuk Mankaw**, **Bubuan and Cagingaan**. Such journeys should only be tackled by wanderlust loving adventurers with plenty of time to spare, as boat connections are infrequent and hotel accommodation almost non-existent. It's an entirely different kind of Philippine experience and one that will linger long after memories of other trips have faded.

HOTEL GUIDE

Hotel address	Phone	Fax	Telex	Cable	〰	🍴	🍽
A (US$80 or above) **B** (US$50-80)	**C** (US$30-50)		**D** (US$30 or below)				
ALBAY **D**							
La Trinidad Rizal St, Legazpi City	2951 (-55) 503306 (Manila)		2359 CS (PT&T)	LATRINIDAD LAGAZPI	▲	▲	
Casa Blanca Hotel Penaranda St, Legazpi City	3744						▲
Kagayonan Sa May Dagat Padang, Legazpi City	817-6276 (Manila)				▲	▲	
Legazpi Plaza Lapu-Lapu St, Legazpi City	3344 (-45)						
AKLAN **A**							
Club Panoly Boracay Island, Malay **C**	886241 (Manila)	8160747	660664 PANOLY PN		▲	▲	▲
Boracay Beach & Yacht Club Boracay Island, Malay	588809 (Manila)						
Friday's Boracay Island, Malay	5215440 (Manila)					▲	▲
Pearl of the Pacific Boracay Island, Malay	990947					▲	▲
Sand Castles Boracay Island, Malay	595678 (Manila)					▲	
BASILAN **D**							
Basilan J. S. Alano St, Isabela							▲
BATAAN **C**							
Montemar Beach Club Pasinay, Bagac	888391 8153490 (Manila)		63799 CACHO PN		▲	▲	▲

Hotel address	Phone	Fax	Telex	Cable	〰	🍴	☕
BATANES D							
Casa de Tolentino Basco							▲
Lily's Lodge Washington, Basco							▲
BATANGAS C							
Taal Vista Lodge National Rd, Tagaytay City	8102016 (Manila)				▲	▲	▲
Matabungkay Beach Club Barrio Matabungkay, Lian	8080054, 8186254				▲	▲	▲
Punta Baluarte Calatagan D	8183185 (Manila)		RCA23314		▲	▲	▲
Villa Adelaida Foggy Heights, Tagaytay City	871898				▲	▲	▲
Maya-Maya Reef Club Balaytigue, Nasugbu	8159289, 8106865			MAYAMAYAMLA			
Anilao Seasport Centre Mabini, Anilao	872292 (Manila)				▲	▲	▲
Ligpo Island Hotel & Resort Ligpo Island, Bauan	481985 (Manila)				▲	▲	▲
Aqua Tropical Resort Mabini, Batangas	583289 (Manila)				▲	▲	▲
BENGUET C							
Hyatt Terraces South Drive Rd, Baguio City	4425670 (-77), 4425780 074-4425760 loc. 105		27202 HYATTPH		▲	▲	▲

Hotel address	Phone	Fax	Telex	Cable	〰️	🍴	🍽️
BENGUET – *Cont'd* **D**							
Baguio Park Harrison Rd, Baguio City	4425627 (-28), 5220541 (Manila)		7420329 RAJAH PM 7424008 RAJAH PN 7427472 RTIPH	RAJTOUR		▲	▲
Hotel Montecillo Mary Heights, Kennon Rd, Baguio City	4426566, 4426690						▲
Hotel Nevada 2 Loakan Rd, Baguio City							
Belfranit Gen. Lun		(82)62959			▲	▲	▲
Apo View Hotel J. Camus St, Davao City	74861 (-69) 857911 (Manila)		24853	APOVIEW	▲	▲	▲
Davao Anteliz Hotel Km 7 Lanang, Davao City	74440, 78110, 77017				▲	▲	▲
Cuison Hotel J. P. Laurel St, Davao City	79011			RESORTELS	▲	▲	▲
Hotel Maguindanao 86 Recto Ave, Davao City	78401 (-05)					▲	
IFUGAO **C**							
Banaue Hotel Banaue	8104741		63457 IPOC PN				
ILOCOS NORTE **C**							
Fort Ilocandia Resort Hotel Calayab, Laoag City	8104741 (Manila) 221166		63457 IPOC PN		▲	▲	▲
Texicano Hotel Rizal St, Laoag City	220990					▲	▲
Hotel Casa Llanes P. Burgos St, Laoag City	2304, 2305					▲	▲
Villa Lydia Inn San Nicolas	220284				▲	▲	▲

Hotel address	Phone	Fax	Telex	Cable	≋	🍴	🍽
ILOILO							
B							
Isla Naburot c/o Philippine Air Lines, Iloilo City	76112						
C							
Sicogon Island Resort Sicogon Island, Iloilo City	818-2284 (Manila) 79291		22695 SDCO PH				
Hotel del Rio M. H. del Pilar St, Iloilo City	75585			HOTEL DEL RIO	▲	▲	▲
Sarabia Manor Gen. Luna St, Iloilo City	72731, 79127					▲	▲
Iloilo Case Plaza Hotel Gen. Luna St, Iloilo City	73461, 76964					▲	▲
Amigo Terrace Cor. Iznart-Delgado Sts, Iloilo City	74811			AMIGOH	▲	▲	▲
ISABELA							
B							
Cauayan Grand Rizal Ave, Cauayan	22023					▲	▲
Isabela Hotel Miranate, Cauayan	22058					▲	▲
D							
Helen's Lodge Jolo Buyon St							▲
LAGUNA							
C							
Hidden Valley Resort Alaminos	898205, 893561				▲	▲	▲
D							
Villa Escudero San Pablo	5201830 (Manila)				▲	▲	▲
Pagsanjan Rapids Hotel Gen. Tinio, Pagsanjan	885474					▲	

Hotel address	Phone	Fax	Telex	Cable	〰	🍴	🍽
LAGUNA – *Cont'd* **D**							
Pagsanjan Tropical Hotel Barrio Sampaloc, Pagsanjan	6451267, 6451698				▲	▲	
LANAO DEL SUR **C**							
Marawi Resort Marawi City	8010-14 (Davao)				▲	▲	▲
LA UNION **D**							
Bali Hai Baringan, Bauang	412504				▲	▲	▲
Cresta del Mar Paringao, Bauang	413297		29001 PX OHA PH		▲	▲	▲
Cabana Resort Paringao, Bauang	412824				▲	▲	▲
LEYTE **C**							
Leyte Park Hotel Magsaysay Blvd, Tacloban City	8104741 (Manila)		63457	IPOC PN	▲	▲	▲
MacArthur Park Beach Palo, Leyte	8104741		63457	IPOC PN	▲	▲	▲
METRO-MANILA **A**							
Century Park Sheraton Vito Cruz St	5221011	5213413	27791 CPH PNI 0489	SHERMLA PM/ CENPARK			
Hotel Intercontinental Makati Commercial Centre, Makati	894011, 8159711	8171330	RCA-233-144	ICH PH, ETPI-63597 ETPHIM PM, ITT-45005 TXBOOTH PM/ INHOTEL	▲	▲	▲

Hotel address	Phone	Fax	Telex	Cable	〰️	🍴	🍽️
METRO-MANILA – *Cont'd* **A**							
Hyatt Regency 2702 Roxas, Blvd, Pasay City	8312611	8179742	PN3344 PN3462	HYATT MANI			
Manila Hotel Rizal Park, Manila	470011	471124	ITT-40537 MHOTEL PM/ETPI- 63496	MHOTEL PN	▲	▲	▲
Mandarin Oriental Hotel Makati Ave, Makati	8163601	8172472	ETPI-MAND PN63756 ITT-MANDA 7425073	MANDAHOTEL MANILA	▲	▲	▲
Manila Peninsula Ayala Ave, Makati	8193456	8154825	22507 PEN PH	PENHOT MAN	▲	▲	▲
Philippine Plaza Hotel Cultural Centre Complex, Roxas Blvd, Manila **B**	8320702	8323845	40443 FILPLAZA	FILPLAZA MANILA	▲	▲	▲
Holiday Inn 1700 Roxas Blvd, Pasay City	597961	5223985	63487 HOLIDA PEN, 40437 HOLIDAY- PM	HOLIDAY IN MANILA	▲	▲	▲
Nikko Manila Garden Makati Commercial Centre	857911	8171330	45883 GARDEN PM	GARDENHO MNL	▲	▲	▲
Manila Pavilion United Nations Ave, Manila	573711	5223531	ETPI-6338 HILTELSPN RCA-27538 HILTNPH, ITT-40773 HILTNPM	HILTELS MANILA	▲	▲	▲
Manila Midtown Hotel Pedro Gil St, cor. Adriatico, Ermita, Manila	573911	5222624	27797 MMRPH	MIDTOWN MANILA	▲	▲	▲
Philippine Village MIA Rd, Pasay City	8338081	5215328	63074	PVH PN	▲	▲	▲
Silahis International 1990 Roxas Blvd, Manila **C**	573811	2502526	63163 SILTEL PN	SILATEL MANILA	▲	▲	▲
Asian Institute of Tourism Don Mariano Marcos Ave, Quezon City	969071 (-78) 3536				▲	▲	▲
Hotel El Oriente Real St, Dumaguete City	3436					▲	▲

Hotel address	Phone	Fax	Telex	Cable	≈	❧	⬹
NUEVA ECIJA **C**							
Manrio's Hotel Maharlika Rd, Cabanatuan City	9632804						
PALAWAN **A**							
El Nido Resort Miniloc Island **C**	8182623 (Manila)				▲	▲	▲
Jack Gordon's Pangalusian Island Resort El Nido						▲	▲
Rafols Hotel San Miguel St, 05012 Puerto Princesa **D**	8176514 (Manila)		2212, 2022		▲	▲	▲
Emerald Plaza Hotel Puerto Princesa	241				▲	▲	▲
Badjao Hotel 182 Rizal Ave, 2761 Puerto Princesa					▲	▲	▲
PAMPANGA **C**							
Clarkton House B. Juico Ave, Angeles City	3939, 3434				▲	▲	▲
Maharajah Hotel Villa Sol Subdv., Angeles City	3681, 2371, 2372				▲	▲	▲
Angeles Tropicana Hotel San Pablo St, Angeles City	7321, 5075					▲	▲
Oasis Hotel Clarkville, Balibago, Angeles City	3301, 5075				▲	▲	▲
Marlim Mansion Hotel Balibago, Angeles City	27030, 2002, 2393					▲	▲
Jet Hotel Rizal St, Balibago, Angeles City	6341 (-45)				▲	▲	▲

Hotel address	Phone	Fax	Telex	Cable	〰	🍴	🍷
PAMPANGA – *Cont'd* **C**							
Swagman Narra Hotel Diamond Subdv., Balibago, Angeles City	5133, 5231				▲	▲	▲
Bowliseum Hotel San Fernando	612701, 612725						
PANGASINAN **C**							
Hotel Victoria A. B. Fernandez St, Dagupan City						▲	▲
Hotel Mil-Excel A. B. Fernandez St, Dagupan City	4463					▲	▲
Pangasinan Village Inn Bued, Calasiao	2525				▲	▲	▲
Hotel Cadena de Amor Calasiao	3878, 4151					▲	▲
San Carlos Plaza View Hotel Bonifacio St, San Carlos City	127					▲	▲
SOUTH COTABATO **C**							
Matuum Hotel 47 Acharon Blvd, General Santos City						▲	▲
Pioneer Hotel Pioneer Ave, Gen. Santos City	2422 (-23)					▲	▲
QUEZON PROVINCE **C**							
Lucena Travel Lodge Barrio Iyam, Lucena	611581, 603829				▲	▲	▲
Lucena Fresh Air Hotel Isabong Iyam, Lucena City	712424, 703031				▲	▲	▲

Hotel address	Phone	Fax	Telex	Cable	≋	🍴	🥣
TAWI-TAWI **C**							
New Southern Hotel Datu Halun St, Bongao						▲	
ZAMBALES **C**							
White Rock Resort Subic, Zambales	2225555 7215245 (Manila)		63554 EPPIMK PN	LINCPHIL	▲	▲	▲
Marmont Resort 15 Barretto St, Olongapo City	2225572					▲	▲
Cora Hotel National Rd, Kalaklan, Olongapo City	2224403					▲	▲
Riza Hotel 20 Afable St, Olongapo City	2225561						
Admiral Royale Hotel 2 & 4 West 17th St, WBB, Olongapo City	2222400						
ZAMBOANGA **B**							
Oakak Park and Beach Resort Dapitan City Zamboanga del Norte **D**	7210426 (Mla)	7222463	29001	PXO PN	▲	▲	▲
Lantaka Hotel by the Sea N. S. Valderroza, Zamboanga City	3931 (-34)				▲	▲	▲
New Sultana Hotel Canelar St, Zamboanga City	3031, 5531					▲	▲
Zamboanga Hermosa Hotel Mayor Julio St, Zamboanga City	2071 (-75)					▲	▲

SINGAPORE

The few reminders of the colonial past together with patches of Somerset Maugham atmosphere and the island's immigrant Asian heritage are no longer endangered in this vigorously modern city state. Conservation has won a hard fought battle despite the unrelenting growth of high-rise buildings, new roads and air-conditioned shopping complexes. The preservation of historic districts in the central area delineated along ethnic lines has continued since 1977, accounting for 4% of the central land area. The ever-pragmatic authorities see conservation as having a dual purpose: reminding Singaporeans of their heritage and also attracting the highly valued tourists.

Singapore — a crossroads for aviation (boasting one of the best modern airports in the world) — shipping, business and commerce in much the same way as Hongkong — continues to fashion a new lifestyle for its people. The city-state owes much of its charm to the mixture of Chinese, Malays, Indians and Eurasians. It is still a place in which the varied customs of different people are continued; a place where the East often lives in a very Western, albeit tropical, setting. And it is an Asian country where orderliness is a national characteristic, as are its parks and greenery. It is also justly proud of its cleanliness, in marked contrast to some other Asian countries.

The life-blood of Singapore is its harbour, and this has been changing considerably of late, in order to serve the types of ships typical of any modernised port, mostly tankers and container vessels. Ships awaiting a berth stretch in their hundreds towards the islands of neighbouring Indonesia and Malaysia. The country in general enjoys a standard of living well above that of its neighbours, but, of course, only has a fraction of their populations and no rural poor.

The government has consistently — and to a large part successfully — cultivated a sense of nationhood. The numerous events and songs which commemorated the 25th anniversary of the republic's founding on August 9, 1990 saw a blossoming of national pride as striking as the national flower, a native mauve orchid.

The republic consists of the island of Singapore, measuring 42 km by 23 km and 57 smaller island, the whole area being 626 km². Lying 136.8 km north of the equator, Singapore is just across the Johor Straits from the southern tip of the Malay Peninsula, and is connected to it by a 1,056-m causeway carrying a road, railway and water pipeline.

In this multi-racial state, Chinese account for 77% of the 2.5 million population, Malays 15%, Indians 6% and Eurasians 2%. This conglomeration makes race, language and religion sensitive issues, but in general Singapore has turned this into an asset. Certainly for visitors, it is one of the republic's great attractions.

Vigorous economic growth, with a rate averaging 8% a year since the republic recovered from a brief but serious recession in 1985-86, has made labour shortage a grave problem to future growth. Private enterprise has flourished, sometimes in partnership with the government. With very little rural sector to complicate planning, the city-state has been able to push ahead rapidly into steel milling, shipbuilding and high technology. The industrial estate of Jurong is well established

◁ *Singapore's modern skyline.*

227

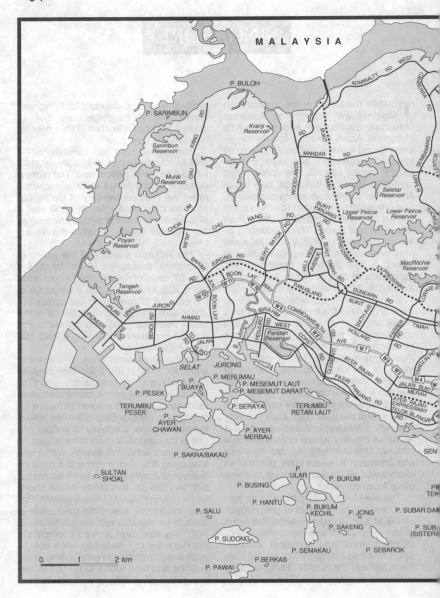

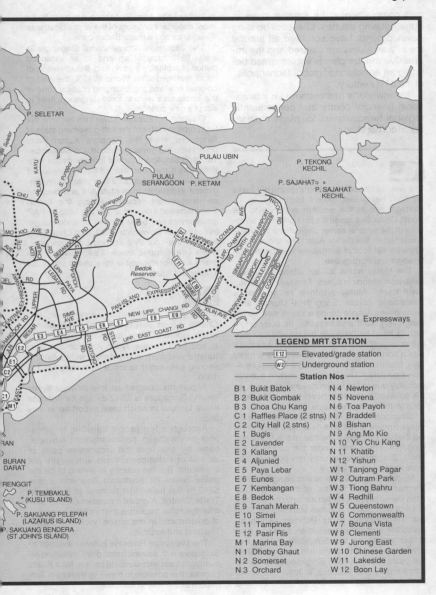

Expressways ·········

LEGEND MRT STATION

E 12 Elevated/grade station	
W2 Underground station	

Station Nos

B 1 Bukit Batok	N 4 Newton
B 2 Bukit Gombak	N 5 Novena
B 3 Choa Chu Kang	N 6 Toa Payoh
C 1 Raffles Place (2 stns)	N 7 Braddell
C 2 City Hall (2 stns)	N 8 Bishan
E 1 Bugis	N 9 Ang Mo Kio
E 2 Lavender	N 10 Yio Chu Kang
E 3 Kallang	N 11 Khatib
E 4 Aljunied	N 12 Yishun
E 5 Paya Lebar	W 1 Tanjong Pagar
E 6 Eunos	W 2 Outram Park
E 7 Kembangan	W 3 Tiong Bahru
E 8 Bedok	W 4 Redhill
E 9 Tanah Merah	W 5 Queenstown
E 10 Simei	W 6 Commonwealth
E 11 Tampines	W 7 Bouna Vista
E 12 Pasir Ris	W 8 Clementi
M 1 Marina Bay	W 9 Jurong East
N 1 Dhoby Ghaut	W 10 Chinese Garden
N 2 Somerset	W 11 Lakeside
N 3 Orchard	W 12 Boon Lay

and complemented by smaller ones in huge housing estates. Low-cost housing developments have sprouted all around the city as slums are cleared and the impressive master plan is implemented befitting an envisioned "global technopolis" of the 21st century.

Meanwhile, it has become an international financial centre and consequently regional headquarters for many multinational corporations.

The year 1819 saw the island's rebirth but it was far from being Singapore's beginning, for its strategic site at the western entrance to the South China Sea made it a linchpin in the ambitions of the several earlier civilisations that have flourished in Southeast Asia. The Indians and Chinese set foot in Singapore well before the Spanish and Portuguese.

The Malay name for the island in ancient Javanese chronicles was *Temasek*, meaning "sea town." Malay histories record that a Palembang prince, Sang Nila Utama, after being driven ashore during a storm, saw something "very swift and beautiful, its body bright red, its head jet black, its breast white, in size rather larger than a goat." Nila Utama was told it was a lion, which he considered to be a lucky sign, founded a city and called it Singapura — "the Lion city." This is almost certain a myth, probably due to the Indian cultural influence, as it is believed there have never been any type of lions on the Malay peninsula.

Singapore was a Malay capital within the Sri Vijaya Empire until it was destroyed in the fighting that accompanied the rise of the Majapahit Kingdom. For a time, under the control of the Thais, Singapore eventually ran down to little more than a fishing village.

Modern Singapore came into being when Sir Thomas Stamford Raffles, of the British East India Company, concluded a treaty on February 6, 1819 with Sultan Hussein Mohammed Shah and Temenggong Abdul Rahman, which allowed the company to establish a trading post at the mouth of the Singapore River. Full sovereignty over the island was ceded to Britain five years later. In 1826 Singapore was joined with Penang and Malacca to form the Straits Settlements, first administered from Penang

but, after 1832, from Singapore. It grew to be the most important entrepot of the whole Southeast Asian area and a major British base.

The Japanese occupation of Singapore in early 1942 brought an end to an extended period of profitable trading and, though entrepot trade resumed after World War II, the end of colonial rule and the changing political state of the whole area were to force Singapore itself to adopt a new outlook.

On June 3, 1959 Lee Kuan Yew became the first prime minister of the self-governing state of Singapore when the People's Action Party (PAP) won the general election. On September 16, 1963 Singapore gained independence from Britain as a member state of the Federation of Malaysia, but on August 9 two years later, Singapore separated from Malaysia and became an independent republic, joining the British Commonwealth on December 22, 1965. A PAP government has been elected by wide margin ever since. In Novemebr 1990, Goh Chok Tong became the country's second prime minister, when Lee stepped down. Lee, however, remains a senior minister in the cabinet and is still a dominant figure.

Most visitors arrive in Singapore by air, and Changi airport serves 48 scheduled airlines which operate more than 100 flights daily to and from Europe, North America and Australasia and from many points within Asia. A second passenger terminal was completed in 1990.

Airport tax charged on international flights leaving Singapore is S$12 except for flights to Kuala Lumpur in which case airport tax is only S$5.

Although a few people travelling to Singapore on the cheap, particularly from Australia, come by sea from the Indonesian ports of Jakarta or Palembang, these arrivals are not significant. But the country is aiming to be the cruise centre for Southeast Asia with a new S$40 million passenger terminal at the **World Trade Centre**. A growing number of firms now offer fly/cruise packages that include a number of destinations in the region, including Japan, Thailand and Australia.

The Malaysian Railways network extends to Singapore with several trains daily, including an overnight train with sleeping berths, from Kuala Lumpur. It is possible to travel by train from Singapore all the way to Bangkok.

Hindu devotee carrying kavadis at Thaipusam festival. ▷

Singapore

Everyone entering or leaving Singapore must be in possession of valid passports or internationally recognised travel documents endorsed for Singapore when necessary. The following require no visas for both social visits or employment: Commonwealth citizens, British protected persons, and citizens of the Irish Republic, nationals of Liechtenstein, Monaco, the Netherlands, San Marino and Switzerland. US nationals entering Singapore in transit or for a temporary stay for any purpose other than residence or employment do not require a visa.

Visas are not required by the following if the visit is for social purposes for a stay not exceeding three months: holders of valid passports issued by the governments of Austria, Germany, Italy, Belgium, Denmark, Finland, France, Iceland, Japan, Luxembourg, Norway, Spain, Pakistan, Sweden and South Korea.

Visas are required by nationals of Afghanistan, India, Cambodia, Laos, China, Soviet Union, Vietnam, holders of refugee travel documents issued by the Middle East countries to Palestinian refugees and Hongkong certificates of identity. Stateless persons must in all cases be in possession of valid visas for Singapore.

Holders of valid Soviet or Chinese passports may visit for a maximum of 24 hours without visas provided they hold confirmed onward/return bookings and tickets. Holders of Taiwan passports do not require visas as tourists but they must have visa cards which can be obtained free from any Singapore overseas mission, airline or shipping company.

Visitors are no longer required to have an international certificate of health showing smallpox vaccination or inoculation against cholera. Valid certificates of vaccination against yellow fever are required for any one above the age of one who has passed through any endemic zone which include: Angola, Benin, Bolivia, Brazil, Burkino Faso, Burundi, Cameroon, Central African Republic, Chad, Colombia, Congo, Ecuador, Equatorial Guinea, Ethiopia, French Guyana, Gabon, Gambia, Guinea Bissau, Ghana, Ivory Coast, Kenya, Liberia, Mali, Mauritania, Niger, Nigeria, Panama, Peru, Rwanda, Sao Tome, Senegal, Sierra Leone, Somalia, Sudan, Surinam, Tanzania, Togo, Uganda, Venezuela, Zaire, Zambia.

Singapore is free of virtually all tropical diseases, including malaria, and boasts an exceptionally modern and efficient hospital system. Among its many other ambitions, the republic wants to become a regional medical centre. Well-trained physicians and specialists are readily available.

Singapore remains a relatively free port. Despite a number of remaining protective duties, the government is generally trying to lift as many of these as it thinks possible. Tourist goods such as radios, watches, clocks, cameras, record players, radio-games, cassettes, curios, plastic articles, footwear, jewellery and precious stones, arts and crafts, toys and TV sets remain non-dutiable exports. Prices for these are lower than those in London or New York, and occasionally Hongkong, though the range of items is much smaller.

Dutiable items are garments and clothing accessories, tobacco, refrigerators (alone among electrical appliances), cars, leather bags and wallets, imitation jewellery, chocolates, sweets, pastries, cakes and alcoholic beverages.

However, bona fide travellers other than those coming from Malaysia may bring in duty-free one litre of wine, one litre of beer or stout or ale or port, and a litre of spirits; 200 cigarettes or 50 cigars or 250 grams of tobacco; reasonable quantities of food preparations not exceeding S$50 in value; reasonable quantities of personal effects and household goods.

Import permits are required for arms, ammunition, animals and birds and their by-products, live plants and seeds; poisons, vaccines, serum and controlled drugs, arms and explosives, bullet-proof clothing; toy guns, pistols, revolvers and walkie-talkies; weapons such as daggers, spears and swords; cartridges, cassettes and pre-recorded film, video tapes or disks, telecommunication and radio communication equipment.

Motor vehicles and motorcycles can only be brought temporarily into the country under a *carnet de passage*. However, such vehicles cannot be sold in Singapore and must be taken out within one year. An inward declaration is required and this document can be obtained from the **Automobile Association** of Singapore, 336 River Valley Rd, Singapore 0923.

Vehicles brought temporarily into Singapore will be issued with a free International Circulation Permit for a period of 90 days by the association on production of a current certificate of insurance. Minimum coverage is third party.

The following are prohibited; controlled drugs, obscene publications, seditious and treasonable material, endangered species of wildlife and their by-products, including ivory and reproductions of copyright publications, video tapes or discs, records or cassettes.

The mandatory death sentence applies to people convicted of carrying more than 15 g of dimorphine, 30 g morphine, 30 g cocaine, 200 g cannabis resin, 500 g cannabis or 1.2 kg opium. This law is strictly enforced and many executions have been carried out. There is no exemption for foreigners.

There is no currency restriction in Singapore. The unit of currency is the Singapore dollar (S$) exchanging in early 1991 at approximately S$1.73:US$1. The Singapore dollar is divided into 100 cents, $10,000, $1,000, $500, $100, $50, $25, $10 and $1 notes are in circulation, along with $1, 50c, 20c, 10c and 5c coins. The Singapore dollar is at parity with the Brunei dollar and is now worth roughly 35% more than the Malaysian dollar. Money may be changed at banks or with official or unofficial money-changers. The best rates are from the unofficial ones on Raffles Place and Collyer Quay. Hotel exchange rates are always bad, so try the licensed money-changer located in almost every shopping complex.

Singapore is the best place in Southeast Asia for purchasing Asian currencies on the free market. Traveller's cheques denominated in Singapore dollars can be bought at any of the local banks.

English is the language of business, administration and the law, and is widely understood. There are three other official languages: Mandarin (Chinese), Malay and Tamil. The main Chinese dialects are Hokkien, Cantonese, Teochew, Hainanese, Hakka and Foochow, though their use is being officially discouraged in favour of Mandarin. Languages of those originally from India are Telegu, Urdu, Malayalam, Punjabi, Gujarah, Hindi and Bengali. However, most Singaporeans are bilingual and frequently multilingual. The lingual versatility is impressive.

Conditions are tropical. Daily temperatures are uniformly high, though rarely above 75°F (24°C) at night. There is no distinct wet or dry season but from November to January during the northeast monsoon, it rains frequently. Showers are sudden and heavy, but in most cases brief.

Shirt and tie usually suffice for daytime office appointments. Some of the more up-market hotels and restaurants will require a man to wear a jacket at dinner. National dress is useful and sometimes can replace jacket and tie. Women's formal dresses are lounge wear. There is a need for frequent changes of clothing due to the tropical climate, so a reasonable supply is advised to allow time for laundering.

Government offices and commercial firms keep staggered hours, starting between 7:30 am and 9:30 am and closing between 4 pm and 6 pm Monday to Friday and between 11:30 am and 1 pm on Saturday. It is advisable to telephone the department or company and check their business hours. Bank hours are from 9:30 am to 3 pm Monday to Friday, and from 9:30 am to 11:30 am on Saturday. Two **United Overseas Bank** branches and three **Overseas-Chinese Banking Corp.** branches open on Sundays. Two of these are in the Orchard Rd tourist belt. Post offices are open 8 am to 5 pm Monday to Friday and 8 am to 12 noon on Saturday. However, the airport and Orchard Point post offices are open seven days a week, including public holidays from 8 am to 8 pm. The General Post Offices at Fullerton Bldg and Comcentre at Somerset Rd are open 24 hours. Most shops open at 10:30 am. Many stores catering to tourists stay open until 9 pm, though other shops close at 6 pm. Some local shops and some of those in the big shopping malls are open on Sunday. The **Metro** chain of department stores, **Chinese Emporiums**, the **People's Park Complex** and Japanese department stores such as **Sogo** are open daily until 9 pm.

FROM THE AIRPORT: The taxi fare from **Changi Airport** to the city proper and to most hotels should be around S$15, including a S$3

Across five Continents impressio

the Singapore Girl

3S91

surcharge for any trip to or from the airport. A bus service runs from the airport takes you to the **Orchard Rd — Scotts Rd** area, while a number of others travel to various points on the island.

The fastest and most comfortable way to get around is by the S$5 billion **Mass Rapid Transit** which operates from 6 am to midnight. There are two easy-to-use routes: north-south and east-west. S$10 stored value tickets are recommended if you want to spare yourself the effort of figuring out the local currency each time you take a trip. Fares of 50 S cents–S$1.20 are cheap for the comfort and efficiency of the service.

Taxis are plentiful. In most central locations they may only stop at designated ranks, where queues at rush hours are long enough to cause a half-hour or more wait. The charge is a standard S$1.90 for the first 1.5 km and 10 S cents for each additional 275 m thereafter. There is an extra S$1 charge for trips originating in the central business district (CBD) at 4-7 pm weekdays and 12-3 pm on Saturday. Between midnight and 6 am there is a surcharge of 50%. Multiple-loading taxis operate from the city to the **Johor causeway**, charging S$2-3 per passenger. These can be hired at **Queen's St**. Nowadays, it is possible to dial a taxi but you should allow yourself plenty of time and be patient. A booking fee of S$3 is charged. For the **24-hour dial-a-taxi service** , call 452-5555, which is the service run by the National Trades Union Congress, or any of the privately operated services listed under taxis in the Yellow Pages of the telephone directory.

BUSES: The Singapore Bus Service (SBS) fleet runs from 6 am to 11:30 pm and fares are low. Check the numbers in the very useful **Singapore Bus Guide**. However, the bus ride is recommended only for the adventurous as the bus service in Singapore is not on a par with modern development in the country. SBS operates a few air-conditioned services. Singapore Explorer Tickets costing S$5 for a one-day ticket and S$12 for a three-day ticket will take you to most of the tourist attractions.

Bus services to Peninsula Malaysia are readily available. Buses cross the causeway to the Malaysia's southern state capital, Johor Baru. Buses also run from Johor Baru and other towns in southern Peninsula Malaysia to Singapore. Express buses to **Malacca** direct from Singapore leave seven times a day from the Lavender St depot and fares are S$11 for adults and $5.50 for children. There is a twice-daily bus service to the Malaysian capital, Kuala Lumpur, costing S$16, and departing from Rochor Rd. Express buses to **Malacca** leave from the Lavender St terminus seven times a day. Fare is S$11.

A few pedal driven trishaws remain on Singapore's streets. A group cluster in the shady nook around the **Queen St/Bras Basah Rd** junction. Prices are comparable to those of taxis. You should negotiate the price before you start the trip. With the trishaw, you can see the town better. They are still used by locals, and one often sees children on their way to school in them, but they are increasingly becoming a tourist attraction. Trishaw drivers seen to think they have right of way anywhere and ignore vehicles, which can make for an exhilarating — and sometimes hair-raising experience.

SELF-DRIVE CARS: Self-drive cars can be hired in Singapore and are admitted in Malaysia. To hire a car, all that is needed is a valid driver's licence from your own country or an international driving permit. Self-drive rates: from S$60 per day (mileage unlimited) and S$12 per day for insurance. Major car hire chains charge around S$150 a day. Fuel is extra. A permit is required by Malaysia for entry, which can easily be obtained at the causeway. Traffic uses the left-hand side of the road in both countries.

Because petrol is cheaper in Malaysia than in Singapore, to prevent Singaporeans crossing the border merely to fill their tanks and return, no vehicle is allowed across the causeway from Singapore unless its tank is at least three-quarters full, and this is strictly enforced, so make sure you conform or you will be turned back. Chauffeur-driven air-conditioned cars are available from S$350 a day.

Boats may be hired from **Clifford Pier** on **Collyer Quay**. Naturally the price depends on the size of the craft. A junk tour costs about S$20 for a two-and-a-half-hour run around the harbour. One can also cruise on a Chinese junk touring the harbour and island with buffet dinner on board, at a cost of about S$36; half-price for children. Motor boats for water skiing (with driver) rent for about S$55 per hour at **Ponggol** on the island's northern side.

Boat charters are available to Malaysia and Indonesia. Book two weeks ahead for weekend charters but weekday cruises can be arranged at shorter notice.

Cruises are organised by **The Port of Singapore Authority**, **Water Tours Ltd**, **J&N Cruise**, **Island Cruises** or **Eastwinds Organisation**. All these are operated from **Clifford Pier**.

Many operators run package tours of the city, harbour or the island or across to Johor and up into Malaysia for trips lasting several days. See the classified ads in local press, or enquire through travel agents or from the hotel lobby you can get information concerning various kinds of tours which operate almost daily. A simple city tour lasting three-and-a-half hours by coach costs S$21. For privately arranged tours, visitors are advised to use only **Singapore Tourist Promotion Board** licensed tourist guides who wear special badges and carry licences which must be shown on request, as no other person is allowed by law to act as a tourist guide. English-speaking guides charge S$40 for a half-day tour. Guides hired for individuals or small groups, charge S$40 an hour (or S$80 a hour if you need one who speaks a foreign language other than English).

Singapore is fast becoming a resort and convention city. Its hotels and the booming tourist facilities in the Orchard Rd area are changing the lifestyle of this affluent city. These facilities come under siege by the local population whenever Orchard Rd is closed off to allow the street to be used for parades. Annually in August in the **Swing Singapore** celebrations, up to a quarter of the population will pour on to a few kilometres of road just to bop along with music blasting from the loudspeakers. It is arguably the safest street party in the world.

Hotel facilities are excellent though accommodation rates, like prices generally over the past several years, have risen to levels comparable with the most expensive cities in the world. Do not hesitate to ask for a discount, however.

The centre of gravity of the top-class hotels has shifted slightly away from Orchard Rd with the develops on or near the land reclaimed from the harbours, which include the twin towers of the **Westin Stamford** and **Westin Plaza** and the the **Pan Pacific**, the **Marina Mandarin** and the **Oriental** all in Marina Square on the reclamation.

Most hotels have shopping arcades, several bars, swimming pools and even art galleries. Guests at other slightly less luxurious hotels are scarcely handicapped since the city offers any missing service within a reasonable distance.

For the romantics, old-timers and Somerset Maughamers, the renovated **Raffles Hotel**, almost a national monument, is reopening in mid-1991, having been up-graded and a S$51 million extension added, much in the way that the famous Manila Hotel in the Philippines has been modernised.

Owing to personal taste and cultural preference, you will find certain nationalities tend to cluster in certain hotels. For instance, Americans tend to go for the known quantities — **Holiday Inn** and **Hilton** whereas the French gather themselves around the **Marco Polo**, the **Meridien** or **Novotel Orchid Inn** in Dunearn Rd.

The Japanese tend to go to the **Harbour View Dai-Ichi** (located in the business district), the **New Otani**, the **Crown Prince** and **King's Hotel**.

The older hotels, such as the **Ming Court**, **Cockpit** and **Oberoi Imperial** are still good. Again, some people would prefer the cosy atmosphere of, say, the **Boulevard Hotel**, **Chequers**, the **Garden Hotel**, the **Ladyhill** or the **Tanglin Court**. All hotels have a 10% service charge and add a 3% government tax on room charges and on food, drink and other items.

For variety, quality and fair price, food is one of the main attractions of Singapore and eating a national pastime. The island's mixed racial population, plus the country's position on the sea/air routes between East and West over the past 150 years has enabled its cooks to take wisely a little of this and a pinch of that to add to the collection of dishes that today constitute great Singapore food. Sometimes national dishes have been modified under the influence of the new environment — as happened to southern Chinese cooking subjected to the spices of the Malay people and which is now known as *nonya* food. Nonya food is Straits-born (from Penang and Malacca) Chinese cooking which has become the indigenous cuisine. Nonya restaurants have sprouted and the more popular nonya dishes such as *laksa* are available in most hotel coffee shops. **Kedai Kopi** (Malay for coffee shop) in **Peranakan Place**, and the Apollo Hotel's **Luna Coffee House** offer nonya food of a consistently high standard, the latter in buffet form.

Some dishes, despite their names, are unique to Singapore. No one on China's Hainan island, for instance, has ever heard of a dish called **Hainanese chicken rice**. Conversely, while "Singapore noodles" is a common dish in

Hongkong, no one in Singapore knows what it is. You have to specify whether it is Cantonese, Hokkien or Teochew fried or soup noodles. Apart from noodles, one can try Cantonese, Peking, Sichuan, Shanghainese, Hunan, Hokkien, Teochew, Hakka and Hainanese food in a range of settings, from simple, cheap — and clean — hawker stalls to expensive restaurants. The stalls are regularly inspected for hygiene and nobody need hesitate to use them. Most are in modern "food centres" where stalls serving Chinese, Malay and Indian food can all be found. Simply find a table (which is numbered), walk from stall to stall selecting the dishes you fancy, and they will be brought to you within minutes.

The Guide to Singapore Hawker Food by James Hooi (S$2.80 or US$2) is indispensable to food lovers who want to work their way through the virtually limitless range of hawker food.

Armed with this guide, a visit to the **Satay Club** on **Queen Elizabeth Walk**, **Newton Circus** car park and **Rasa Singapura** (which has moved to the **Bukit Turf Club**) food stalls are a must. Smokers who must light up before/during/after meals now frequent these and other open-air spots as they are the only eating places where smoking is allowed. Having banned smoking in all public places which are air-conditioned, the government is aiming to make Singapore a smoke-free state.

Chilli crab is a famous Singapore dish. The **Long Beach** restaurant and many other places which used to be along Upper East Coast Rd and Bedok Rd and provide wonderful seafood, have mostly been relocated to the **Seafood Centre** along the **East Coast Parkway**, affording a view of sea. There is excellent seafood to be had at **Ponggol Point**. This makes a marvellous ending to an afternoon's water-skiing there. The supermarket-style restaurant at the **Big Splash** amusement centre in the **East Coast Park** — where you choose your raw seafood at a counter and it is then cooked for you — also offers fresh seafood in an outdoor setting. **Marina South**, a recreational development on reclaimed land, has **Beach Garden** which serves good seafood at reasonable prices.

As the Chinese represent nearly 80% of the republic's population, Chinese restaurants are more abundant than others. The restaurant scene is changing constantly in Singapore — establishments open and close or remodel and change their menus constantly. It is best to consult the daily newspapers or periodicals aimed at visitors for the current favourites. Although Hokkiens predominate, more Chinese restaurants serve Cantonese food than any other dialect group's cuisine.

Some of the better Cantonese restaurants in hotels include:

Shang Palace in the Shangri-La Hotel; **Li Bai** at the Sheraton Towers; **Tang Court** in The Dynasty ; **Canton Garden** at the Westin Plaza; the **Summer Palace** at the Regent; **Inn of Happiness** at the Hilton; **Lei Garden** at the Boulevard; **Fragrant Blossom** at the Holiday Inn Park View; **Full Moon** at the Glass Hotel and **Tsui Hang Village** at the Hotel Asia.

Many of them, such as the **Garden Seafood Restaurant** in the Goodwood Park, serve *dim sum* for lunch.

For **Peking** food, try the **Jade Room** in Lucky Plaza shopping complex, **Pine Court** in the Mandarin Hotel, **Eastern Palace** in Supreme House and the revolving restaurant in **Prima Tower** in Keppel Rd.

After Cantonese, the hot and spicy **Sichuan** food is the next most popular cuisine. It is served in the following hotels: **Tai Pan Ramada**, **Novotel Orchid Inn**, **King's Hotel**, **Crown Prince Hotel**, **River View Hotel**, **Equatorial**, **Royal Holiday Inn**, **Grand Central**, **New Otani Goodwood Park** and **Westin Plaza**.

Hokkien, **Teochew**, **Hakka** and **Hainanese** foods are found mostly in small coffee shops and food stalls plus such restaurants as the **Moi Kong** (Hakka) or **Beng Hiang** (Hokkien) in **Food Alley** on Murray St, or Teochew havens such as the **Ban Heng** on Boon Keng Rd, the **Ellenborough Market** stalls on Teochew St, or the "Guan Hin" on Whampoa West. Occasionally, plush hotels pick some favourites from these types of food to add to their menus in the coffee shops under the heading of local dishes.

Malay food is best described as something between *nonya* (except that no pork is served) and Indian cooking. **Aziza's** in Emerald Hill Rd is about the most up-market Malay restaurant. **Bintang Timur** in Far East Plaza is a more modest establishment. The most well-known Malay dish, *satay*, is served in nearly all hotel coffee shops and pool sides as well as the **Satay Club**. Tasting very similar to Malay food but with more places serving it, is the Singapore version of Indonesian food, for which try the restaurant in the **Apollo Hotel**, **Jawa Timur** at Chint Hong Bldg.

The Singapore penchant for adapting food also applies to Indian cuisine. **Fish head curry** is one of the most popular local Indian dish and several modestly priced restaurants Race

Fish head curry: local speciality.

Course Rd. **Banana Leaf Apolo** is world famous for its curries, eaten with the hands off, of course, banana leaves. A folk and spoon will be provide on request. The more humble eating establishments offer south Indian food, which tends to be hotter than its northern counterpart, including vegetarian dishes. Try the **Keralan Restaurant** in Food Alley on Murray St, or **Jubilee** on North Bridge Rd.

For Indian vegetarian food, the **Komala Villas** and the **New Woodlands** on Serangoon Rd are recommended. Northern Indian cuisine is usually served in expensive restaurants. **Omar Khayyam** on Hill St and **Shalimar** in Tanglin Shopping Centre are long-established as serving delicious food in air-conditioned and elegant surroundings.

Singaporeans have adventurous taste-buds and so **Korean**, **Japanese**, **Vietnamese** and **Thai** food provide interesting Asian varieties. The **Han Do** in the Orchard Shopping Centre is well known for Korean food. The **Chao Phraya Thai Seafood Market & Restaurant** at Block 730, Ave 6, Ang Mo Kio is one of the oldest of the Thai favourites. **Saigon** in Cairnhill Place is a little hard to find but its Vietnamese food is excellent.

There are quite a few good Japanese restaurants, many in the Japanese-owned hotels. **Fujiya** in the multi-storey carpark in Market St is one of the oldest and best. Then there is the **Yamagen** in Yen San Bldg. Japanese food in Singapore, as elsewhere, is very expensive.

Western food is readily available. The decor, food and service are unmistakably Olde English at the **Jockey Pub** on the first floor of Shaw Centre and **Fosters** in the Specialists' Shopping Centre. Royal Holiday Inn has Austrian and German restaurants. The **Brasserie** in the Omni Marco Polo is famous for its French atmosphere, serving simple but good French food. **Belvedere** in the Mandarin Hotel provides another variety. **Le Restaurant de France** in Hotel Meridien is expensive, as is **Maxim's** in the Regent. **Nutmeg** in the Hyatt Regency is excellent for its food, its New York art deco atmosphere and (on Sunday until 3 pm) its jazz.

Of the Italian restaurants, **Prego** in the Westin Stamford, **Grand Italia** in the Glass Hotel and **Pete's Place** in the Hyatt are the most popular. **Pasta** in **Holland Village** is small and trendy. The more well-known Continental restaurants serving the most popular of French, Italian, Swiss and German dishes are **Latour** (Shangri-La), **Compass Rose** in the Westin Stamford, **Gordon Grill** in the Goodwood Park and **Harbour Grill** in the Hilton. **Le Grand Bouffe** in Sunset Way is popular among locals, particularly for its souffles.

Swiss food is served at the **Movenpick** in Scotts Rd and its branch in the Standard Chartered Bank Bldg in Battery Rd is popular among businessmen.

For Mexican food try **El Felipe's** at Orchard Towers.

The Western restaurants serve all the usual alcoholic drinks as well as a few special cocktails such as the Singapore Sling. Anchor and Tiger beers are the regular drinks around town.

Hotels and cabarets provide ample opportunity for a good night out. The entertainment features excellent music from a number of imported bands and local groups. Once in a while international stars give performances in Singapore, (see the daily newspaper for entertainment news) but tickets can be hard to come by, especially during the biennial Arts Festival in June. In general, the entertainment scene in Singapore is in keeping with the clean-cut mould into which the population has been eased. Perhaps because of this, it lacks the excitement one would find in other less structured cities. Singapore is building tourist entertainment in line with Western tastes. But Chinese cultural events are growing with the heightened consciousness of their cultural heritage among Chinese. The theatre scene has moved away from the expatriate-run amateur drama groups to one where near full-time local actors and directors stage good productions regularly. *Theatreworks* productions at the **Drama Centre** in Fort Canning are usually first rate.

Piano bars are quite popular, but the rage is *karaoke*. **Java Jive** in Holland Village is one of many karaoke bars. But if you want professional musicians rather than often soused amateurs, go to **Bill Bailey's** in the Dynasty Hotel. **Brannigan's** at the Hyatt Regency has jam sessions, while jazz is played at the **Saxophone** in Cuppage Terrace.

The **Neptune Theatre Restaurant** on Clifford Pier offers the big night out — dinner, dancing and a floorshow. These are top class with prices to match. There is no cover charge at the Neptune. The **Oasis** at Kallang Park offers a slightly less traditional evening out with girls available for chatting and dancing in addition to the food and music.

The proliferation of discos ensures at least a dozen choices. They range from **Scandals** in Westin Plaza, where Singapore meets the space age, to Shangri-La's **Xanadu**, with girl bartenders, and **Caesar's** and **Top Ten** in Orchard Towers and **Rumours** in Forum Galleria. The **Red Leaf**, a more up-market disco at the Centruy Park Sheraton, has a S$15 cover charge on weekdays and S$20 on weekends, but only for men.

Singapore is a most enjoyable and safe place in which to simply walk around, especially in the relative cool of the evening. You might come across an outdoor eating place and sample some local foods and, if you are lucky, there might be a *wayang* (Malay for Chinese street opera) going on which you can see free. (See *Singapore This Week* for places and times). *Wayang* is usually performed during festive occasions or for religious thanksgiving.

There are a number of air-conditioned cinemas screening Western, Chinese, Indian and Malay or Indonesian films.

In keeping with the government's emphasis on a clean-living image and lack of corruption, there certainly is no equivalent to the raunchy "girlie" bars of Bangkok or Manila, though there are a few vestiges of the old red light districts, one in Geylang, which are free from police harassment. The notorious Bugis St, once famous for its transvestites, has been demolished and redeveloped. The transvestites have mostly dispersed, but some are still found around town late at night, mostly in the Orchard Rd tourist area, but move their venue from place to place because they are subject to arrest for soliciting. By far the best and safest way for a tired businessman to find female company is through the several escort agencies which advertise in the Yellow Pages of the telephone directory.

Singapore enjoys much the same duty-free status as Hongkong, but is no match for the colony's prices or variety on items such as cameras and watches. However, Singapore is the handicraft centre of the region. If you cannot visit those countries, then buying in Singapore is wise. Although the range is never as wide as you can get in the source countries, at least the prices are fair.

The delicate silver filigree work and silk (*kain songket*) from Kelantan, northeast Malaysia, are beautiful. The silk can cost up to S$200 a piece and can be found in the shops along **Arab St**. Pewterware is made from Malaysia's locally mined tin and is elegant and long-lasting. Kelantan *batik* cloth is another quality product, though the Indonesian fabrics may have more to offer in richness of colour and design. There is a great deal of machine-printed batik on the market, so be careful in your selection. The colours are closely matched and you will have to feel the cloth (for its waxy touch in the original) and look for cracking marks on the border. True batik is made with waxing as part of the process, and wax used tends to crack on the edge of the part being worked, giving a clue to the buyer that the product is genuine. However, handmade batik costs much more than the machine-made variety and needs special care in washing and drying. Never dry batik in the sun. Indonesian wood-carvings from Bali are another excellent buy.

It is best to buy at a shop displaying the Merlion sticker, since that retailer is approved by the Consumers' Association of Singapore and the Singapore Tourist Promotion Board. For photographic and sound equipment, electrical goods and watches, buy at a store which is accredited to the manufacturer of the item you are buying and always get the manufacturer's guarantee rather than the shop's. As elsewhere in the region, copies are sometimes offered as designer merchandise.

For those interested in paintings and art by locals, there are several art galleries in which to browse — usually in shopping centres and hotels. Alpha Gallery is another place for browsing. In many of the shops selling Chinese artefacts, one can buy Chinese scroll paintings.

It is wise to buy gold, silver, pearl, jade and other precious stones in Singapore because of the low prices. You should buy these in a reliable shop unless you are an expert in jewellery. Goldsmiths along **North Bridge Rd** and the **People's Park Complex** offer competitive prices. Nothing is priced because gold items are sold by weight, set according to the day's gold price. While you cannot bargain over the gold price, feel free to knock down the workmanship fee for the item.

Products from China are sold in Singapore, though in a very limited range compared with Hongkong. Tientsin carpets and rosewood furniture in Chinese style are wonderful buys. The modern Chinese often have a sense of taste which is foreign to the discerning visitor, thus some of their simple and elegant products are cheap while their garish items are expensive. If your taste runs to the simple, you can often pick up a real bargain.

Persian, Afghan and Baluchi carpets are sold in shops along Orchard Rd and Tanglin Rd. Carpets are duty-free items, both machine and hand-made. Taiping carpets are manufactured locally. Singapore-made cane furniture is sought after because of its low price.

Orchard Rd is the main shopping area for tourist and its 23 shopping complexes are served by one of three MRT stations — **Dhoby Ghaut**, **Somerset** and **Orchard**. But Orchard Rd is only the mecca for fashionable items. Look for spices in **Little India**, which leads off Serangoon Rd. For Chinese herbs and foodstuffs try **Chinatown** off South Bridge Rd.

Some tourists tend to think that places like the **People's Park Complex**, **Rochor Plaza** or **Sim Lim Towers** are the cheapest places to shop. But once in a while they will find, after some hard bargaining, that the item they have just bought is priced even lower in a departmental store. However, bargaining is good fun and provides a way of communicating between foreigners and locals. It is best to bargain only if you really want the item. A touch of humour is always helpful. Shopkeepers loathe people who waste their time haggling and walk away after the price has been lowered.

Squash and tennis courts costing S$3-6 an hour are available at the **Clementi Recreation Centre** in West Coast Walk, the **East Coast Recreation Centre**, and at **Farrer Park**. One usually has to book a few days in advance for a court, but the day courts are relatively easy to get.

There are 17 golf courses (13 with 18 holes and three with nine, and a driving range). Visitors should contact the Singapore Island Country Club or one of the other clubs directly and request permission to play. Be prepared for high green fees (S$40-100) on weekdays. A beautiful course on **Sentosa** has a spectacular view of the sea.

In the heart of the city, on the padang opposite the Town Hall, visitors can enjoy sports being played by the local people late on most

A Chinese street barber's chair.

afternoons, and at weekends there is often a cricket match in progress. Polo matches can be seen at the **Singapore Polo Club** field, Thompson Rd, on Tuesdays, Thursdays, Saturdays (5:45 pm) and Sundays 5:30 pm during the season from mid-January to late October. Horse riding at S$30 for 45 minutes is offered at the polo club. Horse racing at the **Bukit Turf Club** is on most weekends. Race meetings alternate between Singapore and Malaysia.

Changi Beach and **East Coast Park** lagoon at the eastern end of the island provide the best swimming facilities. On **Sentosa** there is a swimming lagoon and a good picnic area. Also, bikes can be rented on the island. If you swim on the beach check the tide information in the daily press and swim only at high tide to avoid mud. For water-skiing go to **Ponggol Point** on the north of the island where there are speedboats and skis for hire. But the water there is not particularly clear.

Flying fans should contact the **Singapore Flying Club** which offers Cessna, Piper or Twin Comanche aircraft. The Flying Club is near **Seletar Air Base**.

And then, there's jogging: Singapore's green surroundings and pavements make it a jogger's paradise. Apart from the tracks around the reservoirs and **Botanical Gardens**, you can even run around the huge public housing estates in the districts outside of city.

Singapore's calendar of festivals points up the multiracial nature of the republic's community. Chinese festivals are most common, though Indian festivals compete as intriguing spectacles and the Muslim community offers its solemn occasions of prayer. To offset the watering down of tradition behind such celebrations which have taken place, organisations have begun to put on events like the *Chingay* procession down Orchard Rd during *Chinese New Year*. The success of the Chinese, Malay and Indian cultural months in 1990 as part of the celebrations of the republic's 25th anniversary has ensured their being repeated in future, once the debate over the sensitive issue of ethnicity is settled.

The West adds Christmas, Easter and the

New Year. Most festivals change their date of celebration from one year to the next because of the lunar calendar. Not all festivals are public holidays. Those dates listed below for celebration subject to the lunar calendar are the closest approximation for 1991. In Singapore as well as Malaysia, where a holiday falls on a Sunday, the day following is a public holiday.

January 1: New Year's Day (public holiday).

January: Ponggal: The southern Indians' thanksgiving, using rice in offerings to the gods. Go to the Sri Srinivasa Perumal Temple in Serangoon Rd to observe these rites.

February: Thaipusam. On this day Hindu devotees doing penance for their sins and those who have made pledges during serious illness carry *kavadis* (spiked frames) through the streets on their shoulders. Thaipusam honours Lord Muruga and the festival begins at dawn in the Perumal Temple in Serangoon Rd. Then follows a long journey to the Chettiar Temple in Tank Rd.

At the Sri Mariamman Temple in South Bridge Rd some devotees drive steel skewers through parts of their bodies. Fire walking also takes place in this temple. All these might be frightening for the unfamiliar but devotees feel no pain and draw no blood as their minds are exalted towards thoughts of God. There are kavadi-carrying processions, dancing and the beating of drums along Serangoon Rd, Selegie Rd, Dhoby Ghaut, Orchard Rd and Clemenceau Ave. In the evening processions go through Maxwell Rd, Robinson Rd, Market St, Cecil and Cross Sts, New Bridge Rd and River Valley Rd.

Chinese New Year: The first two days are public holidays for a celebration which lasts for 15 days. The Chinese parade about town in new clothes visiting friends and relations. Children and unmarried youngsters are given *ang pow* (red packets) containing money and no unlucky words are spoken. A week-long festival on the Singapore River has become a regular Chinese New Year event.

Birthday of the Monkey God: He is one of the most famous Chinese mythological characters and the event is celebrated at the Monkey God Temple in Seng Poh Rd, with a procession of mediums in a trance who cut or pierce themselves and smear paper charms with their blood which are then distributed to devotees. His birthday is also celebrated in October.

March-April: Hari Raya Puasa (public holiday). The major Muslim festival, to celebrate the end of *Ramadan*, the month of fasting which begins in March. Bussorah St in the Arab St area, is full of stalls selling post-dusk meals to fasters.

Good Friday (public holiday). A candlelight procession takes place in the grounds of the Church of St Joseph on Victoria St.

Qing Ming: Chinese families visit graves of relatives to sweep and clean up the ground.

May 1: Labour Day (public holiday).

Vesak Day (public holiday) is celebrated by Buddhists to honour the birth, death and enlightenment of Lord Buddha by eating only vegetarian food or fasting and attending prayers. The Temple of 1,000 Lights on Race Course Rd and Phor Kark See on Bright Hill Drive are crowded with worshippers. It is a day of charity.

July: Hari Raya Haji (public holiday) has special significance to those who have completed their *haj* (pilgrimage) to Mecca. However, all Muslims celebrate by praying in the mosque and sacrificing goats and other animals.

August 9: National Day (public holiday). In the daytime there are processions and displays; in the evening fireworks light up the sky. Look out for the Orchard Rd dance party, Swing Singapore, usually a fortnight later.

August: The seventh lunar month celebrates the festival of the hungry ghosts. The Chinese believe that during this month, the souls of the dead are released from purgatory to roam the earth. Incense and joss sticks are burned and food is offered to appease the ghosts. Wayang and other street shows are performed during the festival especially around the carpark and food stall areas.

September: Navarathi. A festival which celebrates the consorts of the Hindu trinity of dieties through music. At the Chettiar Temple in Tank Rd over nine nights.

Thimithi: At the Sri Mariamman Temple in South Bridge Rd, devotees walk over a 4-m pit of burning coals to show their faith (and courage).

Moon Cake Festival: According to the Chinese, the moon is at its roundest and brightest on the 15th night of the eighth moon so they celebrate by eating moon cakes and persimmons. On the night of the festival, children light lanterns.

October: Festival of the Nine Emperor Gods is celebrated in a similar fashion to the Monkey God's birthday.

Pilgrimage to Kusu Island: A month-long festival celebrated by both Malays and Chinese who visit shrines on the island said to have been a turtle who saved the lives of a Malay and a Chinese fisherman. The *Tua Pek Kong* temple and the *kramat* are where offerings are made.

November: Deepavali (public holiday) is also known as the Festival of Lights, and is celebrated by the Hindus to commemorate the slaying of the mythical tyrant Ravana by Lord Rama. This marks the victory of light over darkness, the triumph of good over evil. Hindus decorate their houses with oil lamps and visit friends.

December 25: Christmas Day (public holiday).

Addresses

Singapore Tourist Promotion Board: Raffles City Tower, #37-00, 250 North Bridge Rd (0617). Tel: 3396622.

Immigration Dept, Pidemco Bldg, 95 South Bridge Rd (0105). Tel: 3396622.

Publications

The STPB produces many informative publications for distribution free to visitors. These can be obtained from the airport and from the board's office in Raffles City. Publications include *Tour It Yourself* and *101 Meals*. The *Singapore Street Directory* is worth buying for those who intend to stay some time.

The **Times Bookstore** is a huge chain and has a comprehensive selection of books on Singapore. *East Meets West* is a comprehensive summary of Singapore affairs and is well illustrated. *Singapore Reflections*, *Streets of Old Chinatown*, and *Singapore Mementoes* are very useful. **Select Books**, on the third floor of Tanglin Shopping Centre, is a more scholarly store, especially strong on Asian subjects.

ABN, 18 Church St. Tel: 5355511; Fax: 5323108.

Asia Commercial Bank, 60 Robinson Rd. Tel: 2228222; Fax: 2253493.

Ban Hin Lee Bank, 15 Philip St. Tel: 5337022; Fax: 5338490.

BNP, 20 Collyer Quay, Tung Centre. Tel: 2240211.

Bangkok Bank, 180 Cecil St, Bangkok Bank Bldg. Tel: 2219400; Fax: 2255852.

Bank Negara Indonesia, 158 Cecil St, Dapenso Bldg. Tel: 2257755.

Bank of America, 78 Shenton Way, Tel: 2236688; Fax: 3203068, 2233310.

Bank of China, 4 Battery Rd. Tel: 5352411; Fax: 5343401.

Bank of East Asia, 137 Market St. Tel: 2241334; Fax: 2251805.

Bank of India, 108 Robinson Rd, GMG Bldg. Tel: 2220011; Fax: 2252976.

Bank of Singapore, 101 Cecil St. Tel: 2239266; Fax: 2247407.

Bank of Tokyo, 16 Raffles Quay, #01-06 Hong Leong Bldg. Tel: 2208111; Fax: 2244965.

Banque Indosuez, 2 Shenton Way. Tel: 2207111; Fax: 2242140.

Chase Manhattan Bank, 50 Raffles Place, Shell Tower. Tel: 5304111; Fax: 2247950.

Chung Khiaw Bank, 1 Bonham St, UOB Bldg. Tel: 2228622; Fax: 2254404.

Citibank, 5 Shenton Way, UIC Bldg. Tel: 2242611; Fax: 2249844.

Deutsche Bank, 8 Shenton Way, Treasury Bldg. Tel: 2228388.

DBS, 6 Shenton Way, DBS Bldg. Tel: 2201111; Fax: 2211306.

Far Eastern Bank, 1 Bonham St, UOB Bldg. Tel: 2225411; Fax: 2235620.

First National Bank of Chicago, 76 Shenton Way, Ong Bldg. Tel: 2239933.

Four Seas Bank, 19-25 Cecil St. Tel: 2249898; Fax: 2244936.

Hongkong & Shanghai Banking Corp., 21 Collyer Quay, Hongkong Bank Bldg. Tel: 5305000; Fax: 2250663.

Indian Bank, 2 D'Almeida St, Bharat Bldg. Tel: 5343511; Fax: 5331651.

Indian Overseas Bank, 64 Cecil St, IOB Bldg. Tel: 2251100; Fax: 2244490.

Industrial & Commercial Bank, 2 Shenton Way, ICB Bldg. Tel: 2211711; Fax: 2259777.

International Bank of Singapore, 50 Collyer Quay, #02-01 Overseas Union House. Tel: 2234488; Fax: 2240236.

Kwangtung Provincial Bank, 60 Cecil St, Kwangtung Provincial Bank Bldg. Tel: 2239622; Fax: 2259970.

Lee Wah Bank, 1 Bonham St, #01-00 UOB Bldg. Tel: 2258844.

Malayan Banking Bhd, 2 Battery Rd, Malayan Bank Chambers. Tel: 5352266; Fax: 5327909.

Mitsui Bank, 16 Raffles Quay, #01-04 Hong Leong Bldg. Tel: 2209761; Fax: 2250962.

OCBC, 65 Chulia St, OCBC Centre. Tel: 5357222; Fax: 5326007.

Overseas Union Bank, 1 Raffles Place, OUB Centre. Tel: 5338686; Fax:5332293.

Security Pacific Asian Bank, 6 Raffles Quay, #01-01 Denmark House. Tel: 2243363; Fax: 2256316.

Societe Generale De Banque, 30 Robinson Rd, Tuan Sing Towers. Tel: 2227122.

Standard Chartered Bank, 6 Battery Rd. Tel:

2258888; Fax: 2259136.

Tat Lee Bank, 63 Market St, Tat Lee Bank Bldg. Tel: 5339292; Fax: 5331043.

UCO Bank, 2 D'Almeida St, #01-01 Bharat Bldg. Tel: 5325944; Fax: 5325044.

United Malayan Banking Corp, 150 Cecil St, Wing On Life Bldg (0106). Tel: 2253111; Fax: 2247871.

United Overseas Bank, 1 Bonham St, UOB Bldg (0104). Tel: 5339898; Fax: 5342334.

CHAMBERS OF COMMERCE

American Business Council, Shaw Centre, #16-07, 1 Scotts Rd. Tel: 2350077.

British Business Assoc., 450/452 Alexandra Rd. Tel: 4754192.

Indonesian Business Assoc., 158 Cecil St, #07-03. Tel: 2215063.

Japanese Chamber of Commerce & Industry, 10 Shenton Way, #12-04. Tel: 221 0541; Fax: 2256197.

Singapore Chinese Chamber of Commerce, 47 Hill St. Tel: 3378381; Fax: 3390605.

Singapore Indian Chamber of Commerce, #23-01 Tong Eng Bldg. Tel: 2222855; Fax: 2231707.

Singapore International Chamber of Commerce, Denmark House #05-00, 6 Raffles Quay. Tel: 2241255.

Singapore Malay Chamber of Commerce, #24-07 International Plaza, 10 Anson Rd. Tel: 2211066; Fax: 2235811.

Singapore Manufacturers' Assoc., 20 Orchard Rd. Tel: 3388787; Fax: 3383358.

Singapore Pakistan Chamber of Commerce, 171 Tras St, #07-177. Tel: 2248562.

DISCOVERING SINGAPORE

Singapore is a convenient place in which to wander on your own since it is not very large and English is widely spoken. It is fairly safe to walk alone at night. The city has grown up around its harbour which remains the focus of much of its activity. Although most areas on the island have been developed, around the city centre and commercial areas you will be able to see pre-

served areas with traditional shophouses — a reminder of early Singapore like **Peranakan Place** off **Orchard Road**, **Telok Ayer Street** and **Tanjong Pagar**. Chinatown will remain a mess until 1992 because it is undergoing restoration.

To discover Singapore, start with the main artery, the **Singapore River**, which runs through the heart of the city. In pre-modern Singapore at all hours of the day and night lighters used to move up and down the narrow channel between the moored boats, supplying and emptying the warehouses that lie a little further upstream. The lighters have now been banished to an outlying industrial wharf (in **Pasir Panjang**) in the name of Singapore's self-sanitisation crusade. Nonetheless, a boat ride in the harbour at dusk is still a beautiful introduction to the city. One can take a small craft which may be hired at **Clifford Pier** on **Collyer Quay**.

Queen Elizabeth Walk is a wide pedestrian way near the pier facing the harbour. At its western end is the **Merlion Statue** — the symbol of Singapore — near the water. Its eastern end is connected to the massive **Marina Centre** (a shopping area) and the **Marina Park**. Queen Elizabeth Walk in the morning is the venue for a number of Chinese who engage in the graceful exercise and discipline known as *tai chi chuan*. Every day they are there, stabbing the air and thrusting into space. The area is inhabited throughout the day: in the evening it becomes crowded as the people come to take a little air by the water's edge and enjoy the good food to be bought at the **Satay Club**.

Across Connaught Drive from Queen Elizabeth Walk is the green expanse of the **padang**, the city's playing field, which has at one end the **Singapore Recreation Club** (where Eurasians hang out) and the **Cricket Club** (the British colonial club now mostly used by lawyers). At the eastern end of the padang rises the tall column of a war memorial to all those who lost their lives in World War II. Many of the city's public buildings stand round or near the padang. Opposite is the **City Hall**, which used to be the seat of the elected government. This has been converted to house courts which have outgrown the **Supreme Court** building next door and the **Academy of Law**. The core of the original building was built in 1827 as a private residence, but was later taken over by the government and altered extensively. Little of the original structure is now visible, though the present 1926 remodelled building retains much of the original dignity; here on National Day and

Singapore

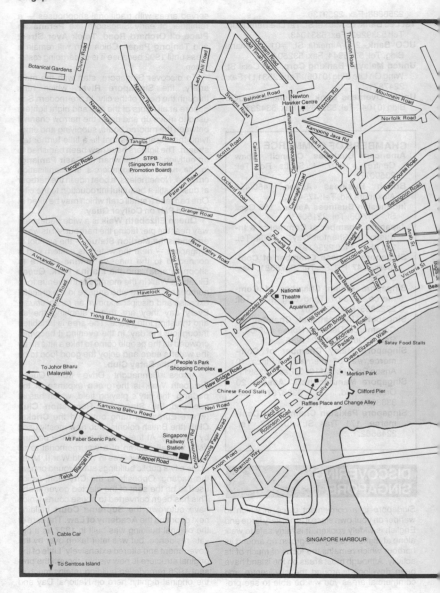

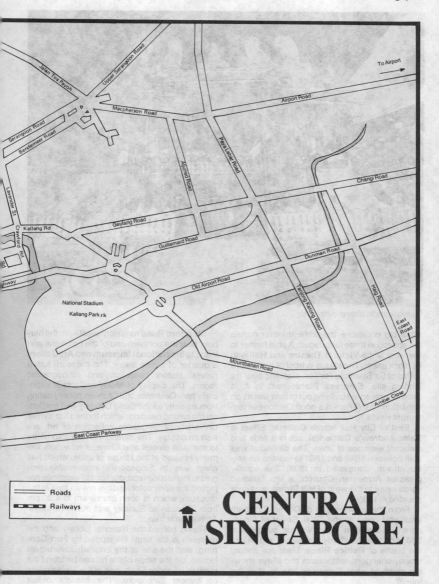

CENTRAL SINGAPORE

Roads

Railways

National Stadium

Kallang Park rk

To Airport

Airport Road

Macpherson Road

Serangoon Road

Bendemeer Road

Upper Serangoon Road

Jalan Toa Payoh

Lavender St.

Crawford Rd.

hway

Kallang Rd

Geylang Road

Guillemard Road

Old Airport Road

East Coast Parkway

Aljunied Road

Paya Lebar Road

Changi Road

Dunman Road

Tanjong Katong Road

Haig Road

Mountbatten Road

Amber Close

East Coast Road

Traditional model offering to the dead.

other big occasions the prime minister makes his speech in three languages. A little further to the west is the **Victoria Theatre and Hall** with its clock tower. The statue in front of the theatre is that of Sir Stamford Raffles, standing near his landing site. **Empress Place**, next to it, is another preserved building put to new use as an exhibition site. (There is a good Cantonese restaurant inside.)

East of City Hall across Coleman Street is **Saint Andrew's Cathedral**, set in a wide and pleasant expanse of lawn. The cathedral was built between 1846 and 1861 to replace an earlier church, completed in 1837. The equally pleasant **Armenian Church**, a few hundred yards away to the west of **Hill Street**, was constructed in 1835.

From the western end of Queen Elizabeth Walk you come to the "Wall Street of Singapore" — **Shenton Way**. Via the suspension bridge go past the sturdy grey banks and on into the bustle of **Raffles Place**. Here are shops, money-changers, restaurants and alleys showing much of what Singapore has to offer the tourist.

Stamford Road runs northwest from the harbour past the northern end of the cathedral and leads to the **National Museum** and **Art Gallery** a quarter of a mile away. The museum has a natural history collection and ethnographic rooms. The display of Malay artifacts is especially fine. Ceramics and Chinese pottery dating from as early as the Sung Dynasty and textiles, sculpture and painting, which formed the former University of Singapore collection of art, are also on display. The museum is now also home to the jade pieces and Chinese art works formerly housed at the House of Jade, which has given way to Singapore's irrepressible progress. Interesting reproductions of paintings depicting the early colonial days are on sale at the museum, which is open from 9 am to 4:30 pm from Tuesday to Sunday and public holidays. Admission is free.

Rising behind the National Library and the museum is the small hill topped by **Fort Canning**, and the site of the original Government House. On the slope of the hill can be found the tomb of Iskander Shah, one of the Malay rulers of ancient Singapore. The island's oldest cemetery, dating from 1822, rests on the hilltop.

Running parallel to Stamford Road is **Bras Basah Road** on which is the **Saint Joseph's Institution**, an old Catholic establishment whose architectural style is beautiful — but is to be demolished to make way for redevelopment. Turning to **Queen Street**, **Victoria Street**, **Middle Road** and **Waterloo Street**, you will come across churches of many denominations as well as Chinese temples and Muslim or Hindu places of worship. All these sacred places stand amid rundown shophouses and crowded residences.

North Bridge Road runs roughly north from the Singapore River (south of the river it becomes South Bridge Road), and is one of the main reference roads in the city. **South Bridge Road** leads into **Chinatown** and if you follow it for a little over a mile you reach **Sago Lane**, noted for the buildings to which old and improverished Chinese came to await death. But Chinatown does not stop here. There are more streets to be explored. From **Smith Street**, **Temple Street** to **North Canal Road** and the whole area of **New Bridge Road** can be considered as Chinatown. Despite the move away from these crowded tenements, many families still live here and hang their laundry out of windows on long poles. Chinatown is fast giving way to ambitious building programmes that are replacing the slums with new blocks of flats — though still with their windows bedecked with laundry poles and their colourful flags of shirts, trousers and underwear.

At the northern end of North Bridge Road is the **Arab Street** area and near its southern edge is where the infamous night-time hangout of transvestites, **Bugis Street**, once was. But Bugis Street as it once was has been wiped off the map (though there is an underground station called Bugis) and it will present its rebuilt, cleaned and spruced up face again in 1991. An official press release says "modern, hygienic kitchens will serve the street restaurants, airconditioned dining upstairs for those who want to observe the fun but not necessarily take part . . . and a special platform is being prepared for the more colourful performers whose early morning antics made the streets such a drawcard." Make what you will of this.

Little India is the area enclosed by the lower end of Bukit Timah Road extending to Sungei Road, Jalan Besar and Race Course Road. Serangoon Road runs through Little India. The scent of jasmine flowers and spices wafts through this charming area.

Around the **Orchard Road** area, especially from the **Mandarin Hotel** to the **Marco Polo**, is a comfortable exile for the tourist, provided one is not overwhelmed by its consumer atmosphere. The few old outdoor cafes have been torn down since they were connected with shophouse-style establishments, but there are two at the start of Orchard Road — at the **Ming Court Hotel** and across the road at **Orchard Hotel**. The coffee shop at the Mandarin is open 24 hours — night owls take note, since it is one of the few such establishments in Singapore.

Scattered about the city are the several places of worship associated with one or other of the religious groupings. The **Shuang Lin Buddhist Monastery** in Kim Keat Road near Toa Payoh is the most complete and largest among the Buddhist monasteries in the area. Shuang Lin Temple, meaning Twin Grove Temple, was built in 1898 and it took 11 years to complete. It has been restored and is in good order, in contrast with other Chinese temples located in Telok Ayer Street. The largest Buddhist temple, however, is **Kong Meng San Phor Kark** temple complex in **Bright Hill Drive**. **Thian Hock Keng** (Temple of Heavenly Happiness) is a typical old Hokkienese temple built in 1840. The **Sakya Muni Gaya Temple** on Race Course Road displays a large reclining Buddha. Because of its wealth of surrounding lights, it is also called the Temple of a Thousand Lights. There is also a replica of the Buddha's footprint, carved from teakwood and inlaid with mother-of-pearl.

The oldest place of Hindu worship in Singapore is the **Sri Mariamman Temple** on South Bridge Road. The building was constructed some time before 1843 and about 30 years ago the facade was modified with the addition of many lifelike carvings of gods and animals. The Sri Subramaniam Temple is another important Hindu place of worship in the city, and can be found on Tank Road.

Completed in 1928, the **Sultan Mosque**, north of the city along **North Bridge Road** in one of the Malay quarters, is the centre of worship for the island's 100,000 Muslims. Observe custom by washing your face, ears, hands and feet in holy water and then, barefoot, follow the man who will show you around the building.

For a scenic and refreshing view of the island, go to **Mount Faber**. On Mount Faber Ridge stands the **Alkaff Mansion**, once the home of a rich Arab trader and now preserved and refurbished at the cost of S$3 million as an "entertainment facility" and reopened in late

A traditional Malay wedding.

1990. From Mount Faber you can take a cable ride to **Sentosa**, overlooking the blue Straits of Singapore. Sentosa itself is a beautiful resort featuring a lagoon, camping ground, joggers' track, 18-hole championship golf course and one hotel — the **Apollo Sentosa**.

Several reservoirs outside the city make pleasant parks, such as **MacRitchie**, **Pierce** and **Seletar Reservoirs**. The **Botanic Gardens** are near the Tanglin road area, while **Orchid Farm** and the **Zoological Garden** are both near **Mandai Road**. The **Crocodile Farm** is on the East Coast Parkway and the **Kranji War Memorial** (where the graves of 24,000 dead overlook the Straits of Johore) is off Woodlands Road. A special **World War II** tour will take in the memorial, **Changi Prison** and the **Sembawang Naval Base**. **Bukit Timah Nature Reserve** is a popular tourist spot. The **Tiger Balm Gardens**, a kind of Buddhist/Taoist/Confucian Disneyland teeming with gaudily daubed moral tableaux, has been given a sprucing up and re-opened in September 1990.

A visit to **Jurong**, the most important industrial area on the west of Singapore, will also reveal the tallest man-made waterfall in the world. The landscaped **Chinese Garden** and **Japanese Garden** are also in Jurong. The former is based on the style of Peking's Summer Palace and architectural traditions of the Sung Dynasty. Both gardens are open from 9:30 am to 6 pm daily. The **Science Centre** with its **Omni-theatre** with three multi-dimensional screens and **Bird Park**, are also in Jurong. To get to Jurong, try to hire a car or join a tour, as the area is vast and it is difficult to go from one spot to another because taxis are difficult to get.

While going from place to place in Singapore, one should bear in mind that in 1977 the Singapore Government introduced a traffic law with special regard to pedestrians. They may cross roads only at designated sections. Watch out for signs along the road concerning this. Pedestrians who violate the traffic regulation are fined S$50. In many parts of town, especially in the central business district and shopping centres, there are designated taxi stands, but their locations are so sparse and out-of-the-way as to make it virtually impossible to get a cab speedily at peak hours, except at an hotel entrance.

HOTEL GUIDE

Hotel address	Phone	Fax	Telex	Cable	≋	🍴	🍵
A (US$108 and above)　　**B** (US$86-108)　　**C** (US$48-86)							
A							
Boulevard 200 Orchard Rd	7372911	7348449	RS 21771	BOUTEL	▲	▲	▲
Carlton 76 Bras Basah Rd	3388333	3373394	RS 42076	CARLHO	▲	▲	▲
Century Park Sheraton 16 Nassim Rd	7321222	7322222	RS 21817	CPSSIN	▲	▲	▲
Crown Prince 270 Orchard Rd	7321111	7327018	RS 22819	HCROWN	▲	▲	▲
Dynasty 320 Orchard Rd	7329900	7335251	RS 36633	DYNTEL	▲	▲	▲
Goodwood Park 22 Scotts Rd	7377411	7328558	RS 24377	GOODTEL	▲	▲	▲
Hilton 581 Orchard Rd	7372233	7376849	RS 21491	HILTELS	▲	▲	▲
Holiday Inn Park View 11 Cavenagh Rd	7338333	7344593	RS 55420	HIPV	▲	▲	▲
Hyatt Regency 10-12 Scotts Rd	7331188	7321696	RS 24415	HYATT	▲	▲	▲
Mandarin 333 Orchard Rd	7374411	7322361	RS 21528	MANOTEL	▲	▲	▲
Marina Mandarin 6 Raffles Blvd	3383388	3394977	RS 22299	MARINA	▲	▲	▲
Melia at Scotts 45 Scotts Rd	7328855	7321332	RS 36811	FEDPAC	▲	▲	▲
New Otani 177A River Valley Rd	3383333	3392854	RS 20299	SINOTA	▲	▲	▲
Omni Marco Polo 247 Tanglin Rd	4747141	4710521	RS 21476	OMPS	▲	▲	▲
Oriental 5 Raffles Blvd	3380066	3399537	RS 29117	ORSIN	▲	▲	▲
Pan Pacific 7 Raffles Blvd	3368111	3391861	RS 33821	PPSH	▲	▲	▲
Regent 1 Cuscaden Rd	7338888	7328838	RS 37248	REGSIN	▲	▲	▲

Hotel address	Phone	Fax	Telex	Cable	〰	🍴	🍜
SINGAPORE – *Cont'd*							
A							
Royal Holiday Inn Crown Plaza 25 Scotts Rd	7377966	7376646	RS 21818	HOLIDAY	▲	▲	
Shangri-la 22 Orange Grove Rd	7373644	7337220	RS 21505	SHANGLA	▲	▲	▲
Sheraton Towers 39 Scotts Rd	7376888	7371072	RS 37750	SHNSIN	▲	▲	▲
Westin Plaza 2 Stamford Rd	3388585	3382862	RS 22206	RCHTLS	▲	▲	▲
York 21 Mt Elizabeth	7370511	7321217	RS 21683	YOTEL	▲	▲	▲
B							
Amara 165 Tanjong Pagar	2244488	2243910	RS 55887	AMARA	▲	▲	▲
Cairnhill 19 Cairnhill Rd	7346622	2355598	RS 26742	CANHIL	▲	▲	▲
Excelsior 5 Coleman St	3387733	3393847	RS 20678	EXCELH	▲	▲	▲
Furama 10 Eu Tong Sen St	5333888	5341489	RS 28592	FURAMA	▲	▲	▲
Glass 317 Outram Rd	7330188	7330989	RS 50141	GLHTL	▲	▲	▲
Harbour View Dai-Ichi 81 Anson Rd	2241133	2220749	RS 40163	DAISIN	▲	▲	▲
Imperial 1 Jln Rumbia	7371666	7374761	RS 21654	IMPHTL	▲	▲	▲
King's 403 Havelock Rd	7330011	7325764	RS 21931	KINGTEL		▲	▲
Ladyhill 1 Ladyhill Rd	7372111	7374606	RS 23157	LADYTEL	▲	▲	▲
Le Meridien Changi 1 Netheravon Rd	5427700	5425259	RS 36042	HOMRA	▲	▲	▲
Ming Court 1 Tanglin Rd	7371133	7330242	RS 21488	MINGTEL	▲	▲	▲
Miramar 401 Havelock Rd	7330222	7334027	RS 24709	MIRAMAR	▲	▲	▲
New Park 181 Kitchener Rd	2915533	2960719	RS 33190	NPHTL	▲	▲	▲

Hotel address	Phone	Fax	Telex	Cable	〰	🍴	🍷
SINGAPORE – *Cont'd*							
B							
Novotel Orchid Inn 214 Dunearn Rd	2503322	2509292	RS 21756	NOVSIN	▲	▲	▲
Orchard 422 Orchard Rd	7347766	7325061	RS 35228	ORTEL	▲	▲	▲
Plaza 7500A Beach Rd	2980011	2963600	RS 22150	HOTPLA	▲	▲	▲
Phoenix Somerset Rd	7378666	7322024	RS 23718	FEENLX		▲	▲
River View 382 Havelock Rd	7329922	7321034	RS 55454	RVHTEL	▲	▲	▲
Tai-Pan Ramada 101 Victoria St	3360811	3397019	RS 21151	TAIPAN	▲	▲	▲
Westin Stamford 2 Stamford Rd	3388585	3382862	RS 22206	RCHILS	▲	▲	▲
C							
Apollo 405/406 Havelock Rd	7332081	7331588	RS 21077	APOLLO		▲	▲
Asia 37 Scotts Rd	7378388	7333563	RS 24313	HOTASIA		▲	▲
Bayview Inn 30 Benccolen St	3372882	3372721	RS 26965	BAYSIN		▲	▲
Cockpit 115 Penang Rd	7379111	7373105	RS 21366	COCKPIT	▲	▲	▲
Equatorial 429 Bt Timah Rd	7320431	7379426	RS 21578	EQUATOR	▲	▲	▲
Garden 14 Balmoral Rd	2353344	2359730	RS 50999	GARTEL	▲	▲	▲
Golden Landmark 390 Victoria St	2972828	2982038	RS 38291	LANMAK	▲	▲	▲
Negara 15 Claymore Drive	7370811	7379075	RS 34788	NEGARA	▲	▲	▲
Royal 36 Newton Rd	2534411	2538668	RS 21644	ROYAL	▲	▲	▲
Paramount Marine Parade Rd	3445577	4474131	RS 22234	PARTEL	▲	▲	▲
Peninsula 3 Coleman St	3372200	3393847	RS 21169	PENHOTE	▲	▲	▲
Seaview 26 Amber Close	3452222	3451741	RS 21555	SEAVIEW	▲	▲	▲

CENTURIES OLD TRADITIONS.

STATE OF THE ART TECHNOLOGY.

THAI. WE REACH FOR THE SKY.

THAILAND

Thailand, formerly Siam, means "land of the free." Unlike other Asian nations it was never colonised by a foreign power, a fact which swells the Thais with pride. Although only a semi-democracy — the military has a large say in its government — its people enjoy a large degree of personal freedom, especially compared with some of their neighbours.

Thailand's landscape, like its 57 million people, is remarkably varied and often beautiful. The people, easy-going and tolerant, are arguably the most physically attractive in Asia. A visitor sees at once why it is called "The land of smiles" and has become one of the most popular tourist destinations in the world. There are 5 million tourists a year and tourism brings in more foreign exchange than rice or any other export.

Tourism and economic development though are exacting a price. The Thais still smile but prospective visitors should not delay if they want to see the old Thailand. Traditional values and culture are disappearing and much natural beauty has already been lost. Bangkok's particular crisis, traffic, noise and air pollution, is one of the horrors of the modern world. The capital's population exceeds 7 million and May reach 12 million by 2000.

Thus seasoned travellers now give themselves only two or three days in Bangkok before heading for delights which are still abundant upcountry and along the coast. However, even in Bangkok, old Thai ways still exist behind the concrete towers and beyond the roar of the bulldozers and pile drivers.

Soon after dawn Buddhist monks in robes which may vary in colour from dark saffron to bright orange can be seen making their way across building sites, along the banks of the *klongs* (canal) and down narrow (streets) where people wait to fill the monks' bowls with food and provide other essentials, a practice which Buddhist teaching says will make merit for the giver.

Thailand is predominantly Buddhist and signs of that are visible everywhere. Many young men still become monks for a short time, thereby honouring their parents, and older men spend time in a temple on retirement. Every Thai house has its own spirit house to accommodate the spirits from the land on which the house stands. The custom owes more to animism than Buddhism but that does not bother the tolerant Thais whose religion is the gentlest and most liberal form of Buddhism.

What is left of traditional Thai architecture is mainly visible in the glittering Buddhist temples and shrines and the simpler, wooden houses in which the monks live and study. Stylish domestic houses of beauty and interest in Bangkok and other cities have all but gone. Thais now prefer to live in air-conditioned, concrete structures.

Some old ways and superstitions do remain. It is common for Thai government and military leaders to consult their astrologers before making important decisions. Astrologers nominate a propitious time for a new minister or general to take up his post or to make an important journey. On election day politicians seeking success can be seen making offerings of a pig's head at the popular **Erawan Shrine** (corner of Ploenchit Rd and Rajdamri Ave, Bangkok). Buddhist shrines provide good luck numbers for

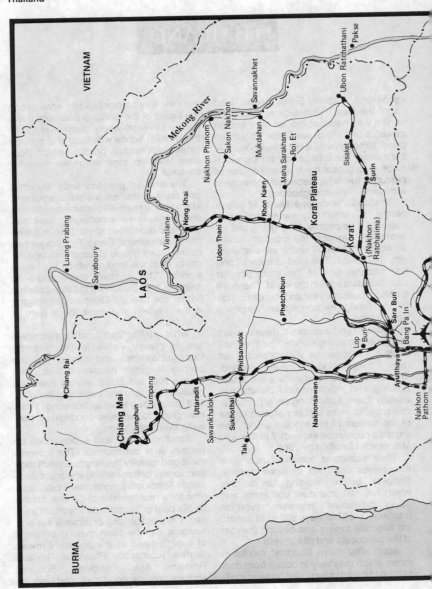

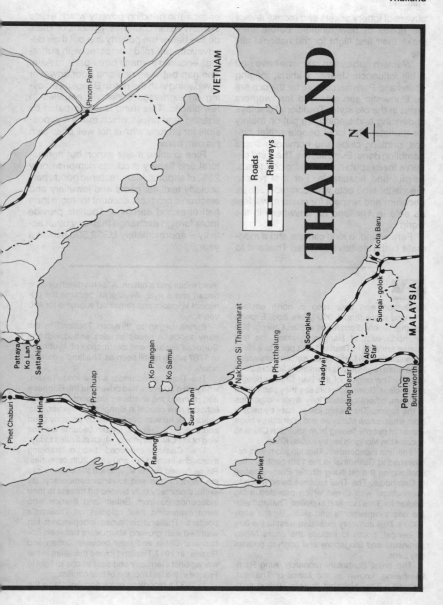

N

THAILAND

Roads

Railways

VIETNAM

Phnom Penh

MALAYSIA

Kota Baru

Sungai-golok

Songkhla

Alor
Star

Padang Besar

Haadyai

Phatthalung

Nakhon Si Thammarat

Penang

Butterworth

Surat Thani

Ko Phangan

Ko Samui

Ranong

Prachuap

Hua Hin

Phet Chabun

Pattaya

Ko Lan

Sattahip

Phuket

buyers of lottery tickets and monks anoint the noses of new airliners before they make their first flight for the national airline.

Western habits and fashions have had a big influence. Jeans, T-shirts, jogging shoes and Parisian couture for the rich are in. Domestic servants and farmworkers dress in the old style. Traditional displays of dancing and singing are put on mainly for tourists. The local people prefer discos, drinking clubs and nominally illegal gambling dens. Even so, the Thais still deserve their reputation for being courteous, helpful and hospitable. For that reason the visitor who acts with common sense, decorum and respect for custom, will feel as safe in Thailand as anywhere in the world.

Fertile land, a kind climate and a moderate birth rate have enabled Thailand to escape the grinding poverty which exists in many Asian countries. Millions of Thais do live below the poverty line but their deprivations are mild compared with sufferings endured in many other parts of Asia. The gap between rich and poor however is widening with the rich in Bangkok enjoying an extravagant lifestyle equalled in few places. This trend is exacerbated by soaring land prices which make it impossible for anyone who is not well off to own his own home.

Rice is still a major export but agricultural and fishery products comprise only 21% of exports. Manufactured goods particularly textiles, gems and jewellery and electronic products account for more than half of export earnings. Tourists provide more foreign exchange than any other activity – approximately US$2,500 million a year.

Civilisation was flourishing in north eastern Thailand more than 5,000 years ago. Experts say that recent discoveries at Ban Chieng, 500 km north east of Bangkok yielded the first human artifacts in Thailand and point to a civilisation older than Middle East settlements which have been regarded as mankind's first cradle of culture. The origins of the Ban Chieng people are unclear. Some scholars say they came from Vietnam, others contend they were indigenous to the region. They were joined later by people from what is now Malaysia and later still by huge waves of people fleeing from southern China to escape the Mongols led by Kublai Khan.

The first independent Thai kingdom was established at Sukhothai in the 13th century after challenging the far-flung Khmer Empire based in Cambodia. The Thai success owed much to connections with China which provided a big market for Thai rice and supplied Thailand with the latest implements and skills. By the early 1300's Thai authority extended west to the Bay of Bengal, south to include the entire Malay peninsula and Singapore and north to present day Laos.

The great Sukhotahi monarch, King Ramkamhaeng, known as the father of Thailand, created a Thai alphabet thereby uniting scattered tribes into a nation. After his death decline began and a rival, Ayutthaya, became the dominant kingdom and remained supreme for 400 years.

Burma began to threaten Thailand in the early 1500s. A series of wars ended with the Burmese capture and destruction of Ayutthaya in 1767 which is still seen as Thailand's darkest hour.

The Thais rallied under a new king, Taksin, who within 10 years had driven out the Burmese and reunited the shattered kingdom and established a new capital in Bangkok. However, four years later he was overthrown by an army coup and executed. General Chakri became the first king of the Chakri dynasty which still rules today.

The Chakris produced two outstanding monarchs in the 19th and early 20th centuries, Rama IV and Rama V, who led the country into the modern age and towards democracy. By skilful diplomacy they fended off threats to their independence from Britain and France who were expanding their colonies on Thailand's borders. Thailand remained independent but watched with growing alarm wars between Britain and China and later between Japan and Russia. In 1917 Thailand joined the allies in the war against Germany and sent troops to fight in France in the last months of that conflict.

In 1932 a bloodless revolution overthrew the

A Thai floating market. ▷
Photo: Tourism Authority of Thailand

absolute monarchy, but the king was invited to be a constitutional monarchy on the British pattern. What emerged however was a military dictatorship rather than a parliamentary democracy. In the past 60 years Thailand has had few elected civilian governments. Field marshals and generals have sustained their power with coups and counter coups, many of them violent.

One of the most notable dictators was Field Marshal Sarit Thanarat who made a name for himself by summarily executing arsonists and also by the mistresses and wealth he acquired during six years in power.

In 1973 and 1976 many hundreds of civilians were killed in clashes between the army and democrats. The army leaders fled into exile but later returned to cause another uprising.

Since the late 1970s, national affairs, much influenced by King Bhumibol, have changed for the better. Coming to the throne in 1946 the king is the longest-ruling monarch in Thai history. He is revered as a man dedicated to his people, and there are heavy punishments, including imprisonmnent for any insult to the throne.

Most visitors arrive by air at Thailand's five international airports. The major gateway is Bangkok's **Don Muang International Airport** 25 km from the city. More than 50 airlines from all parts of the world use the airport. Some also fly to airports at **Phuket** and **Hat Yai** in the south, **Chiang Mai** in the north and **U-Tapao** southeast of Bangkok. Charter flights operate from Europe, North America and other parts of Asia.

There is a departure tax of Baht 200 for international flights and Baht 20 for domestic.

Travellers also can arrive by sea at Bangkok's **Klong Toey** port just south of the city. A cruise ship, **Adaman Princess**, operates a regular passenger service between Singapore and Bangkok. Details from Siam Cruise Co. Ltd, Bangkok. Tel: 255-8950-7; Fax: 255-8961.

Travellers may enter Thailand overland from Malaysia and Laos but Burma and Cambodia are accessible only by air. Trains run daily both ways between **Butterworth** in northern Malaysia and Bangkok. The Bangkok-Butterworth journey takes 21 hours. Fares: second-class seat US$19; second-class sleeping berth (with fan) US$25; second-class berth (with aircon.) US$29; first-class sleeping berth (aircon.) US$49.

Malaysian trains run from Singapore and Kuala Lumpur to Butterworth. Those operating from the east coast also connect with Bangkok trains. Times should be checked carefully to ensure connections.

Provided strict customs regulations are observed, it is possible to drive between Thailand and Malaysia. The border is open daily only between 5 am and 5 pm (Thai time) and 6 am and 6 pm (Malaysian time) but these hours probably will soon be extended to 10 pm (Thai time).

Many visitors may enter without a visa. Travellers from nearly 40 countries in Western Europe, North America, Australasia, the Pacific and Southeast Asia may stay for up to 15 days without a visa but travellers from most other Asian countries and from Africa and the Middle East do require entry visas.

All visitors must carry passports or certificates of identity. Holders of Hongkong certificates of identity may travel on them in lieu of a passport and they are exempted from the guarantee clause. Malaysians carrying a border pass may travel up to 50 km into Thailand and stay 15 days. Taiwanese residents can obtain an entry permit from the Taipei office of Thai Airways International or process their papers through the Thai Embassy in a third country.

Foreign nationals wishing to stay longer than 15 days should obtain visas in their own countries. Travellers from countries without a Thai embassy or consulate should apply to missions in neighbouring countries or apply with supporting evidence to: Immigration Division, Soi Suan Phlu, Sathorn Tai Rd, Bangkok 10120. Tel: 286-9176, 286-9230.

All visas must be used within 90 days of issue. Visitors without visa may stay 15 days, tourist visa 60 days, transit visa 30 days, non-immigrant visa 90 days. Non-immigrant visas may be extended at the Immigration Division in Bangkok. Normally it is easier for visitors to extend tourist visas by travelling to the Thai Consulate at Penang in northern Malaysia. A person leaving Thailand who wishes to return during the validity of a visa must obtain a re-entry visa at the Immigration Division. Visa extensions and re-entry permits cost US$20.

Tax clearance: foreign nationals staying in Thailand for 90 continuous days are required to produce a tax clearance on departure. Inquiries should be made at the Revenue Department in Bangkok.

EMBASSIES IN BANGKOK

	Tel	Fax		Tel	Fax
Argentina	2590401-2		Netherlands	2526103	254-5579
Australia	2876890	2582589	Norway	2580533	259-1010
Austria	2863011		Pakistan	2530288	
Bangladesh	3918069-70		Philippines	2590139	
Belgium	2330840-1		Poland	2584112	
Brazil	2566023		Portugal	2340372	
Brunei	2515766	2535951	Romania	2510280	
Bulgaria	3143056		Saudi Arabia	2350875	2350879
Burma	2332237, 2342258		Singapore	2861434	
			Spain	2526112	2589990
Canada	2341561-8	2369469	Sri Lanka	2512789	251-1960
Chile	3918443		Sweden	2343891	2364699
China	2457030-44		Switzerland	2530156	255-4481
Czechoslovakia	2341922	2365843	Turkey	2512987	
Denmark	2863930		USSR	2342012	
Egypt	2530160	254-9489	United Kingdom	2530191	2537124
Finland	2569306	2515986	US	2525040	2861977
France	2340950-6	213-1291, 236-7973	Vatican	2118709	
			Vietnam	2515838	
Greece	2521686		West Germany	2864223	287-1776
Hungary	3912002	259-3166	Yugoslavia	3919090	2581066
India	2580300	2584627			
Indonesia	2523135		## CONSULATES		
Iran	2590611	259-9111			
Iraq	2785225		Bolivia	2141501	
Israel	2523131	254-5518	Dominican Republic	5210737	
Italy	2864844		Honduras	2512862	
Japan	2526151	258-6877, 258-9716	Iceland	2491300	
Korea	2340723		Ireland	2230876	
Laos	2860010		Jordan	3917142	
Malaysia	2861390	213-2126	Mexico	2451415	
Nepal	3917240		Oman	2367385	
New Zealand	2518165	2539045, 254-9488	Peru	2335910	
			Senegal	5731976	

No inoculations or vaccinations are required unless travellers are coming from or passing through a contaminated area.

THE DEATH PENALTY IS THE PUNISHMENT FOR THOSE ATTEMPTING TO SMUGGLE ENOUGH NARCOTIC DRUGS FOR TRAFFICKING AND THIS PENALTY HAS BEEN APPLIED TO FOREIGNERS. BE WARNED.

Obscene literature and pictures are prohibited imports. Import of firearms and ammunition is permitted only if a permit is granted by the Police Department or Local Registration Office.

Customs authorities are liberal towards visitors. They permit the import of personal effects, professional instruments and used household effects in generous quantities free of duty. One still camera or one movie camera with five rolls of still camera film or three rolls of movie film are permitted, as are not more than 250 grams of tobacco products or 200 cigarettes, one litre each of wine and spirits.

Certain species of plants, fruit and vegetables are prohibited, so importers should make inquiries from the Agricultural Regulatory Division, Bangkhen, Bangkok. Permission of entry for animals may be obtained at the airport on arrival or from the Department of Livestock Development, Bangkok, for sea arrivals. Animal vaccination certificates are required.

Tourists may import motor vehicles free of duty for up to six months but in most cases cash or bank guarantees are required. Full details can be obtained from the Customs Department in Bangkok or from Thai embassies or tourist offices before departure.

EXPORTS: Thailand imposes stringent controls on the export of art objects. NO BHUDDA IMAGE OR FRAGMENT THEREOF, IRRESPECTIVE OF ITS AGE, MAY BE TAKEN OR SENT OUT OF THE COUNTRY. All other art objects, irrespective of whether they are originals or reproductions, require export licences from the Fine Arts Department. Permission takes at least two weeks. Details from the Bangkok National Museum, Bangkok, or from reputable art dealers and shops.

Foreign visitors may bring in any amount of foreign currency but amounts in excess of

US$10,000 should be declared. Travellers may be prevented from taking out more than US$10,000 though this restriction is rarely enforced. Regulations also say that a visitor should bring in no more than Baht 2,000 and take out no more than Baht 500, but currency imports and exports are in practice almost never questioned.

Major credit cards are acceptable almost everywhere now that Thais use them widely.

When cashing travellers' cheques or foreign currency, visitors should avoid hotels where the offered rate is substantially less favourable than rates available at banks.

Thai Baht come in 500, 100, 50, 20, and 10 Baht notes and 10, 5, and one Baht coins. The Baht is divided into 100 satang; 50 and 25 satang coins (yellow in colour) are in circulation.

Thai is spoken everywhere with only minor differences from north to south. In the northeast where ethnic Lao are predominant, they speak their own language as well as Thai but the two are closely related. Some southerners speak a mixture of Thai and Malay. The large ethnic Chinese population in Bangkok speak various south China dialects but mainly Teochew.

English is widely spoken in Bangkok and in the major tourist resorts.

Tropical with an annual temperature of 28°C (82°F). Temperatures as low as 11°C (52°F) occur at night in rural areas during the November-February cool season. Day-time temperatures even in the hottest season (March-June) rarely reach 38°C (100°F).

Humidity is high at most times. Annual average rainfall is 1,500 mm. The dry, hot season is from about late February to early June and the wet season runs from around June until late October. The relatively cool, dry, sunny season is early November until the end of February and the best time of year to visit Thailand.

The weather in the far south is less predictable as thunderstorms occur all year round.

Do not buy a new tropical wardrobe for the trip. Instead buy it in Bangkok where light, casual garments are cheap but good quality. Thais are paragons of neatness and style, therefore some

formality is advisable for business appointments and similar occasions. Shorts and T-shirts are frowned upon in government offices and men should keep their shirts on at all times, except on the beach. Jackets and ties are required in some hotel restaurants. Pullovers are useful in the cool season at night and early morning, particularly in rural areas, when temperatures drop to 11°C (52°F). Dress discreetly at temples and national monuments. Wear slip-on shoes for the temple visits — and socks without holes.

Government and most commercial offices are open from 8:30 am until 4:30 pm Monday to Friday. Most government offices close for lunch between noon and 1 pm.

BANK HOURS: 8:30 am-3:30 pm Monday to Friday. Banks in major centres operate automatic teller machines long hours seven days a week.

Post offices keep government hours though many, including the General Post Office in New Road, Bangkok, open on Saturday mornings. The GPO also provides telegraph, telex and international telephone services at all times.

SHOPS: Most shops open from 8/9 am until 9 pm or later and remain open during weekends. Department stores: 10 am to 7/8 pm seven days a week.

RESTAURANTS: Open early and generally stay open until business comes to an end. Eating places open 24 hours a day can be found in hotels, generally coffee shops and in markets in Bangkok and other big towns.

LIQUOR: On sale at all times except religious holidays, when it is available only in hotels and Western-style restaurants.

BANGKOK

From the airport a limousine to a city hotel costs Baht 300 (US$12). The airport bus which runs to the Asia Hotel is Baht 60. Tickets available at the desk inside the terminal.

Transport can also be arranged at a taxi desk in the terminal. Fares must be negotiated and should be about half the limousine fare. Avoid the touts who operate derelict vehicles outside the law.

TAXIS: There are few taxi ranks anywhere but a cruiser is generally quickly available. Fares must be negotiated so a stranger is at a disadvantage. About Baht 40 has become the

minimum fare for a *farang* (Westerner).

Higher fares will be demanded during heavy traffic and when it is raining. No tipping is expected. Many drivers speak English but it is wise to carry a hotel card to explain your destination.

SAMLORS: Three-wheeled vehicles whose constantly increasing engine power give them astonishing speed. They are called "tuk tuks" because of their noise. Minimum fare is Baht 20 and generally they cost two-thirds of a taxi.

BUSES: Extensive routes all over the city. The Tourist Authority of Thailand has route maps. Services can be irregular with long delays. The vehicles at most times are overcrowded. Fares range from Baht 2 to 3. Air-conditioned buses which are more comfortable and less crowded cost Baht 5.

BOATS: Regular boats on the river and *klongs* (canals) cost only Baht 4 or 5 for quite long journeys. Negotiate for hire of a personal boat.

UPCOUNTRY

AIR: Thai Airways International's domestic service provide flights to all the main centres:

Chiang Mai — several flights daily. Fare: Baht 1,335-1,635.

Phuket — flights every day. Fare: Baht 1,620-1,920.

Samui — one flight daily. Fare: Baht 1,745.

Hat Yai — several flights daily. Fare: Baht 1,850-2,150.

BUSES: These are cheap and frequent to all parts of the country. Some are air-conditioned and comfortable but the accident rate is high. Many roads are too narrow to cope with the heavy vehicle traffic and the authorities admit that drivers work overlong hours and take drugs to keep awake. Bangkok has several special terminals where buses begin their journeys. For example, a southern terminal for those going to the south, an eastern terminal and so on. Sample fares:

Bangkok–Chiang Mai: Baht 242 (air-conditioned coach), Baht 370 (VIP coach).

Bangkok-Phuket: Baht 299 (air-conditioned coach), Baht 450 (VIP coach).

Buses without air conditioning are much cheaper.

TRAINS: Day-time trains give visitors the most thorough view of Thailand. Most long distance services however run at night though there are some day services. Trains are comfortable and run on time. Bookings can be made through travel agents or at the Bangkok main railway station, 8:30 am to 5:30 pm weekdays and 8:30 am to noon at weekends and holidays.

Bangkok's Wat Phra Kaeo.

Photo: Tourism Authority of Thailand

The daily express from Bangkok to Butterworth in Malaysia takes 21 hours. Fares range from Baht 481 for a second class seat to Baht 1,227 for a first class air-conditioned sleeper. Lower berth second class sleepers are good value and comfortable.

The extensive rail network covers most of the country. Trains are dearer than buses but are favoured by many because of their safety. Sample fares:

Bangkok–Hat Yai (south) one way: Baht 960 first class, Baht 363 second class.

Ubon Ratchthani (north east): Baht 696 (air-conditioned sleeper), Baht 480 second-class sleeper.

Most Bangkok hotels catering for tourists have tour offices to arrange visits in the city area and beyond. **The Tourist Authority of Thailand** (TAT) can provide appropriate publications and advice at their offices in Sydney, Singapore, New York, Los Angeles, London, Frankfurt, Paris, Rome, Kuala Lumpur, Hongkong and Osaka.

Head Offices: Ratchdamnoen Nok Ave, Bangkok 10100. Tel: 282-1143–7, Tlx: 72059 TAT BKK TH, Fax: 280-1744.

TAT offices are located outside Bangkok in:
Chiang Mai: Tel: 235334, Fax: 252812
Phitsanuloke: Tel: 252742–3
Kanchanaburi: Tel: 511200
Pattaya: Tel: 428750, 429113
Nakhon Ratchasima: Tel: 243427, 243751
Phuket: Tel: 212213, Fax: 213582
Hat Yai: Tel: 243747, Fax: 245986
Surat Thani: Tel: 281828, 282828, Fax: 282-828
Ubon Ratchathani: Tel: 255603

TRAVEL AGENTS
Bangkok:
Diethelm Travel, 140/1 Wireless Rd, Bangkok 10330. Tel: 255-9150–79, Fax: 250-0248, 256-0429.

Boonvanit Travel Agency, 420/9 Siam Square Soi 1, Bangkok. Tel: 251-0526–7, Fax: 254-1158.

Arlymear Travel, CCT Bldg, 109 Surawong Rd, Bangkok. Tel: 236-9317, Fax: 236-2929.

SEA Tours, 4th Fl., Siam Centre, 965 Rama I Rd, Bangkok. Tel: 2514862–9, Fax: 236-9317.

Siam Travel Consultant, Maneeya Centre, Mezzanine Fl., 518/5 Ploenchit Rd, Bangkok 10330. Tel: 250-0364, 251-2074, 251-5026, 251-5027.

Chiang Mai:

Centrepoint Holidays: Tel: (053) 244938
Northern Trekking Centre: Tel: (053) 222-174
Intco: Tel: (053) 211910
Alita Travel: (053) 236737

Phuket:

Atlas Travel: Tel: (076) 212569
Phuket Centre Tour: Tel: (076) 212892
Queen's Tour: Tel: (076) 321250

Songkhla:

Angel Travel Service: Tel: (074) 243918
Erawan Travel: Tel: (074) 313253

Surat Thani:

Bandon Travel: Tel: (077) 272267
Best Air Booking: Tel: (077) 421411

Tak:

Aswin Tour: Tel: (055) 531146

BANGKOK

Despite a hotel building boom in recent years rooms can be hard to find in the peak tourist season. Advance booking is essential. There is an enormous choice from luxury five star of the highest international standards to middle-range establishments which can be clean, comfortable and modern and cheaper places including many agreeable guesthouses. Male travellers may stay in temples where there is no set rate for accommodation but guests should make a cash donation on leaving.

Travellers should bear in mind that hotels levy a government tax of 10% on bills plus another 11% service charge.

Bangkok's top class hotels provide the fullest range of facilities including swimming pool, tennis courts, gymnasium, massage service, sauna, television and video in rooms, shopping arcades, interpreters and office/secretarial services. Major hotels will send a representative to the airport to escort guests if that service is requested at the time of booking.

At the **Oriental**, Bangkok's most famous hotel, guests may even take lessons in Thai cooking. There is little to choose in terms of luxury among the top hotels. The convenience of location does differ though. The Oriental owes mush of its popularity to its river location though now there are other riverside hotels of similar distinction notably the **Shangri-La** and the **Royal Orchid Sheraton**. However travelling between the riverside and business and govern-ment centres in other parts of the city can be a nightmare during peak traffic periods and in the wet season.

The Regent, the **Dusit Thani**, **Hilton International**, **Imperial**, **Montien**, **The Landmark** and the new **Hyatt Erawan** are located more centrally. Close to the airport are the **Airport Hotel**, the **Rama Garden** and the **Central Plaza**.

Inquiries about staying in temples should be made at **Wat Samphya** off Samsen Rd, **Wat In**, Visutkasat Rd and **Wat Maha Tahd**, opposite Thammasat University.

Extremely good value are the **YMCA** and **YWCA** hostels in Sathorn Tai Rd, the **Executive Penthouse**, Suriwongse Rd and the **Sukhumvit Crown**, Soi 8, Sukhumvit Rd.

For those on small budgets, clean rooms can be found in a variety of establishments often above a shop, in and around Khaosarn Rd between the Democracy Monument and the Grand Palace. These are usually family-run where a meal of good Thai food can be had for US$1 and a room for US$2-3 a night.

UPCOUNTRY

Hotels of international standard can be found only at major resorts such as Phuket, Pattaya, Jomtien, Chiang Mai, Hua Hin, Cha-am, Songkhla, Hat Yai and Ko Samui. However, many provincial capitals and big towns have Western-style hotels with swimming pools and tennis courts which offer some of the best accommodation bargains in Thailand. Such hotels can be found in Mae Sot, Chiang Rai, Surin, Ubon Ratchathani, Ayutthaya, Nakhon Pathom (**Rose Garden Country Resort**), Kanchanaburi, Bang Saen, Rayong, and Chantaburi.

Thai food provides quite a different adventure from Chinese and Indian cuisine which it may appear to resemble. It is a blend of five distinct tastes: sweet, sour, salty, bitter and hot. When it is very hot the dish probably contains the yellowy-orange Phrik Leung, the hottest of all chillies. Thais say some chillies are mild, but few are safe to chew.

Thai cooking is simple compared with the complicated dishes of China, India and France. Essentials are fresh, local ingredients and fragrant and pungent spices and herbs, including lemon grass, basil, garlic, ginger, turmeric and coriander.

Thailand

A typical meal is built around steamed rice; in the north it will be glutinous, sticky rice eaten with the fingers. Then there are five or six dishes of soup, fish, a curry blended with coconut milk, vegetables, perhaps grilled dried beef or an omelette stuffed with pork. Shrimp paste, fish sauce, tamarind sauce and other condiments are on the side.

Thailand produces and exports huge quantities of seafood but Bangkok eating places cannot be depended upon for fresh supplies, especially the huge establishments specialising in them. However, near the coast, shrimps, prawns, crabs, lobster and mussels are fresh and sweet.

Thai desserts sometimes are too sweet and sticky for visitors but in the season (March to May) mango with sticky rice blended with coconut milk is a treat for all. There are other desserts made from egg, mung beans, lotus seeds and palm sugar, and sticky rice mixed with peanut and baked in a short length of bamboo.

Local fruit is probably the finest food to be had in Thailand. The mangosteen, which resemble a small purple tennis ball, pomelos (citrus), jackfruit, rambutan and durian are the best in the world. Durian is foul-smelling, but the Thais call it the King of Fruits and its rich, custardy flavour is unforgettable. It has increasingly become popular in the whole of Southeast Asia and now even in Hongkong. (Warning: airlines will not permit passengers to carry durians aboard because of the pungent smell.)

In the northern mountains enterprising growers now produce temperate fruits, especially strawberries. Pineapple, banana, papaya and oranges are available throughout the year.

Some of the most popular Thai dishes include:

Tom Yum: A soup of shrimp, white fish or chicken with vegetables, made sharp and hot with lemon grass, chillies and other herbs. This is the nearest thing to a Thai national dish.

Khao Tom: Clear white soup.

Tom Ka Kai: Chicken soup with coconut milk.

Kaeng Som: Sweet/sour fish curry.

Som Tam: Papaya salad.

Kaeng Khiew wan kai: Chicken coconut curry.

Khao Phad mangsawirat: Vegetable fried rice.

Masaman mangsawirat: Vegetable curry.

Tod mun pla: Fishcake.

Boo nueng: Steamed crab.

Phad priew wan moo: Sweet and sour pork.

Phad kana nue num mun hoy: Fried beef with green vegetable.

Some of the best Thai food is served in open-fronted shop houses or in outdoor markets in Bangkok and other cities and towns. When there is a language problem just point and you will almost certainly get what you want. Good areas for these places in Bangkok are **Pratunam Market** (near the junction of Phetchaburi road and Rajprarop road); in the vicinity of the **Ratchadamnoen Boxing Stadium** (Ratchadamnoen road); along **Silom and Sukhumvit** roads and in the area between the **Democracy Monument** and the river.

Some of the riverside restaurants have boats which sail on the Chao Phya river for dinner. Excellent Thai food is served during the two-hour voyage. One of the best floating restaurants sails from the **Yokyo Restaurant**, Visuthikasat road, near the Bank of Thailand. Tel: 282-7385.

The Oriental Hotel has vessels which make longer voyages up river but they are much grander and more expensive. On the Thonburi side of the river opposite the Oriental Hotel the **Sala Rim Nam** puts on a nightly show of classical Thai dancing with dinner.

There is also Thai music and dancing at **Tumpnakthai**, 131 Ratchadapisek Rd. Tel: 277-8833 or 277-8855. This claims to be the biggest restaurant in the world. It covers 10 acres and employs 1,000 waiters and waitresses bringing dishes to tables on roller skates.

On a smaller scale, **Lemongrass Soi**, 24, Sukhumvit Rd (Tel: 258-8637) and **Bussaracum**, Soi Pipat (Tel: 234-2600) have a pleasant, intimate atmosphere popular with visitors.

Genuine Royal Thai cuisine is available at the **Thanying**, Pramuan Rd, off Silom Rd (Tel: 236-4361) and vegetarian food at the **Whole Earth**, Langsuan Rd, off Ploenchit Rd (Tel: 252-5574). Two of Bangkok's most famous Thai restaurants are **D'Jit Pochana**, Soi 20 Sukhumvit Rd (Tel: 258-1597), and the **Galaxy**, 19 Rama IV Rd (Tel: 235-5000). The latter is renowned as the "no hands" restaurant because pretty girls feed the male diners.

Chinese restaurants are numerous and good and offer cuisine from several regions of China. **White Orchid** (New Petchaburi Rd, Tel: 253-7528) is good for Peking duck. One of the oldest Chinese restaurants is **Yim Yim**, corner of Yaowapanich and Padsai Rd in Chinatown, Tel: 224-2205. There are three branches of the **Shangrila**, Thaniya road, Silom road and Rama IV road. **The Chinese Seafood Restaurant** (Suriwong Rd under Wall St Tower) also specialises in Dim Sum (Tel: 235-7591).

WESTERN FOOD: There is no point in coming to Thailand for European or American-style food because it is far better at home. There are a few French, Italian, German or Scandinavian restaurants which seem good to resident foreigners but visitors will not rate them too highly.

Western food in most hotels, even five-star establishments, can be indifferent. Among the better places are **Ma Maison** (Hilton Hotel), **Normandie Grill** (Oriental Hotel) and **The Fireplace Grill** (Meridien President Hotel).

The cooking is possibly better at smaller restaurants including:

French:

Le Bordeaux, 1/38 Soi 39, Sukhumvit Rd. Tel: 258-9766; **La Grenouille**, Soi 1, Sukhumvit Rd. Tel: 252-0311; **Le Metropolitain**, Gaysorn Rd. Tel: 252-8364; **Two Vikings**, 2 Soi Charoennives, Soi 35, Sukhumvit Rd. Tel: 258-8843.

Italian:

L'Opera, Soi 39, Sukhumvit Rd. Tel: 258-5605; **Pan Pan**, Soi 31, Sukhumvit Rd. Tel: 391-7276; **Madrid Bar**, Patpong Rd has the best Pizza in Town. Tel: 234-6905.

German:

Wiener Wald, Sukhumvit Rd. Tel: 252-3240; **Bei Otto**, Soi 20, Sukhumvit Rd. Tel: 252-6836, 258-1496.

English:

Angus Steak House, Thaniya Rd (off Suriwong Rd). Tel: 234-3590; Soi 33 Sukhumvit Rd. Tel: 259-4444; and also at Pattaya and Chiang Mai; **Bobby's Arms**, Patpong 2 Rd (off carpark bldg). Tel: 233-6828.

Scandinavian:

Mermaids Restaurant, Soi 8, Sukhumvit Rd, Tel: 253-3648.

Indian and Muslim:

Royal India, 392/1 Chakrphet Rd. Tel: 221-6565; **Himali Cha Cha**, 1229/11 New Rd, near corner Suriwong Rd. Tel: 235-1569. **Moghul Room**, Soi 11, Sukhumvit Rd. Tel: 253-4465.

Burmese:

Mandalay, Soi 11, Sukhumvit Rd. Tel: 250-1220.

Vietnamese:

Le Cam Ly, 2nd fl., Patpong Bldg, corner of Patpong and Suriwong roads. Tel: 234-0290; **Le Dalat**, Soi 23, Sukhumvit Rd. Tel: 258- 4192.

Indonesian:

Bali, Ruamrudee Village, Soi Ruamrudee, Ploenchit Rd. Tel: 2500711.

Japanese:

Hanaya, 683 Siphya Rd. Tel: 234-8095; **Kikusui**, 133 Pan Rd. Tel: 234-4031; **Daikoku**, Asoke Rd, Sukhumvit Rd. Tel: 254- 9980; **Go Ro**, near Bangkok Bank Head Quarters, Soi 7, Silom Rd.

The *Bangkok Restaurant Guide*, available at Asia Books (221 Sukhumvit Rd; Peninsular Plaza, Ratchadamri Rd; and Landmark Hotel, Sukhumvit Rd) is an invaluable publication.

Bangkok's notorious nightlife is as male-oriented as ever, but fears about AIDS have reduced the scale of business. There are hundreds of bars, discos, clubs and massage parlours open until the early hours of the morning. The main areas for them are Patpong Road (there are two parallel streets linking Silom and Suriwong roads) and the surrounding quarter; Soi 4 Sukhumvit Road; and Soi Cowboy, off Soi 21, Sukhumvit Road. Japanese bars can be found in Soi Thaniya between Silom and Suriwong roads.

What might be called "real" bars, where customers may drink and talk without too much noise and hassle, are few and far between in these streets. Probably the best of them is the **Crown Royal** (Patpong 2, near the carpark and the **Madrid** on Patpong 1). Most male visitors go to Patpong and similar places for girls. They will not be disappointed at the **Safari**, **King's Castle**, or the **Superstar** in Patpong 1. The speciality at the **Cleopatra** (Patpong 2) is body painting.

Apart from singles, some couples go to Patpong just for the experience of the "live shows" and other "attractions." Live shows are put on every night at the **Lipstick**, **Kangaroo**, **Rose** and the **Supergirl**, which has a surprising motor cycle act.

Some live show establishments make an extra charge for "entertainment" but do not announce that fact in advance. Customers often complain when the unexpected charge appears on the bar bill.

The proliferation of bars and other drinking places makes this section of the guide almost superfluous. Nobody will ever die for want of a drink in Bangkok, but it can be an expensive activity. A glass of local beer varies from US$1.20 in a noodle shop to US$4 in a luxury hotel. Local whisky is the cheapest alcoholic drink.

The most popular is Mekhong whisky at less than US$2 for a half bottle. Try it with ice, soda

Classic Thai Tom Yum Soup.

Photo: Tourism Authority of Thailand

and a squeeze of lemon. Foreigners find Kloster the best of the beers though the big beer with Thais is Singha. Amarit Draught from the cask is not easy to find but it is palatable and the cheapest beer on the market.

Some bars are inclined to mix imported whisky and gin with local products. Imported wine in restaurants and liquor stores is expensive, as the government taxes it at the same rate as imported spirits.

Bangkok is not strong on other forms of entertainment. Most big hotels have music bars where musicians, mostly from the Philippines, provide Western-style music.

Thai classical dancing is presented nightly at the **Sala Rim Nam** restaurant opposite the Oriental Hotel and interesting northeastern Thai music and dancing in a big open air establishment alongside **Florida Hotel**, Phyathai Rd.

Western jazz is widely played in Bangkok. Sunday nights at **Bobby's Arms** (Patpong 2). **Brown Sugar**, Soi Sarasin (opposite Lumpini Park), is a top spot every night of the week.

Massage parlours can be found all over Bangkok. There is one that employs 1,500 girls. The classified yellow pages of the telephone di-

rectory list more than 100 parlours. Depending on the service required and the plushness of the establishment, prices range from Baht 300 to Baht 1,500.

In a very different style, the relatively new **Thai Cultural Centre**, Ratchadapisek Rd, Bangkok: offers a fine variety of Thai, Asian and Western music, dance and drama.

Bargaining is a way of life in Thailand so join in as almost every shop except department stores will offer discounts. Obtain receipts, especially for jewellery and antiques. Antiques and genuine works of art need export licences. Export of Buddha images is forbidden. Anyone with a complaint about a purchase should write to the Tourism Authority of Thailand (TAT), Ratchadamnoen Nok Ave, Bangkok 10100.

Shoppers may feel confident of shops which display the TAT emblem as they have passed the scrutiny of the tourist authority. The performance of each shop is monitored regularly.

Bangkok: The chief duty-free shop in Bangkok is in Ploenchit Rd (between Wireless

Rd and the railway line) but compared with Hongkong and Singapore, Thailand has little to offer in the way of duty-free electrical and photographic goods. What it does have are traditional Thai articles in silk, cotton, silver and nielloware, lacquer and bronzeware, celedon and woodwork. There are many "antique shops" but genuine articles are rare and very expensive. Some of the craftsmen making these articles ask dealers "do you want your pieces present day or antique?" They can do them one way as easily as the other.

Genuine Thai silk is a good buy. The pure stuff is bulky and rough, almost un-silk-like to unfamiliar buyers, while the material mixed with Japanese silk is more silky to look at and touch. Most silk on sale in Bangkok is mixed and is regarded as a good buy as both varieties of silk have their own special value.

The thing to avoid is rayon mixed with the silk. Many Indian merchants sell these products. Burning a fragment will reveal the truth: pure silk forms into droplets while the synthetic rayon vaporises. Buy from well-established people like the **Jim Thompson Thai Silk Company**, 9 Suriwong Rd or Design Thai, 304 Silom Rd. Your will pay more but will get the real thing. Thai handicrafts can be bought from the government shop **Narai Phand** on Ratchadamri Rd, Bangkok. Shops in the **Oriental Plaza** near the hotel are also worth browsing through.

Thai tailors and dressmakers are outstanding for quick, made-to-measure suits, shirts, dresses, etc.

The main shopping centres in Bangkok are Silom, Suriwong, Sukhumvit roads and Siam Square. The Banglumphu district near the Grand Palace and Pratunam market are best for lower priced goods.

Chiang Mai: The night bazaar has some of Thailand's finest handicrafts. Outside the city San Kamphaeng (13 km from town) is noted for silk and Bo Sang village for parasols.

Precious stones: Thailand is a treasure trove of gems, gold and silver. Rubies and sapphires are mined here and also come in from neighbouring Burma and Cambodia. Burma sends its jade to Thai workshops whose skills are universally acclaimed. Every type of precious stone and metal can be bought in Bangkok, which has thousands of reputable retailers, where prices compare favourably with those in other countries. Customers may order pieces to be made to their own design though Thai designers and cutters are unsurpassed anywhere.

Buyers should patronise only shops which display the TAT emblem which guarantees the retailer's integrity. They should obtain from the shop a detailed receipt and a certificate guaranteeing the authenticity of the gemstone or precious metal which they have bought. They should also try to establish if the shop is a member of the **Thai Gems and Jewellery Traders Association** (Tel: 233-2490-2). **The Asian Institute of Gemological Science** (AIGS) (Tel: 513-2112) conducts tests for the identification of stones. Visitors with complaints may also contact the Tourist Police (Tel: 221-6206-10 in Bangkok).

Never buy from a peddler or from a guide who promises bargains at a particular shop.

Outside Bangkok the best place for gems is **Chantaburi** (280 km from Bangkok) on the coast beyond Pattaya. Rubies and sapphires are mined nearby and the town, which still has a French air about it, is famous for its gem cutters.

The AIGS occasionally holds seminars on buying gems and jewellery in Thailand. Tuition fees are approximately Baht 500. The AIGS is at 484 Rachadapisek Rd, Bangkok.

The Thais love their sport and love to gamble on the outcome of any contest. The traditional conflicts between Thai boxers, fighting fish, cocks, bulls and kites in the sky still go on everywhere, but today there are also football, tennis, sailing and golf. The richer Thais have taken up golf with a passion scarcely equalled anywhere in the world.

New golf courses and driving ranges are opening. Entrance fees and membership in some cases exceed US$25,000. More than 20 public courses in or near Bangkok however are open to visitors. The English-language The Nation newspaper publishes details every Friday.

Thai boxing: This unique sport combines orthodox punching with kicking and kneeing. In the clinches anything seems to go. Its elements can be found in other forms of unarmed combat in Asia. Bouts are of five three-minute rounds with two minutes between rounds. Each fight begins with an elaborate dance and prayer ritual in which the fighters invoke the aid of spirits, pay respect to their teachers and work themselves up to a high state of aggression. As the fight begins so too does frantic Thai music that sends fighters and crowd into a frenzy. The fighting can be vicious and damaging because of the powerful kicking. Serious injuries, occasionally fatal, occur frequently.

Top venues in Bangkok are **Lumpini Stadium** and the **Ratchadamnoen Stadium**. Bouts take place at one or the other every other week. Admission varies from Baht 30 to Baht 200.

Cock and fish fighting: Traditional rural pastimes but not easy to locate because they are officially illegal — not because of the fighting between the creatures but because the gambling involved is against the law.

Bull fighting: Between beast and beast without direct human involvement. Confined to the south of Thailand.

Tennis: Some major hotels have courts. Public courts for hire are listed in the classified section of the Bangkok telephone directory.

Horse racing: Meetings on Saturday and Sunday either at **Royal Bangkok Sports Club** or the **Royal Turf Club**.

The date of many of the Thai festivals, particularly those connected with Buddhism, are determined by the lunar calendar and thus vary from year to year.

The most interesting for visitors are the **Songkran** festival which marks the traditional Thai new year in April and **Loi Krathong** in November when Thais wash away their sins.

February: Makha Bucha Day, on full moon day. It commemorates the occasion when 1,250 disciples spontaneously gathered to hear Lord Buddha preach (public holiday).

April 6: Chakri Day commemorates the founding of the present ruling dynasty in 1782. This is the only day of the year when the Royal Pantheon, containing statues of the kings at the Temple of the Emerald Buddha, is open to the public. (Public holiday.)

April 13-15: Songkran Festival. The Thai new year marked by religious merry-making, beauty parades and nationwide water throwing. In Chiang Mai, the best place to experience the occasion, there is a procession of local beauties wearing Thai dress and carrying silver bowls of perfumed water. Westerners are favourite targets for the water throwers. (Three public holidays.)

May 1: Labour Day. The government provides free film shows and other public entertainment for the workers. (Public holiday.)

May 5: Coronation Day: The reigning monarch, King Bhumibol, was crowned on this day in 1950. (Public holiday.)

May: Royal ploughing ceremony: Near the beginning of the month. This marks the official beginning of the rice-planting cycle and involves elaborate Brahma ritual to produce predictions about the forthcoming rice harvest. The King and Queen preside over the ceremony at Sanam Luang in Bangkok.

Rocket festival: Second weekend of the month at Yasothorn in the northeast. Villagers construct large rockets to fire into the sky to ensure plentiful rice season rains. Folk dancing and other revelry are part of the festival.

Wisaka Bucha Day: Full moon day in May. The holiest of all Buddhist days marking Lord Buddha's birth, enlightenment and death. In the evening a procession of Buddhists, and tourists too, carries candles, incense and flowers three times around the temples. The Temple of the Emerald Buddha and the Marble Temple are among the best places to view the festival in Bangkok. (Public holiday.)

July: Full moon day: Asalaha Bucha Day: Commemoration of Lord Buddha's first sermon to his first five disciples and the beginning of Buddhist Lent when monks retire to their monasteries to study and meditate. (Public holiday.) The same day marks the candle festivals at Ubon Ratchathani in the northeast. Beautifully embellished beeswax candles are paraded before presentation to temples.

August 12: Queen's birthday. Queen Sirikit was born in 1932.

September: Late September–early October on both sides of the full moon at Phuket in the south a Vegetarian festival is held, during which people of Chinese descent commit themselves to a vegetarian diet for nine days. They also dress in white and inflict pain upon themselves by piercing their cheeks and tongues with metal skewers and walking on fire.

October: The end of the rainy season near the full moon day is celebrated with boat races wherever a suitable stretch of water is available. The illuminated boat procession on the Mekong river at Nakhon Phanom in the northeast is spectacular.

October 23: Chulalongkorn Day, Honours King Chulalongkorn who reigned from 1868-1910. He led feudal Siam towards present-day Thailand. He abolished slavery, introduced railways and established personal contacts with foreign monarchs. (Public holiday.)

November: Phra Pathom Chedi Fair at Nakhon Pathom (80 km from Bangkok). First weekend of the month a colourful festival of drama, dancing, sideshows and popular entertainment. Loi

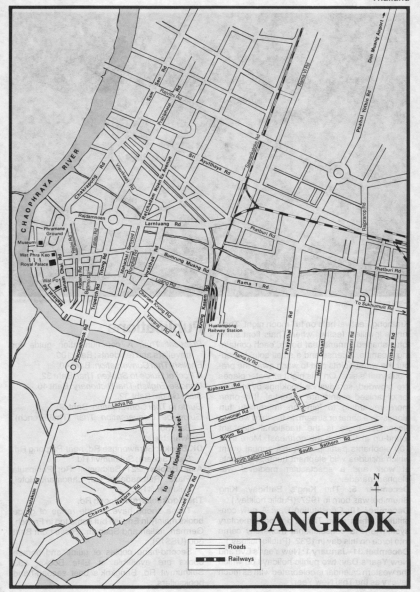

BANGKOK

Roads
Railways

Para sailing at Pattaya.

Photo: Tourism Authority of Thailand

Krathong Festival held on full moon night. Thailand's loveliest festival when Thais float small lotus-shaped banana-leaf boats, each containing a candle, incense and a small coin, to honour the water spirits and to wash away the previous year's sins. On this night all water places are crowded, so advance bookings by tourists for organised events are essential. It is often more rewarding to join the impromptu fun alongside a canal or stream. In the third week of November there is the traditional elephant round-up at Surin in the northeast. More than 100 elephants participate in this annual event which includes wild elephant hunts, elephants at work and a spectacular medieval war elephant parade.

December 5: The King's Birthday. King Bhumibol was born in 1927. (Public holiday.)

December 10: Constitution Day: A new constitution which gave Thailand a parliamentary system and a constitutional monarchy came into force on this day in 1932. (Public holiday.)

December 31–January 1: New Year's Eve and New Year's Day: two public holidays on which the western calendar is celebrated with as much revelry as the Thai New Year.

Publications

Practical Thai: A communication guide for travellers and residents: Baht 100.

English-Thai Conversation: Baht 40.

A Pocket Guide to Spoken Thai: Baht 32.

Concise English-Thai Dictionary: Baht 40.

Siam Guide: Baht 32.

Guide to Thai Conversation: Baht 60.

Guide de Conversation Thai (Thai-French): Baht 30.

Available at:

DK Books: Surawongse Rd, near Patpong Rd; Siam Square; Sukhumvit Rd.

Asia Books: 221 Sukhumvit Rd; Peninsula Plaza; Ratchadamri Rd; Landmark Hotel, Sukhumvit Rd.

The Booksellers: Patpong Rd.

These shops have a wide range of guide books mainly in English but some too in French, German, Italian and Spanish. Prices from Baht 300 (US$12).

Second-hand copies of guide and phrase books are available at Elite Books, 593 Sukhumvit Rd, Bangkok's best second-hand booksellers.

Ancient and modern: Bangkok skyline. ▷

Photo: Gary Knight/APSARA

STOCK EXCHANGE

The Securities Exchange of Thailand, Sinthorn Bldg, Wireless Rd, Bangkok. Tel: 250-0001 – 8; Fax: 254-9470 – 4; 254-4078.

CHAMBERS OF COMMERCE

American Chamber of Commerce, 140 Wireless Rd, Bangkok. Tel: 251-1605.

Australian-Thai Chamber of Commerce, 17th floor, Ocean Insurance Bldg, 163 Suriwong Rd, Bangkok. Tel: 233-4476; Fax: 235-7166.

British Chamber of Commerce, Tel: 255-8866 – 8; Fax: 255-8869

German-Thai Chamber of Commerce, 699 Kongboonma, Silom Rd. Tel: 236-2369; Fax: 236-4711.

India-Thai Chamber of Commerce, 13 Soi Attakarnprasit, South ʻSathorn Rd, Bangkok. Tel: 286-1506.

Japanese Chamber of Commerce, 518/3 Ploenchit Rd, Bangkok. Tel: 251-7418; Fax: 256-9621.

Thai-Chinese Chamber of Commerce, 233 South Sathorn Rd, Bangkok. Tel: 212-3916.

Thai Chamber of Commerce, 150 Rajbophit, Bangkok. Tel: 225-0086; Fax: 225-3372.

DISCOVERING THAILAND

BANGKOK

After what often seems to be an endless wait at immigration, then dodging airport touts offering a taxi ride into town or a pretty girl — or boy — you may wonder if it is all a mistake. The run in from the airport through traffic jams and pollution will not dispel those early misgivings. Bangkok is an ugly city sprawling over low-lying land. It has no obvious geographical centre but it has a lot of heart. It is a friendly, vibrant place and, thus, visitors quickly brush aside the hassles and ugliness.

The city scarcely possesses a building much more than 100 years old but there are many older works of art brought in from earlier settlements.

Bangkok was founded more than two centuries ago on the site now occupied by the Grand Palace, an array of temples and shrines which has been called "a dazzling fairy tale of dreams." **Chakri Palace**, the Royal Family's original home, is also there but the King now lives in the more modern **Chilada Place** nearby.

Inside the Grand Palace complex is Thailand's most famous and sacred Buddhist shrine — the **Temple of the Emerald Buddha**. It is so sacred that nobody may photograph the green image which is made of jasper. Only 76 cm high, the Budda is linked by the Thais with the very survival of the royal house.

The **Temple of the Reclining Buddha** offers an astonishing sight as the recumbent figure symbolising the passing of the Lord Buddha from this life into Nirvana is 48 m long and 15 m high.

Tickets costing Baht 100 each admit visitors to both temples. Mornings from 8:30 am are the best time for a visit.

Discreet dress is essential in the Grand Palace; skirts for women, long trousers for men. In some sections a jacket is required and may be hired on the spot.

The **Temple of Dawn** on the banks of the river is one of Bangkok's striking landmarks. Parts of it are 90 m high and are covered with fragments of porcelain and pottery. Traditional Thai massage is available at the temple. Nearby, on the Thonburi side of the river, is the dock for the King's barges on which monarchs for centuries have travelled on state occasions. These 45-m-long craft are brilliantly decorated in red, gold and black and are manned by 60 oarsmen on ceremonial occasions.

Wat Benchamabophit (Marble Temple), on Sri Ayutthaya Rd, near the Dusit Zoo, is a perfect place to rest and enjoy the cool of Italian marble underfoot.

Wat Traimit (Temple of the Golden Buddha), near the Hualamphong railway station, contains a Buddha statue made from 5.5 tonnes of solid 18-carat gold. For nearly 200 years the image was encased in plaster, but the gold was revealed when it dropped from a crane 40 years ago.

The National Museum near the Grand Palace is not to be missed by those who want to know how Thailand became what it is today. The huge, grassy expanse outside the museum, known as **Sanam Luang**, is the stage for great occasions — state funerals, political meetings and even revolutions. In the breezy early months of the year children and grown men engage in a favourite, traditional pastime of flying colourful kites.

Journeys along the Chaophraya river offer probably the most fascinating sightseeing in Bangkok. There are regular boat services and other craft are available for personal hire.

Tourist offices in hotels and tour agents will organise trips, visits to floating markets and cruises along the *klongs* (canals).

Jim Thompson's house, off Rama 1 Rd is worth a detour for anyone interested in Asian art. The owner, who disappeared in Malaysia more than 20 years ago in circumstances never explained, revived the Thai silk industry after World War II, making Thai silk popular all over the world. His enchanting home, perhaps the most beautiful house in Bangkok, was built from six old teak houses brought from upcountry. It is filled with exquisite works of art from Thailand, Cambodia, Burma and China. The garden is an oasis of beauty and peace. Thompson's original silk factories are across the *klong*. Open 9 am to 5 pm every day except Sunday. Entrance fee Baht 100.

Bangkok markets provide not only good shopping and eating but also a panorama of city life. **Pratunam** is the most central. Many restaurants and some shops stay open most of the night.

The Weekend Market (Chatuchak Park, opposite the northern bus terminal), open from 7 am to 6 pm on Saturday and Sunday, is the biggest in the city. On sale is everything from live animals to old books.

Chinatown is one bustling market specialising in imports from China, gold, festival decorations and Swiss watches — mostly fakes. For antiques try the so-called **Thieves' Market** (Woeng Nakhon Kasem).

The Snake Farm (Rama IV Rd) is open every weekday at 11 am. Entry Baht 40. You can watch keepers handle the snakes, including lethal cobras and pythons nearly 20 ft long. The serum extracted from two or three cobras into a glass vessel is enough to kill 20 humans. Tourists like to be photographed with pythons draped around their necks.

DAY TRIPS FROM BANGKOK

The Rose Garden Country Resort, only 30 km from Bangkok on the road to Nakhon Pathom, has large and beautiful gardens, a hotel as well as bungalows for rent, several restaurants and every afternoon a Thai cultural show. As well as dancing there is boxing, sword fighting, cock fighting and a display of rural life. **The Crocodile Farm** and **Zoo** is nearby, housing the world's largest albino crocodile and other wild animals. The highlight is a wrestling match between a crocodile and a keeper.

Further on, 50 km from Bangkok, is **Nakhon Pathom** one of Thailand's oldest settlements and site of the **Golden Chedi**, a bell-shaped shrine visible from afar. Rising 115 m, it is the largest pagoda in Southeast Asia and the tallest Buddhist monument in the world.

Ayutthaya, only 80 km from Bangkok, can be reached by road, rail or river. The capital of old Siam, Ayutthaya was razed by Burmese invaders in 1767. The city's canals were said to have run red with blood. Red-coloured ruins are just about all that is left now of the old capital, though a few buildings have been restored.

The principal ruins lie around the former royal palace. There is a teak pavilion still standing where the kings paid homage to their predecessors. The gardens are delightful, particularly in January and February when "flame of the forest" trees are in bloom.

The newly opened **Ayutthaya Historical Centre** presents an exciting picture of Thailand's "golden age" and is a unique information and research centre.

Boats which may be hired at the landing stage in the modern town will take you to some of the most interesting of the ruins and to a number of good restaurants on large boats or floating rafts near the main bridge.

On the way back to Bangkok you can stop at the summer palace of **Bang-Pa-In**. It was here that an early king met and fell in love with a beautiful girl called In. The place was therefore called the village (bang) where he met (pa) In.

Now rarely used, the palace has a melancholy air though the buildings and gardens have great beauty. One of the garden buildings is a Victorian observation tower built by King Chulalongkorn in memory of one of his wives, Queen Sunanta, and their child, who were drowned on their way to the palace in the 1870s.

To go further north from Ayutthaya to **Lopburi** and Saraburi is a long day trip, but it is worth it as you leave the flat plain and enter hilly country. At **Saraburi**, 130 km from Bangkok, there is a shrine said to contain the Buddha's footprint, **Phra Buddha Bhat**. The footprint was found, the local story goes, by a hunter who had wounded a deer which disappeared into a copse and then emerged completely healed. Nearby is the **Muak Lek** botanical park which is rich in plants and flowers.

Pattaya, which has been dubbed "sin city," is still the most popular weekend resort for Bangkok residents. It is described as one of Asia's major beach resorts, yet the sea is officially classified as too polluted for safe swimming. Many hotel swimming pools are also dubious because fresh water supplies have not kept

Ancient Kmer stone lintel.

Photo: Tourism Authority of Thailand

up with the enormous growth of hotels and high-rise apartments. But it is only 120 km from Bangkok and on the super highway the drive takes less than two hours.

Pattaya has an enormous range of hotels, guesthouses and restaurants at every price. The night life is a repeat of all that is available in Bangkok plus transvestite shows. The most popular of these places are **Tiffany's**, **Alcazar** and **Simon**.

Over the hill from Pattaya is the new resort of **Jomtien Beach** which is less crowded and strident. The sea is also cleaner. Further down the coast is **Koh Samet** which is less developed than similar resorts.

Across the Gulf of Thailand is **Hua Hin** and just north of it **Cha-Am**, two popular weekend resorts on the coast. They can be reached by road in about three hours or by train. There is also an air service from Bangkok to Hua Hin which takes less than half an hour. Both places are expanding but are restrained compared with Pattaya.

UPCOUNTRY

Kanchanaburi, the centre of the province of the same name, is only 130 km west of Bangkok. The area running up to the Burmese border at Three Pagodas Pass is worth a stay of two or three days. The town is prosperous and just outside stands the infamous so-called **Bridge over the River Kwai**, built by prisoners of the Japanese army during World War II to carry the Thailand-Burma railway. The bridge was basi-cally destroyed by Allied bombers in 1945. Only the curved spans are part of the original structure. The railway today runs up to Nam Tok where the line ends. It is a popular journey for tourists and the trains are also used by farmers to bring their produce, mostly chillis, to market. The Kanchanaburi war cemetery is in the centre of the town and holds the graves of almost 7,000 POWs, most of them British, Australian and Dutch, who died working on the railway. A smaller war cemetery, Chungkai, is on the other side of the river. Near the centre of town a museum contains photographs, POWs' possessions and tools and tells the story of the railway. It is called the "Jeath" museum — made up of the first letters of the nations mainly involved (Japan, England, Australia, Thailand and Holland) because many people felt "death" was too stark a name.

Son et Lumiere shows are held at the bridge every November. Good hotel accommodation is available in Kanchanaburi and further up-river. Cruises are available on the river, as are river rafts. The road to the Burmese border at Three Pagodas Pass is good all the year round and limited accommodation is available at the Pass. **Chiang Mai**, called "the rose of the north" is 1,023 ft above sea level and lies in a valley ringed by mountains. Because of its fresh cool air, its flowers, mountains, colourful festivals and beautiful women, it is one of the most popular places in Thailand for Thais and foreigners alike. Chiang Mai is the home of Thai handi-

◁ *Elephant power at Chiang Mai.*
Photo: Hilary Andrews

277

Fruit vendor: bargaining a way of life.

Photo: Tourism Authority of Thailand

crafts — silk and cotton weaving, pottery, umbrella making, silverware, lacquerware and wood carving. Artists and craftsmen can be seen at work everywhere. Varied groups of hilltribe people live in the nearby mountains. Visitors may observe them at work and in their villages and homes.

Chiang Mai means "city of a thousand temples." There are more than 1,100 in the city area, though many are now obscured by modern buildings. The oldest temple is **Wat Chiang Man** built about 1300 AD. The largest, **Phra Singh**, houses the most venerated Buddha image in the north. Wat Koo Tao has one of the strangest towers in Thailand. It was built in 1613 in the form of gourds in five tiers and decorated with coloured porcelain. The most famous structure in the north is **Wat Doi** Suthep a 14th-century temple outside Chiang Mai. Nearby the Royal Winter Palace's gardens are open Fridays, weekends and public holidays, except when the royal family is there. There is a Thai saying that if you do not climb **Doi Suthep** or eat *kow soy* you have not been to Chiang Mai. *Kow soy* is a noodle dish served in a curry sauce. You do not have to look far for the dish. **Chiang Rai**, close to both Burma and Laos, can be reached from Chaing Mai by road and air. Just beyond it are the opium poppy fields of the infamous Golden Triangle, but it is an ideal spot to begin a jungle trek or a rafting trip on the river. **Mae Hong Son**, a remote hill-town, has become more popular with improved access by road and air. Some of Thailand's last big, natural forests

are in the vicinity. The town of wooden buildings is still unspoiled. Communist insurgents kept tourists away until recently, though bandits occasionally make trouble. Half-way between these northern resorts and Bangkok are **Sukhothai**, site of the first Thai capital, and **Phitsanuloke**, a convenient area for breaking the long journey. Two fine national parks and spectacular waterfalls are easily accessible. **Korat**, a thriving commercial centre, is the gateway to the northeast's 17 provinces. Attractions include wild scenic beauty in the **Khao Yai National Park**. There are outstanding Khmer ruins at **Pimai**, 60 km from the town. Although the northeast is the poorest region of Thailand there are many attractive places to visit. The towns on the Mekong river, **Nong Khai** and **Nakhon Phanom**, where Laotian and other outside influences are evident; **Surin** and **Buri Ram** where Khmer influence is strong. Surin stages the annual elephant round-up which people from all over the world attend every year. **Udorn Thani** province is famous for **Ban Chiang**, site of the birthplace of the Thai race 7,000 years ago. Loei province has winters and mountains which attract many people dried out by the tropics. It is the only place in Thailand to record frost.

THE SOUTH

Stretching down the narrow peninsula and beyond the isthmus of Kra to Malaysia lies some of the most scenic country which is increasingly popular with foreign visitors. Most of Thailand's muslim population lives in these southernmost provinces. Traditionally the big business operations concerned rubber and tin, but tourism is now the most valuable. The hub of that industry is the island of **Phuket**, off the coast in the Andaman Sea. It is connected to the mainland by a causeway and it is 800 km^2 in area. It has magnificent coves and bays, sparkling sea and white beaches and hotels of the highest international standards, including some of the best in Southeast Asia. The best beaches are on the west coast. But building and other development for tourists are spoiling the ambience, polluting air and sea and destroying the coral reefs. Patong beach has become a mini-Pattaya, and those not looking for a "good time in the old town tonight" would be advised to seek the more remote resort hotels with private beaches. Further north, **Krabi** with its famous Phi Phi islands offshore remains unspoiled, but large-scale developments are already evident. On the edge of Malaysia, Satun has a new marine national park with magnificent coral and crystal clear water. **Songkhla**, a seaside town with long, white beaches, has managed to escape the worst excesses of tourism. Not far away is **Hat Yai**, a rip-roaring frontier town noted for its smuggling, cheap shopping and sex. **Koh Samui**, a large island 40 km off Surat Thani, is a popular resort for Thais and foreigners. Discovered by the hippies in the 1960s, it has gone up-market with expensive hotels and restaurants and, as well as the boat from the mainland, now has direct flights from Bangkok, Hongkong and other Asian cities. The two major beaches are among the most beautiful in Southeast Asia but are crowded in high season.

Thailand has no fewer than 50 national parks all over the country. **Khao Yai National Park**, which has more than 100 wild elephants and is one of the finest wildlife reserves, is in the southeast of the country.

There are also marine parks based on islands in the south. Two of these are **Ang Thong**, near Samui island, and **Tarutao** off the southwestern coast in the Andaman Sea.

Limited accommodation is available in some of the parks. Details from the Tourist Authority of Thailand offices.

LOCAL CUSTOMS

The King is deeply revered, so offensive remarks about the monarchy can be dangerous. When the national anthem is played in the cinema and other public places everybody is expected to stand silently.

Shorts and sleeveless garments are forbidden in parts of the Grand Palace in Bangkok and other holy places. Jackets are available for hire at the Palace.

Never cross your legs so your feet point at another person, at a Royal portrait or Buddha image. Do not climb over or sit on Buddha images.

Thais often laugh to hide their embarrassment when something goes wrong. So on those occasions their mirth should not be regarded as derision.

Never raise your voice, thump the table or lose your temper in other ways no matter how extreme the provocation. Thais feel contempt for such behaviour. So smile. It is impossible to be too polite.

The best greeting of all is a smile though a wave will do no harm. In this traditional Thai greeting the hands are placed together as in Christian prayer and you bow to the person you are greeting. The higher the hands the deeper the respect.

Thais rarely kiss each other in public though they do walk hand in hand. Anything more extreme is frowned upon.

Except for the fortnightly state lottery and horse racing, gambling is illegal. Reject invitations to play cards. Police even raid private homes and arrest gamblers playing for money.

Smoking is forbidden on buses and in cinema and some other public places.

Buddhist monks are forbidden to touch or be touched by a woman. If a woman has to give anything to a monk or novice she must hand it to a man who will pass it on. Otherwise the woman can place the item on the ground in front of the monk.

Although tap water is now officially "potable," visitors should drink bottled water which is available everywhere.

Electricity: current throughout Thailand is 220 volts, 50 cycles.

Tipping: hotels and major restaurants add service but this is not the case in smaller Thai eating places. Baht 10-20 as a tip is adequate in those places. Taxi drivers are not tipped. Give hotel porters Baht 5 or Baht 10.

HOTEL GUIDE

Hotel address	Phone	Fax	Telex	Cable	〰	🍴	🥣

The Hotel Information Centre has information about hotels all over Thailand. Tel: 254-2799.
Because of the disparity between prices in various parts of Thailand, the ratings are listed separately for each area.

A (US$125-200) **B** (US$80-125) **C** (US$50-80) **D** (US$10-50)

BANGKOK

A

Hotel address	Phone	Fax	Telex	Cable	〰	🍴	🥣
Dusit Thani 946 Rama 4 Rd	236-0450	236-6400	Th 81170, 82027	DUSITOTEL	▲	▲	▲
Central Plaza 1695 Phahoyothin Rd	541-1234	541-1087	20173 Centel Th		▲	▲	▲
Airport 333 Choet Wudhakat Rd	566-1020-1	566-1941	Th-87424 Th 87425	APINTERHTL	▲	▲	▲
Hilton International Wireless Rd	253-0123	253-0680	Th 72206 Hilbkk	HILTELS	▲	▲	▲
Crowne Plaza Holiday Inn Silom Rd	238-4300	238-5289	82998 Hibkk		▲	▲	▲
Hyatt Erewan Ratchadamri Rd	252-9100	2535856			▲	▲	▲
Landmark Sukhumvit Rd	254-0404	253-4259 254-0439	Th 72341 Th 87474		▲	▲	▲
Meridien President Ploenchit Rd	253-0444	253-7565	81194, 20874 Homro Th	HOMRO BANGKOK	▲	▲	▲
Oriental Oriental Ave	236-0400 236-0420	236-1939	Th 82997	ORIENHOTEL	▲	▲	▲
Regent Ratchadamri Rd	251-6127 251-6370	253-9195	20004 Reg Th		▲	▲	▲
Royal Orchid Sheraton Captain Bush Lane	234-5599	236-8320	84491, 84492 Royorch Th	ROYORCH BANGKOK	▲	▲	▲
Shangri-La New Rd	236-7777	236-8579	84625 Shangla Th	SHANGRILA BANGKOK	▲	▲	▲
Siam Inter-Continental Rami 1 Rd	253-0355-7	253-2275	Th 81155 Siamint	INHOTELCOR BANGKOK	▲	▲	▲
Somerset Soi 15, Sukhumvit Rd	254-8500	254-8534	72631 Somrset Th	JAGTARJI BANGKOK	▲	▲	▲
Imperial Wireless Rd	254-0111 254-0023	253-3190	82301, 84418 Imper Th	IMPERHOTEL	▲	▲	▲
Novotel Siam Square	255-2444-7	255-1824	22780 Novotel Th		▲	▲	▲

BANGKOK – *Cont'd*

B

Hotel address	Phone	Fax	Telex	Cable	〰	🍴	🥣
Ambassador Sukhumvit Rd	254-0444 255-0444	253-4123	82910 Amtel Th	AMTEL	▲	▲	▲
Asia Phayathai Rd	2150808	215-4360	82722, 81177 Asiatel Th	ASIA HOTEL	▲	▲	▲
Bangkok Palace New Phetburi Rd	253-0500	253-0556	84278, 84279 Banghtl Th	BKK PALACE	▲	▲	▲
Impala Soi 24, Sukhumvit Rd	259-0053	258-8747	21146, 84056 Impa Th	IMPAHOTEL	▲	▲	▲
Menam Charoenkrung Rd	289-1148-9	291-1048	21098, 87423 Menam Th		▲	▲	▲
Montien Surawongse Rd	234-8060	236-5219	Th 81160 Th 82938	MONTELBKK	▲	▲	▲
Narai Silom Rd	233-3350	236-7161	81175 Naraihotel Th	NARAIHOTEL	▲	▲	▲
Princess Larn Luang Rd	281-3088	280-1314	87688 Th		▲	▲	▲
Rama Gardens Vibhavadi Rangsit Rd	579-5400	561-1025	84250 Gardens Th	Ramagarden	▲	▲	▲
Royal River Charansanitwong Rd	433-0300-19	433-5880	22048 Roriver Th		▲	▲	▲
Silom Plaza Silom Rd	236-8441-53	236-7562	21625 Silompla Th		▲	▲	▲
Tara Soi 26, Sukhumvit Rd	259-2900	259-2896	22612 Tara Th		▲	▲	▲
Tawana Ramada Surawongse Rd	236-0361	236-3738	81167 Tawaram Th		▲	▲	▲
Indra Regent Rajprarob Rd	252-1111	253-3849	82723 Indra Th	INDRAHOTEL	▲	▲	▲
Boulevard 5017 Sukhumvit Rd	255-2930	255-2950					

C

Hotel address	Phone	Fax	Telex	Cable	〰	🍴	🥣
First Hotel New Phetburi Rd	252-5011	251-7040	827027 Firstht Th		▲	▲	▲
Majestic Ratchadamnoen Rd	281-5000		82114 Th	MAJESTIC BANGKOK	▲	▲	▲
Mandarin Rama 4 Rd	233-4980	234-1399	87689 Mandarin Th	MANOTEL	▲	▲	▲

Hotel address	Phone	Fax	Telex	Cable	〰	🍴	🥣
BANGKOK – *Cont'd*							
C							
Manohra Surawongse Rd	234-5070		82114 Manohra Th	MANORAOTEL	▲	▲	▲
Plaza Surawongse Rd	235-1760	237-0746	72152 Plaza Th	PLAZATEL	▲	▲	▲
Windsor Soi 20, Sukhumvit Rd	258-0160	258-1491	82081 Windhtl Th	WINDHOTEL	▲	▲	▲
Manhattan Soi 15, Sukhumvit Rd	255-0188	255-2331	87272 Th	HOTELMAN	▲	▲	▲
Swissotel Convent Rd	233-6721	2369425	20582 Swissgh Th		▲	▲	▲
D							
Christian Guesthouse Saladaeng Soi 2	233-6303 233-2206					▲	▲
Century Hotel Rajprarob Rd	246-7800	246-7197	87119 Centhtl Th	CENTURY HTL	▲	▲	▲
Florida Phayathai Rd	245-3221			FLOHOTEL	▲	▲	▲
Golden Dragon Damrongrak Rd	589-5141	5898305	82133 Ngdtel Th	GOLORATEL	▲	▲	▲
Mermaids Rest Soi 8, Sukhumvit Rd	253-2400 253-5122 253-3410		20235 Surveys Th		▲	▲	▲
Nana Soi 4 Sukhumvit Rd	252-0121	255-1769	84401 Nana Th	NANA HOTEL	▲	▲	▲
New Fuji Surawongse Rd	234-5364		20939 Fujiho Th		▲	▲	▲
New Peninsula Surawongse Rd	234-3910		84079 Peninho Th	PENINHO	▲	▲	▲
Opera Soi Somprasong, New Phetburi Rd	252-9754	253-5360			▲	▲	▲
Rose Surawongse Rd	233-7695			ROSEHOTEL		▲	▲
Royal Ratchadamnoen Rd	222-9111	224-2083	84252 Royalho Th	ROYALHOTEL	▲	▲	▲
Trocadero Surawongse Rd	234-8920		81061 Newtroc Th		▲	▲	▲

Hotel address	Phone	Fax	Telex	Cable	〰	🍴	🍲
BANGKOK – *Cont'd*							
D							
Victory Silom Rd	233-9060	233-9071	87379 Shertrv Th	VICTORYHTL		▲	▲
Viengtai Tanee Rd, Banglumpoo	282-8119	280-3527	82976 Th	VIENGTAI	▲	▲	▲
YMCA/YWCA Sathorn Tai Rd	287-2727	287-1996	72185 Bymca Th	YOUTH BANGKOK	▲		▲
C (US$38)							
BAN SAEN							
C							
Bang Saen Beach Resort Bang Saen Beach	(038) 376675		75513		▲	▲	▲
B (US$45-100) **C** (US$20-45)							
CHA-AM							
B							
Methavalai On the Beach Rd	(032) 471028	(032) 471590	78302 Metha Th		▲	▲	▲
Regent Cha-am On the Beach Rd	(032) 471480	(032) 471492	Th 78306		▲	▲	▲
Suan Buak Haad Hotel Phetkasem Rd	(032) 471334		82965 Th		▲	▲	▲
Dusit Resort (Opening 1991) Beach Rd					▲	▲	▲
C							
Cha-am Cabana Hat Khlong-Thian	(032) 741614					▲	▲
Cha-am Garden Beach Rd	(032) 471046-7					▲	▲
Cha-am Holiday Lodge Beach Rd	(032) 471595					▲	▲

Hotel address	Phone	Fax	Telex	Cable	〜	🍴	🛏
C (US$15-25)							
CHANTABURI							
C							
Eastern Hotel Tha-Chalab Rd	(039) 312218				▲	▲	▲
Travel Lodge Raksak-Chamun Rd	(039) 311531				▲	▲	▲
B (US$45-70) **C** (US$30-55) **D** (US$15-28)							
CHIANG MAI							
B							
Chiang Inn Changkhlan Rd	(053) 235655	(053) 234299	Th 43503	CHIANGIN CHIANG MAI	▲	▲	▲
Chiang Mai Orchid Hotel Huay Kaeo Rd	(053) 222099	(053) 221625	43537, 49337 Chior Th		▲	▲	▲
Chiang Mai Plaza Sridonchai Rd	(053) 252050	(053) 252230	Th 49329		▲	▲	▲
Dusit Inn Chang Klan Rd	(053) 251033	(053) 251037	Th 49325		▲	▲	▲
Mae Ping Sridonchai Rd	(053) 251060	(053) 251069	Th 49343		▲	▲	▲
Poy Luang Siyake Poy Luang	(053) 242633	(053) 242490	Th 43502		▲	▲	▲
Rincome Huay Kaeo Rd	(053) 221044	(053) 221915	Th 49314		▲	▲	▲
Suriwongse Changkhlan Rd	(053) 236733		Th 49308	SURIWONGSE CHIANGMAI	▲	▲	▲
C							
Chiang Dao Hill Resort 28 Mu 6, Amphoe Phiang Dao (100 km from Chiang Mai)	(053) 236995	(053) 47573	47573 Hillresth			▲	▲
Chiang Mai Hills Hotel Huay Kaeo Rd	(053) 221255		Th 49316			▲	▲
President Witchayanon Rd	(053) 251025					▲	▲
Erawan Resort 30 Mu 2, Amphoe Mae Rim	(053) 251191					▲	▲

Hotel address	Phone	Fax	Telex	Cable	~~~	🍴	🍽
CHIANG MAI – *Cont'd*							
C							
Porn Ping Hotel Charoenprathet Rd	(053) 235099					▲	▲
D							
Little Duck Hotel Huay Kaew Rd	(053) 222122	(053) 221750			▲	▲	▲
Mae Sa Valley Hill Resort Hotel C/ North West Tour, Suriwongse Hotel, Chiang Mai	(053) 236789					▲	▲
Muang Mai Hotel Huay Kaew Rd	(053) 221392					▲	▲
Phet Ngam Hotel Charoenprathet Rd	(053) 234153	(053) 233947				▲	▲
Sri Tokyo Hotel Boonruangrit Rd	(053) 213899					▲	▲
Wang Tarn Resort 35/1 Mu 2, Tambon Luang Nua, Amphoe Doi Saket, Chiang Mai	(053) 221185		Th 72377		▲	▲	▲
C (US$30-50)							
CHIANG RAI							
C							
Dusit Island Resort Kraisomsithi Rd	(054) 711865				▲	▲	▲
Wangcome Hotel Pemaviphat Rd	(054) 711800	(054) 713844	Th 41307		▲	▲	▲
Wiang Inn Phahonyothin Rd	(054) 711543	(054) 711877	Th 41308 Wiang Inn		▲	▲	▲
C (US$28-48) **D** (US$16-25)							
HAAD YAI							
C							
JB Hotel Jootee Anusorn Rd	(074) 234300	(074) 243499	62113 Jbhtl Th		▲	▲	▲

Hotel address	Phone	Fax	Telex	Cable	≈	🍴	🥣
HAAD YAI – *Cont'd*							
C							
Lee Gardens Lee Phatana Rd	(074) 245888					▲	▲
Montien Hotel Niphat Uthit Rd	(074) 245399					▲	▲
Nora Hotel Thammanun Rd	(074) 244944					▲	▲
D							
Ambassador Phadung-Phakdi Rd	(074) 246665		60213			▲	▲
Asian Hotel Niphat Uthit Rd	(074) 245455	Th 62173	Asian Ho			▲	▲
President Hotel Phetkasem Rd	(074) 244477				▲	▲	▲
Kosit Hotel Niphat Uthit Rd	(074) 235710	(074) 232365	62149 Kosit Th			▲	▲
B (US$75-100) **D** (US$18-35)							
HUA HIN							
B							
Hotel Sofitel On the Beach Rd	(032) 512021	(032) 511014	78313 Th		▲	▲	▲
Royal Garden Resort Phetkasem Rd	(032) 511881	(032) 512422	78309 Th		▲	▲	▲
Royal Garden Village Phetkasem Rd	(032) 512412	(032) 512417	78314 Th		▲	▲	▲
D							
Golf Inn Damnoen Karem Rd	(032) 512473				▲	▲	▲
Hua Hin Highland Resort Klongcholapratarn Rd	2112579					▲	▲
Thanam Chai Damrongrat Rd	(032) 511755					▲	▲
Sailom Hotel Phetkasem Rd	(032) 511890				▲	▲	▲

Hotel address	Phone	Fax	Telex	Cable	〰	🍴	🍽
D (US$15-20)							
KAMPHAENG PHET **D**							
Navarat Hotel On Mse Ping River	(055) 711211					▲	▲
Phet Hotel Wichit Rd	(055) 712810	(055) 712927	87200		▲	▲	▲
Chakungrao Hotel Thesa Rd	(055) 711315					▲	▲
C (US$28-48)							
KANCHANABURI **C**							
Kasem Island Resort Chaichumpon Rd	(034) 513359	Bangkok 236-7455	82156			▲	▲
Kwai Yai River Huts	Bangkok 258-1322					▲	▲
River Kwai Hotel Saeng Chuto Rd	(034) 511184	(034) 511269	78705 Ramarkh			▲	▲
River Kwai Village Hotel Sai Yok	Bangkok 2157828	Bangkok 2552350			▲	▲	▲
River Kwai Jungle Rafts	Bangkok 3923641					▲	▲
C (US$18-30)							
KOH SAMET (*SAMET ISLAND*) **C**							
Wongduan Resort Wongduan	Bangkok 3210731					▲	▲
Wongduan Villa Wongduan	Bangkok 3210789					▲	▲
Diamond Hotel Sai Kaew Beach	Bangkok 3210814					▲	

Hotel address	Phone	Fax	Telex	Cable	〜〜	🍴	🥣
C (US$35-70) **D** (US$12)							
KRABI							
C							
Krabi Resort Phatthana Rd	(075) 611389		67201 Th Sripong			▲	▲
Tonsai Village Uttarakij Rd	(075) 611496	(075) 612251				▲	▲
D							
Thai Hotel Issara Rd	(075) 611122						▲
C (US$15-80)							
MAE HONG SON							
C							
Mae Hong Son Resort 24 Ban Huaiduca	(053) 611504	(053) 249133				▲	▲
Holiday Inn Khun Cumprapas Rd	(053) 611231				▲	▲	▲
D (US$10-32)							
MAE SOD							
D							
Mae Sod Hill Hotel Asia Rd	(055) 532601		Th 48214 MS Hill		▲	▲	▲
Siam Hotel Prasatvithee Rd	(055) 531376					▲	▲
D (US$15-25)							
NAKHON RATCHASIMA *(KORAT)*							
D							
Chom Surang Hotel Mahad Thai Rd	(044) 257088	(044) 252897			▲	▲	▲
Khao Yai Motor Lodge Pak Chong	Bangkok 2813041					▲	▲

Hotel address	Phone	Fax	Telex	Cable	～	♙	♙
C (US$50-90) **D** (US$20-40)							
PATTAYA **C**							
Ambassador City Jomtien	(038) 231501-40	(038) 231731	Th 85902		▲	▲	▲
Asia Pattaya Beach Hotel Pattaya City	(036) 428602	(036) 423496	Th 85902	ASIA PATTAYA BANGKOK	▲	▲	▲
Dusit Resort Pattaya Beach Rd	(038) 429901	(038) 428239	Th 85917	DUSITOTEL	▲	▲	▲
Grand Palace Pattaya Beach	(038) 418541				▲	▲	▲
Merlin Pattaya Pattaya Beach	(038) 428755		Th 82197		▲	▲	▲
Montien Pattaya Pattaya Beach	(038) 418155		Th 85906	MONTELP	▲	▲	▲
Nipa Lodge Pattaya Beach	(038) 428195	(038) 429097	Th 85903 Siamlux	NIPALODGE	▲	▲	▲
Novotel Pattaya Beach Rd	(038) 428645		85910 Novtrop		▲	▲	▲
Ocean View Hotel Pattaya Beach	(038) 428084	(038) 428551	85912 Ocean Th	OCEANVIEW	▲	▲	▲
Orchid Lodge Pattaya Beach	(038) 428161	(038) 428165	Th 85903 Siamlux	ORCHID LODGE	▲	▲	▲
Pattaya Park Beach Resort Jomtien	(038) 423000	(038) 423009	85956 Pty Park Th		▲	▲	▲
Royal Cliff Pattaya Beach	(038) 421421	(038) 428511	85907 Cliffex Th	CLIFF PATTAYA	▲	▲	▲
Royal Garden Pattaya Beach Rd	(038) 428126	(038) 429926	85909 Rogaden	ROGADEN	▲	▲	▲
Siam Bayshore Pattaya South	(038) 428678		20119 Bayshor Th		▲	▲	▲
D							
Diamond Beach Pattaya Beach	(038) 428071					▲	▲
Koh Larn Resort Larn Island	(038) 428422		84904 Goldtel			▲	▲
Little Duck Hotel North Pattaya	(038) 428065	(038) 426043	85914 Resort Th			▲	▲

Hotel address	Phone	Fax	Telex	Cable	≈	¶¶	⌣
PATTAYA – *Cont'd* **D**							
Palm Villa Pattaya Beach	(038) 428153		85923 Palmhtl Th			▲	▲
Pattaya Palace Pattaya Beach	(038) 428066	(038) 428026	75904 Palpatth	·	▲	▲	▲
Sea View Hotel Naklua Rd	(038) 429371		85913 Seaview Thpty		▲	▲	▲
Weekender Hotel Pattaya Rd	(038) 428720					▲	▲
D (US$15-30)							
PHITSANULOK **D**							
Amarin Nakorn Chaophraya Rd	(055) 258588		Th 46253			▲	▲
Phailin Hotel Baromtrilokanart Rd	(055) 252411	(055) 258983	Th 46258			▲	▲
Nanchao Hotel Baromtrilokanart Rd	(055) 252510					▲	▲
A (US$80-130) **B** (US$35-70)							
PHUKET **A**							
Boathouse Inn Kata Beach	(076) 215185	(076) 214028	69532 Yacht Th			▲	▲
Club Mediterranee Kata Beach	(076) 214830		69526 Clubmed Th		▲	▲	▲
Dusit Laguna Resort Chemgtalay	(076) 311320	(076) 311174	69554 Dlaguna Th		▲	▲	▲
Holiday Inn Patong Beach	(076) 321020	(076) 321435	69545		▲	▲	▲
Karon Villa Karon Beach	(076) 214820	(076) 214822	69571 Karonpk Th		▲	▲	▲

Hotel address	Phone	Fax	Telex	Cable	≈	🍴	🥣
PHUKET – *Cont'd*							
A							
Karon Beach Resort Karon Beach	(076) 214828	(076) 214828	69534 Katasea Th		▲	▲	▲
Le Meridien Tambon Karon	(076) 321480	(076) 321479	69542 Merihkt Th		▲	▲	▲
Phuket Arcadia Karon Beach	(076) 214841	(076) 214840	69503 Arcadia Th		▲	▲	▲
Patong Merlin Patong Beach	(076) 321070		69541 Pamelin Th		▲	▲	▲
Pearl Hotel Montree Rd	(076) 211044	(076) 212911	69510 Pearl Th		▲	▲	▲
Phuket Yacht Club Hotel Nai Harn Beach	(076) 214020	(076) 214028	69532 Yacht Th		▲	▲	▲
Pansea Hotel Rasada Centre	(076) 216137	(076) 214668	69522 Pansea Th		▲	▲	▲
Thavorn Palm Beach Karon Beach	(076) 214835	(076) 215556			▲	▲	▲
B							
Banthai Beach Resort Patong Beach	(076) 321329	(076) 321330	65509 Banthai Th		▲	▲	▲
Club Andaman Patong Beach	(076) 321102				▲	▲	▲
Kataka Inn Rasda Rd	(076) 214828-9	(076) 214828			▲	▲	▲
Patong Bay Garden Patong Beach	(076) 321297		69573 Bgarden Th		▲	▲	▲
Patong Beach Hotel Patong Beach	(076) 321286		69521 Patong Th		▲	▲	▲
Patong Resort Patong Beach	(076) 321333	(076) 321189	69535 Presort Th		▲	▲	▲
Thara Patong Beach Resort Patong Beach	(076) 321135	(076) 321446	69539 Tharaho Th		▲	▲	▲

Hotel address	Phone	Fax	Telex	Cable	≈	🍴	🥣
A (US$90-160) **B** (US$32-100)							
RAYONG							
A							
Swiss-Purinas Beach Hotel Ban Chang	Bangkok 3927883-4	Bangkok 3916829					▲
B							
Rayong Resort Ban Phe	Bangkok 258-4461				▲	▲	▲
Sinsamut Village Ban Phe	Bangkok 2529467					▲	▲
Suan Wang Kaew Ban Phe	Bangkok 2525053					▲	▲
Amornphan Villa Ban Phe	(038) 612918					▲	▲
Princess Hotel Opening mid-1991 Ban Chang	Bangkok 236-0450	Bangkok 2366400					
B (US$65-135) **C** (US$10-40)							
SAMUI ISLAND							
B							
Imperial Ban Chaweng	(077) 421390	(077) 421390	67431 Imsamui		▲	▲	▲
Tongsai Bay Hotel Ban Plailem	(077) 421451	(077) 421462			▲	▲	▲
Pansea Samui Hotel Chaweng Beach	(077) 421384	(077) 421385				▲	▲
C							
Chao Ko Bungalow Na Thong Bay	(077) 421214					▲	▲
Coral Bay Resort Bo Phut	(077) 272222					▲	▲
Samui Ferry Inn Thong Yang Beach	(077) 273130					▲	▲

Hotel address	Phone	Fax	Telex	Cable	〰	🍴	🍽
C (US$30)							
SONGKHLA							
C							
Samila Hotel On the Beach Rd	(074) 311310		64204 Samila Th		▲	▲	▲
D (US$20-30)							
SUKOTHAI							
D							
Rajthanee Charodvitheetong Rd	(055) 611031	(055) 611602	Th 47206			▲	▲
Thai Village House Charodvitheetong Rd	(055) 611049					▲	▲
D (US$15)							
SURIN							
D							
Petchkasem Hotel Jitbumrung Rd	(045) 511274	(045) 514041			▲	▲	▲
D (US$12-20)							
UBON RATCHATHANI							
D							
Pathumrat Hotel Chayang-kul Rd	(045) 241501					▲	▲
Bordin Hotel Palochai Rd	(045) 255777					▲	▲

VIETNAM

Stretching over 1,600 km from the misty mountains on the Chinese border to the fertile delta of the Mekong River, Vietnam is one of the most beautiful countries in Asia. Its physical infrastructure still bears the scars of more than 30 years of warfare and since the victory of the North in 1975 and reunification, reconstruction has been painfully slow. Obstacles have included rigid adherence to policies Vietnam's leaders now acknowledge as mistaken and by the embargo on business imposed by the US after Vietnam's 1978 invasion of Cambodia.

But Vietnam opened up rapidly to visitors in 1989 and 1990 as part of a drive by communist party elders to liberalise and re-invigorate the economy. The authorities even declared 1990 a "year of tourism" to coincide with a number of important anniversaries, among them the centenary of former president Ho Chi Minh's birth, and hoped to attract close to

150,000 visitors, more than 15 times the level of the mid-1980s. Already thousands of former refugees are visiting every year including in 1989 around a thousand American veterans of the war.

The desire to attract tourists, however, is offset by lack of amenities in a country whose economy, starved of capital, is several decades behind such prosperous Southeast Asian neighbours as Thailand or Malaysia. Internal political uncertainties and a tightening of security in the south in 1990 also led to occasional constraints on tourists' movements. The main difficulties range from shortages of hotel rooms to the limited capacity of both internal transport and international flights to and from Vietnam. Access improved in 1989-90, however, with the start of flights to Ho Chi Minh City by some neighbouring countries and a sharp rise in the frequency of existing services, particularly by Air Vietnam.

The Vietnamese (ethnically a blend of Sinitic and Indonesian stocks) have their roots in southern China (Guangdong province) and the Red River Delta (now northern Vietnam). By the middle of the third century, the main Viet tribes had coalesced into the kingdom of Au Lac, later renamed Nam Viet. In 111 BC, Nam Viet fell under the authority of Han China and remained an outer province of China until 938 AD. Even after independence, the Vietnamese recognised the power of China by the payment of a regular tribute.

Chinese influence continued for a long period in Vietnam. The country's scholars were imbued with Confucian values and Chinese characters were used for the written language,

while many elements of government were also borrowed. Yet, though long under the sway of such a powerful, all-pervading culture, the Vietnamese always retained their identity.

The country was ruled by several Vietnamese dynasties until the early 15th century when the Chinese — under the pretext of removing a usurper — returned to power. They were driven out in 1428 after a brief rule and were replaced by a new Vietnamese dynasty, the Le (1428-1776) under Le Loi. The country's name was again changed, this time to Dai Viet.

The Vietnamese, prior to the Le dynasty, found themselves competing for power with the kingdom of Champa, which was immediately to their south. The Chams, like the Khmers to the west, had adopted the Hindu religion of India and had more than once inflicted military defeat

◁ *Buffalo power: tradition farming continues.*

295

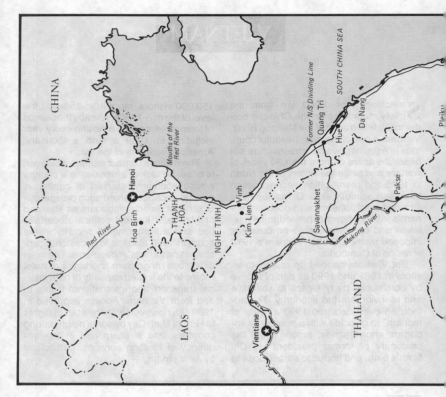

on the Vietnamese. During the 15th century, however, the Vietnamese began to gain the upper hand, capturing more and more Cham territory. They then pushed southwards and eventually overran all of Champa and even went as far as the Camau Peninsula in the far south, which the Vietnamese were to take from the Khmers.

Although the Le dynasty lasted until 1776, much of the real power was not held by the emperor. The Trinh family controlled the north of the country and the Nguyen family were in power in the south. After a lengthy period of civil war, the country was officially divided in 1672 in the vicinity of the present 17th Parallel.

National reunification came with the Tay Son peasant rebellion which began in 1776, and with the defeat of both the Trinh and the Nguyen

families the Le dynasty was finally removed. The Tay Son emperor died in 1792. One of the Nguyen successors, Nguyen Anh, came to power and under the royal name of Gia Long founded the Nguyen dynasty in 1802. The country was renamed Vietnam.

European missionaries and traders had for some time gained entry to the country, though it was risky. The French had a privileged position because of the help given to Nguyen Anh in his early years by the Bishop of Adran. Successive emperors, however, were far less appreciative of foreign intervention. Attacks on Christian missionaries gave the French an excuse to take Saigon by force in 1861.

Independence came to an end in 1883 when French control was extended to the north. The French divided the country into three sections

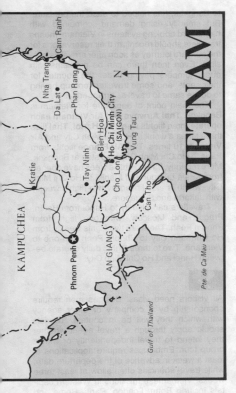

Minh, who took effective control. They were soon displaced by Chinese and British forces and the country was handed back to France. This began the long post-war struggle by the communists, first against the French for control of the country.

The country was divided in 1954 into North Vietnam and South Vietnam after the Geneva Agreements brought an end to the fighting with the French, who eventually withdrew completely, leaving the communists in control of the North and a non-communist regime in the South. Theoretically this was all to be subject to a national poll, which was never held. US intervention in Indochina was limited at first to "advisers" to the South Vietnamese over what was regarded as a minor communist insurgency. But it gradually escalated into a full-scale war (though war was never officially declared) between National Liberation Front (Vietcong) forces and North Vietnamese infiltrating from the North into the South and gradually increasing numbers of US combat troops. The full weight of the US military machine was swung against the communists by President Lyndon Johnson in 1965 and continued through the start of President Richard Nixon's administration.

When the US used B-52 heavy bombers to bomb North Vietnam, the advance of the communists seemed for a while to have been halted, even if not actually turned. North Vietnamese and US officials met in Paris for what became a long drawn-out series of apparently fruitless peace talks, starting in March 1968, with the US offering the sweetener of having stopped the bombing of the North.

In November 1968, Johnson suspended all military action against North Vietnam and in mid-1969 Nixon began the phased withdrawal of US troops. When in March 1972 the North launched its so-called Spring Offensive across the partition line, Nixon ordered bombing of the North to resume.

A peace accord eventually signed in Paris on January 27, 1973, provided for an international control commission to supervise observance of a ceasefire and withdrawal of remaining US forces. After they had left, the North resumed its offensive making rapid advances. The US, however, refused to become involved on the ground again and the Saigon government defences caved in. On April 30, 1975, after frantic evacuation of foreigners, communist tanks crashed through the gates of the Presidential Palace in

for administrative purposes; Cochinchina, the southernmost section, was made a French colony while the remainder, Tonkin in the area of the Red River Delta and Annam in the central reaches of the country surrounding the capital of Hue, were made protectorates. With Cambodia and Laos, Vietnam made up what was known as French Indochina.

Nationalist movements increasingly marked the period of foreign rule before World War II. The Japanese occupied Indochina in 1941 but left the Vichy French in control. In March 1945, with defeat inevitable, Japan overthrew the French and granted independence to Vietnam with the last of the Nguyen emperors, Bao Dai, as head of state. But with the sudden surrender of the Japanese in August that year, it was the communists, under the leadership of Ho Chi

Saigon and the war was over.

For the first year, military management committees set up in all southern cities carried on day-to-day administration. In April 1976, Vietnam staged nationwide elections for a unified national assembly and in July 1976 the country was formally reunified under the name of the Socialist Republic of Vietnam.

But peace for Vietnam's army was short-lived. In December 1978, after savage cross-border attacks ordered by Cambodia's Khmer Rouge rulers, Hanoi invaded, quickly capturing Phnom Penh and driving remnants of Pol Pot's forces back to the mountains and jungles bordering Thailand. Hanoi then installed a Cambodian regime in Phnom Penh, backed by more than 200,000 Vietnamese troops.

China, Pol Pot's supporter, reacted by launching a fierce attack into northern Vietnam to "teach it a lesson." Chinese troops pulled back after only a few months but hostilities in the form of cross-border artillery bombardments continued sporadically long into the 1980s as Peking sought to keep up the pressure on Vietnam to reach a compromise settlement over Cambodia.

The Vietnamese army left Cambodia in a series of phased withdrawals culminating in September 1989. But though Hanoi by then had softened its position on international verification, no agreement was reached on an appropriate mechanism. Most governments accepted Vietnam had pulled out all but technicians and perhaps a hard core of special forces.

Economic liberalisation since 1986 produced rapid improvements in living conditions and attracted some foreign investment. The gains were insufficient, however, to offset the crippling obstacle posed by a US veto of IMF and World Bank funding for Vietnam. This, combined with drastic cuts in Soviet and East European aid after 1989, left Vietnam's reform-minded leaders struggling to sustain the initial impetus of their economic restructuring and helped to strengthen resistance to political liberalisation among party hardliners.

A sharp rise in the number of businessmen and tourists seeking access to Vietnam has put flights under considerable pressure — particularly flights out of Vietnam, which also cater to tens of thousands of Vietnamese emigrating annually to the West. A leap in the number of flights during 1990, particularly those by **Air Vietnam**

to Bangkok, has helped to ease the pressure. But steadily rising demand, combined with haphazard booking systems in Vietnam, means travellers should reconfirm their reservations for the outward journey as soon after arrival as possible. Even then there can be problems with queue-jumpers paying under the counter for their seats, and some travellers end up having to do the same to travel as arranged.

The main point of departure for Vietnam is Bangkok. **Thai Airways** and **Air Vietnam** each operate three flights weekly to **Hanoi**, **Thai** flies three times a week to Ho Chi Minh City and **Air Vietnam** 10 times. Two **Air France** flights from Paris to Ho Chi Minh City also stop at Bangkok. More recently, three flights a week have opened from Kuala Lumpur and Manila to Ho Chi Minh City, which is also linked by two flights weekly with Jakarta and Singapore.

Travellers can also fly to Hanoi from Berlin, Prague and Moscow, with one flight from Phnom Penh. There are two flights weekly from Ho Chi Minh City to Phnom Penh and one to Vientiane. Two to three flights daily operate between Hanoi and Ho Chi Minh City.

All visitors need visas. Businessmen require sponsorship by a company or other agency with which they will be in contact. Tourists should apply through a travel agent whether they intend to travel independently or with a group tour. Embassies require applications at least a week in advance of the departure date, while travel agencies often allow at least three weeks. Vietnamese missions in Western capitals include Bonn, London, Paris, Rome and Stockholm. Other major embassies include Bangkok, Canberra, Jakarta, Kuala Lumpur, Manila and Vientiane. Travel agencies in Bangkok offer tours of three, four and five days to Ho Chi Minh City only and tours of seven to nine days also visiting Da Nang, Hue and Hanoi, prices ranging up to US$640, inclusive of air fare.

Visitors travelling in the countryside are well advised to take precautions against malaria, which may require taking pills well ahead of their journey, and injections against hepatitis, endemic in Vietnam.

Travellers may also wish to be vaccinated against cholera. Avoid drinking tap water.

Vietnam's currency, the dong, was valued in April 1991 at an official rate of Dong 7,900:US$1. The government switched to a unified and floating rate of exchange in place of the previous multiple rate system in 1988, wiping out most of the differential between official and black-market rates of exchange. Travellers will find the US dollar still used in many transactions, notably hotel bills (services such as food, laundry etc. may be payable in dong but not rooms), taxis and car rental, international telephone calls, telex and fax, and often for shopping. Visitors can change traveller's cheques in Hanoi and Ho Chi Minh City but may have difficulty trying to do so anywhere else.

Vietnamese is the national language. The version spoken in the south differs slightly from that of the north. A Roman script with added marks indicating vowel changes and tones is used for the written language. French and/or English are spoken by a large number of educated people.

It is best to visit the northern part of the country (if it is possible) between October and March. However, in late January and February the crachin, a continuous drizzly rain, makes conditions unpleasant. Winters are cool and sometimes chilly. Summers are very hot and rainy.

Conditions in the southern half of Vietnam are warm to hot throughout the year with the average daily maximum exceeding 31°C (88°F). At night temperatures drop to around 23°C (73°F). March, April and May are the hottest months and temperatures often reach as high as 35°C (95°F). The humidity is usually high.

The more pleasant months are between November and March. The rainy season in Ho Chi Minh City is from May to late November, but further north near Da Nang and Hue it is from October to March. Temperatures in the highlands are considerably lower than those at sea level. The annual average temperature at Da Lat is 19.4°C (67°F).

Lightweight clothing is sufficient in Ho Chi Minh City all year round. A jacket may be necessary in some of the air-conditioned restaurants.

Warmer clothing will be necessary during the winter in the Hue region and certainly in the highlands, especially at night when it can become cool. In winter, the north of the country gets pretty cold, in some places the temperature dropping below 0°C. If the visitor intends to go to Hoa Binh mountain resort or Ha Long Bay during the winter, he should carry an overcoat and wind-resistant jacket. In Hanoi, too, one should wear fairly heavy winter clothing.

Working hours for government offices all over the country are from 8 am to noon and from 1 pm to 4:30 pm from Monday to Saturday. Sunday is a holiday. Private shops and restaurants, however, commence business at 8:30 am and close rather late in the evening. Banks are open from 8 am to 4:30 pm from Monday to Friday and are also open on Saturday mornings. However, tourists must note that money changing is not possible after noon. Since the end of 1977, there has been a midnight curfew in Ho Chi Minh City.

Taxis are available at Hanoi and Ho Chi Minh City airports, but the fare into the city (US$20 and US$10 respectively) should be agreed before entering the vehicle. For touring Hanoi and Ho Chi Minh City, transport can be arranged with **Vietnam Tourism** on an hourly or daily basis. Trips outside the cities are charged on a per kilometre basis. In most cities, visitors can hire pedicabs (cyclos) for a modest fare, but should ensure the driver understands the destination.

Visitors are encouraged by Vietnam Tourism to travel between Hanoi and Ho Chi Minh City by air. The one-way fare is US$150. Travel by train is now open to visitors and cheaper than flying even on the most expensive of the three classes of train. But trains are frequently congested, comforts minimal and journey times extremely variable. Buses also operate between major cities but, though cheaper still, are even more rugged.

Hotel reservations can be made directly in Ho Chi Minh City but there, as everywhere else, are best left by tourists to travel agencies and by other visitors to the individuals or agencies host-

Can Tho rice market.

Photo: John Spragens, Jr

ing their trip. The increasing number of visitors has put pressure on existing hotel accommodation, prices are rising and to find a confirmed room may require some searching. Since late 1988, licences have been issued to some private individuals to receive guests and a number of small guesthouses now operate in Hanoi and Ho Chi Minh City. Information should be available from **Vietnam Tourism**.

In Hanoi, since the closure of the **Thiong Nhat** for renovation, the main hotels are the **Thang Loi**, rather remote, and the **State Guesthouse**, centrally located, where single rooms are available at about US$40-50 a night. Smaller and less expensive are the **Hoa Binh** and the **Hoan Kiem**.

In Ho Chi Minh City, the **Saigon Floating Hotel** offers rooms at US$115 a night and boasts its own generator, insulating it from power cuts. The more comfortable **Continental** has single rooms available at US$71. Hotels offering less elegance but a comprehensive range of facilities (including telex and fax) at single room rates of approximately US$35-50 a night include the **Cuu Long** (often referred to by its former name the **Majestic**), the **Rex** and the **Doc Lap** (**Caravelle**).

There are reasonable hotels at Ha Long Bay, Do Son sea resort in the north and at Hue (limit-ed), Da Nang, Nha Trang, Dalat, and Vung Thau in central and southern areas and at Can Tho, My tho and Ben Tre in the Mekong Delta.

Many Vietnamese restaurants are small, insignificant spots where the visitor would have trouble making himself understood and may be put off by the modest hygiene. But recent economic liberalisation has spawned a dramatic increase in the number of restaurants and better quality.

Vietnamese cooking, comparable to Chinese but often more spicy, offers considerable variety. Visitors soon become aware of *cha gio* (pronounced cha yor), deep fried rolls of rice paper filled with crab meat, egg, vermicelli and chopped vegetables. Smaller than Chinese spring or egg rolls, they should be dipped in the strong local fish sauce called *nuoc mam*.

Bo bay mon (beef served in seven varieties) is excellent, each variety accompanied by its own traditional sauce and vegetables. *Com tay cam* is a casserole dish with finely sliced pork, chicken, mushrooms and rice in ginger sauce.

Vietnamese soups are also excellent. *Pho*, the most common, comes in many varieties depending on the meat, noodles and other ingredients used. *Soupe chinoise* is similar. The fish soup called *canh chua* is also a tasty dish.

All the hotels in Hanoi and Ho Chi Minh City serve some sort of Western food but are facing increasing competition from the burgeoning number of private restaurants. In Hanoi, the **Piano Bar, 2-0-2** restaurant (at 202 Hue Ave), the **Cha Ca** (Cha Ca St) and the **Quan An Duc San** (Nha Chung St) are all well patronised (and well known to cyclo drivers) along with **Chau Thanh** in Phat Loc St.

In Ho Chi Minh City, **Mme Dai's**, near the Cathedral, with a long-established clientele, and the nearby Tennis Club's **Thanh Nien**, face competition from newer restaurants like the **Mekong**, offering a service far better than expected from an establishment owned by Saigon Tourism.

Doing good business with locals as well as visitors are the **Dang Phat**, a few blocks from the **Majestic Hotel**, and the **Jianj Nan** in Cholon's Tan Da St. The **Doc Lap's** restaurant compares favourably with those of other hotels while the continental provides an up-market setting for business engagements.

There is a plentiful supply of wines, liquor and other alcoholic drinks, many locally made, available from Ho Chi Minh City shops, such as those in Tu Do St, and a host of street stalls. Mekong Champagne is eminently avoidable.

Ho Chi Minh City remains the entertainment capital of Vietnam boasting a variety of discos and dancing establishments. Massage parlours and more risque bars still exist but are subject to intermittent closure by police. Among the most fashionable dancing establishments are the discos in the **Floating Hotel** (admission US$5 and drinks about the same), the **Majestic** and the nightclub of the **Rex**, all well-patronised by locals as well as foreign visitors. **Maxim's** (next door to the **Majestic**) offers a band and singers with food of rather modest quality.

Hanoi, more austere and without Saigon's experience or exposure to modern Western tastes, is only just beginning to develop any semblance of nightlife. Apart from the burgeoning number of small cafes, where young locals sit in near darkness listening to local and Western music, nightlife revolves almost entirely round a handful of dance halls where quicksteps and foxtrots are still as popular as disco dancing. Most frequented by foreign residents of Hanoi are the dancing at the **Thanh Loi Hotel** and the **International Club**, noted for dense weekend crowds and deafening music.

Traditional Vietnamese handicrafts, promoted by the government, include lacquerware, carved tortoiseshell, mother-of-pearl inlaid panels and jewellery, ceramics, bamboo products, jewellery and silk goods. Lacquerware is ubiquitous but the quality variable.

Handmade silver bracelets, pendants and earrings make attractive purchases and if the silver content should not be overestimated the prices are still modest. Hanoi and to a lesser extent Ho Chi Minh City offer a large number of art shops selling modestly priced paintings. Ho Chi Minh City is also awash with radios, stereo cassette players and other electronic goods, many of them smuggled in, and selling at cheaper prices than in Bangkok, where they carry heavy duty.

In Hanoi, many arts and crafts shops are located in streets around the south side of the Hoan Kiem lake (close to the Post Office) and in the old quarter on the north side. Ho Chi Minh City's shopping area is concentrated around Tu Do. Le Loi and Le Thanh Ton streets, Nguyen Hue Blvd and the central market.

Some items, such as lacquerware or household goods, may be purchased in local currency but most, particularly more costly items such as antiques, will be priced in dollars. Visitors should bear in mind that they may face duty on antiques, assessed rather arbitrarily by customs officers at the airport.

The Vietnamese festival calendar reflects both Chinese, French (Christian) and communist influences. Some holidays, including Tet, vary from year to year. Although in recent years many of the festivals were not observed because of the war, now normal conditions have been restored in both sections of the country and festivals are being celebrated once more.

January-Febraury: Tet (Vietnamese New Year) is the major festival. A traditional ceremony, Giao Thua is celebrated at midnight. Gifts are exchanged, well-wishing calls made and pagodas and temples are visited. The third day is highlighted by unicorn dance (public holiday, three-and-a-half days).

March-April: Easter (public holiday).

April 12: Anniversary commemorating the emperor-founder, Hung Vuong (public holiday).

April 30: Anniversary of the incorporation of North and South Vietnam.

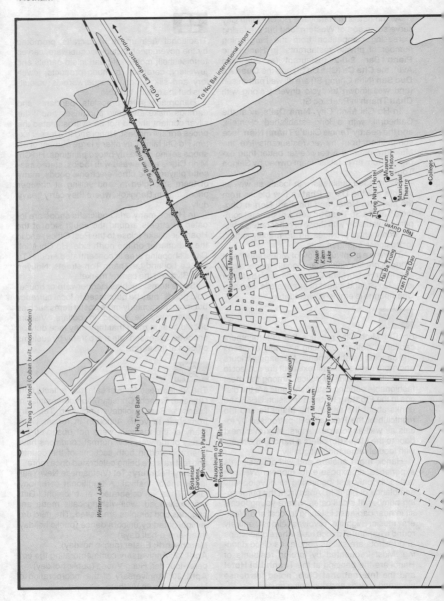

To Noi Bai International airport

To Gia Lam domestic airport

Long Bien Bridge

Thang Loi Hotel (Cuban built, most modern)

Western Lake

Ho Truc Bach

Botanical Gardens

President's Palace

Mausoleum of President Ho Chi Minh

Municipal Market

Hoan Kiem Lake

Army Museum

Art Museum

Temple of Literature

Museum of History

Thong Nhat Hotel

Municipal Theatre

Colleges

Ngo Quyen

Hai Ba Trung

Tran Hung Dao

May 1: May Day (public holiday).

May: Buddha's birthday, celebrated on the full-moon day of the fourth lunar month, is observed at temples and pagodas. Homes and temples are festooned with lanterns and processions are held in temples in the evening (public holiday).

July-August: Wandering Soul's Day falls on the full moon of the seventh lunar month. Offerings of food and gifts are made at homes and temples for the wandering souls of the forgotten dead.

September-October: Mid-Autumn Festival falls on the full-moon day of the eighth lunar month. It is mainly a Chinese festival and the bakeries in Cholon — the Chinese section of Ho Chi Minh City — are filled with moon cakes and many shops sell colourful lanterns for the children.

September 2: Independence Day.

December 25: Christmas Day (public holiday).

DISCOVERING VIETNAM

HANOI

Under French rule, Hanoi became one of the most attractive cities in Asia and there is still charm in its broad, tree-lined boulevards and shady parks. The wartime bombing left its scars for a while, but now there are few visible traces remaining to spoil the city's charm — even the famous one-man bomb shelters dug into the pavements have been filled in.

Places to visit in Hanoi include: the **Petit Lac** in the centre of the city, a charming willow-pattern lake with a small island on which stands the **Turtle Pagoda** marking the spot where, in a legend, a turtle rose from the water bearing a sword with which an ancient Vietnamese hero drove out the Chinese invaders of the time.

The **One-Pillar Pagoda (Chua Mot Cot)**, also in the middle of a lake, which is shaped like a lotus to commemorate the birth of an heir to an emperor; a **mausoleum** opened to the public in late 1975 in honour of the late president Ho Chi Minh, near the One-Pillar Pagoda; the **Two Sisters Pagoda**, commemorating the sisters who led a rebellion against the Chinese in 40 AD; **Citadel Square**, the site of an ancient Vietnamese fort; and the **Covered Market**.

Other places worth visiting particularly on Sunday or public holidays are the **Reunification Park**, the **Zoo** and the **State Circus** (which usually performs in the Reunification Park). Visitors will nowadays encounter no restrictions if

Hue Citadel.

Photo: J. G. Gerrand

they wish to wander unescorted in central Hanoi, but special permits are needed for travelling outside the city. Interested tourists can ask to visit a farming cooperative on the outskirts of Hanoi.

UPCOUNTRY

One of the most scenic spots to visit in Vietnam is **Ha Long Bay** — 164 km by road from Hanoi. Strangely shaped, lime-rock mountains jutting out of the emerald sea and fishing junks plying in and out of them are a remarkable sight. **Hoa Binh** town, in a mountainous zone 76 km west of Hanoi, offers a majestic view of jungle-covered mountains. One can visit a village inhabited by national minorities as well as a primeval tropical forest that has been preserved. **Haiphong**, 105 km east of Hanoi, is a major port and industrial centre. Visitors not interested in the industrial scene may prefer to spend time in the beach resort of **Do Son** which is nearby.

Driving west from Hanoi towards the Lao border the traveller can view some of the most beautiful scenery in the world. Sea-blue mountain ranges, lush, green, hidden valleys and craggy outcrops come straight at you as if they were transposed from some giant Chinese silk screen. The area between **Son La** (where there is quite a reasonable government guesthouse) and Dien Bien Phu is populated by the Black T'ai hill tribes. They still follow the slash-and-burn cultivation of the land and dress in their traditional costumes. These people are a beautiful race without the Mongolian features of their distant cousins in Thailand. They still live high up on the slopes to be close to hill spirits, but are gradually being colonised by the Vietnamese who are forcing them down from the hills and into government-run cooperative farms in the valleys.

Dien Bien Phu itself is well worth a visit. Howitzers and tanks abandoned by the French in 1954 litter the valley fields and one may visit the famous hills — named after Legionnaires' girl-friends — where French positions were overrun by human-wave attacks from the Vietnamese.

There are several government guesthouses in Dien Bien Phu and Hanoi is hoping to encourage tourism in the area. Construction has been completed on a hotel right on a lake some 20 km from town and it is open for business.

If the visitor motors down south, he can see numerous cooperatives in **Thanh Hoa** and **Nghe Tinh** provinces on the way as well as the famed **Ham Rong (Dragon's Jaw) Bridge**. The city of **Vinh**, once a major industrial centre, was destroyed during the war, but it is fast coming back to life. The late **Ho Chi Minh's** native village, **Bong Sen**, is just half an hour's drive from Vinh and is worth visiting.

HO CHI MINH CITY (SAIGON)

The city centre runs from the west bank of the Saigon River. It extends southwest along the western bank of the Ben Nghe Canal and merges with the Chinese section, known as Cholon. The major hotels are in Tu Do and Nguyen Hue Sts, which run parallel to each other. The **Notre Dame Basilica** which stands at the opposite end of Tu Do from the river is one of the city's most prominent landmarks though it has no special architectural merit. The building was completed in 1883. Across the road to the north is the Central Post Office built about the same time. Other impressive buildings of a similar style are the **Gia Long Palace** (on Gia Long St) and the **Town Hall** (on Le Loi St), both only a short distance from Tu Do St.

At the junction of Le Loi and Tu Do is the **National Assembly** — once the National Theatre. The Dong Khoi (**Continental Hotel**) overlooks the plaza in front of the assembly and its front verandah is the next best thing to a sidewalk cafe for taking in the sights. Opposite is the **Doc Lap** and the view from its roof shows the closeness of the countryside. Le Loi, south of the assembly, is often crowded with street stalls and leads to the **Central Market** which is near the railway station.

Thong Nhut St, which runs past the western end of the Basilica, leads from **Independence Palace** (now called the office of the Military Management Committee) in the south to the grounds of the **zoo and park** in the north. Just inside the entrance to the park is the excellent **National Museum** with a collection of Vietnamese, Khmer and Cham cultural pieces. It also houses Chinese and Japanese object d'art. Opposite the museum is the interesting Vietnamese-style **Souvenir Temple**, which is usually shut. However, it might be possible to find an open door enabling you to take an unobtrusive look inside.

The **Xa Loi Pagoda**, a modern concrete structure and scene of agitation against ex-president Diem, is located about a kilometre to the southwest of Independence Palace.

Ho Chi Minh's Chinese sister city, **Cholon**, has far less respect for appearances. Its streets are narrower and its numerous shop-houses resemble a bazaar in parts. There are a number of Chinese temples in the area. The **Temple of Marshal Le Van Duyet** contains the tomb of the military hero who served the first Nguyen emperor — Gia Long. It is about 3 km from the centre of Ho Chi Minh City in Gia Dinh district. Destroyed by emperor Minh Mang in 1831, it

was rebuilt by his successor Thieu Tri; each year during the Tet festival, it is filled with devotees. A visit to the site provides a good view of the traditional Vietnamese cult of ancestors. The facade of the temple is decorated with innumerable fragments of porcelain and glass, and relics of the hero are preserved for viewing in the main hall.

UPCOUNTRY

Special permits are required for travelling outside Ho Chi Minh City. The easiest way to travel is with an organised party. **Bien Hoa**, 32 km north of the city along an American-built highway, is a centre of pottery manufacture. **Thudaumot**, to the west on the road to Tay Ninh, is known for its lacquer work and all stages of the long, complicated process can be seen at the workshops.

Tay Ninh, 96 km northwest of Ho Chi Minh City, is the site of the fantastic **Cao Dai Temple**, whose stylistic kindred can be found in the Tiger Balm Gardens in Singapore and Hongkong. Caodaism, a sect created in the late 1920s, professes to be a synthesis of Buddhism, Confucianism and Christianity. Members allegedly receive messages from the great spirit Cao Dai and from certain historical people including Victor Hugo. Inside, the temple contains pillars entwined with pink plaster dragons, sculpture and embroidered banners, and at one end is the eye of Cao Dai painted on a blue globe which represents the world.

Vung Tau (formerly Cap St Jacques) has undergone something of a facelift from the time it was a rather seedy beach resort and R. & R. base for Australian troops stationed in Vietnam during the war. The hotel is good and the seafood excellent. Vung Tau faces the South China Sea and is backed by the Mekong Delta so it is one of the richest areas in southern Vietnam. The beach is long and clean with sparkling, white sand and unpolluted water. It can be reached in a two-hour drive from Ho Chi Minh City and is well worth a visit.

The vast expanse of flat land known as the **Mekong Delta** begins south of Ho Chi Minh City; it is an area built up over the centuries by the massive loads of silt from the Mekong River, one of Asia's great waterways. The region is criss-crossed by drainage and irrigation canals. Villages are dispersed and individual houses lie along the canal banks sheltered from the fierce sun by banana and coconut trees. Because of the ample rice production, the towns of the Delta are a little more prosperous than elsewhere.

It was previously possible to drive to My Tho, about 65 km southwest of Ho Chi Minh City. Here a long ferry crossing on one of the arms of the Mekong takes you to Bentre. Southwest of Bentre, via the town of Vinh Long and two ferry crossings (across the Mekong and its main arm, the Bassac River), is Can Tho, a major rice trading centre and capital of the region called Trans-bassac.

Small, basic-living-standard hotels offering accommodation for only a few US dollars can be found in all the Delta towns. The best places for a meal, if a restaurant is not recommended, are often the main markets which all have eating stalls — it is usually possible to get steak, fried eggs, coffee and beer in addition to the usual local Vietnamese dishes.

The province of **An Giang**, of which Long Huynh is the capital, is controlled by a militant sect called the Hoa Hao. It was founded in the 1940s by the Mad Bonze, Huynh Phu So, who was killed by the Vietminh in 1947. Some 10% of the population comprises refugee Catholics who came from the North after the 1954 ceasefire, but 60% follow the Hoa Hao faith. West of Long Xuyen is a region populated — rather thinly — by adepts of local cults. The **Vinh Te Canal**, one of the great public works of the past, runs a few yards from the Cambodian border and connects the Bassac River with the sea to the south.

Access to the mountain resort of **Da Lat** is by road (180 km) from Ho Chi Minh City or by train, on a line which branches off the main north-south line at Thap Cham near Phan Rang.

Da Lat was founded in 1893 by a French doctor, Yersin, who recognised its recuperative benefits. Some 1,200 m above sea level, the town overlooks lakes and is surrounded by pine tree–covered hills. The average summer temperature is 20°C (75°F) and in winter 15°C (59°F). The nights are usually cool.

The centre of the town is at one end of a lake, but the residential areas are spread out. Each chalet-style villa, with its carefully tended lawns and gardens of gladioli, hibiscus, roses, mimosa and bougainvillaea, stands virtually in a park of its own.

Moi hill tribes can be seen in the town and it is even possible (security allowing) to visit their villages.

The village of **Dran**, on the road to Phan Rang, is said to preserve relics of the Cham Kingdom in the form of a gold crown, a silk coat and other valuable objects. Other Cham villages are scattered along the coastal plains in Ninh

Thuan province (of which Phan Rang is the capital) and further north. The Cham people are more deeply pigmented than the Vietnamese and speak their own language (which has affinities with Malay) in addition to Vietnamese. The men wear sarongs, short jackets and sometimes colourful head-dresses, and the women, long buttonless indigo-blue dresses.

There is a strong matrilineal element in their social affairs. Some of the Chams are Hindus — they eat no beef and cremate their dead — while others are Muslim who do not eat pork and bury their dead. There are a number of characteristic brick towers located in this area; remnants of the much grander days of the Chams. There is an excellent tower just on the outskirts of Thap Cham. Near Nha Trang is one of the oldest towers, the **Po Nagar**, built by King Saryavarman in 784.

Other notable Cham towers can be found at Hung Thanh, near Qui Nhon further north, and at My Son just south of Da Nang, where the 10th-century shrine of Bhadresvara was the spiritual centre of the Chams.

Some 100 km north of Phan Rang is the coastal city of **Nha Trang** (450 km from Ho Chi Minh City), a beach resort. Nha Trang has a wide beach stretching for 3 km. The waters are blue and calm except between November and early March. **Cape Varella**, one hour's drive to the north, also has an excellent beach.

Da Nang (Tourane under the French) has an interesting **museum of Cham art**. Near Da Nang is the famous **Marble Mountain** which has a Buddhist monastery. Behind the monastery is a passage leading to a cave in the centre of the mountain which has walls of natural marble. It is lit through a gap in the mountain where a small pagoda has been constructed. Other caves have some very fine examples of stalactites and stalagmites.

From Da Nang it is 112 km by road across the Col des Nuages (Pass of Clouds) to **Hue**, the former capital of the emperors. Hue is 13 km from the sea on the Song Huong (Perfume) River; the old city lies to the north of the river and forms a square centred on the **Imperial Citadel**, while to the south is the newer residential and administrative section.

Much of Hue was destroyed during the heavy Tet fighting of 1968.

The Citadel (also known as the Imperial City) is called **Dai Noi (The Great Within)** and occupies a square surrounded by ramparts. Its construction was begun by Gia Long in 1804 and continued by subsequent emperors.

◁ *Ho Chi Minh film studio.*
Photo: Gerhard Joren

Dawn at Cai Tau in the Mekong delta.

Photo: John Spragens. Jr

The principal gate, the **Ngo Mon (Noon Gate)**, is on the south and faces the river. In front is the 34-m **Flat Tower** (on which the communists raised their flag when they held the city in 1968). It was originally built in 1809 and has been rebuilt twice since — the last time being in 1949. On top of the Ngo Mon is the **Ngu Phung (Five Phoenix Bldg)** where the emperor appeared on important occasions — notably for the promulgation of the calendar for the following lunar year. On the main road in front of the gate is a tablet which reads: "Take off your hat and dismount."

From the Ngo Mon a bridge over a lake leads to the courtyards in front of the Thai Hoa (**Palace of the Full Peace**). The upper courtyard was used by mandarins of the highest rank, while the lower one was for lesser officials. The present Throne Hall was built in 1833; the original, built by Gia Long, stood in the centre of the Citadel.

Other buildings in the Citadel include the **Dien Tho (Everlasting Longevity) Palace**, which was built in 1803 as the Queen Mother's residence, and the **The-Mieu Temple**, in the front of which can be found the nine dynastic urns. There are many other buildings in various stages of decay. The buildings would make a very pleasant spectacle if and when the grounds were transformed into parkland.

Beyond the Citadel, some 450 m to the north, is the **Tinh Tam (Serenity of Heart) Lake**, a place embellished with pavilions where the emperors came for recreation.

Five kilometres west of Hue on the north bank of the Perfume River is the seven-storey **Phuoc Duyen Tower** which was built in 1844 in the Linh Mu Pagoda grounds. The original pagoda has disappeared but a huge bell (weighting 2 tonnes) and a cylindrical stone stele remain.

Upstream between 8-16 km, from the Citadel are the impressive **imperial tombs** of the Nguyen emperors. The nearest, that of Tu Duc (1848-83), stands in a dense pine forest, its compound enclosed by a high wall. There is a pavilion on the edge of a small lake and higher on the hill a temple dedicated to the emperor and nearby the tomb proper. Emperor Dong Khanh's (1885-89) tomb lies immediately to the south.

The tomb of Thieu Tri (1841-47) is located to the south and has a splendid temple with relics of the reign inside. Khai Dinh's (1916-25) tomb is further south again.

The tomb of the first Nguyen emperor, Gia Long (1802-20), and of his successor, Minh Mang (1820-40), are both located on the opposite side of the river.

The town of Hue is unremarkable but it is interesting to walk around and note the more traditional atmosphere. The city's men often wear the old traditional clothing. The countryside is dotted with fascinating Buddhist temples on the outskirts of villages.